The Varieties of Consciousness

PHILOSOPHY OF MIND

Series Editor
David J. Chalmers, Australian National University and New York University

Self Expressions
Owen Flanagan

Deconstructing the Mind
Stephen Stich

The Conscious Mind
David J. Chalmers

Minds and Bodies
Colin McGinn

What's Within?
Fiona Cowie

The Human Animal
Eric T. Olson

Dreaming Souls
Owen Flanagan

Consciousness and Cognition
Michael Thau

Thinking Without Words
José Luis Bermúdez

Identifying the Mind
U. T. Place (author), George Graham, Elizabeth R. Valentine (editors)

Purple Haze
Joseph Levine

Three Faces of Desire
Timothy Schroeder

A Place for Consciousness
Gregg Rosenberg

Ignorance and Imagination
Daniel Stoljar

Simulating Minds
Alvin I. Goldman

Gut Reactions
Jesse J. Prinz

Phenomenal Concepts and Phenomenal Knowledge
Torin Alter, Sven Walter (editors)

Beyond Reduction
Steven Horst

What Are We?
Eric T. Olson

Supersizing the Mind
Andy Clark

Perception, Hallucination, and Illusion
William Fish

Cognitive Systems and the Extended Mind
Robert D. Rupert

The Character of Consciousness
David J. Chalmers

Perceiving the World
Bence Nanay (editor)

The Contents of Visual Experience
Susanna Siegel

The Senses
Fiona Macpherson (editor)

Attention Is Cognitive Unison
Christopher Mole

Consciousness and the Prospects of Physicalism
Derk Pereboom

Introspection and Consciousness
Declan Smithies and Daniel Stoljar (editors)

The Conscious Brain
Jesse J. Prinz

Decomposing the Will
Andy Clark, Julian Kiverstein, and Tillmann Vierkant (editors)

Phenomenal Intentionality
Uriah Kriegel (editor)

The Peripheral Mind
István Aranyosi

The Innocent Eye
Nico Orlandi

Does Perception Have Content?
Berit Brogaard (editor)

The Varieties of Consciousness
Uriah Kriegel

The Varieties of Consciousness

URIAH KRIEGEL

Oxford University Press is a department of the University of Oxford. It furthers
the University's objective of excellence in research, scholarship, and education
by publishing worldwide. Oxford is a registered trade mark of Oxford University
Press in the UK and certain other countries.

Published in the United States of America by Oxford University Press
198 Madison Avenue, New York, NY 10016, United States of America.

© Oxford University Press 2015

First issued as an Oxford University Press paperback, 2019

All rights reserved. No part of this publication may be reproduced, stored in
a retrieval system, or transmitted, in any form or by any means, without the
prior permission in writing of Oxford University Press, or as expressly permitted
by law, by license, or under terms agreed with the appropriate reproduction
rights organization. Inquiries concerning reproduction outside the scope of the
above should be sent to the Rights Department, Oxford University Press, at the
address above.

You must not circulate this work in any other form
and you must impose this same condition on any acquirer.

Library of Congress Cataloging-in-Publication Data
Kriegel, Uriah. The varieties of consciousness / Uriah Kriegel.
pages cm.—
(Philosophy of mind series) Includes bibliographical references and index.
ISBN 978–0–19–984612–2 (hardcover : alk. paper); 978–0–19–094598–5 (paperback : alk. paper)
1. Consciousness.
2. Phenomenology. 3. Philosophy of mind. I. Title.
B808.9.K755 2015
128'.2—dc23
2014033966

CONTENTS

Preface vii

Introduction: Phenomenal Primitives 1

1. Cognitive Phenomenology 38

2. Conative Phenomenology 72

3. The Phenomenology of Entertaining 97

4. Emotional Phenomenology 129

5. Moral Phenomenology 159

Conclusion: The Structure of the Phenomenal Realm 184

Appendix: Theses on the Phenomenology of Freedom 205
Notes 245
Bibliography 273
Index 283

PREFACE

This book started out, in early 2010, as a collection of papers on nonsensory forms of phenomenal consciousness. I had a paper on cognitive phenomenology, a paper on the act of entertaining a proposition, two papers on moral phenomenology, an idea for a slightly unusual paper on the phenomenology of freedom, and a couple of half-related papers on the relationship between phenomenology and intentionality. As I was working on putting logical order in this material, certain general principles regarding the study of different types of phenomenology started to emerge in my mind. This made me see what a more systematic book on the subject might look like. In the summer of 2011, I read Paul Ricœur's book on the phenomenology of the will, originally just out of curiosity, and ended up writing a paper on conative phenomenology that takes Ricœur's account as a starting point; a few months later, I taught a module on emotion at the University of Arizona, and found myself writing a paper on emotional phenomenology. All the while, a clearer appreciation of the general framework I was in effect applying continued to form in my mind. I tried to work out this framework as a (long!) introduction to the book.

By mid-2012, I had a real monograph (as opposed to a collection of papers) on my hands: chapters on cognitive phenomenology, conative phenomenology, entertaining, emotional phenomenology, moral phenomenology, and the phenomenology of freedom, with an introduction on the metaphysical and methodological foundations of the entire project. But when, after a couple of months of taking distance from it, I read the manuscript from beginning to end, I found in it too many traces of the collection-of-papers this once was to be. For the past two years, I have been working to unify the manuscript and erase its bastardly origins. The result is below.

In working on this book, I have been tremendously helped by presenting portions at a variety of colloquia and conferences. I have mentioned at the end of each chapter all the relevant ones, and all the audience members I could remember whose input influenced the text in any way. In addition, many people have offered me extremely valuable input on (material from) this or that chapter, and they are mentioned at the ends of chapters as well. I owe special thanks to Eric Schwitzgebel and Mark Timmons, who I believe are the only persons to have read every chapter of the manuscript; their perceptive comments have pushed me to make changes both at the sentence level and in global directions. I am, more generally, deeply grateful to the department of philosophy at the University of Arizona, where I spent a decade of my life learning from my colleagues about matters both philosophical and not. I often experience an occurrent phenomenology of gratitude upon contemplating all that the Arizona department had given me over the years. Finally, I am grateful to my current employer, France's CNRS (the Centre National de la Recherche Scientifique), whose full-time research positions allow members to progress at their own pace in their understanding of the world.

When good things happen to me—I get a paper accepted for publication, say, or I see an excellent exhibition—my mood goes up for a day or two, but eventually gravitates back down toward its standard baseline. When bad things happen to me—I have an unpleasant interaction with a stranger on the subway, I have a fight with a friend—my mood dips for a while, but then eventually gravitates back up to the baseline. Over the years, I have become good at knowing what is likely pull me above the baseline and what might push me below it. But how do you move the baseline itself? That is still a mystery to me, and in my own life I have found only two things that move the baseline itself: love and creative work. In that respect, one of the paramount events of my life occurred when I met my now-wife Lizzie, on 19 September 2009 at 3:20 p.m. just outside the Neue Galerie in New York. On that afternoon, my mood just shot up way above the baseline; but in the long run, that event slowly dragged the baseline itself up and up and up.

It is hard to overestimate the influence of calm love on a person's steady level of concentration. A certain restlessness of spirit dissipates and a clearer distinction between the urgent and the important emerges. Letter by letter and chapter by chapter, this book owes an indefinable debt of gratitude to Lizzie—to whom it is dedicated.

Paris, August 2014

The Varieties of Consciousness

Introduction

Phenomenal Primitives

Recent work on consciousness has featured a number of debates on the existence and character of controversial types of phenomenology. Perhaps the best-known is the debate over the existence of a sui generis, irreducible *cognitive phenomenology*—a phenomenology proper to thought. Another concerns the existence of a sui generis phenomenology of agency. Such debates bring up a more general question: how many types of sui generis, irreducible, basic, primitive phenomenology do we have to posit to just be able to *describe* the stream of consciousness? This book attempts to make some contributions toward answering this question. The purpose of this introduction is to clarify the question and how one might approach it, laying relevant metaphysical (§§2–5) and methodological (§§6–8) foundations.

1. Before (and after) Philosophy

About a century ago, stream-of-consciousness literature started being promulgated by such writers as James Joyce, Marcel Proust, and Arthur Schnitzler. Instead of the traditional well-organized, cleaned-up, highly processed presentation of characters' thought and conduct, these writers attempted to describe inner life in a realistic, hence somewhat chaotic and confused, fashion. We might say they were seeking a more phenomenologically adequate rendering of inner life. The technique has quickly gained popularity and renown. It is a good question what is so compelling about it, but one immediate thought is that it offers insight into questions of the form "What is it like to be this kind of person, in this kind of situation?" Outside fiction, we have *direct* insight only into our own consciousness; this epistemic loneliness is broken by stream-of-consciousness narratives that offer a believable peep into another consciousness.

Typical stretches of stream-of-consciousness prose often feature sensory perceptions, bodily sensations, and visceral aspects of emotional feelings. However, they are *never* restricted to such elements. On the contrary, they also feature—at least as centrally—thought processes, hopes and desires, and more intellectual aspects of emotion. Without the latter, the resulting narratives would be extremely boring. The technique would have exhausted itself long ago. Nobody wants to read about an interminable sequence of sensory occurrences. But many of us want to read about stretches of inner life as described by stream-of-consciousness writers. This is because in describing also the thought processes, hopes and desires, and more intellectual aspects of emotion, these narratives manage to shed light on what it is like to occupy a different subjective perspective. Without including such elements, no real insight into what it is like to be someone else would be gained.

Consider an early example. In his 1897 short story "The Dead Are Silent," Arthur Schnitzler explores a stretch of inner life of a married woman who flees the scene of an accident in which her lover just died. The accident occurs in a countryside corner just outside Vienna, and much of the story takes place "inside her head" as the protagonist makes her way back home to her husband and child. Here is Schnitzler's description of her approach to Vienna's city center:

> The noise of the city grows louder, the street is lighter, the skyline of the Prater street rises before her, and she knows that she can sink into a flood tide of humanity there and lose herself in it. When she comes to a street lamp she is quite calm enough now to take out her watch and look at it. It is ten minutes to nine. She holds the watch to her ear—it is ticking merrily. And she thinks: "Here I am, alive, unharmed—and he—he—dead. It is Fate." She feels as if all had been forgiven—as if she had never sinned. And what if Fate had willed otherwise? If it were she lying there in the ditch, and he who remained alive? He would not have run away—but then he is a man. She is only a woman, she has a husband, a child—it was her right—her duty—to save herself. She knows that it was not a sense of duty that impelled her to do it. But what she has done was right—she had done right instinctively—as all good people do. If she had stayed she would have been discovered by this time. The doctors would question her. And all the papers would report it next morning; she would have been ruined forever, and yet her ruin could not bring him back to life. Yes, that was the main point, her sacrifice would have been all in vain.

This passage starts with an enumeration of sensory elements: loud noises, brighter lights, and so on. Soon the action moves to the emotional domain, as a summary battle with a sense of guilt takes place; importantly, we do not grasp the phenomenology of the protagonist's guilt through descriptions of her visceral sensations, but through descriptions of highly conceptual thought processes. Finally, a sort of emotional clarity dawns on the protagonist as a purely cognitive, intellectual event takes place: she manages to articulate to herself something she was feeling when she *realizes* what matters in the situation, namely, that if she had stayed by her lover's side and sacrificed her reputation and her family's happiness, her sacrifice would have been in vain. Again, we would not really grasp what it is like to be her at that moment if we were told that her stream of consciousness included visual sensations of the shapes my^sacrif ice^would^have^been^in^vain, or that it included auditory imagery of the corresponding sounds. It is the *meaning* of those shapes and sounds, the *proposition* present before her mind, that gives us the kind of insight that makes it worth reading stream-of-consciousness literature. And in any case, it is presumably not my^sacrifice^would^have^been^in^vain that floated before her mind's eye, but für^nichts^hätte^sie^sich^zu^Grunde^gerichtet. Yet readers who cannot read German still gain insight into the protagonist's inner life by being described this episode. The reason is that the correct description of the episode focuses not on any shape-sensations the protagonist may experience, but on the *thought*, as a contentful conscious event, that occurs to her.

Much of this book will be dedicated to philosophical arguments to the effect that there *exist* forms of nonsensory (phenomenal) consciousness, including cognitive and conative. I am alive to the possibility, however, that the opposite view may require therapy more than argumentation. My therapeutic prescription is a healthy daily dose of stream-of-consciousness literature. Just as Harman (1990) predicted that when you introspect seeing your hands you will become aware of nothing but the hands you are seeing, I issue the following prediction: the longer you immerse yourself in stream-of-consciousness literature, the odder would seem to you the notion that phenomenal consciousness involves no pure, irreducible cognitive and conative elements.

I. Metaphysical Foundations
2. Phenomenal Primitives and Phenomenal Grounding

According to eliminativists about phenomenal consciousness (e.g., Rey 1988), there are no phenomenal properties—at least no instantiated ones. Most philosophers of mind are not eliminativists here. They accept the existence of *some* types of phenomenology. In particular, there are two types of phenomenology traditionally thought relatively uncontroversial: the phenomenology of perceptual experience and the phenomenology of pleasure and pain ("algedonic" phenomenology). Mainstream philosophy of mind tends to accept those.

What about other types of phenomenology, neither perceptual nor algedonic? For example, what about a phenomenology of thinking, or of agency? One perfectly coherent and stable position is to deny the existence of any such, accepting *only* perceptual and algedonic phenomenology; this would be a sort of eliminativism about the phenomenology of thought, of agency, and so on. On this view, there is nothing it is like to think, for example. Another option is to accept some further types of phenomenology, but claim that ultimately they result from combinations of perceptual and algedonic phenomenology; this would be a sort of reductivism rather than eliminativism. On this view, there *is* something it is like to think, but *what* it is like is just the right combination of sensory experiences. A third option, however, is to accept these more adventurous types of phenomenology and furthermore claim that they go beyond perceptual and algedonic phenomenology, constituting *sui generis* or *primitive* types of phenomenology; this would be a sort of *nonreductivism* or *primitivism*.

In fact, for each putative type of phenomenology, these three options are prima facie open. For each there is an eliminative, a reductive, and a primitivist option. Consider cognitive phenomenology. Some deny that there is any distinctive phenomenology associated with thinking that 2 + 2 = 4 (Nelkin 1989 *inter alia*). Others accept the existence of a phenomenology of thinking that 2 + 2 = 4, but argue that ultimately it amounts to some type of already familiar sensory phenomenology; often the idea is that it is the phenomenology of auditory imagery in "inner speech," whereby the sounds "two plus two equal four" float by one's mind's ear, so to speak (Carruthers 2006 and Prinz 2011 *inter alia*). Still others, however, insist that there exists a sui generis cognitive phenomenology that goes beyond the phenomenology of inner speech, and in fact cannot be captured by any form of perceptual (or algedonic) phenomenology (Siewert 1998 ch.8 and Pitt 2004 *inter alia*). The first view is *eliminativist* about cognitive phenomenology, the second *reductivist*, and the third *primitivist*.

The choice among these three options can be appreciated through an inconsistent triad:

1) There exists cognitive phenomenology.
2) Cognitive phenomenology is irreducible to perceptual and algedonic phenomenology.
3) Perceptual and algedonic phenomenology ultimately exhaust all phenomenology.[1]

The eliminativist about cognitive phenomenology denies 1, the reductivist denies 2, and the primitivist 3.

(It should be stressed that the debate over reductivism here is orthogonal to the debate over physicalism. The issue is not whether cognitive phenomenology reduces to *physical* properties, but whether it reduces to other *phenomenal* properties. One could be a primitivist about cognitive phenomenology in the sense of holding that it is irreducible to any other phenomenology and still reduce cognitive-phenomenal properties to some neural properties. Conversely, one could hold a reductivist account of cognitive phenomenology in terms of perceptual phenomenology but be a dualist about phenomenal properties in general, thus denying the physical reducibility of cognitive-phenomenal properties. The two issues are logically independent. My concern here is with the *phenomenal* reducibility, not *physical* reducibility, of certain types of phenomenology.)

Similar choices face us with respect to other putative types of phenomenology. Consider emotional phenomenology. It is odd, but not incoherent, to maintain that there is nothing it is like to undergo emotional episodes; the eliminativist about phenomenal consciousness is presumably committed to this. More commonly, it has often been argued that the phenomenal feel of emotion is nothing but proprioceptive (or kinesthetic, or somatic) feeling (James 1884 and Armstrong 1968 *inter alia*). This is to claim that emotional phenomenology reduces to a species of perceptual phenomenology. At the same time, it is also possible to hold that whatever other elements emotional experiences involve, there is also a more basic sui generis element that constitutes a primitive emotional phenomenology (Stocker 1996 and Montague 2009 *inter alia*). The choice among these views can again be captured in a triad:

1) There exists emotional phenomenology.
2) Emotional phenomenology is irreducible to perceptual and/or algedonic phenomenology.
3) Perceptual and algedonic phenomenology ultimately exhaust all phenomenology.

Similar triads can be formulated for other types of phenomenology—the phenomenology of agency, for instance (see Bayne 2008).

It is worth noting that the three theoretical options do not *have* to be formulated relative to perceptual and algedonic phenomenology as potential reducers. A primitivist about cognitive phenomenology who considered the status of emotional phenomenology should include cognitive phenomenology among the potential reducers. At the same time, someone could deny that perceptual or algedonic phenomenology is primitive. For example, she might hold that pain is just tactile perception of tissue damage, effectively reducing algedonic to perceptual phenomenology. For someone who accepted cognitive phenomenology but not algedonic phenomenology as primitive, the question of emotional phenomenology would become this: does emotional phenomenology exist, and does it reduce to some combination of perceptual and cognitive phenomenology?[2]

The general issue for any putative phenomenology P, then, is whether it reduces to whatever primitive phenomenologies one already recognizes. Put in terms of an inconsistent triad, the general form of the question, for any given putative phenomenology P, and phenomenologies $P_1, \ldots, P_n$ recognized as primitive, is what to reject among:

1) There exists phenomenology P.
2) P does not reduce to phenomenologies $P_1, \ldots, P_n$.
3) $P_1, \ldots, P_n$ exhaust all phenomenology.

Call this the *generalized triad* for phenomenology.

With this generalized triad, we can answer straightforwardly the question "How many types of phenomenology do we need to posit to just be able to *describe* the stream of consciousness?" The answer is: as many types as primitivism (rather than reductivism or eliminativism) is true of. There is a view, which we may call "mainstream stingy-ism," that is primitivist only about perceptual and algedonic phenomenology.[3] My starting point in this book is that mainstream stingy-ism is likely false, and there probably exist some non-perceptual, non-algedonic types of irreducible phenomenology. The question is which ones they are.

The generalized triad can help us put in place an *idealized*, or *rationally reconstructed*, "procedure" for generating coherent and stable accounts of the scope of primitive phenomenology. To a *first approximation*, the "procedure" is this. In Step 1, we produce a comprehensive inventory of *putative* types of phenomenology. In Step 2, we feed each item in this inventory into the generalized triad just described, with that item serving as a substitution instance for P and all other items functioning as $P_1, \ldots, P_n$; going through each of these triads, we attempt to establish which values of P are such that the primitivist position is the most plausible for them. (*How* we do so is the topic of §§6–8.) This produces a first outcome: a list of all phenomenal primitives. That is, it divides the set of all putative phenomenologies into two subsets: the primitive ones and the rest. Moving now to Step 3, we feed each member of the non-primitive subset into a new triad in which $P_1, \ldots, P_n$ are given by all and only the members of the primitive subset; here we attempt to establish which values of P are such that reductivism is more plausible for them than eliminativism. This produces a second outcome: a list of all "phenomenal derivatives." That is, it divides the non-primitive subset into two further subsets: those that are derivative upon the phenomenal primitives and those that are not.[4] The overall outcome is a structure we might describe as $(S_1, (S_2, S_3))$, where S_1 = the set of all phenomenal primitives, S_2 = the set of all phenomenal derivatives, and S_3 = the set of *mere putatives*.[5] This structures the phenomenal realm along an important dimension, presenting all phenomenal properties and all reduction or "grounding" relations among them. It tells us what the phenomenal primitives are and what other phenomenal properties they ground/reduce.[6]

(I will be using "grounding" as interchangeable with "reduction." In truth, this is quite incorrect, as grounding is typically taken to be an in-virtue-of relation, whereas reduction is not.[7] In a way, though, my real interest is in the *disjunction* of grounding and reduction.)

⁂

As noted, this is only a first approximation of the "procedure," and I will offer refinements shortly. Already in this form, however, we can appreciate that the project at hand is a special case of a more general metaphysical project. According to Schaffer (2009), the central mandate of metaphysics is to tell us what grounds what. Although philosophers commonly profess to be eliminativists about this or that putative entity, often closer inspection reveals that their view is better classified as reductivist, claiming that the relevant putative entity is "nothing but" some other entity or collection of entities (and thus is not *fundamental*, and no *addition of being*). The true goal of metaphysics, according to Schaffer, is to identify the basic, ungrounded entities in terms of which all other entities can be accounted for—the ungrounded grounders of reality, if you will.[8] At the same time, genuine eliminativism is a real *option*, and sometimes it is clearly adopted—as when the atheist goes eliminativist with respect to gods. Arguably, metaphysics always presents us with a choice between primitivist, reductivist, and eliminativist positions. The present project can be seen as a metaphysic of phenomenology.

In an ostensibly more epistemological vein, Chalmers (2012) proposes that a central goal of philosophical worldviews is to produce the minimal base of truths from which the totality of truths could be derived *a priori* by an ideal reasoner (see already Jackson 1998). This is, in Chalmers' terms, a "scrutability project." (When *p* can be derived from *q a priori* by an ideal reasoner, we say that *p* is "scrutable" from *q*.) I describe the vein as only *ostensibly* epistemological because on the "Australian view" of ontological reduction (Chalmers and Jackson 2001), a necessary condition on the ontological reduction of entity E_1 to entity E_2 is that all truths about E_1 be scrutable from truths about E_2. Against this background, questions of phenomenal *reducibility* implicate questions of phenomenal *scrutability*: which phenomenal truths are scrutable from which, and which types of phenomenology are such that truths about them form the scrutability base of all phenomenal truths? So against the background of the Australian view, the present project can also be seen as a scrutability project restricted to the phenomenal realm.

It might be objected that certain features of the phenomenal realm make this kind of project, legitimate in other areas of inquiry, unviable for phenomenology. For example, it might be argued that the kind of project outlined above presupposes that the putative entities up for elimination, reduction, or recognition as primitive must be discrete and separate from each other; but that there is a perfectly reasonable view, which we may call *phenomenal holism*, that denies this. In other words, the project under discussion is beholden to a rather naïve sort of phenomenal atomism.

It is clear, however, that the project is fully consistent with phenomenal holism. But to see why, we need a more precise formulation of phenomenal holism. Chudnoff (2013a: 562) offers the following: "All partial phenomenal states of a subject at a time metaphysically depend on the subject's total phenomenal state at that time." Consider the overall experience of a bite of peanut-butter and jelly sandwich. This involves as parts (i) a gustatory experience of peanut butter, (ii) a gustatory experience of jelly, (iii) associated olfactory experiences, (iv) tactile experiences of wet bread, perhaps (v) a motivational experience of wanting the next bite or (vi) an aesthetic experience of appreciating the sandwich's taste, and much more. According to holism, the overall experience does not metaphysically depend on (i)–(vi), but on the contrary (i)–(vi) depend on it: (i)–(vi) exist in virtue of the overall experience existing, not the other way round. We can see now that phenomenal holism does not exclude distinguishing different parts of an overall experience, it just makes a claim about metaphysical priority or dependence between the parts and the whole. As long as we have well-defined parts on our hands, we can then ask whether primitivism, reductivism, or eliminativism is the right view of them. Thus, even if the aesthetic experience of the sandwich metaphysically depends on the overall experience, we can wonder whether it involves a sui generis phenomenology or not.[9]

The objector might insist that there is also a stronger kind of phenomenal holism that denies the possibility of distinguishing different parts within a dated overall experience. On this view, (i)–(vi) is an artificial, pragmatically driven decomposition of the bite experience. In and of itself, the experience is strictly *indivisible*. Compare: in the metaphysics of material objects, there is a distinction between two kinds of "monism." According to "priority monism," individual objects metaphysically depend on the overall universe, such that facts about this dog or that tree obtain in virtue of facts about the overall universe obtaining (Schaffer 2007, 2010). According to "existence monism," by contrast, there are simply no individual objects other than the overall universe—the latter is the only material object (Horgan and Potrč 2008). The phenomenal holism just considered is analogous to priority monism, but there is also a version of phenomenal holism analogous to existence monism. On that version, there are no partial experiences, characterized by a discrete phenomenology about which we can debate the merits of primitivism, reductivism, and eliminativism.

However, this stronger phenomenal holism faces a dilemma. On the face of it, the overall experiences we have at a time normally seem *structured*, not homogeneous blobs. It is natural to accommodate this by adverting to parts: the structure of a dated overall experience is fixed by the properties of its parts (even if these parts metaphysically depend upon the overall experience). The strong holist faces a dilemma: either (*a*) she attempts to accommodate structure in some other fashion, or (*b*) she denies the datum of structure. If (*a*), then presumably some other notion will be invoked ("*dimension* of experience"?), but then our project could be framed in terms of that notion. If (*b*), then the view is truly implausible—implausible enough that its rejection is no longer a meaningful liability on our project.[10]

3. Phenomenal Determinables and Determinates

The project does face an immediate complication, however. Consider the difference between the phenomenology of seeing yellow and the phenomenology of seeing blue. Both are species of visual phenomenology, which in turn is a species of perceptual phenomenology. The fact that there is quite a bit of variety within perceptual phenomenology might induce some to reconsider its status as phenomenally primitive. After all, there is a sense in which perceptual phenomenology is but the collection of all its possible species: seeing yellow, seeing blue, seeing circles, hearing trumpets, and so on. At the same time, there is also a sense that the internal variety in perceptual phenomenology is irrelevant to its status as primitive: the mere fact that it does not reduce to phenomenologies algedonic, cognitive, emotional, and so on guarantees the status. We are tempted to say that perceptual phenomenology is primitive because it is irreducible to any phenomenology *at the same level of generality*.

Unfortunately, this way of putting things is somewhat vague. The true moral, it seems to me, is that the notion of phenomenal primitiveness is relative—it must be relativized to those "levels of generality." One way to think of this is as follows: the structure of the phenomenal realm must refer not only to grounding relations but also to "determinable/determinate" relations or "genus/species" relations. Two phenomenologists may agree on which emotional experiences instantiate which phenomenal properties, but disagree on whether emotional phenomenology should be taken to have twelve species or fourteen. This appears to be a disagreement about the structure of the phenomenal realm, but not about grounding.

If this is right, then the above procedure for generating accounts of phenomenal primitives and derivatives requires modification. Recall that Step 1 in the procedure drew an inventory of putative types of phenomenology, Step 2 identified the phenomenal primitives in it, and Step 3 identified the phenomenal derivatives. It would now seem that the procedure requires two major modifications. First, an intermediary step is needed between Steps 1 and 2, whose purpose is to figure out the determinable/determinate and genus/species relations among the items in the inventory. Secondly, when we feed items into triads in Steps 2 and 3, we should consider as potential reducers only phenomenologies from the same level.

Before expanding on these two modifications, a word on the relationship between the determinable/determinate and genus/species relations. Both relations can be found in the phenomenal realm: visual and auditory are two different species of perceptual phenomenology, but reddish$_{16}$ and reddish$_{17}$ are two different *determinates* of visual phenomenology. There are two main differences between them. First, there is a continuum between determinates of the same determinable (such as reddish$_{16}$ and reddish$_{17}$ qualities) but not between species of the same genus (such as auditory and visual qualities). Secondly, determinates of the same determinable necessarily exclude each other, whereas species of the same genus do not (an experience of a loud blue airplane overhead can be both visual and auditory but not both bluish$_{23}$ and bluish$_{24}$).[11] It would be useful to have a term for the generic relation two species of which are the determinate/determinable and genus/species relations: "encompassing/encompassed" might be an option.[12] Instead, however, I am going to use "determinable/determinate" technically to cover both relations.

The highest phenomenal determinable is *phenomenality per se* (what-it-is-like-ness as such, if you will).[13] It is the phenomenal property that is not a determinate of any other phenomenal property. The second-highest phenomenal determinables are those phenomenal properties which are determinates of no other phenomenal property but phenomenality *per se*. They are determinates of only one phenomenal determinable. Third-layer phenomenal determinables are determinates only of phenomenality *per se* and of phenomenal properties that are determinates only of phenomenality *per se*. And so on and so forth. Presumably, there is also a bottom layer of *maximally determinate* phenomenal properties. These are phenomenal properties that do not serve as determinables of any other phenomenal properties. Brentano, Wundt, and the early introspectionists called these the *elements of consciousness*. One task, then, is to stratify the initial inventory of putative phenomenologies into the number of determinable layers between the highest determinable of phenomenality *per se* and the maximally determinate "elements" of consciousness.[14] (There is a question as to how we might *establish* which phenomenal determinables a putative type of phenomenology is a determinate of; I will return to this in §4.)

This stratification alters the "procedure" from §2. Suppose we are concerned to establish whether some phenomenology P is primitive. This requires that the reducibility of P be considered within the right "layer" of phenomenal properties. More precisely, it requires that we (i) determine the *n*-layer P belongs to, (ii) identify in our inventory all the other *n*-layer putative phenomenologies $P_1, \ldots, P_n$, and (iii) feed P into a triad in which $P_1, \ldots, P_n$ serve as P's potential reducers.

A *second approximation* of the "procedure" would thus involve *four* steps. Step 1 creates the initial inventory of putative phenomenologies. Step 2 stratifies these into layers of determinate-ness. Step 3 identifies the phenomenal primitives in each layer. Step 4 identifies the phenomenal derivatives in each layer.

The overall outcome is a conjunction of lists each of which specifies phenomenal primitives, derivatives, and mere putatives in different layers of phenomenal determinate-ness.

❧☙

Again certain worries about the viability of the envisaged project may arise. One is that, for all we know, there are several equally good ways to organize phenomenal properties into layers of determinacy, and there are no objective facts of the matter as to which one is the "real one." This is certainly a fair worry, which will be taken up in §5.

Another possible worry is that talk of phenomenal determinables can be indulged as a *façon de parler*, but cannot be taken literally. In general, an objector might contend, there are no determinable properties at all. Although we have *concepts* for such properties, there is an immediate causal-preemption threat: determinable properties' causal powers are presumably exhausted by their determinates', rendering the former explanatorily redundant (Gillet and Rives 2005). Thus the only real properties are maximally determinate ones: in the phenomenal case, the aforementioned phenomenal "elements."

There are three responses to this objection. First, the debate over the ontological status of determinables is by no means resolved. Wilson (2012) argues (roughly) that determinables have certain modal properties that cannot be accounted for by their determinates, and are therefore irreducible to them. Consider a red car that is in fact red_{17}. The car's redness has the property that it could have been another shade of red (say, red_{21}). This modal property of the car's redness is inexplicable in terms of the car's red_{17}-ness. For it is not true that the car's red_{17}-ness could have been a red_{21}-ness. To imagine that the car is red_{21} rather than red_{17} is to imagine that the car's red_{17}-ness does not exist at all, not that it exists but with a different character or quality. But to imagine this is *not* to imagine that the car's *redness* does not exist at all; rather, it is precisely to imagine that the car's redness has a different quality.[15] This is not the place to pursue a close examination of the cogency of Wilson's modal argument. The argument is at least initially compelling and bears further consideration, especially since it parallels modal arguments about material constitution.[16] Accordingly, it is far from settled that there are no determinables.

Secondly, *concepts* for phenomenal determinables are of great value even if it turns out that there are no *properties* they pick out. As natural, evolved creatures of limited cognitive resources, in grasping a realm of phenomena we cannot operate with concepts for maximally determinate properties only. Putting order in the phenomena at the level of determinacy at which we interact with them requires that we develop concepts for determinables. This is why we operate in everyday life mostly with the concept of red and not red_{17}. And while a scientific framework is supposed to refine the prescientific grain, no existing science does away with concepts for determinables altogether. Thus insofar as the present goal is to develop a framework through which to study the phenomenal realm and put order in its phenomena, determinable-concepts are indispensable. The project could always be recast as concerning the structure of the conceptual scheme for making sense of the phenomenal realm (rather than as concerning the structure of the phenomenal realm itself).

Thirdly, the absence of phenomenal determinables would not vitiate the part of the project concerned with grounding relations. We could ask whether there is sui generis cognitive or conative phenomenology and mean by that no more than whether there are irreducible maximally determinate cognitive-phenomenal or conative-phenomenal properties.

In conclusion, assessment of the status of putative phenomenologies as primitive, derivative, or *merely* putative must be conducted relatively to a layer of determinate-ness. This book purports to make first steps on one sliver of this overall project. The contribution envisaged is to the following question:

(Q) Which putative types of phenomenology are primitive second-layer phenomenal determinables?

The bulk of this book addresses Q by considering five putative types of phenomenology.

4. Putative Phenomenal Universals

We have discussed two dimensions of structure in the phenomenal realm: grounding relations and determinable/determinate relations. There are surely many others. Some phenomenal properties may bear one-way dependence relations to other phenomenal properties. Other property pairs may bear two-way dependence relations. Some phenomenal properties bear structural resemblance relations to some but not all other phenomenal properties. There is thus a group of highly general relations, which we may call *metaphysical relations*, that defines the *overall structure of the phenomenal realm*.[17]

In this book, my concern is only with those dimensions of the overall structure of the phenomenal realm that bear on Q. This involves in the first place grounding and determinable/determinate relations. To fully understand these dimensions of phenomenal structure, however, we must also understand the *relata* bearing grounding and determinability relations. This is the topic of the present section.

The relata are the different putative types of phenomenology. It would be convenient if it were entirely uncontroversial what these are. In reality, an element of theorization is involved even in fixing the inventory of putative phenomenologies. After all, in its concrete unfolding the stream of consciousness consists in the succession of token phenomenal events and processes, but when we speak of a putative phenomenology, we speak of a phenomenal *type* or *property*. The question arises, then, where these putative phenomenal types or properties come from.

In one respect, the question is not special to phenomenology: in its concrete unfolding, the spatiotemporal universe consists in individual objects and events and the particular ways they are. According to the nominalist about properties, such individuals exhaust what the universe contains. Realists postulate also *universals*, entities simultaneously wholly present in distinct places. Most often, these are construed not as Platonic, transcendent, *ante rem* universals that exist outside space and time and that spatiotemporal entities bear a relation of sharing-in to, but as Aristotelian, immanent, *in re* universals that inhere in the spatiotemporal entities themselves (Armstrong 1978).[18]

The epistemology of positing such universals is rather straightforward for Armstrong. When we notice what appear to be objective similarity relations among different concrete particulars, we may infer that there is a universal that they share. This inference is abductive: the fact that completely distinct concrete particulars sometimes resemble calls for metaphysical explanation, and the best explanation is that there is a single entity wholly present in all of them.

The machinery of Armstrongian universals can be applied to the phenomenal realm as well. We may consider that one's stream of consciousness includes in fact not only a succession of token phenomenal states, but also *phenomenal universals* wholly present at temporally disjoint points in that stream (and perhaps in other streams), that is, fully inhering in distinct token phenomenal occurrences. Thus the inventory of putative phenomenologies is just an inventory of putative phenomenal universals—a list of *epistemically possible* phenomenal universals (phenomenal universals there may be).

From this perspective, the epistemology of coming up with the initial inventory of putative phenomenologies is fairly straightforward. It is a matter of seeking phenomenal similarities among individual experiences and inferring from noticed similarities the existence of phenomenal universals shared by them. Presumably, the seeking is through introspection, the inferring through abduction.

Note that this exercise, although straightforward, is doubly fallible. First, one may (perhaps due to attentional overload) mistakenly come to believe that a certain phenomenal similarity holds where in fact it does not, or conversely miss out on a phenomenal similarity that does hold. Secondly, one's abductive inference may be epistemically justified and yet lead to a false conclusion. Still, introspective observing of similarities and abductive inferring from them can be reasonably expected to be *reliable*: although they may lead to false conclusions, they do tend, in the normal go of things, to lead to true ones. (The reliability of introspection will be defended in §§7–8.)

We are now in a position to articulate a *third approximation* of the procedure from §2. This approximation involves decomposing Step 1 into two more basic steps, an introspective step and an inferential step. The former involves introspectively noticing token phenomenal occurrences and recording apparent objective (observer-independent) similarities among them. The latter involves inference from these apparent phenomenal similarities to putative phenomenal universals.

There is a further complication we need to address. It concerns the fact that similarity comes in degrees. There is greater similarity between two experiences as of yellow$_{17}$ than between an experience as of yellow$_{17}$ and an experience as of yellow$_{14}$. The latter similarity is in turn greater than the similarity between an experience as of yellow$_{17}$ and an experience as of blue$_{23}$, which in turn is greater than the similarity between an experience as of yellow$_{17}$ and an auditory experience as of trumpet sounds, which in turn is greater than that between an experience as of yellow$_{17}$ and a cognitive experience as of 2 + 2 = 4 (if such there be). One approach to this problem is to accept only *exact similarity* among tokens as indicating the existence of universals. Armstrong himself adopted this view, thus embracing only maximally determinate universals. But this seems to ignore the genuine similarity between inexactly similar tokens (e.g., experiences as of yellow$_{17}$ and as of yellow$_{14}$). Another approach is therefore to posit an extra dimension along which universals may differ, depending on the degree of similarity among the particulars they inhere in. Lewis (1983) suggests that universals differ in their degree of *naturalness*: the more objectively similar its instances, the more "natural" the universal. Thus there exist both the universal of phenomenal yellowness and the universal of phenomenal yellow$_{17}$-ness; the latter is simply more natural than the former.

Happily, the epistemology of establishing the degree of *naturalness* of a phenomenal universal is essentially the same as that of establishing the *existence* of a phenomenal universal. It is a matter of (introspectively) noticing a degree of similarity among token phenomenal states and (abductively) inferring a degree of naturalness in the universal.

Interestingly, this epistemology of naturalness may offer an entry point into the question, raised in the previous section, of how we might establish determinable/determinate relations among putative types of phenomenology. Consider that maximally determinate phenomenal universals are maximally natural: their instances have the greatest possible similarity among them. At the same time, the highest phenomenal determinable, *phenomenality per se*, has the lowest degree of naturalness of all phenomenal universals: its instances are similar only insofar as there is something it is like to have them at all. Thus establishing relative degrees of naturalness in putative phenomenologies may be at least a partial guide to establishing determinable/determinate relations among them. Using this guide, we can establish that phenomenal yellow$_{17}$-ness is a determinate of phenomenal yellowness, because (i) the degree of naturalness of the former is higher than the degree of naturalness of the latter (because the former's instances resemble each other more than the latter's), and (ii) instances of the former are also instances of the latter. More generally, for any putative phenomenal universals P and P*, we are justified in taking P to be a determinate of P* if (i) P's instances are similar to each other more than P*'s and (ii) P's instances are also instances of P*.

Setting aside the issue of similarity and naturalness, the third approximation of the overall procedure for producing an account of phenomenal structure would involve five components: 1) introspective noticing of apparent phenomenal similarities; 2) abductive inference from said similarities to putative phenomenal universals; 3) ordering of said universals into layers of phenomenal determinables; 4) identifying the phenomenal primitives in each layer of determinables; 5) identifying the phenomenal derivatives in each layer. The result is a web of phenomenal universals bearing grounding and determinability relations.

5. Realism and Anti-realism about Phenomenal Structure

The picture presented thus far is pleasantly but somewhat dogmatically optimistic in its realism about the various dimensions of structure in the phenomenal realm. It assumes that there are objective, observer-independent facts of the matter about phenomenal similarity, grounding, and determinability relations. Such a pleasantly realist picture may be defensible, but there are also reasonable anti-realist positions on similarity and universals, on grounding, and on determinables.

Start with similarity. Although from our vantage point it is natural to take the similarities we detect around us to be *objective*, it is a recurring idea in the history of philosophy that such similarities may at least sometimes be artifacts of our idiosyncratic cognitive architecture. For example, we can (with difficulty!) envisage a kind of creature C such that instances of green strike C as less inherently similar than instances of grue (Goodman 1954). One might dismiss C's similarity impressions as falsidical, but it would not be easy to fend off a charge of chauvinism here. Although we have a strong sense that finding greater similarity among grue than green instances is perverse, this may simply be because we are insufficiently imaginative. For the anti-realist about similarity, there is no fact of the matter as to which group of instances is *really* (objectively, absolutely, inherently) more similar (Gärdenfors 2004). According to the realist, there are—they are the naturalness facts mentioned in §4. This debate is as old as philosophy itself, and this is not the place to make meaningful contributions to it. I mention it merely to bring up the epistemic possibility that the phenomenal similarity relations underlying our carving of the phenomenal realm into putative phenomenal universals may be observer-dependent.

One could reach such anti-realism about phenomenal similarity by simple application of global anti-realism. Alternatively, one might consider there to be something special about the phenomenal realm that lends it to anti-realist treatment. For example, one might hold that, in the phenomenal realm more than elsewhere, some similarity disagreements may be "blameless." Imagine three phenomenal tokens φ_1, φ_2, and φ_3, of which two counterfactuals are true: (*a*) if they occurred in Luciana's stream of consciousness, it would introspectively seem to her that φ_1 and φ_2 resemble each other but do not resemble φ_3; (*b*) if they occurred in Ada's stream of consciousness, it would introspectively seem to her that φ_2 and φ_3 resemble each other but not φ_1. Let us further stipulate, as we seem entitled, that Luciana and Ada are both healthy adults with well-functioning introspective faculties, and that these similarity judgments were issued in favorable epistemic circumstances. It is at least antecedently reasonable to maintain that, at least in some cases fitting this description, neither Luciana nor Ada is wrong: φ_2 resembles φ_1 relative to Luciana's introspective apparatus but φ_3 relative to Ada's. This would suggest that phenomenal similarity relations are introspection-dependent.[19]

The resulting anti-realism could play out in different ways. One view might be that phenomenal tokens φ_j and φ_k resemble iff an ideal introspector would (under ideal conditions) introspectively take them to. Another might be that φ_j and φ_k resemble iff normal introspectors (under normal conditions) do introspectively take them to. Other variants are possible. What they would all have in common is a certain *a priori* tie between phenomenal similarity and introspective impression thereof.

It is not my purpose here to settle any debate over realism and anti-realism about phenomenal similarity. But note that the debate has implications for the status of phenomenal universals: whether they are observer-dependent or -independent. A full theory of the structure of the phenomenal realm should take a position on the matter.[20] It would also take a position on a similar debate about determinability relations. The discussion above assumed that such relations are fully objective. But a more conventionalist or pragmatist approach would not be unreasonable here. On such an approach, the classification of phenomenal universals into determinacy layers is not exactly a matter of tracking observer-independent facts; rather, it is a subtler exercise involving choice of a *useful* scheme to adopt (where the usefulness of a scheme is relative to interests, goals, and so on). In a particularly radical form, the idea might be that a "correct taxonomy" of phenomenal properties is not waiting to be *discovered*, it is waiting to be *created*. Hybrid options would take classification to involve an elusive admixture of discovery and creation. These hybrids cast classification as *partly observer-dependent*.

Consider an analogy. It is apparently a matter of some contention whether Anglican Christianity should be considered a species of Protestantism, a species of Catholicism, or a sui generis branch. The first two views classify Anglicanism as an *n*-layer determinable, but the third as an *n*–1-layer determinable. In this case, it is highly plausible that the choice between the three classificatory schemes is not *just* a matter of accurately tracking some observer-independent facts (historical, doctrinal, or other). There are almost certainly pragmatic and conventional considerations that bear on the choice. It is perfectly respectable to hold that some issues pertaining to phenomenological taxonomy follow the same model. At the same time, a more realist or objectivist approach would be perfectly respectable as well. According to such realism, the phenomenal realm has natural joints and the purpose of phenomenological taxonomy is to capture those accurately. It is by no means immediately obvious which approach is more plausible.

This antecedent uncertainty trickles down to the realm of maximally determinate phenomenal properties—the "phenomenal elements"—such as phenomenal-yellow$_{17}$-ness. Some of the latter's instances occur on the weekend, some during the week. Some occur at night, some during daytime. So the putative properties of weekday-phenomenal-yellow$_{17}$-ness, nightly-phenomenal-yellow$_{17}$-ness, and so on are *more* determinate than just phenomenal-yellow$_{17}$-ness. Phenomenal-yellow$_{17}$-ness is a genus of which they are species. Moreover, the similarity among all instances of weekday-phenomenal-yellow$_{17}$-ness cannot be lower than that among all instances of phenomenal-yellow$_{17}$-ness. Nonetheless, it seems absurd to deny phenomenal-yellow$_{17}$-ness its status as a phenomenal element for this reason. The realist and the anti-realist offer different explanations of this absurdity. The realist claims that phenomenal-yellow$_{17}$-ness is more *natural* than weekday-phenomenal-yellow$_{17}$-ness. The anti-realist maintains that it is much more *useful* to us, given our interests and purposes.[21] The realist explanation is perhaps more initially attractive, but faces difficulties. In particular, if the realist claims that phenomenal-yellow$_{17}$-ness is more natural than weekday-phenomenal-yellow$_{17}$-ness, she must offer some criterion of naturalness that goes beyond similarity. Thus an anti-realist take on what makes a certain phenomenal property "elemental" is far from incredible.

Some grounding relations, such as mereological composition, have sometimes been claimed to be contingent (Rosen 2006, Cameron 2007). Suppose for the sake of argument that the grounding relations among phenomenal properties are likewise contingent. Then there should be distinct metaphysically possible worlds which are qualitatively indistinguishable but which differ with respect to what grounds what. Take any (same-layer) phenomenal universals P_1, P_2, and P_3. If phenomenal grounding is contingent, then there are three otherwise similar possible worlds W_1, W_2, and W_3, such that: in W_1, P_1 and P_2 are primitive, while P_3 is grounded in their combination; in W_2, P_2 and P_3 are primitive, while P_1 is grounded in their combination; in W_3, P_1 and P_3 are primitive, while P_2 is grounded in their combination. But this seems a little odd. There is some intuition, I think, that in fact W_1, W_2, and W_3 are one and the same world, differently described. Since W_1, W_2, and W_3 contain all the same particulars, and moreover these particulars have all the same nonrelational properties, they are in truth indistinct worlds. This may well be the view of some meta-metaphysical anti-realists (see Sidelle 2002). However, there are also capable defenses of meta-metaphysical realism that would insist on an objectivist take on grounding and would treat W_1, W_2, and W_3 as genuinely different worlds (Schaffer 2009, Sider 2011).[22] As before, I raise the issue only to register the multiplicity of possible approaches to the project of understanding phenomenal structure.[23]

In conclusion, phenomenal grounding, determinacy, and similarity each admit of both respectable realist and respectable anti-realist positions. It is even coherent to combine realist and anti-realist positions on different aspects of phenomenal structure (for example, realism about phenomenal similarity with anti-realism about phenomenal grounding and determinability). The most desirable view in this area is robust realism about phenomenal similarity, determinability, and grounding alike. It paints forth an upliftingly objectivist picture of the phenomenal realm as fully and intricately structured in and of itself, suffused with observer-independent structure awaiting discovery. However, it is not improbable that some aspects of phenomenal structure (understood as comprising, *inter alia*, similarity, determinability, and grounding relations) might turn out to partly express our introspective, cognitive, pragmatic, and other predilections. Ultimately, a full theory of the structure of the phenomenal realm would have to take a position on this matter. In this book, though, I stay neutral on this issue and pursue the aspects of phenomenal structure pertinent to the question of primitiveness independently of whether they are observer-(in)dependent.

II. Methodological Foundations
6. The Role of Introspection

If you try to understand the structure of your car's carburetor, you start by *looking* at it. It is extremely hard to make much progress on understanding the interrelations among the carburetor's various parts without looking—a blind person would find the task extremely challenging. Thus *perceptual encounter* with the structure is the starting point for any plausible attempt to decipher it.

Fortunately, the carburetor's concrete physical structure lends itself to perceptual encounter. When a structure is abstract, or mental, it does not lend itself to perceptual encounter. We then hope for some other type of encounter with it. In describing his experience of attempting to understand mathematical structures, the Polish logician Jan Łukasiewicz (1970: 249) extols the virtues of *intuitive encounter*:[24]

> I should like to sketch a picture connected with the deepest intuitive feelings I always get about logistic . . . Whenever I am occupied even with the tiniest logistical problem, e.g. trying to find the shortest axiom of the implicational calculus, I have the impression that I am confronted with a mighty construction, of indescribable complexity and immeasurable rigidity. This construction has the effect upon me of a concrete tangible object, fashioned from the hardest of materials, a hundred times stronger than concrete and steel. I cannot change anything in it; by intense labor I merely find in it ever new details, and attain unshakeable and eternal truths.

If concrete physical structures lend themselves to perceptual encounter and abstract structures offer a sense of intuitive encounter, concrete phenomenal structures may present themselves to *introspective encounter*. Thus in attempting to understand the structure of one's stream of consciousness, it is natural to start by introspectively observing it. On the face of it, understanding the stream's phenomenal structure without introspecting it would be as challenging as understanding a carburetor's physical structure without looking at it.

Unlike perceptual encounter, the notions of intuitive and introspective encounter have faced sustained resistance in much twentieth-century philosophy. Let us set aside intuition, which does not bear directly on our present concerns. When it comes to introspective observation, the very notion that introspection should be understood along observational lines, on the model of perceptual observation, has often been challenged. As I have offered a sustained argument for the observational model elsewhere (Kriegel 2011b ch.1), here I merely wish to draw implications for the study of phenomenal structure. In particular, I want to argue that the model casts introspection as indispensable for such a study.

Consider other areas of inquiry. Zoologists who study zebras pay close attention to the impact of zebras on their environments, the environment's impact on zebra populations, various correlates and indicators or zebra presence, and so on. But in constructing their theories of zebras, zoologist use not only observations of such zebra-indicators. They also use observations of *zebras*. Indeed, given that it is possible to observe zebras, it would be folly for zoologists to refuse to take into account observations of zebras in constructing their theories of zebras. When studying leptons, we must construct our theories without taking into account direct observations of leptons, since we *cannot* observe the leptons themselves. But given that we *can* observe zebras, it would be perverse to construct our theories thereof without taking zebra observations into account. More generally, whenever we *can* observe a type of phenomenon, it is perverse to insist on developing our understanding of it in complete disregard of our observations of tokens.

This general principle has immediate implications for our understanding of phenomenal consciousness. If some conscious phenomena *can* be observed, it would be very odd indeed to insist on bracketing all such observation in developing our mature theories of consciousness. This suggests a straightforward argument for the *epistemic indispensability* of introspection. Let us say that an understanding of P is legitimate just when it is constructed or arrived at in an epistemically responsible manner. Then:

1) When a phenomenon P is observable, any legitimate understanding of P must take account of observations of P;
2) Some conscious phenomena are introspectively observable (and not otherwise observable); therefore,
3) Any legitimate understanding of consciousness must take account of introspective observations of conscious phenomena.

In the remainder of this section, I want to defend this argument from two sources of resistance. From this will emerge a fuller defense of the role of introspection in the contexts of discovering and justifying phenomenological hypotheses.

Before starting, it is worth pausing to draw a distinction between narrow and wide conceptions of introspection. The most straightforward mode of first-person awareness of one's own experience involves turning one's attention inward and attending to one's own concurrent internal goings-on. We may call this "introspection proper." But distinctly first-person awareness may be wider in two ways. First, it may be possible to conjure up a past experience in episodic memory and a future or merely possible experience in imagination, and then use broadly introspective capacities to examine these remembered or imagined experiences. Titchener (1912) called this "indirect introspection." Secondly, it has sometimes been claimed that some or all of our experiences are accompanied by a kind of nonattentive, unimposing, "peripheral" inner awareness (Brentano 1874, Kriegel 2009). To the extent that introspection proper is always attentive, this other inner awareness is not properly introspective. But it is a distinctly first-personal awareness nonetheless: nobody else can have *this* kind of awareness of my own experiences. It may thus be useful to collect under a single heading (i) this nonattentive inner awareness, (ii) introspectively aided examination of remembered and imagined experiences, and (iii) introspection proper. We may use the label "introspection loosely so called" for this wider group of capacities. Most of what I say below is intended to apply to introspection loosely so called. For this reason, when I do not explicitly specify which notion of introspection I am using, I should be understood to speak of introspection loosely so called.

6.1. *Introspective Discovery*

A straightforward objection to introspective indispensability is that the history of cognitive science gives the lie to it. Introspection cannot be epistemically indispensable, since cognitive science has actually dispensed with it.

To my mind, there are two problems with the idea that cognitive science is doing fine without introspection. The first is that it is not doing fine. The second is that it is not doing without introspection. It is a familiar comment—though admittedly a controversial one—that cognitive science has met with limited success when it comes to phenomenal consciousness.[25] This is the sense in which cognitive science is not doing fine without introspection, and I will not belabor the point here. Let me focus instead on my claim that cognitive science is not doing without introspection to begin with.

To appreciate the enduring role of introspection in cognitive science, let us start with the distinction, often attributed to Reichenbach but present already in Bolzano (1837 §15), between the "context of discovery" and the "context of justification." A dramatic example is provided by the German chemist Friedrich Kekulé's discovery of the molecular structure of benzene. The evidence Kekulé (1865) cited in justification of his model of benzene had to do with isomers, derivatives, and so on. But a quarter-century later Kekulé recounted that his initial discovery was due to a daydream in which he "saw" a snake biting its own tail. Clearly, in this case, the manner in which the model was discovered is irrelevant to the manner in which it is justified. Thus the contexts of discovery and justification can come apart, even if typically the gap between them is not this dramatic.

My claim in this subsection is that even *if* introspection has been purged from the context of cognitive-scientific justification, it certainly continues to underlie large tracts of research in the context of cognitive-scientific discovery. In fact, significant portions of modern cognitive science strike me as based on introspective discovery paving the way to non-introspective justification. Often the scientist, being a reflective introspector, experiences an initial introspective insight into some psychological phenomenon, and on its basis forms a hypothesis; s/he then proceeds to devise experimental tasks that ingeniously use exclusively third-person measures (often reaction times) to generate non-introspective evidence for the introspectively formed hypothesis.

A fine example of this is Roger Shepard's seminal work on imagery and the phenomenon of mental rotation (Shepard and Metzler 1971). That we use mental rotation of private images to compare shapes of the objects imaged is of course what introspection teaches—there is nothing surprising there. The ingenuity in Shepard's research was in devising an experimental paradigm in which pairs of similarly shaped but differently oriented three-dimensional "objects" with varying angles of putative rotation were to be judged for similarity by subjects. The fact that subjects took longer to judge the shapes to be similar when the angle of putative rotation was greater suggested that these subjects were mentally rotating imagistic representations of the objects. Thus the purely "objective" (read: third-person) measure of reaction time served to ratify what was already known on the basis of "subjective" (first-person) introspective impression.

A more recent example is Vilayanur Ramachandran's ingenious demonstration of number-color synesthesia (Ramachandran and Hubbard 2001). Ramachandran used panels of numerals printed in a way that made it difficult to distinguish different numerals. Control subjects took significantly longer to identify incongruent numerals than number-color synesthetes, to whom the incongruent numerals presumably appeared incongruously colored. Of course, that number-color synesthesia exists we know on the basis of synesthetes' introspective reports since at least the nineteenth century (see Galton 1880). But Ramachandran's reaction-time-based demonstration had the advantage of purging appeal to introspection in ratifying this knowledge.[26]

From casual observation of cognitive-science conferences and colloquia, my impression is that this sort of gambit is pervasive in vision science and throughout cognitive (neuro-)psychology. Scientists often devise ingenious experimental designs that circumvent explicit appeal to introspection, but the original hunch underlying the research is founded on personal introspection.[27]

It is an open question just how far cognitive science would get if it purged introspection not only from the context of justification but also from the context of discovery. Suppose cognitive science insisted, from its inception, not only on devising non-introspective justification of introspectively formed hypotheses, but also on exclusively non-introspective hypothesis formation. In fact, consider a possible world otherwise like ours but where cognitive scientists lack any introspective capacities. My own suspicion is that we would be shocked to find out just how skeletally poor the scientific understanding of the mind is in such a world. If so, the role of introspection in our own scientific understanding of the mind is greatly underrated in the "official narrative" about cognitive science. For the gap between the state of our knowledge and understanding and the state of knowledge and understanding in that counterfactual world is owed entirely to our implicit ("unofficial") use of introspection.

If all this is right, then introspection is not only epistemically indispens*able*, but also not really dispens*ed* with in cognitive-scientific practice. Still, introspection skeptics may insist that introspection has no role to play in the context of cognitive-scientific justification. This is the topic of the next subsection.

6.2. Introspective Justification

To be sure, there is a long philosophical tradition of over-trusting introspection. In its strongest form, this tendency can be articulated as a conjunction of two converse theses, one asserting the *perfect reliability* of introspection and one the *omnipotence* of introspection. According to the first, introspection is *infallible*:

(II) If subject S introspects having phenomenology P, then S has P.[28]

According to the second, introspection never misses anything that passes within its purview, rendering phenomenology *self-intimating*:

(SI) If subject S has phenomenology P, then S introspects having P.

The conjunction of II and SI casts introspection as perfectly trustworthy. We may call the conjunction *introspective dogmatism* (or perhaps *introspective maximalism*, since it portrays introspection as maximally powerful).

Unfortunately for all involved, introspective dogmatism (or maximalism) is highly implausible. Introspection is far from perfectly reliable and far from omnipotent (Nisbett and Wilson 1977). However, the fact that introspection is not maximally trustworthy does not show that it is thoroughly unreliable and/or entirely impotent.[29] For our present purposes, what matters is whether introspection could be shown to be *minimally* trustworthy, that is, have the least demanding epistemic properties that would be needed for it to play a legitimate role in the context of justification. This requires that we identify these minimal epistemic properties, concerning both reliability and potency.

On the side of reliability, plausibly what is required is that introspection enjoy *above-chance reliability*: it is more likely that one has a phenomenology if one introspects having it. On the side of potency, being minimally justificatory would plausibly require that introspection enjoy *nonnegligible potency*: it is more likely one will introspect a phenomenology if one has it. To a first approximation, we may formulate the claim as follows:

(ACR) If subject S introspects having phenomenology P, then S is more likely to have P than if S does not so introspect.
(NNP) If subject S has phenomenology P, then S is more likely to introspect having P than if S does not have P.

The mere *disjunction* of ACR and NNP already bestows *some* epistemic value on introspection. A more robust yet highly plausible view consists in their conjunction; call it *introspective minimalism*. The idea is that having a phenomenology makes it more likely that one introspect it and introspecting it makes it more likely that one actually has it. I contend that this view, or something very like it, undergirds the legitimacy of appeal to introspection in *justifying* hypotheses about consciousness. Something stronger may yet be true, but the truth of minimalism would suffice to legitimize introspective appeal.

Suppose, for instance, that introspection turned out to be as trustworthy as our sense of smell, that is, as reliable and as potent as a normal adult human's olfactory system. Then introspective minimalism would be vindicated. Normally, when we have an olfactory experience as of raspberries, it is more likely that there are raspberries in the vicinity than if we do not have such an experience. Conversely, when there are raspberries in the vicinity, it is more likely that we would have an olfactory experience as of raspberries than if there are none. So the "equireliability" of olfaction and introspection would support introspective minimalism. Such equireliability is highly plausible.

It is worth noting that introspective minimalism can be refined in various ways. Thus, ACR and NNP do not explicitly contain any quantifiers, suggesting that they are intended as doubly universal, applying to *all* subjects and *all* phenomenologies (all values of S and P). This may turn out to be too strong. Perhaps it would be wiser to restrict these claims to normal subjects normally circumstanced. For it may be that under conditions of cognitive overload, or in psychologically malformed subjects, introspecting a phenomenology does not increase the probability that the phenomenology is present (and/or the presence of a phenomenology does not increase the probability that it be introspected).[30] Likewise, there may be reasons to exclude certain special types of phenomenology from ACR or NNP. Various "exemptions" may need to be carved. For example, according to many phenomenologists, a person's field of consciousness typically involves a "fringe" or "margin" that contributes to one's overall experience very lightly and unimposingly. Thus, as I sit in front of my laptop and visually experience it in an attentive and focused manner, I am also aware, much more peripherally and as it were almost imperceptibly, of the tactile sensation of soles of my shoes, a low-humming anxiety about a looming appointment with a plagiarizer, and so on. Arguably, this fringe phenomenology cannot in principle be introspected, since introspecting a phenomenal occurrence renders it focal rather than fringe (Kriegel 2009 ch.5). Likewise, consider the phenomenology of experiential immersion or engrossment, such as a basketball player experiences when "in the zone." This immersive phenomenology may also be non-introspectible, insofar as turning one's introspective attention onto it would require taking a step back from it and disrupting its characteristic feelings of rightness and flow.[31] More generally, there may be a class of phenomenologies whose very essence requires the absence of introspective attention; we may call these (doubtless suboptimally) "elusive phenomenologies." If so, ACR and NNP would probably need to be restricted to nonelusive phenomenologies.[32]

Taking into account the just-discussed restrictions, we would obtain the following doubly refined thesis of introspective minimalism:

(RIM) For any (normally circumstanced) *normal* subject S and any *nonelusive* phenomenology P: If S introspects having P, then S is more likely to have P (than if S does not so introspect) & If S has P, then S is more likely to introspect having P (than if S does not have P).

Other restrictions may be called for upon closer examination. Still, the fully refined minimalist thesis would very likely be nontrivial yet in a position to undergird the legitimate scientific use of introspection not only in the context of discovery but also in the context of justification.

7. The Problem of Introspective Disagreement

It is sometimes felt that the most important challenge to introspective appeal is not so much the epistemic status of an individual's introspective impressions, but rather the apparent irresolvability of interpersonal introspective disagreements. Suppose S reports her introspective impression that phenomenology P has feature F, whereas S* reports that P does not have F. (We may further suppose that S and S* report the same degree of confidence in their introspective impressions and both have properly functioning introspective faculties.) How is our investigation of P supposed to proceed under such (not uncommon) circumstances?

The question is pressing, because arguably it was precisely the problem of introspective disagreement that has led to the demise of introspectionist psychology. Two disagreements between Titchener's lab and Külpe's have proved particularly intractable, and in the long run particularly damaging to introspectionism. One concerned the existence of imageless thoughts: for Titchener and his students, competent introspection revealed that there are none; for Külpe and his, it revealed there are some. The other concerned the number of phenomenal elements: Titchener required 42,415; Külpe managed with only 11,000 (Revonsuo 2010 ch.2). It is this type of apparently irresolvable dispute that has led Watson (1913: 163) to dismiss introspectionist psychology wholesale:

> Psychology, as it is generally thought of [i.e., by introspectionists], has something esoteric in its methods. If you fail to reproduce my findings, it is not due to some fault in your apparatus or in the control of your stimulus, but it is due to the fact that your introspection

is untrained ... In [the natural] sciences a better technique will give reproducible results. Psychology is otherwise. If you can't observe 3–9 states of clearness in attention, your introspection is poor. If, on the other hand, a feeling seems reasonably clear to you, your introspection is again faulty. You are seeing too much. Feelings are never clear.

Today, similar disagreements bedevil debates over cognitive phenomenology, emotional phenomenology, and so on. One is entitled to worry, therefore, that current phenomenological disputes will prove no more tractable, and in the final analysis no more fruitful, than the original introspectionists'.

In this section, I want to consider three possible reactions to such a predicament. I will call them the *no-fact* view, the *phenomenal variability* view, and the *introspective competence* view. These reactions can be adopted in different circumstances and can be more appropriate in some cases than others. I will argue that the last type of reaction is the most appropriate for the kind of cases at issue in this book.

The most staunchly defeatist reaction to introspective disagreements is that there is *no fact of the matter* as to what the phenomenology is *really* like. In the present case, there is no determinate phenomenological fact that settles the question of whether P is F or not. (This is not to be confused with the eliminativist claim that there is no such thing as P, or F. Such eliminativism does provide for facts that settle the relevant questions.) Call this the *no-fact view*.[33]

The no-fact view can play out in two different ways, depending on whether we adopt descriptivist or expressivist semantics for introspective reports. The more natural version of the view is descriptivist, and claims that both S and S* are attempting to correctly describe the phenomenological facts when they report "P is F" and "P is not F." The upshot is an introspective error theory: since there are no such phenomenological facts, both reports are untrue.[34] There is, however, an expressivist version of the view, according to which the disagreement between S and S* is *merely apparent*, since neither is actually making an assertion. Instead, each expresses a different (noncognitive) attitude toward P's being F: S approves of P being F, S* disapproves.[35] In both versions of the no-fact view, introspective reports do not constitute a source of evidence for theorizing about consciousness.

The main problem with the no-fact view is that, pending further considerations, it comes across as an *over*reaction in virtually every case. In other areas, we do not conclude from the existence of disagreement that there must be no fact of the matter. If S contends that she saw the keys in the living room but S* insists that she saw them in the dining room, we would be disinclined to conclude that there is no fact of the matter as to where the keys really are. So it cannot be just the *existence* of disagreement that leads to the no-fact view. Perhaps what is special about introspective disagreement is that they persist through the end of inquiry, whereas disagreements on key locations tend not to. The problem with this is that there is no meaningful evidence for the claim that introspective disagreements will persist through the end of inquiry. One might suggest that they would *have* to, given the incorrigibility of introspection.[36] But, setting aside the fact that the incorrigibility thesis appears too strong to be plausible, even conceding it could at most lead to an *epistemological* conclusion, namely, that we cannot *know* whether P is F or not. Nothing here entails the stronger *metaphysical* conclusion that there is no fact of the matter as to whether P is F.[37]

A more cheerful reaction to introspective disagreements is what we may call the *phenomenal variability view*. According to it, even the most fundamental features of phenomenology often vary across subjects. The right attitude to our disagreement is to conclude that S's P is F but S*'s it is not F. Their phenomenologies are simply different.[38]

This view may take inspiration from perceptual disagreements. Suppose S and S* are each facing a swan, and S reports that the swan before her is white while S* reports that the swan before her is black. If we know that the swans perceived are numerically different, it would be most natural to conclude that the swans are also qualitatively different: S's is white but S*'s is black. In the phenomenal case, the experiences introspected are definitely numerically different (since one occurs in S and one in S*). So it should be likewise natural to conclude that S's P-experience is F while S*'s is not. This reasoning only requires the plausible premise that introspection is highly reliable. If we know (i) that in S and S* introspection is highly reliable, (ii) that S introspects one instance of P and S* another instance, and (iii) that S's introspective impression is that P is F and S*'s is that P is not F, then we should infer that S's instance of P is F but S*'s is not F.

The phenomenal variability reaction is surely the right one in many cases of introspective disagreement. However, the more basic and general the phenomenal feature at issue, the less plausible the view becomes. If S claims that her phenomenology of frustration involves a tinge of anger, whereas S* claims that hers does not, it is fitting (*mutatis mutandis*) to adopt the variability reaction. But suppose S reports that her emotional phenomenology involves nothing more than feeling certain bodily sensations, whereas S* reports that hers involves an additional element that constitutes a sui generis emotional phenomenology. It would be odd to conclude that S and S* simply differ in their emotional phenomenology, one's being primitive while the other's reducing to bodily sensations. That is, it would be odd to conclude that the James-Lange theory of emotion is true of S but false of S*.[39] We would be more inclined to think that S and S* must have conceptualized differently the same phenomenology, or that one of them did not fully understand what was at issue, or that one committed an introspective mistake or oversight. Likewise if S claimed to have phenomenal properties at all while (otherwise normal) S* professed to be a zombie: a let-a-thousand-flowers-bloom approach would seem misplaced here.

My focus in this book is on second-layer phenomenal determinables. These are the most general phenomenal features other than phenomenality *per se*. To that extent, I am interested in phenomenal features for which the phenomenal variability approach is least appealing. For this reason, I will set it aside here as unlikely to affect the issues to be discussed.

⁂

According to the no-fact view, both S and S*'s introspective reports are untrue. According to the phenomenal variability view, both are true. A third option is that one report is true and the other untrue. On this view, which we may call the *introspective competence* view, introspective disagreements show nothing more than that one of the parties to the disagreement must be wrong. Thus, if S and S* make incompatible introspective judgments on the same type of phenomenology, the right response is to simply seek who is in error.

With perceptual disagreements, this is often the most natural approach. Suppose S and S* smell a bottled extract, and S judges it is gardenia while S* judges it is jasmine. Our natural inclination would be to suppose that one of them must be simply mistaken. One of them is the better nose, the more competent odor-detector. Likewise, at least when subjects introspect the most general features of phenomenology—those for which phenomenal variability is least plausible—it should be natural to suppose that disagreements are due to differences in introspective competence. When S and S* issue conflicting introspective reports (on a very general aspect of phenomenology), the theorist would be justified, *mutatis mutandis*, in endorsing the more competent introspector's report. Such endorsement may result in error, of course, in case the more competent introspector got it wrong. But on the whole, higher competence should be the more reliable guide. So, endorsing competent introspectors' reports would always be epistemically justified, at least by reliabilist lights.

We may think of this as a heuristic for investigating phenomenal structure. *Applying* this heuristic does require that we have a competence measure, one independent of which introspector we theorists happen to agree with. Admittedly, such a measure should be hard to devise. But once it is, introspective disagreements submit to straightforward resolution: we are to endorse whichever introspective report is issued by the more competent introspector.

There is certainly a firm pretheoretic resistance to this approach. But the resistance may be more moral than epistemological. Charles Siewert once pointed out to me that our privileged access to our own phenomenology is a ("the"?) central source of our sense of dignity as separate, inviolable, self-possessing individuals.[40] This is why telling people what they *really* feel, overriding their own claims about what they feel, seems first and foremost *morally abrasive* rather than *epistemically irresponsible*.⁴¹ Conversely, being told what one really feels over one's protestations tends to elicit moral rather than epistemological indignation. The full case for this would have to be prosecuted elsewhere, but my suspicion is that the ethos of first-person incorrigibility is rooted in this sort of respect for the inviolable dignity of others.⁴² It is this ethos, I am suggesting, that accounts for our pretheoretic resistance to the introspective competence view. The view sanctions a domineering attitude toward overridden subjects—which makes us cringe. Conversely, there is a feel-good element to the phenomenal variability view: it respects persons. Nonetheless, we must keep in mind that these pressures away from the introspective competence view are not properly epistemic. They do not provide us with *epistemic* reasons for preferring the phenomenal variability view, only *moral* reasons.

This line of thought effectively provides a *debunking explanation* of our pretheoretic resistance to the introspective competence view (and attraction to the phenomenal variability view).⁴³ All the same, the competence approach is more helpful in principle than in practice. For in practice we have no idea how to devise a sufficiently compelling competence measure. Ideally, the measure would be so compelling that it would be possible for a theorist, who recognized that (*a*) her introspective impressions conflicted with a peer's and (*b*) the peer scores higher on the relevant measure, to let the peer's reported impressions override her own. It is at present unimaginable what such a measure might look like. Wundt reportedly considered an introspector competent only after 10,000 trials (Schwitzgebel 2011: 74). But this does not take into account how attentive and alert the subject is in each trial, how antecedently talented (perceptive and reflective) an introspector she is, and myriad other factors. Yet no better competence measure suggests itself.⁴⁴ In addition, we have no clear standards for when to adopt the introspective competence approach to begin with. It was noted above that the approach is more plausible than phenomenal variability when the phenomenal feature at issue is sufficiently general, that is, constitutes a sufficiently high-level determinable. But this does not yet give us a concrete threshold of generality/determinacy to guide choice between phenomenal variability and introspective competence in practice.

To conclude, I have considered three possible reactions to introspective disagreements. The no-fact view casts the introspective reports of both parties to the disagreement as untrue, the phenomenal variability casts both as true, and the introspective competence view casts one as true and the other as untrue. The correct approach seems to me to be this: when the disagreement is over a relatively specific phenomenal feature, the phenomenal variability view is *prima facie* more plausible; when the disagreement is over a relatively general phenomenal feature, the introspective competence view becomes more plausible (at least *prima facie*).⁴⁵ Unfortunately, however, this provides only the vaguest guide for dealing with introspective disagreements in practice. Methodological developments in this area may yet be possible that would blunt the skeptical effect of introspective disagreements. But until such time we must seek ways to limit or eliminate the potential for introspective disagreement. This is the topic of the next section.

8. Beyond Introspection

Introspective disagreements are especially paralyzing if introspection is considered the end-all and be-all of disputes about the phenomenal facts. But often appeal to introspection is only a first step in theorizing. Reasoning, inference, and argumentation are intended to carry the bulk of the case for or against some phenomenological thesis. The phenomenological thesis is not simply *delivered* by introspection: its proponent does not profess to have directly introspected its truthmaker. Rather, the phenomenological thesis is *suggested* by introspection, in the sense that what introspection delivers can be used in an *argument* for it.

Specially prominent in recent phenomenological discussions have been so-called phenomenal contrast arguments. A classic example is an argument for cognitive phenomenology due originally to Moore (1953) and developed later by Strawson (1994 ch.1). Some philosophers avow direct introspective awareness of a purely nonsensory phenomenology special to cognition; others disagree. The Strawson-Moore argument attempts to provide *indirect* support for the existence of such phenomenology. Imagine two subjects S and S*, such that (i) S and S* are listening to the news in French, (ii) S understands French, and (iii) S* does not understand French. In this scenario, it seems that there is a difference in the *overall* phenomenology of S and S* as they listen to the newscast, but that their strictly sensory phenomenology is the same. It would follow that the difference in their overall phenomenology must be due to some nonsensory phenomenology, presumably a purely cognitive phenomenology of *understanding* present in S's experience but not in S*'s. The argument may be reconstructed as follows:

P1) S and S* have a different overall phenomenology;
P2) S and S* have the same sensory phenomenology; therefore,
C1) There is a purely nonsensory phenomenology that S and S* differ in; and therefore,
C2) There is such a thing as purely nonsensory phenomenology.[46]

The ultimate conclusion of this argument (C2) is a phenomenological claim on which there is clearly no introspective agreement. But the hope is that the phenomenological premises (P1 and P2) are introspectively uncontroversial *in comparison*.[47] Thus an argument can provide indirect introspective support for a phenomenological proposition for which direct introspection has failed to produce widespread agreement.

Notice that the Moore-Strawson argument does appeal to introspection in supporting an irreducible cognitive phenomenology. However, it does not appeal to introspection *of* an irreducible cognitive phenomenology. Instead, it appeals to what it hopes are introspectively less controversial claims. The general strategy, then, is this. When a phenomenological proposition q is met with (wide) introspective disagreement, we seek another phenomenological proposition p, such that (i) p does not tend to induce (as much) introspective disagreement and (ii) there is some argument A whose conclusion is q and whose only phenomenological premise is p.[48] What introspection delivers in A is only p, the relatively uncontroversial phenomenological claim. The route from p to q is not delivered by introspection, but by reasoning. In this fashion, the proponent and opponent of q can isolate some introspective common ground p and debate only the plausibility of $q|p$, that is, *q-given-p* (with introspection playing no role in that part of the debate). This represents, in effect, a fourth possible reaction to introspective disagreements: the theorist remains neutral with respect to introspection's verdict on the phenomenological proposition at stake, and instead seeks a deductive argument with which to bypass direct appeal to introspection. We may call this the *deductive-bypass approach*. (Although the argument leading from p to q need not be deductive, it *may*.)

The obvious drawback in the deductive-bypass approach is that it still makes *some* introspective appeal. Although the proponent of a deductive argument for a phenomenological thesis does not profess to directly introspect the truthmaker of the argument's conclusion, she does profess to directly introspect the truthmaker(s) of at least some premise(s). This is unproblematic as long as the relevant premises succeed in commanding wide introspective assent. But whether they do is not in the proponent's control. The Moore-Strawson argument, for example, has met with significant resistance to P1 and especially P2. Many philosophers have claimed that they do *not* introspect the sameness of sensory phenomenology asserted by P2 (Carruthers 2006, Robinson 2006, Prinz 2011). This does not mean, of course, that such argumentation is "epidialectical": as long as the phenomenological premises garner *more* introspective assent than the phenomenological conclusion, the argument as a whole represents dialectical progress (other things being equal).[49] It produces new dialectical pressure on the opponent.[50] Still, there is a sense in which the possibility-in-principle of a dialectical impasse continues to loom.

∽∾

An ideal solution to this problem would be to devise arguments for phenomenological conclusions that do not involve introspection at any stage. Unfortunately, it is highly implausible that any collection of non-phenomenological propositions could entail a phenomenological proposition. (A proposition is phenomenological just when its truth requires that some phenomenal property be instantiated.) If so, every deductive argument for a phenomenological conclusion would have to involve some phenomenological premise(s). This can be thought of on analogy with Moore's (1903) principle that every deductive argument with a normative conclusion must have a normative premise, i.e., that you cannot derive an "ought" from an "is." To salute Moore's notion of "naturalistic fallacy," I will call its phenomenological parallel the *physicalistic fallacy*:

(PF) A deductive argument with a phenomenological conclusion must have at least one phenomenological premise.

Note well: PF in no way requires us to reject physicalism as such. It only requires us to deny that there are *a priori* connections between physical propositions and phenomenal propositions. That is, it requires us to reject "a priori physicalism," what Chalmers (2002) calls "type-A physicalism." PF is perfectly compatible with *a posteriori* or "type-B" physicalism, according to which there are necessary but merely *a posteriori* connections between physical and phenomenal facts.[51] In what follows, I will assume that *a priori* physicalism is implausible, and concomitantly that PF is plausible.[52] A consequence is that no deductive argument for a phenomenological thesis could proceed without phenomenological premises, and therefore (ultimately) without appeal to introspection.[53]

Importantly, PF does not rule out the possibility of introspection-free arguments for phenomenological theses. It rules out only *deductive* arguments of the sort. It leaves the door open to nondeductive, non-demonstrative arguments. In the recent literature, some *epistemic arguments* have been offered that employ no phenomenological premises but argue through inference to the best explanation for phenomenological conclusions. Perhaps the best known, presented first by Goldman (1993) but developed more fully by Pitt (2004), targets irreducible cognitive phenomenology as well. It proceeds by claiming that our knowledge of some of our cognitive states has certain characteristics that can only be explained, or at least are *best* explained, by the hypothesis that these cognitive states exhibit an irreducible type of phenomenology. Pitt's version of the argument may be reconstructed as follows:

P1) Subject S has immediate, noninferential knowledge of some cognitive states S is in;
P2) If some of S's cognitive states have an irreducible phenomenology, this would best explain S's immediate, noninferential knowledge of them; therefore (by inference to the best explanation),
C1) Some of S's cognitive states have an irreducible phenomenology; and therefore,
C2) There is such a thing as irreducible cognitive phenomenology.

It is not my current concern to evaluate the cogency of the Goldman-Pitt argument. I only wish to point out that it contains no phenomenological premises. Its first premise is epistemological and its second explanatory. Neither makes any claim about any phenomenal property actually being instantiated. The only propositions that make such a claim are the conclusions. Thus although the conclusions are phenomenological, no premise requires appeal to introspection. This represents, in effect, a fifth possible reaction to introspective disagreements: where such occur, they can be bypassed altogether by devising abductive arguments with no phenomenological premises. Call this the *abductive-bypass approach* to the problem of introspective disagreement.

Of the five possible reactions to introspective disagreement discussed here, I have avowed some sympathy for three: the introspective competence view, the deductive-bypass approach, and the abductive-bypass approach.[54] But the abductive-bypass approach is importantly superior in one respect, namely, the scope of putative phenomenal features it can target. Recall that the introspective competence view is most suitable for very general phenomenal features. A putative sui generis cognitive phenomenology would indeed be very general, but epistemic arguments along the above lines can target much more specific features as well.[55] Conversely, as I have pointed out elsewhere (Kriegel 2007), phenomenal features so general that they are present in every possible human experience (perhaps because they are *constitutive* of every experience) elude support by phenomenal contrast arguments. For such arguments require a contrast between two phenomenal episodes only one of which exhibits the feature at issue, but when a feature is universal (or constitutive) no such pair exists. In contrast, epistemic arguments for such features may still be mounted.[56]

My preference for epistemic arguments in matters phenomenological will show itself at various places in this book. But I will develop my own version of this form of argument most fully in Chapter 3, where it will be used to argue that the attitude of entertaining a proposition exhibits its own proprietary phenomenology.

III. Looking Ahead
9. Plan of the Book

The purpose of the preceding has been to lay out the metaphysical and methodological foundations of a first-person inquiry into the scope and structure of the phenomenal realm. This book does not attempt to go very far in pursuit of this project. The core of the book consists in five studies of putative types of phenomenology that, antecedently, might qualify as second-layer phenomenal primitives: cognitive phenomenology, conative phenomenology, the phenomenology of entertaining, emotional phenomenology, and moral phenomenology.

Two other highly general putative types of phenomenology will be discussed in the Conclusion and Appendix: the phenomenology of imagination and the phenomenology of freedom.

To deprive myself of a punch line: I will end up avowing significant credence in cognitive, conative, imaginative, and entertaining phenomenology being second-layer phenomenal primitives. Emotional and moral phenomenology, by contrast, are reducible to combinations of other second-layer types of phenomenology, while the phenomenology of freedom is plausibly a lower-layer phenomenal determinable. Or so I will argue.

In addition to cognitive, conative, imaginative, and entertaining phenomenology, it is taken for granted in this book that perceptual phenomenology and algedonic phenomenology are second-layer primitives. This gives us a tentative list of six second-layer phenomenal primitives. My answer to Q is thus tentative but precise: six!

Chapter 1 is devoted to cognitive phenomenology. Although I support the Goldman-Pitt epistemic argument for cognitive phenomenology, my primary goal in that chapter is to devise a completely new type of argument for sui generis cognitive phenomenology. The argument relies on a thought-experiment in which the mental life of a person lacking any functioning sensory systems still exhibits indicators of phenomenality. A subsidiary goal of the chapter is to sketch an approach to the nonreductive characterization of such a primitive cognitive phenomenology.

Chapter 2 concerns conative phenomenology. The first part of the chapter offers an argument for primitivism about conative phenomenology, based on a series of phenomenal-contrast cases. The second part focuses on the *character* of conative phenomenology. In the functionalist literature that has dominated the philosophy of mind of the last generation or two, the paradigmatic conative state is considered to be desire. But while desire may be *functionally* paradigmatic, it is an open question which conative state is *phenomenologically* paradigmatic. I argue that the mental episode of *deciding and then trying to* φ is the fundamental form of conative phenomenology.

Chapter 3 is devoted to the act of entertaining a proposition. In the first part, I present a sustained epistemic argument for primitivism about the phenomenology of entertaining (which implies it is irreducible to cognitive phenomenology). In the second part, I offer a nonreductive characterization of entertaining in terms of its phenomenal feel and its connections to other propositional attitudes.

Chapter 4 focuses on emotional phenomenology. Part of the problem in discussing this topic is that the very nature of emotion is a controversial issue. I therefore start with a defense of a novel version of the "feeling theory" of emotion, according to which emotions are essentially phenomenal. To do so, I develop an account of emotional phenomenology as involving crucially elements of cognitive and conative phenomenology. It is only once we appreciate emotional phenomenology's full intricacy, I contend, that we are in a position to see emotion as essentially phenomenal. I then consider whether emotional phenomenology is so rich as to involve an irreducible type of phenomenology. Although I reach no decisive conclusion, the weight of evidence seems to favor reductivism.

Chapter 5 is concerned with moral phenomenology, a topic that has garnered quite a bit of attention in recent metaethical research (Kriegel 2008). Here too, the task is complicated by the fact that there is no consensus on what moral mental states are to begin with. The bulk of this chapter is accordingly devoted to developing and defending a specific account of moral commitments, an account I call *dual-process cognitivist internalism*. With this account in place, I proceed to the question of whether the phenomenal feel of moral commitments might be primitive. I conclude that it probably is not: moral phenomenology plausibly reduces to a combination of cognitive, conative, and emotional phenomenology.[57]

In the Conclusion, I address three questions. First, I argue that the phenomenology of imagination is a second-layer phenomenal primitive. Although this book is focused on nonsensory phenomenology, and imagination is typically sensory, I take this question up to "complete the picture" of second-layer primitives. Secondly, I revisit the question of taxonomy raised above. Finally, I briefly discuss a number of potential candidates for a seventh second-layer phenomenal primitive.

There is also an Appendix on the phenomenology of freedom, which plausibly is not a *second*-layer phenomenal determinable at all. My first-order goal is to articulate and defend a substantive characterization of the feeling of freedom. I defend three main theses, perhaps the most important of which is that freedom-experience involves a phenomenology as of compatibilist rather than libertarian freedom. The chapter's second-order goal is to explore some innovative methods for pursuing a first-person inquiry into phenomenal life. For this reason, much of the discussion is dedicated to methodological matters, which I suppose takes us full circle.

10. The Question of (Intellectual) Value

Let me close by addressing a pertinent question: *Who cares*? In other words, why should we expend intellectual energies on discovering the second-layer phenomenal primitives? Why does it matter? What hangs on it?

This is a question about the intellectual value of the project undertaken here. One way of answering the question is by pointing out research areas of recognized intellectual value for which the present project may have implications. Consider research on the nature and structure of epistemic justification. Some philosophers have recently argued that perceptual experiences can confer positive epistemic status on perceptual beliefs purely in virtue of their phenomenal character (Huemer 2001, Pryor 2005). Thus, purely because of what it is like to have a perceptual experience as of a brown table, the experiencer is prima facie justified in believing that there is a brown table before her. Now, if perceptual phenomenology has this kind of justification-conferring power, then a sui generis cognitive phenomenology may as well—provided there is such a phenomenology. Perhaps purely because of what it is like to have a cognitive experience as of identity being a transitive relation, the experiencer is prima facie justified in believing that identity is a transitive relation (Chudnoff 2011a, Bengson forthcoming).[58]

Similarly, the study of conative, emotional, and moral phenomenology may have implications for ethics and metaethics (Kriegel 2008). Thus, many ethicists have held that one is prima facie ethically justified in promoting pleasure and demoting pain (you need not be a consequentialist to hold this). It is, moreover, quite plausible to maintain that the reason it is good to demote pain has to do with the phenomenal character of pain—the unpleasant way it feels like to experience it. If so, the phenomenal character of pain and pleasure have the power to confer prima facie ethical justification on actions that might cause them. Now, if the algedonic phenomenology of pain and pleasure has this power, the same may hold of a sui generis emotional phenomenology involving subtler types of positive or negative affect—provided there is such phenomenology.[59] In this way, the intellectual value of the present project could be demonstrated by its implications for other areas of inquiry.

It may be worth insisting, however, that the project's intellectual value is not *only* instrumental in this way. The project also has *intrinsic, non*instrumental intellectual value. There are reasons to train one's curiosity on the question of phenomenal primitives for its own sake, and regardless of its implications for other questions. Consider that early discussions of phenomenal consciousness in analytic philosophy of mind were concerned primarily with its problematic relation to the physical world, almost never with its internal variety and structure. Such discussions have tended to focus on simple, uncontroversial cases of phenomenal consciousness, most notably visual experiences (especially of red) and algedonic experiences (especially bodily pain). More recently, however, an a-reductive interest in phenomenal consciousness has started to gain traction. It has become apparent that many interesting philosophical questions arise already *within* the realm of the phenomenal, and not only regarding its relation to the physical realm. It has also become apparent that, thanks partly to the prolonged reign of exclusively reductive interest in phenomenal consciousness, our understanding of the internal variety and structure of the phenomena of consciousness has remained limited. It is partly in this context that the debates over cognitive phenomenology, the phenomenology of agency, the richness of perceptual phenomenology, and the like have commanded increasing attention.

The project of searching for the phenomenal primitives is just a generalization from those debates, as is the yet more general project of mapping out the structure of the phenomenal realm. Insofar as there are facts of the matter targeted by these projects, it would certainly be desirable to *know* those facts. There are legitimate questions about whether we *can* know such facts, at least in the same sense in which we know other facts. But it is hard to deny that knowing such facts would be valuable—and valuable in and of itself, that is, intrinsically. After all, they are, more than any others, facts about *us*.[60]

1

Cognitive Phenomenology

My goal in this chapter is twofold. In Part I, I argue for the very *existence* of a phenomenology proper to cognitive states—an irreducible cognitive phenomenology. After introducing the issue (§1), I offer (what I hope are) workable characterizations of the cognitive and the phenomenal (§§2–3). I then present an argument for "cognitive-phenomenal primitivism" (§4). In Part II, I turn to the question of the *character* of cognitive phenomenology: what *is* it like to engage in conscious cognition? After sketching an approach to this question that focuses on what I call phenomenological Ramsey sentences (§5), I produce one for the paradigmatic cognitive activity of *making a judgment* (§6).

I. Cognitive-Phenomenal Primitivism

1. Primitivism about Cognitive Phenomenology

Cognition, as other kinds of mentation, involves both (i) cognitive *processes* and (ii) *products* of such processes, such as cognitive *states* and *acts*. Apparent examples include:

- Judging that p
- Thinking that p
- Believing that p
- Accepting that p
- Suspecting that p
- Surmising that p
- Conjecturing that p
- Hypothesizing that p
- It occurring to one that p
- Being confident that p
- Being convinced that p
- Being sure (certain) that p
- Doubting that p

- Disbelieving that *p*
- Remembering that *p*
- Expecting that *p*
- Predicting that *p*
- Realizing that *p*
- Speculating that *p*
- Deeming that *p*
- Assuming that *p*

Suppose there is a "natural category" in the area of these states, and that there is a property P that conscious occurrences of all and only members of that category instantiate. Then P is a sort of *phenomenal signature of cognition*. It is what we may call "cognitive phenomenology per se." We could then pose the question of cognitive phenomenology by feeding cognitive phenomenology per se into the generalized triad from the Introduction:

1) There exists cognitive phenomenology per se.
2) Cognitive phenomenology per se is irreducible to perceptual and/or algedonic phenomenology.
3) Perceptual and algedonic phenomenology ultimately exhaust all phenomenology.

Primitivism about cognitive phenomenology per se would consist in rejecting 3 and defending 1 and 2.

There may also be no phenomenal signature of cognition. There may be no natural category of cognitive states, or it may not have sharp boundaries, or there may not be any phenomenal feature common and peculiar to conscious occurrences of such a category. None of this would settle the question of cognitive phenomenology. For there to be primitive cognitive phenomenology, only the following needs to hold: there is a phenomenal property P, such that (i) P is instantiated by (conscious tokens of) *some* mental state that unquestionably belongs on the above list, (ii) no mental state that does not belong on the list instantiates P, and (iii) P is irreducible to any other phenomenal properties. Note that this does not require that P be instantiated by (conscious tokens of) *all* mental states belonging on the list.

To my mind, the most paradigmatic cognitive act is that of *making the judgment that p* (say after considering evidence for and against *p*, doing some reasoning and "intellectual exploring," and coming down on the issue of whether *p*).[1] We could of course frame a triad specially for it:

1) There exists a phenomenology of making a judgment.
2) The phenomenology of making a judgment is irreducible to perceptual and/ or algedonic phenomenology.

3) Perceptual and algedonic phenomenology ultimately exhaust all phenomenology.

To reject 3 and endorse 1 and 2 would be to defend the existence of *a* primitive cognitive phenomenology, though not one that constitutes a phenomenal signature of cognition. (Of course, other types of phenomenology might threaten to reduce cognitive phenomenology, such as conative and emotional phenomenology; this possibility will be addressed in due course.)

The literature contains two main types of argument for the existence of *a* primitive cognitive phenomenology.² One is from *phenomenal contrast*.³ Here two conscious episodes are presented, such that (i) it is intuitively clear that the overall phenomenology of the episodes is different, and (ii) it seems that the best explanation of the difference is that one of the two episodes exhibits cognitive phenomenology whereas the other does not. Perhaps the most widely discussed instance of this argumentative strategy is the Moore-Strawson argument (Moore 1953: 58–9, Strawson 1994: 5–13) mentioned in the Introduction. We are enjoined to contrast the conscious experiences of a French speaker and a non-French-speaker when they listen to the news in French. The claim is that there is a phenomenal difference between their overall phenomenologies that is best accounted for in terms of an element of "understanding-experience" present only in the French speaker's stream of consciousness. This understanding-experience is one kind of cognitive phenomenology.⁴

The second type of argument is from *first-person knowability*. Here the strategy is to argue that the knowledge we have of (some of) our cognitive states is the kind of first-person knowledge characteristic of our knowledge of our phenomenally conscious states. An example is the Goldman-Pitt argument (Goldman 1993, Pitt 2004), mentioned in the Introduction. It proceeds as follows: 1) It is possible to consciously, introspectively, and noninferentially identify (i.e., know-by-acquaintance) one's conscious occurrent thoughts; 2) This would not be possible if conscious occurrent thoughts did not have a distinctive phenomenal character; therefore, 3) Conscious occurrent thoughts have a distinctive phenomenal character (see Pitt 2004: 8).

I find myself endorsing both arguments.⁵ Here I will develop a separate argument that has not yet been aired in the literature, one which may sway some readers though is likely to leave cold others. I must say, however, that when I ask myself why I am so certain of the existence of an irreducible cognitive phenomenology, a simple observation presents itself to me: that if there were no cognitive phenomenology, *life would be boring*—more boring than it actually is, at least. In particular, it would be quite irrational to engage in philosophical reflection if none of it "showed up" in consciousness (surely philosophy is not as interesting as it is purely in virtue of affording the imagery that it does).⁶ It is not immediately obvious how to turn this observation into a proper *argument*. Perhaps we could start by unpacking "life" and "boring," to first approximations, as follows: a person's "life" (in the relevant sense) is the sum of all contents of her phenomenal awareness from birth to death (or better: from onset to sunset of phenomenal consciousness); a thing is boring iff it is disposed to elicit differential feelings of boredom towards it in normal subjects under normal conditions (or better, iff it is *not* disposed to elicit differential feelings of *interest* in normal subjects under normal conditions). Then the "life would be boring" argument could be formulated as follows: 1) If we did not have irreducible cognitive phenomenology, the contents of our phenomenal awareness from phenomenal onset to sunset would not be disposed to elicit differential feelings of interest in us; but 2) they do; so, 3) we do have irreducible cognitive phenomenology. There might be better ways to dress the "life would be boring" observation as an argument, but in any case it is the observation itself that convinces me, more than any argument it encapsulates.

As noted, here I will develop a different argument. My sense is that part of the dialectical deadlock around discussions of cognitive phenomenology is rooted in the fact that both "cognitive" and (especially) "phenomenal" are *essentially contested terms* (Gallie 1956)—terms construed differently by proponents and opponents of cognitive phenomenology (Bayne 2009, Siewert 2011). The purpose of the argument I will develop here is to address this issue by taking as its starting point the elucidation of these two notions. I want to argue that with the right characterizations of the cognitive and the phenomenal—characterizations which are informative yet theoretically neutral—one can start to imagine the kind of scenario whose possibility would establish the existence of primitive cognitive phenomenology. The characterizations would be "neutral" in not prejudging the matter of cognitive phenomenology, and "informative" in being substantive and literal rather than ostensive or metaphorical. Ideally, they would provide extensionally adequate *criteria* for phenomenology and cognition, though for our purposes mere *sufficient conditions* would do. In the next two sections, then, I propose such characterizations.

2. The Mark of the Cognitive

In demarcating the cognitive, we must separate cognitive phenomena from two contrast classes. The first is sensory phenomena, such as sense perception. The second is nonsensory phenomena that are not cognitive but (e.g.) conative. A very contemporary suggestion would be that cognitive states are distinguished from sensory phenomena by their *conceptual content*, and distinguished from conative phenomena by their *mind-to-world direction of fit*. On this proposal, a mental state is cognitive just if it is a conceptual representation with mind-to-world direction of fit. Both parts of this are problematic, however.

2.1. The Cognitive and the Conative

A common picture of the attitudes divides them into cognitive and conative, and draws the distinction in terms of direction of fit: a cognitive state is one such that in virtue of being in it, the mind is supposed to fit the way the world is; a conative state is one such that in virtue of being in it, the world is supposed to fit the way the mind is.[7] Thus, in acquiring the *belief* that *p*, S is trying to change her own mind so that it fits the way the world is (namely, a world where *p* holds); in coming to *desire* that *p*, S commits to trying to change the world (into one where *p* holds) so it fits the way her mind is.

One problem with this is that talk of direction of fit and what is supposed to fit what smells metaphorical—and attempts to render it literal have a sketchy track record (Zangwill 1998). A disadvantage specific to our present concerns is that direction of fit does not seem to be a phenomenal property, so appeal to it would not provide a *phenomenal* signature of the cognitive. (Such a signature would simplify the discussion of phenomenal reducibility, as we saw above.)

The deepest problem with direction of fit, however, is that it seems unsuited for an *ultimate* account of the cognitive: the supposed-to-fit facts do not seem to be ultimate facts. More plausibly, there is *something* about a cognitive state that *makes it* supposed to fit the world. Thus, there is something about believing that *p* that makes it fit a world where *p* holds. That "something" would be a more fitting mark of the cognitive. Relatedly, while there is no clear account of what direction of fit is, the leading contender casts it as a functional-role property (Smith 1994 ch.4). (This is often unpacked in terms of a "belief box" and a "desire box" within a boxes-and-arrows functional architecture.) Arguably, however, the facts about states' functional role are grounded in other facts: functional roles are dispositional properties, and those are typically grounded in categorical bases (see Kriegel 2009 ch.6).[8] In separating the cognitive from the conative, we would do well to advert not to functional-role properties such as direction of fit, but to the categorical bases of those properties. This is anyway intuitive: it is not that S judges that *p* because S is disposed to make certain inferences; rather, S is disposed to make those inferences precisely because S judges that *p*.

So: what is it that accounts for the fact that belief that *p* is supposed to fit the way the world is? The answer, it seems to me, is that believing that *p* embodies a *mental commitment to the truth* of *p*. To believe that *p* is to represent *p*, but represent it in a specific *way*, namely, *as true*. In this belief differs from desire, which also represents *p*, but not *as true*. Importantly, belief shares this truth-commitment with other cognitive states, such as assuming, remembering, expecting, and realizing that *p*. It also characterizes suspecting, speculating, surmising, being convinced that, and being certain that *p*, though with varying degrees of confidence. Thus, *part* of what is involved in remembering that today is Wednesday is representing-as-true that today is Wednesday, and *part* of what is involved in suspecting that tomorrow's weather will be nice is representing-as-true that tomorrow's weather will be nice, though somewhat tentatively. Thus mental commitment to truth is a characteristic of cognitive states in general.

How should we understand the idea of "mental commitment to truth"? I propose that we construe it as an *attitudinal* feature, rather than a *content* feature, of mental states. The truth of *p* is not part of *what* the belief that *p* represents, it is an aspect of *how* the belief that *p* represents. The belief exhibits its truth-commitment, we may say, not in virtue of representing *p-as-true*, but in virtue of *representing-as-true p*. The full case for this attitudinal construal of truth-commitment will come through as we go along, but here is an impressionistic motivation. In the opening pages of *Father Goriot*, Balzac (1835: 26) asks us not to treat his book as sheer entertainment, because everything he is about to tell us is true. Yet we are disinclined to do as he asks. This is because the claim that "all is true" is just part of the story. Nothing Balzac can say *inside* the story can make it more than a story. Likewise, nothing going on inside the content of a mental act can embody genuine commitment to the truth of what it represents. Thus when one desires not just that *p*, but that *p* be true, one's mental state still fails to commit one to the truth of *p*. Impressionistic motivation aside, note that animals and infants can believe that *p* even when they lack a concept of truth. Without a concept of truth, however, they would be unable to form propositional attitudes whose contents have the concept of truth as constituent.[9] This is perhaps why our language encodes the attitudinal construal: the surface grammar of belief and desire reports suggests that a belief that *p* and a desire that *p* represent the same thing, but involve a different relation to what they represent.

Importantly for our present purposes, nothing in the notion of representing-as-true rules out phenomenality. It is natural to think that both an unconscious belief that *p* and a conscious judgment that *p* (if such there be) represent-as-true *p*. If so, representing-as-true can occur both consciously and unconsciously. I am going to use the expression "presenting-as-true" to denote the *conscious* occurrence of representing-as-true. We may then put the point as follows: if there are conscious cognitive states, they are distinguished from conscious noncognitive states in exhibiting the phenomenal attitudinal property of presenting-as-true. This property is characterized by Cohen (1992: 11) as follows:

> Feeling it true that *p* may thus be compared with feeling it good that *p*. All credal feelings, whether weak or strong, share the distinctive feature of constituting some kind of orientation on the "True or false?" issue in relation to their propositional objects, whereas affective mental

feelings, like those of anger or desire, constitute some kind of orientation on the "Good or bad?" issue.

It is not my purpose at this point to claim that there *are* "credal feelings" such as presenting-as-true. My current point is just that the notion of representing-as-true *admits* of phenomenal understanding, in a way the notion of direction of fit did not.

With all this in place, let us set out the following *hypothesis* about the mark of the cognitive:

(C$_1$) All and only cognitive states exhibit the attitudinal property of representing-as-true.[10]

The hypothesis has several attractions. First and foremost, presenting-as-good seems to *underlie* and *explain* functional role and direction of fit. The *reason* S is disposed to make certain inferences when S consciously judges that *p* is that S's judgment presents-as-true *p*. If in judging that *p* S were not committed to the truth of *p*, S would not be inclined to reason as he does. In that sense, the judgment that *p* has the characteristic functional role it does precisely *because* it represents *p* the way it does (namely, as true). Furthermore, judgment that *p* is supposed to fit the way the world is precisely *because* it presents-as-true *p*. Because this is how the judgment represents *p*, it is with respect to whether *p* is in fact true that the judgment is to be evaluated. What it is *supposed* to do is *get things right*, because what it *tries* to do is represent how things *are*. In addition, talk of representing-as-true (unlike talk of direction of fit) is perfectly literal. All this recommends seeing representing-as-true as the *categorical basis* of the functional role characteristic of cognitive states.

2.2. The Cognitive and the Perceptual

However, our hypothesis faces a problem of extensional adequacy. For at least some *perceptual* states appear to also exhibit presenting-as-true. Just as I can judge that it is raining, I can also *see* that it is raining. It is natural to think that seeing the rain commits to the rain's reality. In general, when S consciously perceives that *p*, S's perceptual state presents-as-true *p*.[11] It embodies mental commitment to the truth of what is perceived. This commitment may be merely prima facie, and may be overridden by beliefs that "disendorse" the perception. Still, as far as the perception itself is concerned, it carries a commitment to the truth (or reality) of the perceived. Perception too is in the business of getting things right! And yet, it is odd to think of perceiving as a cognitive state. So while appeal to presenting-as-true separates the cognitive from the conative, it does not yet separate it from the perceptual. We must find either an additional feature, or specify a modification of this one that would exclude perceptual states.

The obvious difference between judging that it is raining and seeing that it is raining is this: the latter involves a sensory representation of the rain, the former a nonsensory representation. To that extent, we may say that a mental state is cognitive just in case it presents-as-true *in a nonsensory way*. The question is how to understand the sensory/nonsensory distinction.

The standard appeal here is to conceptual content. One might therefore suggest that a mental state is cognitive iff it presents-as-true *conceptually*. However, conceptuality does not seem like an *essential* difference between cognition and perception. It is true that normal human adults' sense perception tends to outstrip their conceptual resources: we can often discriminate two colors when they are presented to us simultaneously, but if presented with one of them the next day are unable to recognize which one it is. Thus our sensory representations outstrip our recognitional, and therefore conceptual, capabilities: we can sensorily represent shades of color for which we have no concepts. But that seems merely contingent. We can envisage a super-sentient creature who recognizes the next day (and month) any shade of color it can discriminate (Kriegel 2002). Indeed, we can conceive of a creature who possesses a concept for every shade of color it can discriminate, and moreover applies the relevant concept every time it represents a color. If the cognitive/sensory distinction is drawn in terms of the conceptual/nonconceptual distinction, it would follow that this creature does not have sensory states. This seems absurd: for all we have said so far, its color experiences may be qualitatively indistinguishable from ours.

A different attempt to draw the distinction appeals to the contrast between the "receptivity" of the senses and the "spontaneity" of the intellect. The thought is that there is something involuntary and exogenous about our entering sensory states, but voluntary and endogenous about entering cognitive ones. Entering sensory states is something that happens to us, entering cognitive states is something that we do. However, this seems extensionally inadequate. When I deliberately conjure up an image of a smiling octopus, this is something that I do, not something that happens to me. It is a voluntary and endogenous exercise. Yet its result is sensory, since it is a matter of *visual* imagery. Conversely, when the realization that I have yet to pay this month's phone bill suddenly pops into my mind, this is something that happens to me, not something that I do. It is involuntary and exogenous in the relevant sense—and at the same time clearly cognitive.[12]

It may be suggested that sensory states are directed at *sensibles* whereas cognitive ones at *intelligibles*. The sensible/intelligible distinction could then be understood ontologically: sensibles are concrete and/or spatial, whereas intelligibles are abstract and/or a-spatial. However, this too is extensionally inadequate. The thought that the table in the other room is brown is directed at the (concrete) table; it is the wooden, rectangular table itself that one thinks is brown. Moreover, when I perceive that the table is brown and merely *endorse* my perceptual experience, I seem to come to *judge* that the table is brown, with the perception and the judgment having the very same content (otherwise more than endorsement would be needed to generate the judgment). Conversely, though more controversially, it has sometimes been claimed that sensory states involve intentional relations to abstract universals rather than concrete particulars: when one perceives that the table is brown, one bears intentional relations to the universals of tablehood and brownness.[13]

At the same time, there may be some *specific* abstracta to which only cognitive states can be intentionally related. For example, it is plausible (though not unquestionable) that *mathematical entities* cannot be sensed. One cannot perceive that 2 + 2 = 4, only think it.[14] Ditto for *moral* entities: it is impossible to *sense* justice, it is often thought, only to grasp it intellectually.[15] If this is right, then intentional directedness at *some* abstracta, such as mathematical and/ or moral entities, may at least be a *sufficient condition* for a mental state being cognitive.

Another option is to simply characterize cognitive states in terms of (re)presenting-as-true *nonsensorily*. We then need an *extensionally adequate* criterion of the nonsensory. For present purposes, a demarcation by list would do. Just as *x* is Scandinavian iff *x* is a Swede, a Norwegian, or a Dane, so *x* is nonsensory iff *x* is not visual, auditory, olfactory, gustatory, tactile, or proprioceptive. This requires that we know which states are visual, which are auditory, and so on. But vision scientists do not seem overwhelmed by this difficulty: they treat as visual any state causally produced by the visual system, the system that exhibits neurophysiological and/or functional-computational independence and incorporates the right (visual!) sensory organs and/or transducers.[16] By the same token, an auditory state is one produced by the auditory system, construed along similar lines. (Some cerebral real estate could, of course, partake in both the visual and auditory system.) More generally, a state not produced by any of the six sensory systems is thus a nonsensory state. Accordingly, for a mental state to nonsensorily represent-as-true is for it to represent-as-true without being produced by any of these systems. Therefore:

(C_2) For any mental state M, M is a cognitive state iff (i) M exhibits the attitudinal property of representing-as-true and (ii) M is not produced by any sensory system.

This seems an extensionally adequate mark of the cognitive. At the same time, it has the virtue of not prejudging the matter of cognitive phenomenology: there *might* be a primitive phenomenal property of nonsensory presenting-as-true, but there might also not. For all we have said, phenomenal presenting-as-true may consist in the words "the following is true" being rehearsed very quickly in inner speech. The question of phenomenal reduction thus remains open.

3. A Reference-Fixer for "Phenomenal"

The harder question is how to characterize *phenomenal* properties. Part of the problem is the ineffable quality of phenomenal character. A deeper problem is that the nature of phenomenal consciousness appears to be fully appreciated by direct introspective ostension, in a way that makes any explicit articulation seem inadequate. As Block (1978) notes, asked to define phenomenal consciousness we are tempted to respond as Louis Armstrong did when asked to define jazz: "if you have to ask, you ain't never gonna know." My goal in this section is therefore not quite to capture the *nature* of the phenomenal. Rather, it is to provide an extensionally adequate public-language description that could *fix the reference* of "phenomenal" for purposes of philosophical discussions. On the approach I want to pursue, phenomenality is that aspect of consciousness responsible for the philosophical anxiety surrounding consciousness. I proceed in two steps, first giving a sense of the basic idea (§3.1), then developing it more technically (§3.2).

3.1. First Approximation

In trying to put descriptive flesh on the introspectively ostended, the locution "what it is like (for the subject)" is often used to fix ideas. But while this phrase functions well as a wink to insiders, it is unclear how helpful it would be to the uninitiated. For it has a technical usage and a nontechnical usage. In its nontechnical usage, the expression is woefully liberal: as far as acceptability in everyday language is concerned, there is something it is like to play basketball, something it is like to be tall, something it is like to be Jewish, and something it is like to have missed one's exit on the highway. Certainly there is something it is like to *think* that one has missed one's exit—which would settle the question of cognitive phenomenology rather too swiftly. However, this does not seem the pertinent usage of the "what it is like" locution; there seems to be a more specialized (read: technical) usage reserved for what we intend to capture in speaking of *phenomenal* consciousness. There is, in other words, a *phenomenal* usage of the locution (Siewert 2011). Grasping this specialized phenomenal usage, however, would appear parasitic on a prior grasp of phenomenality. Thus intuitions about the applicability of the "what it is like" locution in this specialized sense appear to lie downstream of prior commitments about the scope of phenomenology: cognitive phenomenology enthusiasts will confirm that "there is something it is like to think that 2 + 2 = 4" is intuitive to them, but skeptics will not.

It may be suggested that we proceed by treating uncontroversial cases of phenomenality as paradigms or prototypes and examine whether controversial cases resemble them sufficiently in relevant respects. For this is how we typically proceed when a notion or concept exhibits a prototype structure (Rosch 1973). Thus, according to a prototype account of the concept CITY, something qualifies as a city just when it sufficiently resembles prototypical cities—New York, Paris, and Mumbai, say—along relevant dimensions. Perhaps the same could be said of phenomenology: something qualifies as a phenomenal state just if it sufficiently resembles paradigmatic phenomenal states—visual and algedonic experiences, say—along relevant dimensions. The problem with this is that, in the present context, it is unclear how to specify the *relevant dimensions* in nonphenomenal terms. Requiring mental states to resemble prototypical phenomenal states with respect to intentional content or functional role is unsatisfactory, as it is widely acknowledged that there is no a priori reason why phenomenal and nonphenomenal states could not have similar intentional contents and/or functional roles.[17]

It seems to me that when attempting to characterize phenomenal consciousness, it is worth reflecting on the function of the qualifier "phenomenal," which is a term of art. The everyday, nontechnical term "consciousness" is widely acknowledged to be multiply ambiguous, and plausibly the qualifier came into wide usage precisely as a device for focusing the mind on a particular aspect of consciousness. The reason to focus the mind on that particular aspect is that it is the phenomenon whose status philosophers find bothersome—the phenomenon we find hard to accommodate in the natural order. It is, in short, the phenomenon responsible for the distinctively philosophical anxiety surrounding consciousness. My suggestion is that we characterize phenomenality, for the purposes of making progress in debates over its reach, in terms of this anxiety. To a first approximation: *phenomenal* consciousness is the property responsible for the philosophical anxiety surrounding consciousness. Here, the term "consciousness" (without the adjective "phenomenal") is used as an everyday term; the point is to elucidate the technical term "phenomenal."

Perhaps the most acute expression of this philosophical anxiety is the notion of *explanatory gap* (Levine 1983), the notion that nothing in the physical realm has the resources to reductively explain phenomenal properties.[18] If we take the problem of the explanatory gap to capture the core of the philosophical anxiety surrounding consciousness, we can characterize phenomenal consciousness as the "explanatory-gap-able" property.[19] More formally:

(P_1) For any property F, F is a phenomenal property iff there is an explanatory gap between F and physical properties.[20]

Phenomenality itself ("phenomenal consciousness") can then be characterized as the determinable of all (and only) phenomenal properties.

What this characterization amounts to depends on how we understand the explanatory gap. For there are different ways to diagnose the underlying difficulty that the explanatory gap points at. A full discussion of the matter will take us too far afield, but some preliminary remarks are in order. Consider this quite crisp early articulation of the explanatory gap, due to one John Tyndall:[21]

> Were our minds and senses so expanded, strengthened, and illuminated as to enable us to see and feel the very molecules of the brain; were we capable of following all their motions, all their groupings, all their electric discharges, if such there be; and were we intimately acquainted with the corresponding states of thought and feeling, we should be as far as ever from the solution to the problem, "How are these physical processes connected with the facts of consciousness?" The chasm between the two classes of phenomena would still remain intellectually impassable.

The thought is that a subject may be endowed with complete and perfect knowledge of the physical facts, and complete and perfect knowledge of the phenomenal facts, and still be in no position to know one more set of facts, namely, those pertaining to the relationship between the former and the latter. Two central elements of the explanatory gap come to the fore here. One is *failure of deducibility*: even an epistemic agent with complete knowledge of physical and phenomenal facts (and, presumably, perfect reasoning capacities) would be incapable of reasoning her way to certain further facts.[22] A second element is an explanation of the underlying reason for this failure of deducibility: that the physical facts about the brain concern *structure and function* ("groupings" and "motions"), whereas phenomenal facts essentially go beyond structure and function. This is a recurring theme in articulations of the explanatory gap, from Leibniz to Chalmers.[23] Indeed, it is a central dimension of Levine's (1983: 357; italics original) own presentation:

> [W]e do feel that the causal role of pain is crucial to our concept of it, and that discovering the physical mechanism by which this causal role is effected explains an important facet of what there is to be explained about pain. However, there is more to our concept of pain than its causal role, there is its qualitative character, how it feels; and what is left unexplained by the discovery of c-fiber firing is *why pain should*

feel the way it does! For there seems to be nothing about c-fiber firing that makes it "fit" the phenomenal properties of pain, any more than it would fit some other set of phenomenal properties.

Here the explanatory gap is construed in terms of the inexplicability of subjective feel by structure and function. This is plausibly taken as the deeper diagnosis of the explanatory gap: ultimately, the ideal agent cannot deduce the phenomenal facts from the physical facts because she cannot deduce phenomenal character from structure and function.[24]

If we adopt this diagnosis of the explanatory gap, we can refine the above characterization of phenomenality as follows: a property is phenomenal just in case its instantiation is not deducible, even by an ideal epistemic agent, from structural-functional facts. Let us now consider a number of objections and difficulties to this basic idea, some of which will occasion important modifications.

3.2. Second Approximation

The first objection is that there is simply no explanatory gap. Some materialists concede that there is an explanatory gap, denying only that any ontological gap follows; these are "type-B materialists" (Chalmers 2002). "Type-A" materialists, however, deny the very existence of an explanatory gap. A characterization of phenomenality as explanatory-gap-ability would cast type-A materialists as *eliminativists*: philosophers who deny the existence of phenomenal consciousness. Yet many would insist they recognize the reality of the phenomenal.

My response has two parts. First, we may distinguish two subgroups of type-A materialists. The first deny the existence of an explanatory gap, but recognize that there is a rationally warranted *appearance* of such a gap; we may call these "type-A2 materialists." Type-A2 materialists might debate whether this gap appearance is due to a peculiarity of consciousness, due to peculiar access we have to consciousness, or due to some other peculiarity. But *some* peculiarity in the vicinity of consciousness, they would agree, makes consciousness *appear* to defy reductive explanation in a way other phenomena do not. The other group—"type-A1 materialists"—deny this. They claim that there is not even a rational appearance of an explanatory gap between the phenomenal and the physical. Any such appearance is a philosophical fabrication, a "social construct," or whatnot, but is not rationally warranted. With this distinction in place, we may address the objection by re-characterizing phenomenality in terms the *rational appearance* of an explanatory gap, remaining noncommittal on the issue of whether or not it is *merely* an appearance.[25] This does have the consequence that it casts type-A1 materialists, who deny the rational appearance of a gap, as eliminativists about phenomenal consciousness. But this is not particularly unintuitive: after all, such philosophers deny the existence of any feature that merits a distinctively philosophical anxiety about consciousness.[26]

A converse objection is that explanatory gaps are pervasive in nature, and therefore "explanatory-gap-able" does not pick out phenomenality uniquely. Certain type-B materialists fit this bill. It is possible to interpret Block and Stalnaker (1999), for example, as maintaining that there is just as much of an explanatory gap between water and H_2O as between consciousness and its neural correlate.[27]

Here again, however, we may distinguish "type-B1 materialism," which insists there is no explanatory gap *special* to phenomenal consciousness but allows that there is a rationally warranted appearance of a special gap, from "type-B2 materialism," which claims that any appearance of an asymmetry between the cases of phenomenality and water is founded on sheer confusion. According to type-B1 materialism, then, there is a particularly acute, more pressing, more manifest, or otherwise special appearance of an explanatory gap peculiar to phenomenal consciousness, which accounts for the existence of a (warranted) distinctive philosophical anxiety. My inclination again is to dismiss type-B2 materialists as disguised eliminativists while accommodating type-B1 materialists by requiring the relevant explanatory gap to somehow *appear* special or uniquely pressing.

It is an important question how to understand the specialness of the explanatory gap between phenomenal consciousness and physical properties. This is a difficult question on which I have nothing very satisfactory to say. Two points are worth noting, however. First, some explanatory gaps are ultimately derivative from that stalking consciousness. For example, the philosophical anxiety surrounding free will may ultimately derive from that surrounding consciousness (Nagel 1986 ch.7), since the resilient evidence for libertarian free will is arguably primarily phenomenological.[28] Secondly, some explanatory gaps concern the connection between the empirical realm and something beyond it (this might be the case for normativity).[29] So the explanatory gap for consciousness is special *at least* insofar as it is a *nonderivative* explanatory gap internal to the *empirical* realm. Now, it is highly plausible that consciousness is the *only mental* property for which there is a nonderivative empirical explanatory gap. So at least we could say this: For any *mental* property F, F is a phenomenal property if there is a rationally warranted appearance of an *empirical nonderivative* explanatory gap between F and physical properties.

A third objection complains about my appeal to "appearance" in my responses to the first two objections. The objector contends that any appearance of explanatory gap is entirely contingent: we can readily imagine creatures whose intellects are sufficiently different from ours that to them it simply does not appear that there is an explanatory gap. Indeed, many people in our own world are entirely unconcerned with the place of consciousness in nature! No gap appears *to them*.

My response again involves distinguishing two cases. One case is where the relevant subjects have never *entertained* the proposition that an ideal epistemic agent would be unable to deduce phenomenal facts from physical facts (nor any other gap-reflecting proposition). The other is where the subjects do entertain the proposition but are unmoved by it. This second case is less pressing: any actual subjects of this sort would be just type-A1 materialists, and nonactual subjects can be ruled out by rigidifying the reference-fixing description. To accommodate the first case, we may simply stipulate that we expect a rationally warranted appearance of an explanatory gap to arise for *sufficiently reflective* subjects. (We may operationalize "sufficiently reflective" precisely in terms of entertaining gap-expressing propositions.)

A fourth objection is that the gap-based characterization is *uninformative*, because the notion of reductive explanation is poorly understood in philosophy of science and metaphysics alike (as compared, say, with the notion of *causal* explanation).

One approach to this problem is to simply let work on reductive explanation advance, and trust that whatever comes out of it could eventually be plugged into the gap-based characterization of phenomenality. It would be helpful, however, if we could illustrate what such plugging-in might look like. Let me therefore offer one possible illustration, by considering one relatively developed model of reductive explanation, defended by Chalmers (1996) and Kim (1998) among others. On the Chalmers-Kim model, reductive explanation proceeds, very roughly, by first "functionalizing" the reductive-explanandum (fully specifying its functional role) and then identifying, through scientific inquiry, a reductive-explanans that plays the specified functional role. This approach is particularly congenial in the present context: it suggests that what makes phenomenal consciousness at least *appear* uniquely resistant to reductive explanation is the apparent impossibility of full functionalization (recall the structure-and-function point).[30] This illustrates *one* possible explication of reductive explanation.

Taking into account all the modifications suggested above, we are led to the following characterization of the phenomenal:

(P_2) For any mental property F, F is a phenomenal property iff there is a rationally warranted appearance (to a sufficiently reflective but otherwise normal actual subject) of a distinctive (e.g., empirical and nonderivative) explanatory gap between F and physical properties.

Phenomenal consciousness can still be explicated as the determinable of all and only phenomenal properties. And a phenomenal *state* can be construed either as the exemplification of a phenomenal property or as a bare particular that instantiates a phenomenal property (depending on one's metaphysics of states).[31]

Let me close this section by noting that even this characterization of phenomenality in terms of the explanatory gap is only an illustration of something deeper, namely, the *philosophical anxiety* surrounding consciousness. The problem of the explanatory gap simply happens to be the most acute manifestation of that anxiety.[32] It may be suggested that the source of anxiety is better captured in terms of Jackson's (1982) "knowledge argument" and/or Chalmers' (1996) "zombie argument," and that therefore phenomenality should be characterized in terms of amenability to such arguments. And indeed, some philosophers have argued for cognitive phenomenology precisely on the grounds that some cognitive activity is amenable to a knowledge argument (Goldman 1993) or that some cognition is amenable to zombie argumentation (Horgan 2011).[33] One interesting option is to treat the explanatory gap, knowledge argument, and zombie argument as different *symptoms* of a single underlying philosophical unease regarding consciousness.[34] For the sake of simplicity, I proceed as if a single feature (explanatory-gap-ability) is criterial of phenomenality. But this may be simplification.

4. An Argument for Cognitive-Phenomenal Primitivism

Cognitive phenomenology per se, recall, would be a phenomenal property common and peculiar to conscious cognitive states. With the above characterizations of cognitivity and phenomenality in place, we can say more precisely: it would be an attitudinal property of nonsensory representing-as-true for which there is the right (appearance of) explanatory gap. To be a primitivist about this property is to maintain that it is irreducible to perceptual and algedonic phenomenal properties—as well as to other putative types of phenomenology, such as conative or emotional. We may formulate this "cognitive-phenomenal primitivism" more fully as follows:

(CPP) There is a mental property of nonsensory presenting-as-true, such that (i) there is a rationally warranted appearance (to a sufficiently reflective actual subject) of a distinctive (e.g., empirical nonderivative) explanatory gap between it and physical properties, and (ii) it is irreducible to perceptual, algedonic, emotional, and/or conative phenomenology.

In this section, I present a thought-experiment to support CPP. After presenting the thought-experiment (§4.1), I draw its purported philosophical lesson (§4.2), then consider a number of objections (§4.3).[35]

4.1. The Zoe Thought-Experiment

Imagine that, due to some cerebral malfunction, a person is born blindsighted. She is incapable of any visual perception, and in addition, incapable of visual *imagery*. She is, in Horgan's (2011) phrase, a *partial zombie*—specifically, a *visual zombie*. At the same time, the underlying visual machinery is sufficiently preserved that *some* visual information processing survives. How much? Here I need the individual reader's cooperation: please accord this person as much visual processing power as you can consistently with imagining her lacking any visual phenomenology. Some philosophers seem able to imagine a person without visual experience but with *the same* visual processing power as you and me—a person whose visual states are functionally indistinguishable from yours and mine but lacking in visual phenomenology. Most philosophers are unable to imagine this, but are able to imagine the person having considerably more visual information processing than actual blindsight patients. Please conceive of a person without visual phenomenology but with as much visual processing power as you feel comfortable according them. In every other respect, imagine this person is just like you and me.

Imagine next a parallel condition for audition—a sort of "deafhearing" in which subjects enjoy no auditory phenomenology but preserve quite a bit of auditory information processing. Again, please accord this person in imagination as much auditory information process as you can consistently with lack of auditory phenomenology. Repeat the exercise for all other perceptual modalities.

We may now imagine a more expanded partial zombie—a *sensory* zombie. This is a person all of whose sensory systems are similarly congenitally afflicted, so they fail to produce *any* sensory phenomenology. There is no visual, no auditory, no olfactory, no gustatory, no tactile, and no proprioceptive phenomenology. At the same time, a lot of underlying sensory processing survives, resulting in various sensory states that contribute to our protagonist's overall mental functioning. The protagonist is very different from you and me, but she should not be any less conceivable than a straight-up blindsighter. To be sure, blindsight itself was hard to conceive before its discovery, but in retrospect, this was just a failure of imaginativeness. Now that we have the model of actual blindsight, we should be imaginative enough to conceive similar conditions for other modalities and the co-occurrence of all of them in one personage. To be sure, the deficits in sensory phenomenology, and the impoverished sensory processing power, will surely over time imply further mental differences from us. All the same, a person is perfectly conceivable who has no sensory phenomenology but considerable mental functioning.

Consider next a different partial zombie, one incapable of *algedonic* phenomenology. Congenital analgesia is a condition in which persons are congenitally incapable of feeling any pain (Manfredi et al. 1981). We can envisage a similar condition for pleasure, and a person suffering from both conditions at once, thus forming a positive conception of an *algedonic zombie*.[36] We can further imagine that *some* underlying information processing about pain and pleasure nonetheless survives in this subject.

A third type of partial zombie is an *emotional zombie*. The renowned high-functioning autistic Temple Grandin (1996) reports experiencing only four types of emotion: joy, sadness, fear, and anger. Due to her extraordinary intelligence, she recognizes the existence of other emotions, and understands fairly well their nature, but in a removed and "bloodless" fashion. Those other emotions are *experientially unfamiliar* to her. This kind of limited emotional repertoire is a feature of autism established for quite some time now (Yirmiya et al. 1989). Here we have an instance of congenital *restriction* of one's emotional phenomenology. But we can readily envisage someone suffering from congenital *absence* of such phenomenology. In a first stage, we can envisage a kind of acute autism-like condition in which joy and sadness are absent as well, and another in which fear and anger are absent. We can then put all this together, in an act of imaginative synthesis of sorts, and form a positive conception of a person incapable of *any* emotional phenomenology. This would be an emotional zombie. Presumably, however, the kind of underlying information processing that subserves emotional experience need not be *entirely* destroyed for emotional phenomenology to disappear; some of it may continue, making its contribution to the emotional zombie's overall mental functioning.

Having now conceived in separation partial zombies with sensory, algedonic, and emotional deficits, or rather *lacunas*, we may perform another act of imaginative synthesis and envisage a person lacking all of these phenomenologies at once. This person enjoys no sensory phenomenology, no algedonic phenomenology, and no emotional phenomenology. This is so, we may suppose, because the relevant parts of her brain are deformed, or are lesioned, or because—as they say in the genre—of a "cosmic incident." Nonetheless, we can imagine this person having considerable underlying information-processing power, though one that does not translate into phenomenal experience.

Finally, let us stipulate one more thing about our protagonist: she happens to be a mathematical genius, with a penchant for considering and solving mathematical problems. In her darkened world of sensory, algedonic, and emotional emptiness, she nonetheless formulates mathematical propositions, thinking informally about their plausibility, and then trying to prove them from axioms she has provisionally set. If you find it impossible to conceive of someone with such impoverished processing power getting anywhere with mathematical problem-solving, perhaps the following variant would help. Imagine this person was born healthy, but on her twentieth birthday acquired at once—due to a cosmic incident—all the above deficits: blindsight, deafhearing, and the like for other perceptual, as well as algedonic and emotional, experience. Having acquired all the requisite concepts and capacities before the incident, after it our protagonist spends her time solving mathematical problems without any perceptual, algedonic, or emotional phenomenology. I will develop this variant in §4.3. The point for now is that a person with a lively intellectual life should be possible to imagine who lacks those other types of phenomenology.

This person is quite unusual, and you may feel somewhat alienated from her, but there is no reason to suppose she is logically or conceptually impossible. (I will comment on other kinds of impossibility momentarily.) As a cure for alienation, let me give her a cute name, Zoe, stipulate that in the relevant possible world she is your daughter, and describe her mental life to you a little further. As noted, she spends her days formulating various mathematical problems and attempting to solve them. When the solution is too cumbersome for short-term memory to sustain, the exercise is frustrated; but Zoe is good at recognizing that she is unlikely to solve this or that problem and moving on to others. This is not to say that Zoe gives up easily. Often she struggles to find the solution of some problem—she feels stuck, if you will. But sometimes a nice thing happens next: suddenly "the coin drops" and she can *see*, so to speak, how the solution must go. Often on those occasions, a sudden intellectual gestalt shift makes Zoe realize what the missing element is, which results in a sort of affectively neutral upheaval of thought—a greater vivacity in her thinking.[37] These victorious moments are very distinctive, and Zoe remembers many of them. Thus Zoe's mental life has its own inner rhythm, with new beginnings, stretches of inner flow, slowed down by occasional struggling and feeling stuck, often eventually punctured by breakthroughs of sudden insight and then starting over with a new mathematical problem. At the same time, this life is exhausted entirely by intellectual or *cognitive* activities: thinking, considering, judging, realizing, intuiting, remembering, and so on. Importantly, they do *not* involve phenomenal experiences of satisfaction or frustration, though *some* underlying satisfaction- and frustration-characteristic processing does take place. Indeed, we may suppose that enough such processing takes place to produce the motivational impetus, at a purely functional (unfelt) level, to trigger later rounds of intellectual activity.

The conceivability of Zoe might still be resisted, of course. It might be claimed that we can superficially conceive of her, in that disengaged surveying of the scenario does not reveal any manifest incoherencies, but that when we try to fill in the details, we find ourselves unable to form a positive conception of Zoe.

This kind of objection is hard to assess, but as far as I can tell, it is not only *disengaged* consideration of the scenario that reveals no *manifest* incoherencies—*engaged* consideration does not reveal any *hidden* incoherencies either. Thus the scenario seems genuinely *logically* possible—no contradiction seems to be involved in describing Zoe. If so, it is unclear what is supposed to *prevent us* from forming a conception of someone who does not perceive or emote but only thinks. The objector who contests Zoe's conceivability must do more, then, than proclaim herself unable to imagine Zoe. She must also point out what sort of additional details the fleshing out of the story would require that, according to her, would render the story overtly incoherent.

Here is one attempt to meet this burden. Geometry and arithmetic are plausibly *a priori*, and therefore do not *require* any sensory experience for the establishment of various truths. But, it might be claimed, in the absence of any sensory input, Zoe would be unable to develop the very *concepts* needed to entertain geometric and arithmetic propositions. This includes, primarily, the concept of *shape* and the concept of *number*. Since Zoe has no spatial perception of any sort, and no opportunity to count anything, it is unclear how she could acquire these concepts. If so, Zoe would lack the very concepts with which to engage in the kind of *a priori* reasoning that characterizes her mental life in the thought-experimental scenario.

There are two responses here. First, while sensory perception is plausibly needed to acquire *geometric* concepts, it is less obvious that the same goes for *arithmetic* concepts. Zoe probably does have opportunities to count—she could count, for example, her conscious episodes, or the moments of time passing. Also, we should not forget that Zoe does have sensory information-processing capacities, which might suffice for an elementary grasp of space and of succession, and so for the formation of the relevant concepts. More importantly, the thought-experiment can readily be modified to accommodate the objector's concerns. We can stipulate that Zoe's life is completely normal until her twentieth birthday, whereupon, following a cosmic incident, she instantaneously loses both (i) the capacity to experience sensory, algedonic, and emotional phenomenology (but not all of the underlying capacities required for their production), and (ii) the capacity to remember anything of her life prior to her twentieth birthday. We allow, though, that Zoe is left in possession of all the concepts she has acquired over the first twenty years of her life, including shape and number concepts. We can also imagine that she has been mathematically gifted all along, and that various semi-obsessive mathematical projects have already been underway with her before the incident. It is when the incident occurs that Zoe dedicates her life to proving various geometric and arithmetic theorems—she realized she has nothing better to do at this point.

4.2. The Zoe Argument

It seems to me perfectly possible to imagine such an inner life, even to imagine it from the first-person perspective—to imagine, that is, that it is *one's own* inner life.[38] That said, the exercise of imaginative empathy may not be straightforward, and requires some attention, so that various elements (notably, emotional) not be covertly reintroduced into the scenario imagined. Thus, we must keep in mind that Zoe derives no felt joy from her intellectual activities, though joy-characteristic processing occurs. Furthermore, while arguably our own mental life is always colored by some mood, be it a relatively bland one, in Zoe there is no mood to speak of. It is not *easy* to imagine a mental life devoid of mood and emotion, given their ubiquity in our waking life—just as it is not easy for city-dwellers to imagine absolute silence, given the ubiquity of noise in the city. Nonetheless, nothing *prevents* us from imagining a mental life with much cognitive "action" but no mood/emotional or algedonic dimension (just as nothing prevents the city-dweller from imagining absolute silence). Conceiving of such a life is just as feasible as imagining a life of *perceptual* consciousness without any accompanying mood/emotional or algedonic phenomenology. Both are *weird* but not inconceivable. (Descartes asks us to imagine a scenario where we have no bodies—quite a *weird* scenario, but not inconceivable for that!)

Having imagined Zoe's mental life, we may ask ourselves whether there is a rational appearance of the right explanatory gap for it. It seems to me that there obviously is. Consider an individual episode of sudden realization of how a proof must go. It is entirely natural to be deeply puzzled about how this episode could just *be* nothing but the vibration of so many neurons inside the darkness of the skull. For that matter, how do molecular processes in Zoe's brain translate into her occasional thought that a given proof is complete? How can such thoughts, or such sudden realizations, be not even *brought about*, but *constituted*, by the transmission of electro-chemical impulses among cells? The chasm between these two types of phenomenon appears very much intellectually impassable.

We can appreciate the explanatory gap here by recalling the more specific construal of the explanatory gap from §3. Imagine that an ideal epistemic agent constructs a perfect computer simulation of Zoe's reasoning. This does not seem to capture, for example, the different levels of alertness or vivacity characterizing Zoe's different episodes of realizing how some proof must go. The computer simulation *functionalizes* the relevant episodes, but appears to leave something out.

At the very least, what is left out is the way some arithmetic proposition is present to Zoe's mind, as well as the vivacity or intensity with which it is presented. It is very natural to describe such features of Zoe's mental life in terms of *phenomenal intensity*: the realization is *experienced more vividly* than the more mundane goings-on in Zoe's stream of consciousness. This phenomenal intensity, or vivacity, or alertness, and the variation therein within Zoe's stream of consciousness, represent an interesting commonality with perceptual experience, where phenomenal vivacity often varies independently of the physical properties of the perceptual stimulus (for example, independently of brightness in color experience). I can look at a red surface in a sleepy state of mind and experience its redness with one level of intensity, and a few moments later look at it again in a much more alert state of mind, perhaps after a shot of espresso or a bite of raw chocolate, and experience the same redness with different phenomenal intensity—yet as equally *bright*. The two types of intensity are typically incommensurable and nonadditive: if a red potion is losing its brightness before my eyes, I cannot compensate for the loss by getting more and more alert. This kind of phenomenal intensity is thus separate from sensory intensity even in sensory perception. And it can vary in the intellectual domain as well: a shot of espresso may also make one more vividly aware of the mathematical problem one is attending to, or make a certain mathematical proposition more vivid in one's mind.

Another apparent commonality is naturally described in terms of what Chudnoff (2011b) calls *presentational phenomenology*. When the "coin drops," and Zoe can *see*, as it were, how a proof must go, the way forward with the proof is suddenly present to her mind in much the same way that the aroma of freshly brewed coffee is present to the mind when one has olfactory experience of it.

It is an independent question how to *account* for presentational phenomenology and phenomenal intensity. But it is striking that these clearly phenomenological descriptors are so natural for the relevant episodes in Zoe's mental life.[39] It is not clear how to describe the relevant aspects of Zoe's inner life without appeal to such phenomenal notions. These aspects certainly *seem* not captured by the aforementioned computer simulation. They *seem*, that is, to evade functionalizability. To be sure, they may be ultimately functionalizable. Nonetheless, there is a *rationally warranted appearance* of non-functionalizability here.

We can, of course, imagine a strange possible world where Zoe is the only person. The explanatory chasm brought out above appears to arise *for* that world, even if it does not arise *in* that world. It probably does not arise *in* that world, as it is hard to see how Zoe would come to dwell on the problem of consciousness. But it arises *for* that world in that *we*, sufficiently reflective *actual* subjects, can be puzzled about Zoe's mental life in the way explanatory gaps puzzle.

We can also envisage a world with many people but where *everybody* is like Zoe—a mathematical genius lacking any sensory, algedonic, or emotional phenomenology, but capable of quite a bit of sensory, algedonic, and emotional convert processing. We may stipulate that, on the one hand, this world is *extremely* cooperative and its inhabitants *extremely* lucky, so that many live long lives, and secondly, through a prolonged process of natural selection, the inhabitants' covert information-processing capacities become so elaborate and agile that among other things there arises what from the third-person perspective can only be described as interaction and communication, enabling rudimentary trade, commerce, and other forms of "social" cooperation. People are thus engaged in all sorts of "activities," as these would be described from the third-person perspective, but as far as their inner life is concerned, there is never any sensory, algedonic, or emotional phenomenology implicated. The only thing going on, from the first-person perspective, is *thinking* (i.e., intellectual activity). For this world too, the explanatory gap appears to arise—and have equal bite as it does for our world.

Importantly, the relevant explanatory gap is clearly empirical and nonderivative, and concerns a mental feature. The explanatory gap that arises for Zoe does not concern any property or phenomenon that lies outside the empirical realm, and it is hard to see what other explanatory gap it might derive from. The explanatory gap for Zoe is thus of the *right* variety. Plausibly, then, its rationally warranted appearance to the (actual) human intellect is indicative of phenomenology.

There is good reason to think that the relevant phenomenology is cognitive. When Zoe realizes that she can prove some theorem p, she enters a mental state that presents-as-true p. Since Zoe is a sensory zombie, this cannot be a sensory way of presenting-as-true. By the criterion of cognitivity proposed in §2, then, her realization is a cognitive states. (Recall, furthermore, that §2 proposed intentional directedness at certain abstracta—ones that cannot be sensed—as a *sufficient condition* for cognitivity. Given that mathematical entities are plausibly nonsensible, Zoe's relevant episodes would qualify as cognitive also by this condition.)

Crucially, given that Zoe lacks any sensory, algedonic, and emotional phenomenology, we cannot understand the relevant (appearance of) explanatory gap as pertaining merely to the accidental accompaniments of cognition. For the thought-experiment is set up so that *there are no accompaniments*. In a way, this is the whole point of the thought-experiment. So the phenomenology indicated by the explanatory-gap-able episode of realization must be an irreducible, *sui generis* cognitive phenomenology.

The argument suggested by these considerations proceeds as follows. First, we claim that Zoe's relevant episode of suddenly realizing that some mathematical proposition p is true qualifies as cognitive (on the grounds that it nonsensorily represents-as-true). Secondly, we claim that it qualifies as phenomenal (on the grounds that there is a warranted appearance of an explanatory gap between the property of undergoing it and physical properties). Thirdly, we claim that, by the nature of the thought-experiment, it is irreducible to sensory, algedonic, and emotional phenomenology (since Zoe has none of those). We conclude that there is a cognitive-phenomenal property irreducible to sensory, algedonic, and emotional phenomenology. More fully:

Let Z be Zoe's property of undergoing an episode of suddenly realizing that some mathematical proposition p is true. Then,
1) Z involves nonsensory presenting-as-true p;
2) There is a rationally warranted appearance (to a sufficiently reflective actual subject) of an empirical nonderivative explanatory gap between Z and physical properties; therefore,

3) Z is (i) cognitive and (ii) phenomenal.
4) Z is not accompanied by perceptual, algedonic, or emotional phenomenology; therefore,
5) Z is irreducible to perceptual, algedonic, and emotional phenomenal properties.

The argument's conclusion is essentially CPP, cognitive-phenomenal primitivism. Call it the *Zoe argument*.

4.3. Objections and Replies

One objection is that the Zoe thought-experiment presents a scenario which may or may not be conceivable, but in any case is not metaphysically possible. It is metaphysically impossible for there to be a person whose sensory, algedonic, and emotional systems malfunction in the way described but who nevertheless has the mathematical inner life described.

This is probably not the place to litigate issues in modal epistemology. I want to restrict myself to one remark. Even if we do not embrace the view that certain types of conceivability (e.g., positive conceivability by an ideal reasoner in ideal circumstances) *entail* metaphysical possibility (Chalmers 1996), it is certainly highly plausible that some types of conceivability—including conceivability by an epistemically responsible agent in normal or favorable circumstances—provide *prima facie, defeasible* evidence for metaphysical possibility. Insofar as we accept Zoe's conceivability to such a normal epistemic agent, then, at the very least, the argument produces *defeasible evidence* for CPP. Such defeasible evidence tilts the burden of argument to opponents of CPP. It creates a prima facie presumption in favor of irreducible cognitive phenomenology. After all, if we have defeasible evidence for cognitive-phenomenal primitivism, then pending the provision of an actual defeater, the epistemically responsible stance would be to tentatively embrace CPP.

A second objection might be that it makes no sense to imagine Zoe having *only* mathematical thoughts. In addition, she would need some motivational states that would make her *want* to engage in mathematical reasoning, *seek* mathematical proofs, and so on. But now it would appear Zoe experiences some agential or conative phenomenology, which in turn may serve to reduce her cognitive phenomenology.

My response here is fourfold. First, it is not clear to me that we cannot envisage Zoe as somehow passively finding herself compelled to engage in mathematical thinking, in the manner an addict or obsessive-compulsive person might. That is, it is not clear that we cannot stipulate that Zoe is a conative zombie without altering the dialectical situation in any noticeable manner. Secondly, Zoe's diminished but existent motor-planning and motivational information-processing capacities might suffice to move her. Thirdly, unlike the phenomenology of silent-speech imagery, which is at least a prima facie plausible reducer of cognitive phenomenology, the conative phenomenology of motivational states seems of the wrong kind to reduce *cognitive* phenomenology. (Plausibly, this has to do with the difference in manner of presentation or for that matter direction of fit.) So even if we allow that Zoe has both cognitive and conative phenomenology, it is still plausible that each remains irreducible to the other, hence primitive. Fourthly, cognitive phenomenology skeptics are typically skeptical of conative phenomenology as well. If the Zoe argument were admitted to demonstrate *disjunctive* primitivism about either cognitive or conative phenomenology, it would be an important and worthwhile argument already. This is doubly significant given that, arguably, the fate of irreducible cognitive and conative phenomenology is unlikely to be different: it is more plausible that both are primitive or that neither is than that one is but the other is not. If so, establishing the disjunction should increase our credence in the conjunction.[40]

A third objection is that, whatever else the Zoe argument establishes, it has no resources to establish that cognitive states with different contents have different cognitive-phenomenal characters. Nothing in the argument shows that judging that p and judging that q have different "cognitive feels" associated with them. In fact, the argument does not even show that cognitive states with different *attitudes*—judging that p, suspecting that p, and so on—have different cognitive-phenomenal characters. For all the argument shows, there may be a single cognitive-phenomenal character shared by all cognitive-phenomenal states, a single "intellectual quale."

It is true that the Zoe argument is silent on how finely primitive cognitive-phenomenal characters individuate. However, it is important to appreciate that, sociologically speaking, not all proponents of cognitive phenomenology *believe* that cognitive phenomenology individuates as finely as content (see Koksvik 2011, Chudnoff 2015). So an argument for the big-tent position that there exists a primitive cognitive phenomenology, without commenting on the grain of its individuation, is actually called for. At the same time, the following conditional may be independently plausible: if there is irreducible cognitive phenomenology, then it individuates as finely as content. Arguably, this is antecedently easier to argue for than the existential "there is irreducible cognitive phenomenology." Obviously, the combination of the two constitutes a *modus ponens* for cognitive phenomenology that individuates as finely as content. Its conditional premise is supported by non-introspective considerations. For example, the idea that there exists only a single "intellectual quale" but a great variety of perceptual phenomenal characters introduces an odd disunity into our theory of consciousness. A similar disunity appears if we take perceptual phenomenology to individuate as finely as content but cognitive phenomenology to individuate only as finely as attitude. Thus unity considerations already create dialectical pressure in favor of the conditional premise in the *modus ponens*. Another pressure in the same direction comes from representationalism about phenomenal consciousness. Most representationalists (e.g., Dretske 1995, Tye 1995), though often skeptical of cognitive phenomenology, argue that in general phenomenal character is in fact one and the same as a certain kind of representational content. If one accepts this position on independent grounds (e.g., "transparency"), combining it with the Zoe argument for primitive cognitive phenomenology would generate a prima facie case for content-specific cognitive phenomenology.

There are surely other objections that could be raised against the Zoe argument. I leave the discussion here, as I find that although the case presented here for cognitive-phenomenal primitivism is non-demonstrative, the prima facie, defeasible support it provides is quite strong. Moreover, the argument merely supports what I take to be an already formidable case consisting in phenomenal contrast and first-person knowability arguments, as well as introspective impression and the "life would be boring" observation.

II. A Nonreductive Characterization of Cognitive Phenomenology

5. How Might We Characterize Cognitive Phenomenology?

The Zoe argument, if successful, provides evidence for the existence of primitive cognitive phenomenology. But it tells us nothing about what this phenomenology is *like*. It sheds no light on the *character* of cognitive phenomenology. The problem is vexing, as primitive qualities tend generally to resist informative characterization.

One option is to adduce certain phenomenal contrasts, with the goal not of arguing for the existence of the relevant primitive quality, but of bringing into sharper introspective relief its special character (see Koksvik 2011). We can certainly use this device to illuminate the feature of nonsensory presenting-as-true. The presenting-as-true component can be appreciated when we contrast what it is like to judge that the table is brown (say) with what it is like to merely *entertain* that the table is brown. The nonsensory component can be appreciated when we contrast what it is like to judge that the Eiffel Tower is tall with what it is like to *see* that the Eiffel Tower is tall.

One limitation of this approach is that it does not quite flesh out the richness and variety of cognitive phenomenology. For example, it does not tell us what the difference is between the phenomenology of judging that p and that of suspecting that p, which *ex hypothesi* share the nonsensory presenting-as-true characteristic. Another limitation is that, although helping each of us to privately concentrate his or her mind on the relevant phenomenal feature, it does not offer a public-language articulation.

To obtain a fuller, public characterization of different types of cognitive phenomenology, we might consider constructing various Ramsey sentences for them (see Ramsey 1931, Lewis 1966, 1972). A Ramsey sentence is produced by collecting a large number of "platitudes" about that which one wishes to elucidate, stringing them into a long conjunction, replacing occurrences of the "elucidandum" with a free variable, and prefixing the whole thing with the existential quantifier. (Importantly, "platitude" here need not mean an *obvious* or *pedestrian* statement; it only means a statement about *surface features* of the elucidandum's referent.) The result is a complex description which may be satisfied better or worse by different eligible referents of the elucidandum. Suppose now that the platitudes appealed to are all phenomenological, in the sense that they cite phenomenal features. Then the result may be thought of as a *phenomenological* characterization of the target phenomenon.[41] We may call such sentences *phenomenological Ramsey sentences*.

I propose to seek here a phenomenological Ramsey sentence for the paradigmatic cognitive activity of *making a judgment* (see §2). To that end, in the next section I propose twenty phenomenological platitudes about making the judgment that *p*. This would illustrate how a fuller phenomenological characterization, expressible in public language, could be devised for one central type of cognitive phenomenology.

It might be objected that a phenomenological Ramsey sentence for making a judgment would be hostage to the truth of each platitude it comprises, since if just one of them is false the entire conjunction of them will be. This is a general problem for Ramsey sentences, and fortunately one that Lewis (1972: 256) raises and solves in half a sentence. Lewis suggests that instead of forming the conjunction of all our platitudes, we form a (long!) disjunction of conjunctions of *most* of them. With the twenty platitudes to be offered in the next section, for example, we might produce all possible lists of sixteen among them, make a conjunction of the sixteen items on each list, and then form the disjunction of all of those conjunctions. The resulting Ramsey sentence would be true if at least sixteen of our platitudes are.

A Ramsey sentence can be even more flexible than that, and involve various conjunctions of fewer or more platitudes in the overall disjunction. The more central a platitude is to the concept being elucidated, the more disjuncts in the Ramsey sentence it should appear in. In fact, there may be some platitudes whose truth is nonnegotiable if the relevant notion is to refer; these should therefore appear in *every disjunct* of the Ramsey sentence. There may also be some platitudes so central that satisfying only them would suffice to guarantee reference. If so, some disjuncts could be single-itemed.

I now turn to the business of articulating some phenomenological platitudes about making a judgment. Note well: because in a flexible Ramsey sentence it is not essential that all platitudes be true, I will err on the side of abundance rather than caution, seeking to articulate many different phenomenological platitudes, of varying degrees of plausibility, rather than to ensure that only the most plausible ones make it. The more platitudes we have in our ultimate Ramsey sentence, the more texture does our elucidandum assume.[42]

6. A Phenomenological Ramsey Sentence for Making a Judgment

I am going to assume that making a judgment is always a conscious act. If this is wrong, then the platitudes below concern specifically *consciously* making a judgment. Naturally, my first phenomenological platitudes about making a judgment concerns what I called nonsensory presenting-as-true. Perhaps we should start with the most elemental aspect of the experience: the fact that making a judgment involves a feeling of taking a stand on the question of the truth or falsity of the content judged. This is what Cohen called a "credal feeling" in the passage quoted in §2. We may formulate this first platitude as follows:

1) Making a judgment that p involves a credal feeling, that is, a feeling of committing to the truth of p.

This leads to another platitude, concerning the difference between judging and merely entertaining. Each of us has first-person acquaintance with the experiential difference between the two acts, a difference consisting precisely in the lack of any truth-commitment in mere entertaining. (More on this in Chapter 3.) Thus we may say:

2) There is a felt difference between making the judgment that p and merely entertaining that p.

This formulation suggests that judging and merely entertaining can share the exact same content. They differ only in respect of truth-commitment. If so, truth-commitment cannot be an aspect of the *content* of judgment; it must be an aspect of the *attitude* the subject takes toward the content. This is why presenting-as-true must be considered an attitudinal feature:

3) Credal feelings are attitudinal phenomenal features of making a judgment.

Balzac's futile announcement that "all is true" in *Father Goriot* attests to this (see §2).

The foregoing raises a vexed question about negative judgment: does it involve the different attitudinal feature of falsity-commitment, or simply a truth-commitment toward a negative content? Is disbelieving that *p* just believing that ~*p*, or are the two categorically different? Analogously, we may ask whether a negative judgment about *p* (a "dis-judging" that *p*, if you will) is phenomenally indistinguishable from a positive judgment about ~*p*. One view is that positing two different feels here is phenomenologically and explanatorily extravagant. But some philosophers have insisted that a workable account of judgment requires just that (e.g., Brentano 1874 II ch.6). For my part, I find myself unable to tell which one is *phenomenologically* more plausible. Accordingly, I propose to formulate two alternative platitudes:

4) All acts of making a judgment exhibit the phenomenal attitudinal feature of truth-commitment.
4*) Acts of making a judgment divide in two: those that exhibit the phenomenal attitudinal feature of truth-commitment and those that exhibit the phenomenal attitudinal feature of falsity-commitment.

In our "sophisticated" Ramsey sentence, we may ensure that half of the disjuncts include Platitude 4 and half include 4*.

Other truth-related platitudes may concern the relationship between judgment and various other propositional attitudes. For example, the following relate the phenomenology of judging to that of doubting and suspecting:

5) The feeling of doubting that *p* results from inability to make a judgment as to whether *p* or ~*p*.
6) The feeling of suspecting that *p* is the feeling of being inclined to judge that *p*.

Note well: the inclination cited should be thought of not as a dispositional state but as an occurrent felt inclination. For 6 is meant as a phenomenological platitude.

When we reflect on the process of weighing the evidence/reasons for *p* and ~*p* and finally coming down on the issue, the act of coming down seems to involve a certain feeling of finality and absoluteness. In going ahead and making the judgment, I am deciding to stop my "inquiry," at least for now—I am ruling out further mulling and pondering. Having made the judgment that *p*, I am at least for now fully committed to it being the case that *p*. The truth-commitment feels in some sense absolute, even as the confidence that accompanies it varies. Thus let us add:

7) Making the judgment that *p* involves a feeling of *coming down* on the question of whether *p*.
8) There is a feeling of absoluteness about the coming-down aspect of making the judgment that *p*.
9) Making the judgment that *p* involves a feeling of (provisional?) finality.[43]

This is in many ways the central aspect of making a judgment that distinguishes it from other, more hesitant cognitive acts.

At the same time, typically when one finally decides to make the judgment that *p*, one feels a certain degree of confidence that one has gotten things right. The degree of confidence varies, however, and this may seem to conflict with the felt absoluteness and finality of making a judgment. To relieve this apparent tension, I propose that we construe confidence not as a *modification* of judgments, but as an independent second-order mental state *about* judgments. On this view, it is misleading to say that S judges that *p confidently*. It is more accurate to say that S judges that *p with confidence*, where this means that S harbors two mental states: a judgment with the content <*p*> and a confidence state with the content <my judgment that *p* is very likely true>. The judgment is characterized by absoluteness, the confidence by gradation. We may capture this through the following platitudes:

10) Making the judgment that *p* is typically accompanied by a feeling of confidence about that judgment.
11) The confidence that accompanies making a judgment comes in degrees.

Together, Platitudes 7–11 capture a complex picture of the relationship between judgment and confidence.

In addition to all these truth-related platitudes, there are also epistemically based ones. Perhaps the most salient is that making a judgment feels *rationally compelled*. Horgan and Timmons (2007: 216) write that making a judgment is "experienced as grounded in considerations that serve as sufficient reasons for the [judgment] in question." This is what I call the feeling of rational compulsion:

12) Making the judgment that *p* involves a feeling of being rationally compelled to do so.

Horgan and Timmons note that what one is rationally compelled *by* is the consideration of (epistemic) reasons for and against *p*; as Dorsch (2009) puts it, our judgments phenomenally present themselves as reason-responsive. So we may add

13) Making a judgment that *p* involves a feeling of reason-responsiveness.

Consideration of reasons may or may not amount to the same as consideration of the evidence and counterevidence about *p*. Just in case it does not, let us add

14) Making a judgment that *p* involves the feeling that *p* is sufficiently supported by evidence.

Some of these platitudes may turn out to be redundant, since there may well be a priori connections between the feelings of rational compulsion, reason-responsiveness, and evidence-supportedness. However, potential redundancy is unproblematic in the context of Ramsey sentences: if 13 and 14 amount to the same, say, what follows is only that they could not discriminate among eligible satisfiers of the Ramsey sentence; it remains that if they do *not* amount to the same, they *could*—so there is no harm in adding both to our Ramsey sentence.

The last three platitudes concerned feelings about the epistemic credentials of the judgment being made. Arguably, making a judgment involves also a feeling about the epistemic credentials of the *judging agent*: that she has done her due diligence before making up her mind regarding p, or that she has been epistemically responsible, or something like that. If I commit to the truth of p without feeling that I have done my due diligence, my experience is not as of making a judgment, but as of speculating or suspecting. We may capture this by saying:

15) Making a judgment that p involves the feeling that one has met one's epistemic obligations.

Note that even if meeting one's epistemic obligations just is properly weighing all the evidence, the *feeling* of having met one's epistemic obligations may still be different from the *feeling* of one's judgment being properly supported by the evidence. The former concerns oneself, the latter one's judgment.

These epistemic platitudes bring out a further one, concerning a feeling of involuntariness involved in making the judgment that p. If I consider that the evidence supports $\sim p$, I cannot make the judgment that p (though I may certainly report that I do).[44] So:

16) Making a judgment that p involves a feeling of involuntariness.

More specific platitudes surrounding the same idea could probably be formulated as well.

Horgan and Timmons (2007: 215) mention two other phenomenal characteristics of interest. One is that making a judgment involves the experience of categorizing or sorting items—what we might call a "phenomenology of predication." In this form, the claim may be too strong, insofar as existential judgments do not fit: when I make the judgment that there are no ghosts, this does not feel like categorizing or classifying ghosts with the nonexistents; rather, it feels like simple rejection of a certain sort of thing—ghosts. However, there is a highly plausible weaker claim in the area:

17) Making a judgment always involves the feeling of mobilizing a concept.

When I judge that there are no ghosts, I may not predicate anything, but I do mobilize the concept GHOST.

Connected to this, and arguably more fundamental, is the fact that the phenomenology of cognitive episodes involves a certain *thematic unity* (Nes 2012). When I make the philosophical judgment that zombies are impossible, I undergo visual imagery as of a staggering Hollywood zombie, silent-speech imagery of the words "zombies are impossible," a feeling of relief from anxiety about the possibility of zombies undermining physicalism, and so on. The overall episode is multifaceted, but every part or aspect of it is concerned with a single subject matter: the impossibility of zombies. Crucially, this thematic unity is itself a felt dimension of the overall episode: "the very commonality of the subject matter is a feature of the thought episode's phenomenology" (Nes 2012: 86). We may thus add

18) Making a judgment involves a feeling of thematic unity.

Arguably, this feature underlies that cited in Platitude 17.

Horgan and Timmons's (2007: 216) other claim is that judgments are "naturally experienced as apt for" expression in declarative sentences. Perhaps we can say more simply:

19) Assertion feels like the natural way to express a judgment.

In this formulation, there is no implication that a creature capable of making a judgment must be also capable of expressing the judgment made.

Finally, we may comment on the experienced *temporal* dimension of making a judgment. It is noteworthy that while the process leading up to the making of a judgment may vary in duration, the judgment-making itself seems not to. Still, two views are possible here. One is that making a judgment feels completely duration-less, instantaneous. The other is that making a judgment has an extremely short duration—never longer than the so-called specious present (generally believed to last 2–3 seconds). My own sense is that making a judgment *typically* fits the former model but occasionally (perhaps rarely) fits the latter. So:

20) At least typically, making the judgment that *p* feels instantaneous.

This formulation leaves it open whether the instantaneous feel is *merely* typical or on the contrary universal.

The above platitudes can be straightforwardly Ramsified as follows: "There is an x, such that x involves a credal feeling of committing to truth or falsity & there is a felt difference between x and mere entertaining & the credal feeling is attitudinal phenomenal feature of x & . . ." However, a more sophisticated Ramsey sentence would involve a great multitude of disjuncts of variously lengthy conjunctions. The shortest disjunct in such a Ramsey sentence might be the conjunction of Platitudes 1, 2, 7, 12, and 15: any mental act involving (i) credal feelings, (ii) a felt difference from mere entertaining, and feelings of (iii) coming down on an issue, (iv) rational compulsion, and (v) meeting one's epistemic obligations—*any* such act—would qualify as making a judgment. For these are probably the most central phenomenological platitudes about making a judgment. Accordingly, they are to show up in many of the disjuncts in our sophisticated Ramsey sentence. A second circle of platitudes, still important but less so, might include 3, 4/4*, 8, 9, 13/14, 16, 17, 18, and 20. These concern the feelings of truth- and falsity-commitment (and their attitudinality), absoluteness and finality of coming-down, reason- and evidence-responsiveness, involuntariness, concept-mobilization, and instantaneity. The final circle, of least central platitudes, includes 5, 6, 10, 11, and 19: relations to the phenomenology of doubting and suspecting, being accompanied by a multigradient feeling of confidence, and the feeling of assertibility. These would appear in the fewest disjuncts in our ultimate Ramsey sentence.

A properly structured Ramsey sentence based on the above twenty platitudes (but possibly including many more) would, I contend, offer a useful and compelling *phenomenological* characterization of judging. As a primitive and unanalyzable feature, we can truly grasp the phenomenology of making a judgment only through direct acquaintance with it. But if we want a *theoretical* account of it, public and somewhat informative, this kind of Ramsey sentence is our best bet. If we could then produce many such phenomenological Ramsey sentences, for all the most important cognitive activities, we would have a firmer grasp on the character of cognitive phenomenology.

Conclusion

My *primary* goal in this chapter has not been to characterize cognitive phenomenology, but to argue that there is one and it is irreducible to perceptual, algedonic, and emotional phenomenologies. In particular, I have attempted to develop a new argument for primitive cognitive phenomenology, different from the standard contrast and epistemic arguments already to be found in the literature. A subsidiary goal has been to get clearer on what the cognitive and the phenomenal *are*. I suggested that we characterize the cognitive in terms of an attitudinal feature of nonsensory representing-as-true, and the phenomenal as that which underlies the philosophical anxiety surrounding consciousness (manifested most acutely through the explanatory gap). I then presented a thought-experiment designed to elicit the intuition that a rational appearance of an explanatory gap arises for, or regarding, a person without sensory, algedonic, or emotional states but *with* states characterized by nonsensory representing-as-true. If both the characterizations and the thought-experiment are accepted, we have a prima facie case for the phenomenal irreducibility of cognitive phenomenology.

As suggested above, it is natural to suppose that the status of cognitive phenomenology is similar to that of *conative* phenomenology. The latter is the topic of the next chapter.[45]

2

Conative Phenomenology

Like the previous chapter, this one has two parts. The first (§§1–2) presents a case for primitivism about *conative* phenomenology. This is the claim, roughly, that at least *some* of our conative mental life instantiates phenomenal properties irreducible to any others. The second part (§§3–7) attempts to outline a nonreductive characterization of the relevant phenomenal properties, suggesting that the fundamental form of our conative experience is a proprietary phenomenology of *deciding-and-then-trying*.

I. The Primitive *Conatus*

1. Primitivism about Conative Phenomenology

In orthodox, broadly functionalist philosophy of mind, the paradigmatic conative state is *desire*. Often there are also dedicated discussions of *intention*, sometimes with the claim that intention cannot be reductively accounted for in terms of desire (Bratman 1987). However, the field of conative phenomena is much larger and includes at least most of the following:

- Desiring to φ
- Wanting to φ
- Intending to φ
- Choosing to φ
- Deciding to φ
- Being willing to φ
- Planning to φ
- Needing to φ
- Having φ-ing as a project
- Performing (doing) φ
- Trying to φ
- Striving to φ
- Pursuing φ-ing

- Having a volition to φ
- Wishing that *p*
- Hoping that *p*
- Approving of *x*
- Valuing *x*
- Preferring *x* (over *y*)

This list focuses on *positive* conative states, but there are negative counterparts that qualify equally: disliking, being unwilling, disapproving, refusing to try, and so on.

There might be a sharp natural category of conative states (substantially overlapping this list) with a phenomenal feature common and peculiar to their conscious occurrences. Such a feature would constitute a "phenomenal signature of the conative." But the existence of primitive conative phenomenology requires something much weaker: that *some* phenomenal property is (i) instantiated by some unquestionably conative state, (ii) not instantiated by any nonconative states, and (iii) irreducible to any (combination of) other phenomenal properties. For example, if part of what it is like to decide to φ cannot be accounted for in terms of perceptual, algedonic, and cognitive phenomenal properties, this would suggest a primitive conative phenomenology. In terms of the Introduction's triad:

1) There exists a phenomenology of deciding to φ.
2) The phenomenology of deciding to φ is irreducible to perceptual, algedonic, and cognitive phenomenology.
3) Perceptual, algedonic, and cognitive phenomenology ultimately exhaust all phenomenology.

To reject 3 and endorse 1 and 2 is to defend *a* primitive conative phenomenology. Similarly for parallel triads for other unquestionably conative states, such as desiring, intending, and trying.

In rejecting 3 and endorsing 1 and 2 for some such triad, we make two positive assertions: an existence claim and an irreducibility claim. Primitivism about conative phenomenology is thus equivalent to the following conjunction: there exists a phenomenology of conative mental activity, and that phenomenology is irreducible to any other phenomenology. The existence of conative phenomenology is a matter of some phenomenal property being instantiated by some unquestionably conative state but no nonconative state. Its irreducibility is a matter of outrunning any combination of perceptual, algedonic, cognitive, etc. phenomenal properties. Call this the thesis of the *primitive conatus*:

> (PC) There is a phenomenal property P, such that (i) for any subject S, some conative mental activity instantiates P, and (ii) there are no

phenomenal properties $P_1, \ldots, P_n$, such that P reduces to some combination of $P_1, \ldots, P_n$.

PC states that there is at least one phenomenal property characteristic of conative mental activity that is not grounded in any other type of phenomenology. This claim is not without precedent: it is defended by Brentano (1874 II ch.6) and more recently Ginet (1986).

There may yet be, of course, a phenomenal signature of the conative. In Chapter 1, I highlighted the role of truth-commitment in the nature of cognitive states. What seems to characterize conative states is their *value-commitment* (Brentano 1874: 239). To want ice cream, to wish for ice cream, to like ice cream, to approve of ice cream—all these commit to the goodness of ice cream. The notion of goodness at play here is maximally neutral—a kind of completely generic goodness. It covers both moral and other kinds of goodness (e.g., aesthetic). It covers relative goodness ("good for") and absolute goodness (good *tout court*). It covers the goodness of states of affairs, but also the goodness of actions ("rightness"), mental states ("fittingness"), and persons ("virtue"). It covers intrinsic and final goodness, as well as instrumental goodness. We may call this *generic goodness*, or goodness$_G$ for short. Positive conative states (such as liking or approving of something) are characterized by their goodness$_G$-commitment; negative ones (disliking, disapproving) by their badness$_G$-commitment.

Plausibly, this value-commitment is an attitudinal property as well. Compare desiring that *p* with believing that *p* is good. Arguably, these are two different states.[1] But how can we account for this difference? Both commit to the goodness of *p*, after all. The difference, I suggest, is that the desire represents-as-good *p*, whereas belief represents-as-true *p*'s being good. In the latter, goodness comes in only at the level of content; in the former, already at the level of attitude. Thus the value-commitment built into conative states is attitudinally encoded, if you will: conative states represent-as-good$_G$ or represent-as-bad$_G$. If we use "valuable" as just a label for what is either good or bad, we could demarcate the conative in terms of representing-as-valuable$_G$. For the sake of simplicity, I will conduct the discussion in terms of representing-as-good$_G$.

In the cognitive case, our demarcation appealed to specifically *nonsensory* representing-as-true, in order to rule out perception. Something similar is needed in the conative case, since pleasure and pain seem to represent-as-valuable$_G$ their objects: when one takes pleasure in an espresso, one's pleasure represents-as-good$_G$ the espresso. But pleasure seems too sensory, or sensuous, to qualify as conative. To enjoy something is not an act of the will! Accordingly, we may suggest that conative states are those which exhibit *nonsensuous* representing-as-good$_G$.

If nonsensuous representing-as-good$_G$ is the mark of the conative, then all *conscious* conative states exhibit what we may call nonsensuous *presenting-as-good*$_G$. This is a putative phenomenal attitudinal property for which we can devise a special triad:

1) There exists a phenomenal attitudinal property of nonsensuous presenting-as-good$_G$.
2) This property is irreducible to perceptual, algedonic, and cognitive phenomenology.
3) Perceptual, algedonic, and cognitive phenomenology ultimately exhaust all phenomenology.

Rejecting 3 and endorsing 1 and 2 here would imply the thesis of the primitive conatus as formulated above.

The view that the conative aspect of mental life is basic and irreducible to cognition and perception is rather standard in philosophy of mind.[2] Nonetheless, it may be claimed that although conative states have *some* properties that cannot be accounted for in perceptual, cognitive, and algedonic terms, none of these are *phenomenal* properties.[3] The *phenomenal* properties of conative states, if they exist at all, are reducible to other kinds of phenomenal property. In the next section, I attempt to fend off such eliminativist and reductivist challenges to a *sui generis* conative phenomenology. Through a series of phenomenal contrasts, I argue that there is *a* conative phenomenology unfamiliar from our perceptual, algedonic, and cognitive life.

2. In Defense of the Primitive *Conatus*

This section divides in three, discussing eliminative (§2.1), reductive (§2.2), and primitivist (§2.3) accounts of conative phenomenology.

2.1. Eliminativism

Eliminativism about conative phenomenology is antecedently implausible. Many aspects of our conative mental life seem to have a phenomenal dimension. Consider the following vignette from Bayne (2008: 183):

> You stumble out of bed and reach for the door so as to leave the room and escape the fire. Something is leaning against the door, and you must strain in order to open it. Finally, the door begins to move—you experience yourself as opening the door, and moving into the corridor. . . . Suddenly, you remember that the only copy of your half-finished manuscript is in your study, being threatened by the flames. You deliberate

for a second: should you go back for the manuscript, or continue down the corridor and out of harm's way? You decide to risk it . . .

For the vignette's protagonist, certain states of unmistakably conative character are experientially highlighted: the phenomenology of effortful action (straining to open the door), the phenomenology of deliberation and decision (to save the manuscript), and so on. It would be odd to claim that the protagonist's internal life during this little drama is indistinguishable from that of a somnambulist going through the exact same sequence of movements but having all the same perceptual and cognitive experiences.

Consider a more specific case. Suppose after a training process you learn how to blush at will. For most of us, blushing is something that happens to us, not something that we do. But for you, blushing is something that you do (at least sometimes). We may imagine two subjects whose conscious lives are indistinguishable except that at t, one blushes at will, the other despite himself. Importantly, there is no difference in accompanying experiences: both feel equally embarrassed and helpless, for example. It seems that there is still an important phenomenal difference between the two. The difference is precisely that between feeling like one is doing something and feeling like something is happening to one. Let us call the phenomenal element present only in the former case the *phenomenology of doing*. To deny that there is a phenomenology of doing (to be an eliminativist about it) is to be committed to the complete phenomenal indistinguishability of blushing at will and blushing despite oneself.

I conclude that *eliminativism* about conative phenomenology is almost certainly false. That is, conative states do have a phenomenal character. But what about *reductivism*? In the bulk of this section, I consider six possible reductive accounts of conative phenomenology, arguing that all are flawed. In the process, we will be able to home in on a specific conative residue that I contend is irreducible to nonconative types of phenomenology.

2.2. Reductivism

One straightforward reductive account of the feeling of doing would equate it with a suitable kind of tactile phenomenology. What it is like to strain to open the door, on this view, is given by the tactile feeling of one's arm and shoulder pressing against the door; what it is like to clench one's fist is just what it is like for the hand's different parts to touch each other with a certain pressure.

This account is straightforward, but also straightforwardly falsified. Merleau-Ponty (1944: 93) notes that when we rub our hands together, we can experience, more or less at will, first the right hand doing the rubbing and the left hand being rubbed and then the left hand actively rubbing and the right hand passively rubbed. The strictly tactile phenomenology in those two episodes seems the same, but the *overall* phenomenology is different. A natural explanation of this difference is in terms of which hand is agent and which is patient, so to speak—which hand embodies the active will of the agent and which is merely passive. Thus there appears to be a *phenomenology of agency* built into the experience of doing something that tactile phenomenology fails to recover. (It might be objected that the tactile phenomenology itself is changed by the switch in attention—in the same way visual phenomenology changes depending on whether one attends to the duck or to the rabbit in the duck-rabbit figure. But when we are told that a subject switched her attention from her right hand to her left hand, we have not yet been told whether she has switched her attention from the touching hand to the touched hand or from the touched hand to the touching hand. So there is clearly something more to the experience than the attention-switch.)

A second reductive account might attempt to recover the subject's agentive role through her *awareness* of her own causal efficacy in bringing about the actions she performs. On this view, the difference between the two blushers consists in the presence or absence of a conscious *judgment* to the effect that one is the cause of one's blushing. Both blushers experience warmth in their face, embarrassment, and so on, but the willful one also experiences the *cognitive* phenomenology of judging that it is she who caused the blushing. The unwillful blusher does not have this additional judgment-experience (and may even experience the opposite phenomenology of judging that she did *not* cause the blushing). Likewise, the phenomenal character of the experience of clenching one's fist is nothing but the compresence of (i) the tactile character of one's hand's various parts touching each other and (ii) the cognitive character of thinking something like "I caused the fist to clench." On this account, then, the distinctive phenomenology of agency that accompanies some of our actions is just a combination of tactile and cognitive phenomenology. There is no need to posit a *sui generis* conative phenomenology.

This account goes in the right direction, in that it attempts to take account of the agent's role in causing her bodily motions. But there is an important difference between experiencing the causing and experiencing a judgment about the causing. Conative phenomenology appears more tied to the former. Furthermore, the kind of causal judgment we can make about our own role in bringing about bodily motions we can also make about others' role. Yet clearly we cannot experience others' conative states as we can our own. Suppose you help a friend lift a couch. Just as you make the judgment that you caused your side of the couch to lift, you also make the judgment that your friend caused his side of the couch to lift. Still, there is a straightforward sense in which you *feel* your own causing of your side of the couch lifting but not your friend's causing of his side lifting. The feeling of causing is asymmetric, but the causal judgments are symmetric. The reductive account in terms of causal judgments seems to have no resources to explain this asymmetry.[4]

It might be suggested that a more direct awareness of one's causal efficacy would do here. Perhaps the phenomenology of agency can be accounted for, not in terms of the *cognitive* phenomenology of *judging* that one is the cause, but in terms of the *perceptual* phenomenology of *seeing* one's causal efficacy. This would be a third and distinct reductive account of conative phenomenology, in terms of the combination of tactile and visual phenomenology. Naturally, for this to work there would have to be such a thing as visual awareness of one's causal efficacy. But this is quite plausible. Consider the following story (adapted from Siegel 2005). Jean-Paul and Albert both have a view on the Eiffel Tower, and marvel at the way the Tower's lights come on every night at 21h00. Jean-Paul is eccentric: every night he tries to flip the switch of his living room lights at the exact moment the Tower lights come on. He succeeds about twice a week, and when he does it is a source of great amusement to him, especially when he surprises his guests, who are oftentimes victim to a momentary illusion that he had turned on the Tower's light by flipping his living room switch. Albert is neither eccentric nor humorous. Tonight, both flip their living room switches at the exact moment the Eiffel Tower lights come on. Jean-Paul is greatly amused, but Albert is fleetingly startled: he himself falls victim to the momentary illusion that he had turned on the Eiffel Tower's lights by flipping his living room switch. A split second later he realizes this must be a coincidence. But for that brief moment he did experience himself as having been causally efficacious in lighting up the Eiffel Tower, and the experience was perceptual and direct. The idea, then, is that conative phenomenology might just be a matter of such perceptual phenomenology of causing (coupled with the relevant tactile phenomenology).

There are two main problems with this account. First, it does not make progress with respect to the main problem attending the causal-judgment-based account. Although it provides for a more direct awareness of one's causal efficacy, it does not explain the asymmetry between one's own causal efficacy and others'. For in the same sense in which you can *see* that you are the cause of your side of the couch lifting, you can also *see* that your friend is the cause of *his* side of the couch lifting. Furthermore, even if we agree that *sometimes* one can *see* one's causal efficacy, it may still be that sometimes one cannot. In particular, while one can see one's role in causing nonbasic actions, arguably one cannot with *basic* actions. The notion of basic action comes from Danto (1965). Suppose that seated at café *les deux maggots*, Albert smiles because Jean-Paul just waved hello to him. In waving hello, Jean-Paul has accomplished at least four things: he has made Albert smile; he has greeted Albert; he has moved his own hand (wavily); he has contracted his arm muscles (wave-appropriately). It is natural to say that there are more-basic-than relations among some of these actions.[5] Thus, Jean-Paul made Albert smile *by* greeting him, and in that sense the greeting was more basic than the making-smile. Likewise, he greeted Albert *by* moving his hand, and moved his hand *by* contracting his arm muscles, so the hand-moving was more basic than the greeting and the muscle-contracting more basic yet. We may say, to a first approximation, that action A is *basic* just when no other action is more basic than it, that is, just when there is no action A* such that one performed A by performing A*.[6] Plausibly, although we can see our causal efficacy vis-à-vis nonbasic actions, we cannot see it with our basic actions. Jean-Paul can perhaps *see* that he has greeted Albert, and even that he has raised his arm. But he cannot *see* that he has contracted his muscles (they are occluded by skin and fat). So this fundamental aspect of conative phenomenology—the experience of contracting one's own muscles, and more generally of causing (performing) one's own basic actions—cannot be accounted for in terms of the phenomenology of seeing one's causal efficacy.

※

It might be suggested that both problems can be overcome if we adduce not only tactile and visual phenomenology but also *proprioceptive* phenomenology (see already Dewey 1897). Plausibly, one *can* perceive proprioceptively one's muscle contractions—and one *cannot* perceive proprioceptively others' muscle contractions. So perhaps the conative phenomenology of clenching one's fist could be reduced to the combination of (i) tactile phenomenology of one's hand's various parts touching each other, (ii) visual (or for that matter cognitive) phenomenology of seeing (or judging) that one caused the fist to clench, and (iii) proprioceptive phenomenology of feeling one's fist muscles contracting. The key ingredient is the last: it gives us access to our own basic actions that we have to nobody else's.

This is easily the best reductive account we have considered so far. However, it has an untoward consequence: if it is correct, the phenomenology of doing something should be experienced *after* the doing has been completed, not *during* the doing. For the proprioceptive sensation of muscle contraction cannot occur *before* the muscles have contracted, and indeed must occur quite a bit *after*. Information from the muscles must be detected by receptors, sent to cortex, and processed before a proprioceptive representation of the muscles *having contracted* can form. But the phenomenology of *doing the contracting* of one's muscles takes place *during*, or rather *leading up to*, the muscle contraction. Thus the proposed reductive account gets wrong the temporal order of experience in a standard episode of conative activity.[7]

Perhaps with this temporal concern in mind, James (1890 ch.26) identified the feeling of willing something not with any proprioceptive sensations of actual muscle contractions, but with proprioceptive ("kinesthetic") *imagery* of projected or *anticipated* muscle contractions.[8] This is a fifth reductive account of conative phenomenology, reducing it to the phenomenal combination of tactile perception, visual perception, and proprioceptive imagery. On this view, the key element for capturing the conative dimension of the experience of clenching one's fist is the feel of imaginatively anticipating one's fist's muscles contracting.

The problem with this account is that it puts conative phenomenology too *early* in the order of experience: before the onset of the actual doing. This is something James (1890: 560) himself admitted, almost celebrated:

> The *willing* terminates with the prevalence of the idea; and whether the act then follows or not is a matter quite immaterial, so far as the willing itself goes. I will to write, and the act follows. I will to sneeze, and it does not. I will that the distant table slide over the floor towards me; it also does not . . . [I]n both cases it is as true and good willing as it was when I willed to write. In a word, volition is . . . absolutely completed when the stable state of the idea is there.

But while James is happy with this outlook, it is easy to appreciate how incongruent it seems: the passivity of action that James describes—"I will to write, and the act follows"—seems false to our experience. We experience a representation of the act to follow, but also of the act following, and following because we *make* it follow. That is, we experience not only an anticipation of the act, but also the causing of the act in real time.

This extra phenomenal element, separate from both backward- and forward-looking proprioceptive sensations, might be thought captured by what Wundt (1874) called the "feeling of innervation." This is the idea that when we exert our will we sense a sort of energy current going to our muscles. Not only do we proprioceptively feel our muscles contract, and imagistically anticipate them, we also feel energy traversing our musculature leading up to the contraction. According to a sixth form of reductivism, conative phenomenology may involve a number of different elements, but its distinctive, special characteristic is this feeling of innervation. On the most natural interpretation, the feeling of innervation is proprioceptive, so the account is still reductivist. But instead of backward- and forward-looking proprioception, it appeals to a "present-tense" proprioception (if you will).

The obvious problem with the Wundtian view is that the feeling of innervation is introspectively elusive.[9] There is no question that when I clinch my fist, a current of energy travels from motor cortex to my fist muscles. But as hard as I try, I cannot introspectively track its progress, nor for that matter its onset.[10] We should be open to the possibility that some phenomenal-contrast scenario could make us appreciate the feeling of innervation, or that some abductive argument could support its phenomenal reality. But for now I proceed as though there is no such thing.

2.3. Primitivism

If there is no feeling of innervation, but there *is* a feeling of trying to do something that goes beyond proprioceptive perception and imagery, that phenomenal residue may simply be irreducible. Ginet (1986: 228) attempts to isolate this non-proprioceptive, *proprietary* conative ("volitional") phenomenology in this illuminating passage:

> There is, first of all, *a perceptual* aspect: one perceives the exertion in a certain direct way—not visually or by feeling it with some other part of one's body, but *kinaesthetically*... [However,] The experience of *voluntary* exertion is significantly more than the mere kinaesthetic perception of the exertion. I could kinaesthetically feel my arm's exerting force, in just the same way it does when I voluntarily thrust it forward, without experiencing this exertion as something I control, as my voluntary doing. I could experience it as something that just happens to me, unconnected with my will, while at the same time experiencing the exertion of the bodily part as just like one I might have produced voluntarily. The voluntariness of the experience of voluntary exertion is *a further* part of it (which would be more conspicuous by its absence than it is by its presence), distinct from the perceptual part.
>
> It is, of course, this non-perceptual part that is the volitional part of the experience. This part too could occur all by itself, unaccompanied by any perception of exertion. It could seem to me that I voluntarily exert a force forward with my arm without at the same time its seeming to me that I *feel* the exertion happening: the arm feels kinaesthetically anaesthetized. (Sometimes, after an injection of anaesthetic at the dentist's, my tongue seems to me thus kinaesthetically dead as I voluntarily exercise it: I have then an illusion that my will fails to engage my tongue.)

The experience of contracting one's muscles may seem initially like a simple, incomposite experience. But Ginet offers a double phenomenal contrast to factorize it into two separate phenomenal components. First is a contrast between (i) contracting one's muscles and (ii) muscle contraction not experienced as of one's own volition. A second contrast is between (i) contracting one's muscles and (iii) willing the contraction, exerting the will, without the proprioceptive sensation of muscle contraction. This brings out the internal structure of the experience of contracting one's muscles, as composed of two elements: the exerting of willpower or willing of the contraction, and then the muscle contraction itself. It is in the first element, according to Ginet, that constitutes *sui generis* conative phenomenology (or at least one form of such). The key difference here is between muscle-contraction and muscle-contrac*ting*: the latter brings in the feel of *agency*, of exercising one's will, that characterizes the conative domain. That feel is the distilled, purified experience of the will, or rather of *willing*.[11]

On the face of it, two things are true of Ginet's feeling of willing: (i) it is a phenomenal property instantiated by consciously trying to contract one's muscles, and (ii) it is irreducible to (combinations of) tactile, visual, proprioceptive, and cognitive phenomenology. It is but a short step from this to the thesis of the primitive *conatus*.[12] Note that the experience of willing one's muscle contractions involves presenting-as-good$_G$ those contractions. Crucially, this aspect was missing from all six reductive accounts considered above. Tactile sensations, seeing and judging causal efficacy, proprioceptive perceptions—all these present-as-true (or present-as-real) their intentional objects. They thus seem to be missing the distinctively conative aspect of conative phenomenology. Not so our primitivist account.

It might be objected that the primitivist account conflicts with the celebrated "comparator model" of agentive experience (Frith et al. 2000, Bayne 2011). According to the comparator model, when motor cortex issues a motor command, it also produces a(n "off-line") copy of the command, which it sends (i) to a predictor module that predicts the sensory consequences of the relevant motor action and (ii) to a comparator module that compares these anticipated sensory effects to the actual effects as "conveyed" by a feedback mechanism. This may be taken to challenge the primitivist account defended here and offer a competing account. But this impression is wrong for several reasons. For starters, since the account is couched in subpersonal terms, it has unclear and at most indirect implications for what the personal-level phenomenology might be like. It is thus more relevant to *physical* reduction than *phenomenal* reduction. Furthermore, it seems to target not the character of *doing*, or *trying* to do, but that of being *aware* of doing/trying to do. If it is interpreted as targeting the phenomenology of doing (or trying) itself, then it is vulnerable to the temporal-order worries we already encountered: the comparing of the offline copy with feedback input presumably occurs long after an action is performed, so the phenomenology of doing something would postdate the doing.

There is one respect in which the tension between primitivism and the comparator model is real, namely, that they tend to lead to different predictions about how we *acquire knowledge* of what we are doing. Suppose you consciously try to clench your fist. How do you know that this is what you are trying to do (and that you are trying to do something at all)? Our primitivism suggests a straightforward model: when you consciously try to clinch your fish, you instantiate a primitive conative-phenomenal property, which you may then introspectively encounter. The comparator model suggests a more convoluted but also more parsimonious story: the proper functioning of all the relevant subpersonal modules produces the second-order judgment that you are clenching your fist.

To my mind, the primitivist model is much more antecedently plausible, but I will not argue for this here. Conative self-knowledge is a topic unto itself. Here I wanted to focus on conative phenomenology, making a prima facie case for its (phenomenal) irreducibility. It remains to inquire more fully into the *character* of the primitive conative phenomenology.

II. A Nonreductive Characterization of Conative Phenomenology

3. How Might We Characterize Conative Phenomenology?

In Chapter 1, I approached the task of characterizing cognitive phenomenology by (i) assuming that the act of making a judgment is the most fundamental or paradigmatic experience of cognizing and (ii) offering a phenomenological Ramsey sentence for it. Here I want to invest more energy in (i) showing that the most fundamental experience of exercising the will is that of deciding-and-then-trying to φ; I will then use the results of that discussion to (ii) sketch a potential phenomenological Ramsey sentence for that experience.

In the phenomenological tradition, the existence of both cognitive and conative phenomenology is often taken to be unproblematic. Husserl (1901: 82; my emphasis) declares without fanfare that "percepts, imaginative and pictorial representations, *acts of conceptual thinking,* surmises and doubts, joys and griefs, hopes and fears, *wishes and acts of will* etc., are . . . 'experiences' or 'contents of consciousness.'" Dedicated discussions of conative phenomenology and the associated experiences of the will in this tradition go back at least to Chapters 6 and 8 in Book II of Brentano's (1874) *Psychology from an Empirical Standpoint*. The main themes are further developed in Brentano's (1889) *The Origins of Our Knowledge of Right and Wrong*, but receive a much more thorough treatment in his student Ehrenfels' (1897/8) *System of Value Theory*. Arguably, however, the golden decade of conative phenomenology, so to speak, arrives only in the French philosophy of the 1940s, with a succession of impressive treatments in Sartre's (1943) *Being and Nothingness*, Merleau-Ponty's (1944) *The Phenomenology of Perception*, Jean Laporte's (1947) *The Consciousness of Freedom*, and Paul Ricœur's (1950) *The Voluntary and the Involuntary*.

Ricœur's approach to the will is methodologically interesting. He distinguishes between *empirical* and *phenomenological* psychology: the former studies the will from a third-person mechanistic standpoint, the latter from a first-person experiential one.[13] For Ricœur, this distinction has an all-important foundational implication for the study of the will. Consider that our behavior throughout the day is sometimes determined by conscious personal-level processes of deliberation, decision, choice, and so on, but at least as often by a variety of unconscious processes: reflexes, habits and instincts, needs, subpersonal automatized processes, and so on. Ricœur takes the former to be voluntary (involve exercise of the will) and the latter to be involuntary. The involuntary processes are psychologically and evolutionarily more basic, the voluntary ones more complex and sophisticated. For empirical psychology, this means that the order of investigation must proceed from the involuntary and subpersonal to the voluntary and conscious.[14] However, according to Ricœur our *grasp* of the involuntary is parasitic on our grasp of the voluntary. It is only in light of our understanding of conscious exercise of the will that we can make sense of unconscious conative processes as belonging to the same domain of phenomena. In that respect, conscious volition is *conceptually prior*, even though *causally posterior*, to subpersonal behavior-guiding processes. Although the causal order goes from the bottom up, the order of intelligibility, so to speak, goes from the top down (Ricœur 1950: 22):[15]

> Not only does the involuntary have no proprietary meaning, understanding proceeds from the top down and not from the bottom up . . . I understand myself first as he who says "I want." The involuntary refers itself to wanting as that which gives it motives, powers, foundations, even limits. This reversal of perspective is just one aspect of that Copernican revolution . . .

Given this reversal of perspectives, understanding the will depends in the first instance on phenomenological analysis of conscious, experiential exercise of the will.

Ricœur's analysis leads him to identify three main elements or "moments" in the exercise of the will: deciding, acting, and consenting. Although they *sometimes* appear in temporal order, this is neither essential nor universal. In spontaneous acts, for example, the deciding and the acting are contemporaneous—yet such acts are often *voluntary* (1950: 253). The essential relation between deciding, acting, and consenting is thus not temporal, but compositional: they are components, or aspects, of willing.

In what follows, I use Ricœur's analysis as a springboard for characterizing conative phenomenology. I want to argue that Ricœur is right to focus on deciding (rather than desire and intention) as the fundamental act of the will (§4), but that (i) the role he designates in his account for acting is better played by *trying* (§5) and (ii) consenting is not an additional phenomenal element on a par with deciding and trying (§6). The upshot will be a picture where the phenomenology of deciding-cum-trying is the fundamental form of conative phenomenology (§7).

4. Deciding

Cleaning after a birthday party, Aristide comes across a nice-looking slab of leftover chocolate cake. He likes chocolate cake and would enjoy eating some unceremoniously and unselfconsciously. But he also plans to lose ten pounds by April, and is acutely aware that he ought to be on the guard against fleeting temptations of this sort. The cake is right there—he has to make a decision. He can *feel* the battle of temptation and self-control in him—can feel an inner tension, what James (1890: 529) called the "impatience of the deliberative state"—but eventually decides to throw out the leftover piece without eating it.

The process of deliberation in such an episode has tangible duration to it, but the act of deciding, of making up one's mind, is experientially instantaneous. Yet that instantaneous act is the quintessential conative act, according to Ricœur, and there is something it is like to perform it—a phenomenal character of deciding. According to Ricœur (1950: 66), every decision is experienced as directed toward a *project*. A central characteristic of projects is temporal: they send to the future (1950: 73). Thus decisions have a *character of futurity*. Other conative experiences also have this character of futurity, including commanding, wishing, desiring, and worrying (1950: 74). But what distinguishes deciding is that it presents the project as *in my power*. This "feeling of power," as Ricœur (1950: 78) calls it, is essential to the phenomenology of deciding.[16]

One way to think of this is in analogy to internalism about moral commitments, the idea that such commitments are essentially tied to motivation: unless a mental state involves a pull to action, it is not a genuine moral commitment.[17] Regardless of whether such internalism is true of moral commitment, it is manifestly true of decision: unless a mental state involves a pull to action, it is not a decision. Ricœur (1950: 62, my italics) writes:

> What is remarkable is that the decision, cut off from its execution by a delay, by a blank, is nonetheless not indifferent to its execution; when I have decided to make a delicate move, *I feel myself somehow charged*, in the way a battery is charged: I have the power to act, I am capable of it.

This feeling of charge, of readiness, is clearly essential to—indeed definitive of—the phenomenology of deciding. This creates an internal connection to action (as what would *dis*charge the decision).

It is worth noting that acting on one's decision need not manifest itself in overt behavior. Suppose someone hurts my pride, a barbed retort presents itself to me, but in the end I decide not to respond. My decision results in the *absence* of any overt behavior. Nonetheless, in not responding I do *act on* my decision. A certain *kind* of action is thus still involved—we may call this a *negative action*. Testifying to this is the fact that it is quite *hard* for me to not respond, it requires a distinctive *effort*. Insofar as the mobilizing of effort is an indicator of action, it is clear that not responding is in the present context an action. Sometimes the element of effort disappears and all is left is a negative action, as when I effortlessly decide not to reply to a cryptic email from some vice-dean. Nonetheless, the negative action is still present, and deciding is always deciding *to act*. It features a felt pull to action.

More: decision involves a *special kind* of pull to action, what Ricœur (1950: 70) calls a *categorical* pull to action. Compare desire. Clearly, it is essential to the desire to eat a cake that if no other considerations outweigh it, it would lead to eating the cake. Thus desire appears to involve pull to action as well. However, in desire the connection to action is *hypothetical*: the desire presents the action as to be performed *if* there are no outweighing considerations/desires. In contrast, a decision's connection to action is *categorical*: in making the decision to eat the cake, you commit to acting on it, *period*. The commitment is unconditional. From Ricœur's perspective, this experience of categorical pull to action is the distinguishing mark of decision (Ricœur 1950: 70).

(It is in this respect that decision is arguably the fundamental exercise of the will. It is only when a decision has been made that we experience the will actually being deployed. A desire can be formed without any will-deployment ensuing.)

Importantly, this too is an *attitudinal* feature of decision. For a decision may well have a hypothetical *content*. I can decide that I will visit Grandma next week if my sister does not. The decision's content is hypothetical. But my commitment to it is categorical: for me to not go despite my sister not going, say because of some overriding considerations, is for me to *undo* or *go back on* my decision. By contrast, I can desire to visit Grandma next week if my sister does not and *still* not go through with it without losing the desire (it may simply be overridden). Indeed, I may have a desire with a categorical content (e.g., to visit Grandma) and yet not go—precisely because my commitment to that content is not itself categorical.

The categorical pull-to-action feel is decision's most important phenomenal property. A number of other properties are entrained by it. First, not unlike the experience of making a judgment discussed in Chapter 1, the experience of deciding (or making a decision) has the character of absoluteness: its commitment to the pursuing that which is decided is complete and does not come in degrees. Some desires are stronger than others; decisions cannot be compared for strength. And although people sometimes say "My decision is final," they never say "My decision is *not* final": if one's decision is not final, then one has not really *made* the decision yet. Decision by its nature has a character of finality (analogous to the character of finality of making a judgment).

A related phenomenal property is what we may call *felt stake*: in making a decision to do something, I acquire a stake in what happens. Thus, when I decide to get ice cream, *it matters* to me whether or not I get it. This felt stake creates a certain tension in my consciousness, relieved only by the actual getting of the ice cream (more on this in §5). Arguably, a felt stake characterizes desire as well: already when I want ice cream I have a stake in whether I get it. But the stake seems stronger and somehow less controvertible once the decision to act on a desire has been made. To be sure, a desire to φ may involve a stronger felt stake than a decision to ψ; but a decision to φ will always involve a stronger, or deeper, felt stake than a desire to φ. To that extent, felt stake is more central to decision than to desire.

Recall from §1 that "nonsensuous presenting-as-good$_G$" may well be the phenomenal mark of the conative. If so, different species of conative experience should involve different species of nonsensuous presenting-as-good$_G$. In other words: if the "formal object" of conation is *generic* goodness, then different conative states are directed at different kinds of *specific* goodness. I now wish to argue that decision's categorical pull-to-action feel casts decision as directed at *the right*. If so, it is characterized by the specific attitudinal feature of nonsensuous presenting-as-right.

In the ethical literature, the notion of rightness is connected to the ontology of bearers of ethical properties. Specifically: actions are evaluated primarily for rightness, states of affairs primarily for goodness (moral, not generic!). Suppose you see a one-legged beggar on the subway and give him a dollar. We can distinguish (a) the act of you *giving* the dollar and (b) the state of affairs of the beggar *having* the dollar. You perform (a) in order to bring about (b). What we find natural to say is that (a) is the *right* thing to do and (b) is a *good* state of affairs.[18] Thus the right is primarily an attribute of actions, while the good is primarily an attribute of states of affairs. This contrast is crucial to the intentional difference between decisions and desires. What you decide, in the first instance, is to give the beggar the dollar. What you want, in the first instance, is for the beggar to *have* the dollar. (I use "wanting" as a synonymous with "desiring.") That is, in the first instance you decide on an action and want a state of affairs. To that extent, your decision is primarily directed at the right, your desire at the good.[19] The decision presents-as-right you giving the dollar, the desire presents-as-good the beggar having the dollar. Another example is Aristide's decision not to eat the cake because he wants to lose weight. The desire to lose weight is directed at the good, presenting-as-good the state of affairs of Aristide weighing less. But the decision not to eat the cake does something else—it presents the act of avoiding eating the cake as the *right thing to do* (or rather presents-as-right that act). More generally, decisions appear primarily directed toward actions (or clusters thereof), desires primarily toward states of affairs. Accordingly, desires aim at the good but decisions at the right.[20]

This seems connected to decision's categorical pull to action: since the pull is categorical, action is always that which a decision is "about." What we decide is always to *do* something. Now, since the categorical pull-to-action feel is an attitudinal feature of decision, decision's aiming at the right is an attitudinal feature as well. Deciding to dance involves presenting-as-right dancing rather than presenting dancing-as-right.[21]

5. Acting and Trying

Recall James' (1890: 560) odd contention that a "willing terminates with the prevalence of the idea; and whether the act follows or not is a matter quite immaterial, so far as the willing goes." Something about this feels wrong, and according to Ricœur, we can appreciate that "something" already in the phenomenology of deciding. Although deciding always presents a course of action, there is an unsettled feeling about this presentation—a feeling of "something more" needing to come through. "I 'recognize' the intention's emptiness in the act's plenitude" (Ricœur 1950: 259). Deciding feels *impatient*: its pull to action is unnerving, strongly calling me to act it out. Not only does the decision dispose me to act, but until the decision is acted upon—until the disposition is manifested—there is a subtly unpleasant feeling of tension in my consciousness. Thus by its very nature, a decision desperately wants to be *realized*—realized in action.[22] Phenomenologically, the exercise of the will is not exhausted when a decision has been formed—only when the process of realizing the decision is underway.

This raises a problem, however. Some actions are entirely mental—calculating a tip, comparing lunch options, rotating a mental image. But most actions are not entirely mental phenomena: even when the pensive and sentimental person chases butterflies, picks flowers, or writes a poem, her actions are *overt* and involve a nonmental, bodily aspect. On the assumption that phenomenology is an entirely mental phenomenon, however, it cannot be constituted in part by something nonmental.[23]

Ricœur appreciates the force of this worry and responds by arguing that acting too is possessed of *intentionality*—and so, presumably, is mental. Setting aside the problematic inference from "intentional" to "mental," Ricœur's case for the intentionality of action is underwhelming. It consists in noting that action verbs are transitive in the way "representational verbs" are, expressing "a directedness from a subjective pole to an objective pole" (1950: 261). But of course, transitive verbs far outstrip intentional verbs ("the ball hit the glass," "the ship hit the fan"). A much better criterion of intentionality is Chisholm's (1957): a transitive verb is intentional just when it fails to support certain inferences, notably existential generalization and substitution of coreferentials. By this criterion's lights, action verbs do not fare well. From "Anatole moved his hand" (or

"Anatole moved his painting"), one can validly infer "there is something that Anatole moved"; so existential generalization is supported rather than failed. Further, from "Anatole moved his hand" (or "Anatole moved his painting"), in conjunction with "Simone's favorite object is Anatole's hand" (or ". . . Anatole's painting"), one can validly infer "Anatole moved Simone's favorite object"; so there is no substitution failure either. One would have to conclude that moving, whether proximal or distal, is nonintentional.

We are faced with a difficulty, then. On the one hand, the phenomenology of will clearly includes a component that goes beyond the *making* of a decision and involves the releasing of a process of *implementing* the decision. On the other hand, action is not an entirely mental phenomenon, whereas conative phenomenology is. The solution to this difficulty, it seems to me, is to note that although action itself is not entirely mental, it plausibly contains a purely mental *component*. Wittgenstein (1953 §621) asked: "What is left over if I subtract the fact that my arm goes up from the fact that I raise my arm?" What is left over is the purely mental component of raising one's arm—the mental "core" of action. It is this, I suggest, that must complement a decision in the paradigmatic conative experience.

Arguably, the mental core of action is captured by the notion of *trying*. On the one hand, trying to φ involves initiating the process of implementing the decision to φ. On the other hand, unlike action, trying is genuinely intentional. Thus, from "Anatole tried to move his hand" it does not follow that "there is something that Anatole tried to move" (imagine that Anatole has momentarily forgotten that he lost his arm in battle). Likewise, it does not follow that "Anatole tried to move Simone's favorite object" (imagine Anatole is unaware that his hand is Simone's favorite object). Furthermore, like decision, trying aims primarily at the right: in the first instance, one tries to move a painting, not for the painting to change location.[24] This makes perfect sense if trying has an intimate connection to deciding; in particular, if one tries what one decided.

Indeed, there might be reasons to think that trying is an entirely *phenomenal* state. Or perhaps more cautiously: there is a way of hearing the word "trying" such that a phenomenal duplicate of one is also a trying duplicate. Call this the *phenomenal hearing* of "trying." My brain-in-vat duplicate is not really typing on the keyboard right now, though it is under the impression that it is. But the duplicate is not only under the impression that it is *trying* to type right now, it really *is* trying—at least on one hearing of "trying." The same goes for other actions: the duplicate does not open a door or ride a bike, but it does try to. Thus trying is something that phenomenal duplicates shares, even when (only) one of them is unable to act (see, in this connection, O'Shaughnessy 1973: 369).

In saying all this, I do not mean to deny that there is also a nonphenomenal hearing of "trying" whereby it is false that my envatted duplicate is trying to open the door. It might be objected, however, that trying does not really have the phenomenal hearing I claim on its behalf; that my envatted duplicate is under the illusion that it is trying to type but in fact is not trying to type at all. In response, I would say that to my ear, there still seems to be a(n appropriate) hearing of "trying" in which it does. But even if there is not, we can call the phenomenon I have in mind "seemingly-trying" and insist that it is the mental core of action shared by phenomenal duplicates. I will conduct the discussion below in terms of trying, presupposing a phenomenal hearing throughout, but am open to revising the terminology.

What more can be said about what it is like to try? Plausibly, there is an intimate connection between the phenomenology of trying and the phenomenology of effort: trying always *mobilizes* effort.[25] This is significant, given that dedicated discussion of the feeling of effort has a substantial history, going back at least to Maine de Biran (1812).[26] Laporte (1947) describes the feeling of effort as a phenomenal vector of *force* and *resistance*. We might say, then, that trying involves the experience of mobilizing force in the face of resistance. An impressionistic way to think of this feeling is as a sort of nonsensory analog of Wundtian innervation: an invisible, insentient, but still phenomenally luminous current traveling from will to muscle. We can also use some of the contrast cases in §2 to *point* to, and thus *acquaint* ourselves with, the nonsensory, purely conative element in the experience of trying agents. For example, Ginet's "non-perceptual part of volition" (which goes beyond the feeling of exertion) may well be nothing more than the irreducible phenomenology of trying.

It may be objected that focusing on trying rather than acting, as decision's complement, deforms the phenomenology. In the normal go of things, we do not experience ourselves as *trying* to act, but as acting. When I clench my fist, I normally do not experience myself as trying to clench but as clenching. This is a point Ricœur (1950: 389) emphasizes, arguing that in our actual experience it is action that manifests itself to us first and foremost, while trying is relatively obscured and requires careful and somewhat tutored attention.

This objection rests on a subtle but pernicious confusion. We certainly experience ourselves as *acting*, or in other words as *successfully* trying to do something. But we also experience ourselves as *seeing* the world, that is, as in a good case of visual experience. We do not normally experience ourselves as hallucinating or as being in a state that might be either a seeing or a hallucinating. All the same, our experience is *in fact* a state which might be either a seeing or a hallucinating. When it is a seeing, the phenomenology is veridical, and when it is a hallucinating, it is nonveridical. Likewise with trying: when it is successful, our experience of ourselves as acting is veridical, and when it is unsuccessful, nonveridical. It remains that nothing in the conative experience itself guarantees its success, just as nothing in a visual experience guarantees its veridicality. So the experience itself is just a trying.

A related objection is that the natural complement of deciding is acting, and not trying, because *what* we decide is normally to *do* something, not to *try to do* something. There are marginal cases in which we decide to try something, namely, cases where we are skeptical of our chances of success (I may decide to try to run a marathon). But most decisions are unlike that: one decides to order a salad or to send an email, not to *try* to order a salad or to send an email.

However, it seems to me that the fact that normally we decide to act rather than to try derives entirely from the fact, just discussed, that every trying presents itself as an acting (in the way every experience presents itself as a successful instance of its kind). Compare perceptual belief: normally, I believe that I am seeing my laptop and hearing my wife, not that I am having a visual experience *as of* my laptop and an auditory experience *as of* my wife. The more guarded perceptual beliefs are formed, again, only in conditions of uncertainty. Still, what the belief is *about* is a perceptual experience that may or may not qualify as seeing/hearing. Likewise, what a decision is *about* is a trying, which may or may not qualify as an acting.

I conclude that the feel of deciding to φ inherently requires a complement in trying. This marks a deep difference between decision and desire. Since desire's pull-to-action feel is merely hypothetical, there is nothing phenomenologically problematic about desiring something but trying to do nothing about it. Things are different with decision: given decision's *categorical* pull-to-action feel, it is strictly impossible that one should decide to φ without trying to φ.[27] In that respect, the experiences of deciding and trying are, *au fond*, two components of a single experience, which for want of a better term I will call the "phenomenology of deciding-cum-trying."[28]

6. "Consent"

So far two aspects of conative phenomenology have come through: deciding and trying. The former is perhaps the core act of the will, but has a phenomenal lacuna at its heart, as it calls out for realization; trying offers its phenomenal "filling," as the initiation of realization in action. In these metaphorical terms, we might say that with the combination of deciding and trying, one's conative experience is "phenomenally saturated." Nonetheless, Ricœur maintains that there is one more component of conative phenomenology, what he calls *consent*. In this section, I argue that Ricœur's addition here is a mistake. The section can be skipped by readers who feel no pull to posit a further component, beyond deciding and trying, in the fundamental experience of exercising the will.

It is not straightforward in the text what Ricœur has in mind with the notion of consent. At bottom, consent appears to be the will's relation to that aspect of the world that is outside its control. Ricœur puts this by saying that the formal object of consent is necessity, where by this he appears to mean a kind of practical necessity—*inevitability*. In this section, I present two specific interpretations of the role of consent in Ricœur's picture of the will, which I call the "complement" interpretation and the "alternative" interpretation. I argue that neither makes it plausible that we have here a distinct conative-phenomenal component.

To appreciate the first ("complement") interpretation, recall Aristide's dilemma: he wants to eat a piece of leftover cake, but also wants to lose weight; eventually, he decides to throw away the cake. Observe, now, that the only reason a decision is needed, indeed the only reason he faces a dilemma, is that Aristide is aware of the conflict between his two desires: he realizes that, the way the world works, one normally cannot lose weight by eating chocolate cakes. This is an aspect of the world over which Aristide has no control—it is "necessity" staring back at him. Aristide must *accept* it, *consent* to it, if a conscious act of deciding is to take place at all. Accordingly, we do not *fully grasp* the deciding if we have no grasp of the consenting. Consenting goes to the very meaning of decision-making. In this interpretation, what Ricœur has in mind is that understanding decision requires understanding consent. Although surely very peripheral, the feel of consent is one important element in Aristide's overall phenomenology as he exercises his will in the face of the cake dilemma. Without this element, there is no exercising of the will, no call for decision.

The problem with consent so interpreted is that there is nothing particularly *conative* about it. To *realize* something—say, that the world is set up a certain way—is to have a cognitive representation of it. Even if such realization is a necessary accompaniment to the conative experiences of deciding and trying, that would not make it conative itself. It still involves a theoretical orientation on the world, a mind-to-world direction of fit, a presenting-as-true of its intentional object. This casts consent as one more nonconative element surrounding conative phenomenology, on a par with (e.g.) the proprioceptive perception of muscle contraction.[29] Furthermore, in many cases it seems like the awareness of necessity at issue is not a form of occurrent realization, but of a standing, tacit belief. Certainly the belief that one does not gain weight by eating cake seems to be, in normal subjects, a tacit belief. If so, it is nonconscious and should not show up in the phenomenology.

This suggests to me that the complement interpretation cannot be right. For Ricœur (1950: 431, my italics) is explicit on the need to construe consent as experiential directedness in a practical mode:

> . . . consent is not a *judgment* on necessity, since it does not consider *theoretically* the fact; it does not put it at a viewing distance; it is not

an observational perspective on the inevitable, it is a contemplation without distance, better an *active adoption* of necessity.

There must be another interpretation of consent, one that casts it as a genuinely conative act, an "active adoption."

Suppose that, like Aristide, Adelaide is hit with craving for chocolate cake. Unlike Aristide, however, she has none about—and it is getting late. She decides to drive to her favorite bakery, but discovers that it is already closed. So she heads to another couple of bakeries, which turn out to be closed as well. With a heavy heart, she reconciles herself to the idea of mass-produced chocolate cake, and heads to the nearest grocery store. To her surprise, the grocery store is out of chocolate cake, whereupon she drives to the local supermarket, only to be disappointed again. At this point, she gives up and drives home, exhausted and cakeless. The whole ordeal has taken well over an hour, an hour bustling with a succession of feelings: desire, decision, excitement, disappointment, hope, wish, surprise, frustration, dissatisfaction, more disappointment—and finally, a certain *acceptance* that in this instance the world will simply not yield to her will: she will not have her chocolate cake. In accepting the world's resistance to her will, Adelaide *consents* to the world being the way it is—a world of cakeless Adelaides.

On this interpretation, when consenting happens, trying ceases. The mind no longer attempts to change the world to fit it. Where trying is the relation between the will and the world when one pursues what one takes to be achievable, consent is the relation that ensues when one no longer takes what one wants to be achievable: "consent is even the opposite of effort; it is expressly will without power" (Ricœur 1950: 432). On this interpretation, then, consenting is not really a *complement* of deciding-cum-trying but an *alternative* to deciding-cum-trying. It is not that an act of the will has three "moments" in it, deciding, trying, and consenting. It is that there are two radically different kinds of acts of the will: deciding-cum-trying on the one hand, and consenting on the other.

This interpretation, taking Adelaide rather than Aristide as the paradigmatic consenter, has the exegetical advantage that it casts consent's intentionality as practical rather than theoretical. It also captures a broadly Stoic undercurrent widely recognized to characterize Ricœur's work. However, it has the exegetical disadvantage that it does not integrate consenting with deciding and trying into a single conative experience. It also faces the vexing problem that consent appears to be not just a special kind of act of the will—it appears to be a special kind of *decision*! Adelaide *decides* to give up on the chocolate-cake project. In accepting that the world will not yield to her desires this time, she decides to *refrain* from certain activities. In essence, she decides *not to try* to find cake any more. She decides to revise her expectations, and in the bigger scheme of things, decides to find a way to live in a world where she remains cakeless. This is a radically different kind of decision—a decision to change one's desires to fit (the uncontrollable part of) the world, instead of the more typical decision to try to change (the controllable part of) the world to fit one's desires. But it is a decision all the same. (Indeed, to the Stoic it is the deeper, more autonomous decision.)

More accurately, as a special kind of decision, consent involves a special kind of trying. When Aristide decides to throw away the cake, he proceeds to try to change the world to fit his desire for slimness. When Adelaide consents to cakelessness, she proceeds to try to change her projects so they fit a world where she is cakeless. In doing so, she is acting on certain second-order desires, such as the desire to have as few unrealistic projects as possible or as few frustrated first-order desires as possible. Deciding to act on these second-order desires, and then *trying* to act on them, is what Adelaide's conative phenomenology really comes down to in this instance. Thus consent is not a *sui generis* type of conative phenomenology, apart from the phenomenology of deciding and trying. Rather, it is a *special case* of the phenomenology of deciding and trying—a particularly instructive special case, perhaps, but a special case nonetheless.

I am open to the possibility of a third interpretation of Ricœurian consent that I have failed to isolate or conceptualize. Until I become aware of such an interpretation, however, I provisionally conclude that conative phenomenology is in the first instance a phenomenology as of deciding-cum-trying.

This conclusion may be thought to create a puzzle. If conative phenomenology comes in two varieties, *affirmative* deciding-cum-trying and *consensual* deciding-cum-trying, then the notion that practical intentionality is characterized by world-to-mind fit faces a problem. For it seems that only in the affirmative variety must the world change in order for one's decision's satisfaction conditions to be fulfilled. In the consensual variety, it is precisely the mind that must change itself to fit the world. Yet consensual decisions clearly have a practical, engaged orientation on the world, not a theoretical, removed orientation. They deal with the world not in the context of maximizing the true, but in the context of maximizing the good/right.

The solution to this puzzle lies in keeping in mind that consensual decisions imply *second-order* desires which *are* supposed to change that which they are about, namely, first-order desires. (They may be contrasted, in that respect, with second-order judgments and beliefs.) It is just that in the case of such second-order states, both the state and its intentional object are in the mind. The lesson is therefore that the labels "world-to-mind" and "mind-to-world" are misleading; better labels would be "subject-to-object" and "object-to-subject." Thus, Adelaide's decision to stop pursuing cake has an object-to-subject direction of fit insofar as its intentional object is supposed to change to fit Adelaide *qua* subject of her second-order desire.

7. A Phenomenological Ramsey Sentence for Deciding-cum-Trying

In the course of discussing Ricœur's phenomenology of will, I have made a number of claims (sometimes in agreement with Ricœur, sometimes in disagreement). As in the previous chapter, these can be treated as phenomenological platitudes: platitudes because they concern surface features of deciding and trying, phenomenological because the relevant surface features are phenomenal. Such platitudes yield a characterization of their target phenomenology when collected into a sufficiently sophisticated Ramsey sentence.

Recall that not all platitudes must be true for a sophisticated Ramsey sentence to be (see discussion in Chapter 1). With that in mind, let us list the following eighteen phenomenological platitudes suggested (with various degrees of confidence) in the course of the foregoing discussion:

1) Both deciding and trying involve an attitudinal phenomenal feature of presenting-as-good$_G$.
2) The specific kind of presenting-as-good$_G$ involved in deciding and trying is presenting-as-right.
3) Deciding has a character of futurity.
4) Deciding involves a feeling of in-my-power-ness.
5) Deciding has a pull-to-action feel.
6) The pull-to-action feel involved in deciding is categorical.
7) Deciding involves the experience of the will being deployed.
8) Deciding does not feature degrees of phenomenal intensity.
9) Deciding has the character of finality.
10) Deciding involves a felt stake.
11) Deciding feels impatient, needing to be phenomenally complemented.
12) The phenomenal complement of deciding is trying.
13) Trying is the mental core of action (on the phenomenal hearing of "trying").
14) The experience of trying is what is left over when we subtract from the fact that someone moved the fact that motion has occurred.
15) Trying involves the experience of mobilizing force in the face of resistance.
16) Trying involves a nonsensory analog of innervation (a feeling of a kind of nonsensible current traveling from will to muscle).
17) The experience of trying is the "nonsensory part of volition"—that which goes beyond the feeling of exertion when one acts.

18) Deciding-cum-trying is typically directed at changing the world, but sometimes directed at changing first-order desires deemed unlikely to be satisfied.

We can readily produce an unpolished phenomenological Ramsey sentence from these: "there is an x, and there is a y, such that both x and y involve an attitudinal phenomenal feature of presenting-as-good$_G$; the specific kind of presenting-as-good$_G$ involved in x and y is presenting-as-right; x has a character of futurity; x involves a feeling of in-my-power-ness; . . . the phenomenal complement of x is y; y is the mental core of action; . . ." More plausible, however, would be a *sophisticated* Ramsey sentence that involved disjunctions of conjunctions of variously lengthy subsets of the eighteen platitudes above. And of course there may be many other phenomenological platitudes that could go into the ultimate phenomenological Ramsey sentence of deciding-cum-trying. Such a phenomenological Ramsey sentence would present a nonreductive characterization of the most fundamental kind of conative phenomenology.[30]

Conclusion

Even if we do not accept this broadly Ricœurian take on the nature of conative phenomenology, with its emphasis on the phenomenology of deciding-cum-trying, it is highly plausible that there does exist conative phenomenology, and that it is irreducible to (any combinations of) proprioceptive, visual, tactile, and cognitive phenomenology. At least this is what I argued in §2. If so, in addition to perceptual and algedonic phenomenology, there are at least two other primitive second-layer phenomenal determinables: cognitive and conative. In the next chapter, however, I argue that in fact an adequate first-person account of our mental life requires a *fifth* second-layer primitive phenomenology: the phenomenology of merely entertaining (or apprehending) a proposition, without committing to either its truth or its goodness.[31]

3

The Phenomenology of Entertaining

Functionalist orthodoxy in philosophy of mind is dominated by so-called belief-desire psychology: the idea that behavior is explained by combinations of belief and desire. In seeking to expand the circle of the phenomenal beyond the sensory domain, it is thus natural that we started with cognitive and conative phenomenology. The former corresponds to belief and the latter to desire. But in this chapter, I argue for a third type of primitive nonsensory phenomenology, distinguished from both the cognitive and conative. The paradigmatic phenomenon in this third group is the act of merely entertaining a proposition—without either believing or desiring it to hold. In Part I, I argue that this kind of state exhibits a primitive phenomenology irreducible to cognitive, conative, and perceptual phenomenology. In Part II, I offer a nonreductive characterization of it.

I. Primitive Entertainment

1. The Thesis of Primitive Entertainment

Talk of entertaining can be used to refer to a number of phenomena, including but not restricted to the following:

- Entertaining that p
- Entertaining the proposition that p
- Entertaining the thought that p
- Entertaining the possibility that p
- Entertaining the idea of x
- Entertaining an image of x
- Entertaining the option of φ-ing
- Entertaining φ-ing

My concern here is with entertaining as a propositional attitude, so I will take the second expression as canonical designator of the phenomenon I am concerned with, though also the first as an admissible shorthand.

Entertaining is only the paradigmatic instance of a certain *type* of mental act or episode. Resembling the paradigm in various respects are the following:

- Apprehending *p* (or *x*)
- Grasping *p* (or *x*)
- Thinking of *p* (or of *x*)
- Considering *p*
- Contemplating (that) *p*
- Reflecting on *p*
- Wondering whether *p*
- Pondering *p*
- Examining *p*
- Supposing that *p*
- Conceiving that *p* (or of *x*)
- (Day)dreaming of *x*
- Imagining that *p* (or *x*)
- Visualizing *x*
- Having a mental image of *x*

These differ in important respects, but all seem to have this in common, that what they present they neither present-as-true nor present-as-good. They present it "neutrally," that is, without commenting on either truth or goodness.

There is no good term in everyday English for the entire group. The word "thought" (or the locution "having a thought") is sometimes used in a way that could be interpreted as covering the entire group. When I think of a smiling octopus, I represent neither that it is *true* that some octopus is smiling nor that it would be good if one did. On the other hand, "thought" can also be used to describe a committal cognitive state: I cannot think *that* some octopus is smiling without presenting-as-true the proposition that some octopus is smiling. As far as everyday English is concerned, then, there is a key difference between thinking *of* (which is neutral) and thinking *that* (which is cognitive). We thus cannot unambiguously use the term "thought" for the entire group. Instead, I will call them technically *neutral attitudes*.

It is an open question whether there is a phenomenal property distinctive of neutral attitudes. However, insofar as cognitive attitudes share the attitudinal phenomenal feature of presenting-as-true and conative ones that of presenting-as-good, neutral attitudes plausibly share the attitudinal phenomenal feature of merely-presenting, that is, presenting neither as true nor as good. As before, though, my claim here will be narrower: that there is an irreducible phenomenology characteristic of *some* neutral attitude(s). More formally:

(PE) There is a phenomenal property P, such that (i) for any subject S and proposition p, if S entertains that p then S instantiates P, and (ii) there are no perceptual, algedonic, cognitive, and/or conative phenomenal properties $P_1, \ldots, P_n$, such that P reduces to some combination of $P_1, \ldots, P_n$.

Call this the *thesis of primitive entertainment*. One way to appreciate the thesis of primitive entertainment is in terms of the triad from the Introduction:

1) There exists a phenomenology of entertaining.
2) The phenomenology of entertaining is irreducible to perceptual, algedonic, cognitive, and/or conative phenomenology.
3) Perceptual, algedonic, cognitive, and conative phenomenology ultimately exhaust all phenomenology.

Adopting primitivism about entertaining-phenomenology is a matter of defending 1 and 2 and rejecting 3. (If there are other types of phenomenology that threaten to reduce entertaining-phenomenology, the triad would have to be modified to include them.)

The view is not without precedent. Whitehead's (1929) notion of a basic "propositional feeling" certainly appears to refer to such a *sui generis* subjective experience of merely entertaining. Whitehead (1929: 193) writes:

> A proposition emerges in the analysis of a judgment; it is the datum of the judgment in abstraction from the judging subject and from the subjective form. A judgment is a synthetic feeling, embracing two subordinate feelings in one unity of feeling. Of these subordinate feelings one is propositional, merely entertaining the proposition which is its datum.

In this picture, a judgment is simply a complex subjective feeling involving two component feelings, one of which—the "propositional feeling"—is a matter of simply entertaining the proposition; the other is presumably a feeling of commitment to the truth of the proposition entertained. We will return to this picture in §5, when we discuss the relationship between entertaining and judging.

An earlier precedent is Brentano's (1874) notion of *Vorstellung*, typically translated as "presentation." Brentano divides conscious phenomena into three "fundamental classes."[1] One is "judgment" and covers any conscious state that presents what it does as true or false, real or unreal. This contrasts with what Brentano calls "interest" (or "phenomena of love and hate"), which covers states that present what they do as good or bad rather than as true or false. In addition to these two, Brentano posits a third fundamental category, presentation, covering any state that in itself presents what it does in an entirely neutral fashion, without "commenting" on either its truth or its goodness. For Brentano (1874: 225), these categorical differences are established in the first instance through the "testimony of inner experience." The idea is that there is a phenomenology of doxastic commitment to the truth of something and a phenomenology of axiological commitment to the goodness of something, but in addition there is a phenomenology of non-commitment. When one entertains that *p*, one experiences a phenomenology as of *p* being in some (admittedly elusive) sense simply *present before the mind*, unaccompanied by either assent, dissent, approval, or disapproval.

Brentano's picture of the attitudes is essentially the one I would like to argue for: in addition to the cognitive phenomenology typified by making a judgment, and the conative phenomenology typified by deciding-cum-trying, there is a "neutral" attitudinal phenomenology of entertaining. All three go beyond perceptual and algedonic phenomenology and are mutually irreducible.

2. A *Prima Facie* Case for Primitive Entertainment

The thesis of primitive entertainment, as formulated above, has two clauses: one asserting the very *existence* of entertaining-phenomenology, the other asserting its (phenomenal) *irreducibility*. Accordingly, the argumentative strategy I pursue in its defense proceeds as follows. In a first stage, I adduce a defeasible reason for recognizing a phenomenology of entertaining. In a second stage, I consider a number of potential defeaters and argue against them. This is meant to make the case for the *existence* of entertaining-phenomenology. In a third stage, I consider a number of potential *reducers* and argue against them. This is intended to make the case for the irreducibility of entertaining-phenomenology.

The overall argument is non-demonstrative: it gives us a significant reason to believe in primitive entertainment, but not a *conclusive* reason. Certainty in phenomenological matters is most often produced by direct introspective encounter with the phenomenology, but such direct appeal to introspection is ineffective when disputants profess different introspective impressions. So here I will rest content with an abductive argument—a variation on the Goldman-Pitt epistemic argument for cognitive phenomenology.

2.1. Stage 1: A Defeasible Reason

Goldman (1993) points out that the propositional attitudes are introspectively discriminable: we can often tell by introspection that we believe that *p*, as opposed to desiring that *p* or believing that *q*.[2] This datum needs explaining, and the best explanation, suggests Goldman, is that the belief that *p* has a distinctive phenomenal character for introspection to detect.[3] Pitt (2004) develops a more involved account of the special knowledge we have of our cognitive states—it is immediate, noninferential knowledge (again, both of the attitude and of the content of cognitive states). But for Pitt too, the best explanation of this knowledge is that we are directly acquainted with phenomenal features distinctive of our cognitive states (both attitude and content).[4]

Similar reasoning could be used to support the existence of a phenomenology of entertaining. Suppose you are reading Spinoza's *Ethics* and you come across the following claim: "the order and connection of ideas is the same as the order and connection of things." When presented with this claim, you are probably not immediately in a position to either accept or reject it. More likely, your first act is to merely entertain it. Indeed, just understanding this difficult sentence requires grasping the proposition it expresses, that is, entertaining that proposition. Or suppose an extraordinarily untrustworthy acquaintance tells you that she immasked a starveling. For a second you are unsure what was said, but then you regroup and reason that to immask is probably to put a mask on someone and a starveling is probably someone who is starving; putting this together, you form the proposition that your acquaintance put a mask on a starving person. At the first moment you put this together, you are merely entertaining this proposition, not yet considering its plausibility; this initial moment of sheer entertainment may be prolonged beyond its normal half-life given your acquaintance's untrustworthiness.

Importantly, as you entertain the proposition <the order and connection of ideas is the same as the order and connection of things> (or <Jimmy put a mask on a starving person>), you are not typically inclined to confuse your act of entertaining for belief, desire, or any other attitude. No, you know that what you are doing with the proposition is entertaining it, not believing or desiring it to be the case. Moreover, this knowledge is immediate in Pitt's sense: the second-order belief that you are entertaining that *p* (rather than believing or desiring that *p*) is neither arrived at, nor justified, by any (personal-level) inference. (If there are subpersonal process that can be described as inferences, then I am making no claim about them—clearly, some kind of process must be involved in the formation of any mental state!) That is, it is neither *psychologically* nor *epistemically* based on (personal-level) inference from some other belief. It is natural to say that it is based directly on introspection. You form it (justifiably) by simple *endorsement* of the introspective appearances, somewhat as you form your perceptual beliefs by simple endorsement of the perceptual appearances. Just as you believe that there is a table before you simply because it perceptually seems to you that there is and you endorse that perceptual seeming, so you believe that you are entertaining that *p* simply because it introspectively seems to you that you are and you endorse this introspective seeming. (This is not to suggest, of course, that we would be in a position to apply the public-language expression "merely entertaining" to the episode!)

The possibility of such noninferential, purely endorsement-based formation and justification of second-order beliefs calls for explanation. In other words, we have an explanandum on our hands, a "datum." The datum is that through endorsement, and without inference, we can sometimes form (justifiably) second-order beliefs to the effect that we are merely entertaining a proposition. Note that this "datum" is *not* that we have infallible knowledge, incorrigible knowledge, or otherwise extraordinarily enviable knowledge of our entertainings. In fact, the datum just isolated does not even mention knowledge, only justified second-order belief (true or not).

One straightforward explanation of this datum goes as follows. First, our episodes of entertaining instantiate a distinctive phenomenal property P. Secondly, we sometimes introspectively observe a concurrent mental state to instantiate P, such that it introspectively appears to us that it is P. Thirdly, we can then (justifiably) endorse these introspective observations. The result is a (justifiably formed) second-order belief that we are in a state of entertaining. This basic model can be developed in a number of different ways. Both the notion of introspective observation and that of its endorsement are not unproblematic, and can be accounted for in different ways; I offer my own accounts in Kriegel 2011 ch.1. But the basic observation-*cum*-endorsement model is very natural, so pending special difficulties should be our starting point. Crucially, the model involves the notion that there is a phenomenology distinctive of entertaining that introspection picks up on.

The fact that the observation-*cum*-endorsement model manages to explain the datum, but at the same time requires the assumption that there is a distinctive phenomenology of entertaining, generates a *defeasible reason* for countenancing such a phenomenology. The reason is defeasible, and might ultimately be defeated, e.g. if a *better* explanation of the datum could be provided. But the very fact that a story implicating entertaining-phenomenology has the resources to explain the datum, and so naturally no less, does provide a defeasible, prima facie reason to believe in entertaining-phenomenology. This, recall, is the first stage of my argument for primitive entertainment.

2.2. *Stage 2: Potential Defeaters*

The second stage is to consider potential defeaters. I cannot rule out here every possible defeater. (If I did, the argument would become demonstrative!) Instead, I will consider two particularly promising candidates.

The first potential defeater appeals to functional role. Mere entertaining that *p* clearly does not play the same functional role in our mental economy that believing or desiring that *p* does. It may be suggested that the relevant second-order beliefs are based on introspective observation of the distinctive *functional role* of entertaining, rather than of any phenomenal character. The problem with this suggestion, however, is that the functional role of a mental state is a *dispositional property* of it: the state is disposed to have certain typical causes and effects. It is highly questionable, however, whether dispositional properties can be directly introspected. Many philosophers have thought that dispositional properties are not directly perceptible: even if there is a sense in which we can see *that* the vase is fragile, we cannot *see* the vase's fragility itself—we only see non-dispositional indicators of fragility. Likewise, we cannot see the bullet's explosiveness itself, only certain associated features. If so, it is unclear how we could directly *introspect* dispositional properties such as functional role, and thus unclear how beliefs could be formed by simple endorsement of such introspective observation of functional role.

A second potential defeater appeals to *absence* of phenomenology. Suppose for simplicity's sake that there are three basic propositional attitudes—belief, desire, and entertaining—such that belief is associated with a distinctive phenomenology B and desire with a distinctive phenomenology D, but entertaining is associated with no phenomenology. Then S could tell by introspection that S entertains that *p* simply by noticing that she experiences neither B nor D.[5] Importantly, this explanation is clearly more parsimonious than the entertaining-phenomenology-positing one. However, it faces this problem: S's introspective encounter with the absence of B and D is consistent with S having *no* attitude toward *p* (as opposed to having the entertaining attitude toward it). So we would need an account of how S comes to know that she has some propositional attitude to begin with. If S infers as much from other beliefs, then the ensuing knowledge is not immediate (noninferential) after all. Thus S must be able to tell by introspection alone that she is having *some* attitude. The only way this could work is if there was a general attitudinal phenomenology—call it A—shared by belief, desire, and entertaining (in addition to B and D). In this picture, however, it is no longer true that there is no distinctive phenomenology of entertaining. The phenomenological situation seems to be this: the phenomenology of belief is a composite of A + B, the phenomenology of desire is a composite of A + D, and the phenomenology of entertaining is A. Here S may well be able to tell introspectively that she has some attitude, but then S is also able to tell introspectively that the attitude is that of entertaining. She does so on the basis of introspective observation of A alone, which is distinctive of entertaining.

This concludes the second stage of my non-demonstrative argument for primitive entertainment. By this stage, the argument has established the *existence* of entertaining-phenomenology (pending unconsidered defeaters). The third and final stage attempts to establish the *irreducibility* of such phenomenology. It does so by ruling out potential reducers. Again, I will consider only a subset of all potential reducers. But I will also float a consideration to suggest that other candidates will not fare better.

2.3. Stage 3: Potential Reducers

What are the potential reducers of entertaining-phenomenology? I take it that algedonic and conative phenomenology are non-starters. The phenomenology of perceptual imagery is a better candidate. In particular, the auditory imagery of silent speech so often cited as potential reducer of *cognitive* phenomenology might be recruited in the present context to reduce *entertaining* phenomenology. In one version, the idea might be that both cognitive and entertaining phenomenology reduce to this imagery phenomenology, and therefore there is no phenomenal difference between believing and entertaining. In a more plausible version, the claim would be that entertaining phenomenology alone reduces to imagery phenomenology, and cognitive phenomenology effectively amounts to the compresence of that imagery and truth-commitment—a combination of silent-speech phenomenology and a phenomenology of assent or affirmation. This second version seems more promising. However, it can only work if Zoe from Chapter 1 is impossible, since Zoe appears to merely entertain some mathematical propositions but lack any imagery.[6] Accordingly, here I will focus on attempts to reduce the phenomenology of entertaining to cognitive phenomenology.

In his discussion of the difference between entertaining and judging, Brentano (1874 II ch.7) considers two potential reducers. The first is that the phenomenology of entertaining is simply a very weak (phenomenal-intensity-wise) phenomenology of judging: to entertain that p is to have a phenomenally extremely mild belief that p. Brentano convincingly rejects this reduction as extensionally inadequate: on the one hand, even though the intensity of a presentation can lead us to assent to it, we sometimes recognize that in fact we should dissent from it—without any consequent change in phenomenal intensity. Working on Spinoza for a month, I might undergo an episode of intellectually intense examination of ‹the order and connection of ideas is the same as the order and connection of things›, and after a double espresso the proposition may be before my mind with great vivacity and clarity; nonetheless I have not made up my mind whether to accept or reject it. Conversely, we often find ourselves highly confident in the truth of a weak judgment. Thus, after following a long proof for a complex mathematical theorem, I might experience a somewhat dim grasp of the theorem and yet be completely certain of its truth.[7] For Brentano, this double dissociation is but a manifestation of a deeper underlying phenomenal fact: that the property of phenomenal intensity or vivacity is one thing, while the attitudinal property of presenting-as-true is another. The latter is a constitutive aspect of the phenomenology of making a judgment but is altogether absent in entertaining; this is a difference in kind, not in degree—a qualitative rather than quantitative difference.

Brentano also considers the possibility that entertaining and judging are in fact the same kind of state, but with different sorts of content: whereas judged contents always involve *predication* (a concept or property is predicated of an individual), entertained ones do not. This can be understood as the suggestion that entertaining is a judgment-like state, whose content is not <Fa> however, but <a, F>. Brentano's own response is complex and involves his heterodox theory of judgment. But bracketing Brentano's theory of judgment, it seems clear that we can sometimes come to believe something precisely by endorsing the content of an entertaining. After entertaining and carefully considering Spinoza's thesis for a year, I might finally settle on accepting it. When I do, I simply endorse the content of that which I have been entertaining all along. If so, this particular entertaining and believing must have *the same* content. Indeed, it is for this very reason that, as we saw in Chapter 1, the truth-commitment built into judgment must be construed as attitudinal. There is thus an attitudinal rather than content difference between judging and entertaining: the former does, whereas the latter does not, present-as-true.

One potential reduction Brentano does not consider casts entertaining as belief in mere possibility. On this view, the phenomenology of entertaining that *p* is in reality nothing but the phenomenology of judging that ◊*p*, perhaps with the modality being the least demanding—logical possibility. One problem with this, however, is that arguably one can entertain even propositions one believes to be (logically-)necessarily false. For example, I might entertain Frege's set theory, or perhaps just its axiom of comprehension, even though, being familiar with Russell's Paradox, I believe it to be incoherent.[8] (In one sense, mathematicians entertain impossibilities routinely in the course of proving theorems by *reductio ad absurdum*. Perhaps this is supposition *rather than* entertainment, but recall that supposition too shows up on our initial list of neutral attitudes.[9]) A second and deeper problem, to my mind, is that the "attitudinal neutrality" in the phenomenology of entertaining—the fact that it neither presents-as-true nor presents-as-good—is not replicated in judgments about logical possibility. Even if we were wired so as to be unable to entertain propositions we believed to be impossible, judging that ◊*p* would still involve presenting-as-true ◊*p*, which entertaining that *p* lacks.

A fourth potential reducer is perfect balance between belief and disbelief. The idea might be to reduce the phenomenology of entertaining that *p* to the phenomenology of having exactly 50 percent credence in *p*. This appears more likely to replicate the neutrality of entertaining. Many other problems arise, however. First, I may entertain that *p* precisely with a view to establishing some credence in *p*, with the episode of entertaining spanning moments in which I am inclined to 55 percent credence, moments I am inclined to 45 percent credence, and moments of thorough indecision. Secondly, if it turns out that entertaining-phenomenology individuates as finely as content, then entertaining that *p* and entertaining that ~*p* would feel different; yet arguably having 50 percent credence in *p* and having 50 percent credence in ~*p* feel the same. Finally and most importantly, it is not clear that the phenomenology of attitudinal neutrality is genuinely replicated in 50 percent credence—there is a sense in which the latter involves 50 percent commitment to the truth of *p*, whereas the former involves 0 percent commitment.[10] Consider that a rational subject 50 percent credent in *p* who also experienced great certainty in *q* (say, 90 percent credence) would likely experience significant credence in *p*&*q* (45 percent, say); whereas an equally rational subject who merely entertained that *p*, but also experienced great certainty in *q* (90 percent credence) would be unlikely to experience any separate degree of conviction in *p*&*q* (no credence assignment for the conjunction).[11]

I have considered four potential reductions of entertaining-phenomenology to cognitive phenomenology, finding them all wanting. This in itself does not show that *no* cognitivist reduction is viable. But there is a recurring theme in the difficulties facing these four attempts that threatens to infect all attempted reductions of the kind. This is the fact that cognitive phenomenology is essentially a phenomenology of presenting-as-true some proposition. In consciously making a judgment, we feel committed to the truth of the proposition judged. But it is in the essence of mere entertaining that no such felt commitment to truth occur. We may summarize the problem as the following argument: 1) all cognitive phenomenology involves presenting-as-true; 2) entertaining is attitudinally neutral; therefore, 3) the phenomenology of entertaining is irreducible to cognitive phenomenology.

I conclude, tentatively, that entertaining-phenomenology is phenomenally irreducible—it is a primitive type of phenomenology. This concludes the third and final stage of my (non-demonstrative) argument for PE. The argument proffers a defeasible-but-as-yet-undefeated reason to posit primitive entertaining-phenomenology.

3. Objections and Replies

Various objections to the argument of the previous section are possible. One could contest the datum I claim needs explaining. One could offer alternative explanations of it that do not invoke an entertaining-phenomenology. One could also consider further potential reducers of this entertaining-phenomenology. The only objection I will consider here is that the whole notion of entertaining is an unfortunate folk-psychological error: in truth, there is no such thing as mere entertaining at all. This objection itself can be developed in various different ways. Here I will consider three developments present in the extant literature: what I will call the "Gilbert objection," the "Mandelbaum objection," and the "Hanks objection."

Gilbert (1991) develops and defends a model of thought and reasoning that does away with mere entertaining. According to Gilbert, the traditional model, whereby when presented with a proposition we first entertain it and only later come to believe or disbelieve it, is empirically falsified. In reality, when presented with a proposition, we automatically believe it and only later may suspend or reverse our initial belief.[12] The experimental evidence for this is varied, but the fundamental experimental paradigm is this: two groups of subjects are presented with a number of (identical) propositional statements, but one group's cognitive functioning is interfered with (interference condition) but not the other's (control condition). The findings are consistent: subjects in the interference condition behave in a way that suggests *greater*, rather than lesser, belief in the relevant propositions than subjects in the control condition (Gilbert et al. 1993). The best explanation for this, suggests Gilbert, is that all subjects automatically commit to the truth of the propositions presented to them, and use subsequent cognitive processing to reconsider this initial commitment; when this cognitive processing is interfered with (mostly by creating attentional overload), subjects have less opportunity to reconsider their initial commitments and find themselves more often still committed. It is natural to take such findings, and their attendant model of reasoning, to recommend dispensing with the notion that subjects can entertain a proposition without believing it, that is, can *merely* entertain a proposition (Mandelbaum 2010).[13]

In response, I would argue that there is a superior model of reasoning that accommodates Gilbert's findings but makes ample room for entertaining. Gilbert's model predates developments in cognitive science suggesting that many cognitive functions are subserved by a dual-process architecture. In such architecture, a cognitive function F is performed by both a low-road process and a high-road process. The former is typically fast, efficient, automatic, implicit, unconscious, specialized, and directly tied to action, but not very flexible, not particularly amenable to monitoring and control (because informationally encapsulated), and with limited range. By contrast, the high-road process is flexible, wide-ranged, consciously and explicitly controllable and manipulable, but linked to action only indirectly, slow, and inefficient. This dual-process architecture has been empirically defended for reasoning (Sloman 1996), with the high-road process construed along broadly rationalist lines and the low-road one along broadly associationist ones. I will develop this picture more fully in Chapter 5. My present point is just this: one hypothesis, to which I would subscribe, is that Gilbert's model accurately describes belief formation through the associationist, low-road process, which accounts for the behavioral evidence he adduces. All the same, the rationalist, high-road belief-formation process conforms at least in part to the more traditional model, where conscious acts of entertaining do play a role.

The attractiveness of this hypothesis will not be fully appreciated until Chapter 5. But one immediate advantage is that it makes sense of the introspective impression we first encounter when facing a proposition such as ‹the order and connection of ideas is the same as the order and connection of things›. (As we will see in Chapter 5, the high-road process is generally tied more intimately to introspective access.) The notion that entertaining is a folk-psychological myth, by contrast, has no resources for explaining where this introspective impression comes from.

Mandelbaum's (2010) case against mere entertaining follows in the main Gilbert's. Unlike Gilbert, however, Mandelbaum (2010 ch.4) addresses the introspective evidence for mere entertaining and argues against it. The response is essentially this: beliefs are (often) dispositional states, and dispositional states are not introspectively available, so one cannot tell by introspection that one does *not* believe a certain proposition (say, that the order and connection of ideas is the same as the order and connection of things).

However, regardless of what *belief* is, the episode that I am introspecting (with the content ‹the order and connection of ideas is the same as the order and connection of things›) is certainly not a standing disposition, but an occurrent episode. So even if it is true that we cannot tell by introspection which dispositional beliefs we do and do not have, the act of entertaining is not one of those anyway.

Conceding the introspective evidence for occurrent episodes of entertaining, Mandelbaum could insist that an act of entertaining nonetheless *automatically causes* a dispositional belief (see Mandelbaum 2010: 24). If so, whenever we entertain that *p* we automatically come to believe that *p*; we are therefore not *merely*-entertaining that *p*.

However, if the connection between the entertaining and the ensuing belief is merely causal, and not constitutive, then the view does not really eliminate entertaining. Since there is no constitutive connection between entertaining and belief, the two are still modally separable: there is a possible world where the entertaining occurs but the believing does not, say because the subject died in the middle of the automatic process leading from the former to the latter. In that world, the subject would be merely entertaining that *p*.

To defeat the introspective evidence for mere entertaining, Mandelbaum must argue that when S introspectively seems to herself to merely entertain that *p*, either (i) in reality S does not perform any mental act at all or (ii) in reality S performs a different act, presumably that of *coming to believe* (or judging) that *p*. I take it that (i) is a non-starter: it would be very odd, perhaps incoherent, for someone to be under the impression of being in a mental state without being in one. As for (ii), when most people introspectively seem to themselves to perform the act whose content is that the order and connection of ideas is the same as the order and connection of things, they do not introspectively encounter any commitment to its truth or goodness. So theirs is probably an episode of entertaining.

Mandelbaum may reject the notions of presenting-as-true and presenting-as-good. For he holds that only the contents of propositional attitudes have any phenomenal features associated with them—attitudes do not (Mandelbaum 2010: 91). As a general claim this cannot be right, however: surely I can tell by introspection (and without inference) not only that the content of my current attitude is that I own a private jet, but also that my attitude is desire rather than belief. I am not confused as to whether I *believe* that I own a jet or *would like* to own one. If there is no phenomenal attitudinal properties such as presenting-as-true and presenting-as-good, then some other phenomenal feature must be offered to underwrite this sort of noninferential knowledge.

∽⥿∾

Hanks (2013) is suspicious of entertaining on completely different grounds. The philosophical context in which Hanks operates is somewhat different, and is essentially the following. Recently, some philosophers of language, including Soames (2010 ch.5, 2014) and Hanks (2011), have offered a metaphysical assay of propositions in terms of types of mental act. Different acts are the relevant ones in different versions of the view. Soames' version identifies propositions with types of acts of *entertaining*: the proposition that p just is the type whose tokens are all the individual acts of entertaining p.[14] Soames (2010: 81) proceeds to construe entertaining as a noncommittal act of predication: to entertain that a is F is nothing but to predicate F of a, where predication is understood as a noncommittal act. What Hanks objects to, very reasonably, is the intelligibility of noncommittal predication. Predication, insists Hanks, is inherently committal: to predicate F of a is *eo ipso* to commit to a's being F, hence to the truth of <a is F>. And to mentally commit to the truth of <a is F> is effectively to judge, hence come to believe, that a is F. Thus insofar as noncommittal predication is unintelligible, mere entertaining is unintelligible as well.

Hanks may be right that predicating is an inherently committal act. If so, no mental act grounded in predication could be neutral in the way mere entertaining is supposed to be. Even so, there must also be, in addition, a predication-analog that is noncommittal. If there was no such noncommittal predication-analog, mathematicians could never prove a theorem by *reductio*. When a mathematician supposes for *reductio* that a is F, clearly she is not committing herself to a being F. Indeed, she is persuaded that it is not the case that a is F. Thus it must be possible to think of a's being F without committing to a indeed being F.

This is connected to the fact (argued for in Chapter 1) that nothing in the content of an act can make the act committal. Recall again Balzac's addition to the content of his novel "*all is true*," which failed to change the novel's status from fiction to reportage. Its status as fiction is guaranteed by facts external to its content, and its conversion into reportage would have to be accomplished by such facts as well. By the same token, nothing inside the content of an act can make the act commit to its truth. Only facts external to the content can accomplish this. Thus it cannot be that the very presence of the content before one's mind commits the subject to the content's truth.[15]

It is possible that our linguistic practice misleads us here. When we assert in writing that *a* is F, all we have to write down is "*a* is F." By contrast, when we want to suppose or consider or doubt *in writing* that *a* is F, we have to write down more than that. As a result, when we describe something as the proposition that *a* is F, the very description carries with it a connotation of assertion. However, we can readily imagine a practice in which asserting that *a* is F requires writing "*a* is F" in red ink, supposing that *a* is F requires writing "*a* is F" in green ink, doubting that that *a* is F requires writing "*a* is F" in blue, and so on. This would be an extremely inefficient practice, given how our world is set up. But it would have the advantage of not misleading us to suppose that the content <*a* is F> is somehow inherently committal.

I conclude that none of the three objections is compelling. There may be other objections, but from here on I proceed on the assumption that entertaining-phenomenology is neither eliminable nor reducible. Instead, it must be treated as a third leg in the stool of attitudes, in addition to any cognitive and conative primitives we wish to posit.

It remains to offer a characterization of this phenomenology. As in Chapters 1 and 2, I propose to use a Ramsey sentence that traces out entertaining's relations to other phenomena. For a variety of reasons, here I will not restrict myself to phenomenological relations, but will consider also conceptual relations. (The main reason is that while the very attitudes of belief and desire are well understood in contemporary philosophy of mind, entertaining has long been neglected, so before discussing its phenomenology we should discuss *it*.) In §4, I focus on relations to other "neutral attitudes," in §5 on relations to cognitive attitudes, and in §6 to conative (and mixed) attitudes. I then assemble the results in §7. None of this is intended to deny that we can grasp the nature of the phenomenology of entertaining simply through the right introspective encounter. Still, a more articulated and public portrait is worth seeking.

II. A Nonreductive Characterization of Entertaining
4. Entertaining and the Neutral Attitudes

There is, in fact, a certain ambiguity in the term "entertaining." On one way of hearing the term, believing that *p* excludes the possibility of entertaining that *p*.

A subject cannot entertain that *p* if she already believes that *p*. On another hearing, a subject *can* entertain that *p* who already believes that *p*; what she cannot do is *merely* entertain it. We may call the first the "belief-exclusionary sense" and the second the "belief-inclusionary sense."

If we adopt the belief-*inclusionary* sense, we can treat entertaining as conceptually basic and analyze "mere entertaining" in terms of it—as follows:

(1) S merely-entertains that *p* iff S entertains that *p* & S does not believe that *p*.

If we adopt the belief-*exclusionary* sense, however, we need a new term for the attitude that can cohabit with belief. The word "apprehending" might serve well here. Thus we might say that although a subject cannot entertain that *p* if she already believes that *p*, she can still *apprehend p*. In this terminological regime, 1 is replaced with:

(1*) S entertains that *p* iff S apprehends *p* & S does not believe that *p*.

In 1*, the conceptually basic notion is that of apprehending, and entertaining is analyzed in terms of it.

Here I will adopt the belief-inclusionary way of talking of entertaining. I do so for purely pragmatic reasons, not because I think it reflects better the word's behavior in everyday English; the everyday word's behavior strikes me as equally affording both ways of hearing it.

The ambiguity just discussed concerns the locution "entertaining that *p*." But an analogous ambiguity attends "entertaining φ-ing." On one way of hearing the locution, S cannot entertain φ-ing if she already intends to φ (or already decided to φ). On another, what S cannot do in these circumstances is *merely* entertain φ-ing, but she still can entertain φ-ing *simpliciter*. Call these the "intention-inclusionary" and "intention-exclusionary" senses. They lead to:

(2) S merely-entertains φ-ing iff S entertains φ-ing and S does not intend to φ.
(2*) S entertains φ-ing iff S apprehends φ-ing and S does not intend to φ.

Again I will go with 2 rather than 2* for pragmatic reasons.

Once we adopt this inclusionary way of using "entertaining," we can state the relationship between entertaining and apprehending as follows:

(3) The same phenomenon denoted somewhat equivocally by "entertaining" is denoted more univocally by "apprehending."

This is put in the formal mode of speech for clarity, but the corresponding material claim is clear: apprehending = entertaining (in the inclusionary sense).

A more substantive distinction is between two modes in which entertaining may be done. There is, on the one hand, a kind of entertaining of p that is done with a view to a certain cognitive gain, typically the establishment of some credence in p. I might, for example, entertain the proposition that the order and connection of ideas is the same as the order and connection of things because I am concerned to know whether I should believe it. On the other hand, there is also another kind of entertaining that is purely contemplative, done with no doxastic business in mind and directed at no cognitive achievement. I may have strictly zero interest in whether my untrustworthy acquaintance really did immask a starveling or not; my only cognitive concern here is to understand what she is saying to me. There is a noticeable, if quite subtle, phenomenal difference between these two modes of entertaining. The former involves, whereas the latter does not, a felt element of doxastic or epistemic *engagement* with the proposition that p. Both are in some sense *doxastically neutral*, in that they do not involve commitment to p's truth. But one can be described as doxastically *engaged* and the other as *disengaged*.[16]

With some savagery to ordinary language, we may call entertaining in the engaged mode *considering* and entertaining in the disengaged mode *contemplating*. Here the engaged/disengaged distinction is mapped onto a consideration/contemplation distinction. (I say "with some savagery" because in truth it is perfectly legitimate to use "contemplating" to describe an engaged episode or "considering" to describe a disengaged one. Nonetheless, it would be fair to remark that the engaged usage belongs relatively more on the fringe of the range of ordinary uses of "contemplating" but is relatively more central to the ordinary use of "considering"—and vice versa. This makes it reasonable to introduce quasi-technical usages of "contemplating" denoting all and only disengaged episodes of entertaining and of "considering" denoting all and only engaged episodes of entertaining.[17])

Plausibly, the distinction between considering and contemplating (in this sense) has to do with the presence or absence of certain epistemic desires and/or projects: the desire to know whether p, the project of figuring out whether p, etc. It seems to me that in its ordinary use "to entertain" is neutral on the presence or absence of such desires. In any case this is how I am going to use the term here. So we can now analyze consideration and contemplation, to a very first approximation, as follows:

(4) S considers p iff S entertains that p & S has the project of figuring out whether p.

(5) S contemplates p iff S entertains that p & S does not have the project of figuring out whether p.

These are first passes, which would have to be supplemented with a more precise and more comprehensive understanding of the relevant epistemic goals. For starters, some account would have to be given of "having the project of figuring out." Furthermore, although I have spoken thus far as though the distinction between engaged and disengaged modes of entertaining is binary, it may be more accurate to think that there is a continuum from the fully engaged to the fully disengaged. If so, most episodes of entertaining have something of the considering and something of the contemplating in them. This would not, however, make the distinction between consideration and contemplation any less real (any more than the existence of dimmer-lamps implies that there is no distinction between darkness and light).

Sometimes we entertain that p not because we want to know whether p, but because we want to know whether q. That is, we are interested in the plausibility of some proposition, and our process for figuring out the plausibility of that proposition involves entertaining that p. This seems to be what happens when we *suppose* that p. Typically, we suppose that p in order to figure out what consequences the holding of p might have—or more precisely what is "inferable" from p (see Arcangeli 2014). So a first-pass analysis of supposition might be:

(6) S supposes that p iff S entertains that p & S wants to know what is inferable from p.

In this respect, supposing that p resembles considering p: both involve certain epistemic goals. The difference is that in considering, the goals pertain to p itself, whereas in supposing, they pertain to some other proposition(s).

The analysis of supposition, consideration, contemplation, apprehension, and so on is an extraordinary task. I am fully aware that the above discussion is comically brief. It is *intended* as preliminary and suggestive. Its main function is to illustrate how a web of conceptual interrelations to neighboring notions can give texture to the notion of entertaining. Theses 1–6 trace out a preliminary sketch of a web of interrelations among attitudinally neutral states. The web could be enriched by developing more precise variants of 1–6, or by adding accounts of entertaining's relationship to conceiving, imagining, and other neutral attitudes I have not considered. From this web a portrait of entertaining would emerge that gives the notion clearer and more accurate edges, as it were. Note that the analyzed notion may be partly technical, insofar as 1–6 inhabit the grayish zone between elucidation and stipulation; the stipulative aspect is designed to remove certain ambiguities that attend the everyday terms.

The emerging picture does cast entertaining (in the inclusionary sense) as a fundamental neutral attitude, in terms of which we can understand considering, contemplating, supposing, merely-entertaining, and perhaps other neutral attitudes. As we will see in §§5–6, there may be a case for taking entertaining as fundamental with respect to nonneutral (cognitive and conative) attitudes as well.

A generic phenomenal characteristic of entertaining is what we may call *phenomenal intensity*. To appreciate this claim, we must distinguish two kinds of intensity in experience.

When we consider *sensory* experiences, we note the following two kinds of intensity. A visual experience as of a red surface is intense in one sense to the extent that it presents the surface's redness as very bright. The brighter it presents the redness, the more intense the experience. We may call this *sensory* intensity. In addition, however, the experience can be more or less intense in another sense, to do with the vivacity with which it is present to the subject. The more alert the subject is, for example, the more vivid the experience is liable to be.[18] We may call this *phenomenal* intensity. Compare two cross-world Twins having a visual experience of an identical-looking blue sky. If one is concentrating intensely on the blue expanse before her, while the other is staring more blankly at it, there will be a phenomenal difference between them—even if the sky itself is presented as equally bright.

My claim is that phenomenal intensity characterizes episodes of entertaining as well. Thus, I might calmly entertain the proposition that my acquaintance immasked a starveling, and moments later, with increased interest, concentration, and intellectual energy, suddenly entertain the same proposition more alertly and vividly, that is, with noticeably greater phenomenal intensity. This phenomenal intensity may not be a simple feature—it may consist in a combination of more basic elements. But it is psychologically real nonetheless. Accordingly, we do something to characterize entertaining phenomenologically when we state:

(A) Entertaining exhibits phenomenal intensity.

We can further characterize entertaining by noting that two token entertainings can have different phenomenal intensities but the same intentional content, or different contents but the same intensity. In brief:

(B) The phenomenal intensity and intentional content of entertaining vary independently.

A and B characterize entertaining without describing its relationships to other attitudes.

Entertaining may also be characterized by what Chudnoff (2011b) calls *presentational phenomenology*. Chudnoff argues that certain purely intellectual states, such as intuiting that the taller-than relation is transitive, have this commonality with perceptual states, that they boast a "presentational phenomenology." In perceptual states, this consists in the fact that whenever one undergoes a perceptual experience, in addition to being related to the proposition that is the content of the experience, one is also perceptually aware of a certain item. For example, looking at the clock I can see that it is getting late. Here, although my perceptual state has the propositional content that it is getting late, it also involves a sort of non-propositional item-awareness of the clock. This is the presentational phenomenology of perception. Chudnoff argues that intuitions have a similar feature: when one intuits that p, there is always some abstract object O, such that intuiting that p involves being item-aware of (presented with) O. Typically, says Chudnoff, O is an essence of some property or particular. For example, when I intuit that the taller-than relation is transitive, I am aware of the essence of the taller-than relation. Although the intuition has a propositional content (that the taller-than relation is transitive), it also involves an item-awareness (of the relation's essence). This is the presentational phenomenology of intuition.

The claim I wish to make here is that entertaining often, perhaps typically, involves a presentational phenomenology as well. When I contemplate the proposition that Congress shall make no law respecting an establishment of religion, and examine the phenomenology of my contemplative episode, I find that it is quite complex. It involves, for example, a visual image of the US Capitol building in Washington and an auditory image of the word "establishment" in silent speech. In addition, however, it seems to involve a purely intellectual awareness of certain *items*: religion in general, law in general, government in general. Thus we might say:

(7) If S entertains that p, then typically, there is an x, such that S is aware of x.

Or more generally:

(C) Entertaining involves a presentational phenomenology.

It is not immediately clear how best to describe the *way* items are presented in entertaining's presentational phenomenology: as essences, as abstract objects, as *ante rem* universals, as *in re* universals, as trope clusters, as concepts, as types, or as some other sort of entity. It may well be that the presentational phenomenology itself is simply *silent* on this matter. What is clear is that it presents those items not in any particular spatiotemporal manifestation (this instance of religiosity, that instance of governing), but *in general*. In that sense, but possibly *only* in that sense, it presents them as abstract (or better: presents them abstractly).

The most fundamental characteristic of entertaining, in any case, is surely its attitudinal neutrality, the fact that it involves neither truth-commitment nor goodness-commitment. Unlike belief, entertaining that p does not present-as-true p, and unlike desire, it does not present-as-good p. Instead, it exhibits a third phenomenal attitudinal feature of *merely-presenting p*. We might capture all this by noting:

(D) Entertaining is doxastically noncommittal.

(E) Entertaining is axiologically noncommittal.

To say that entertaining is attitudinally neutral is to say that both D and E are true.

An apparent consequence of attitudinal neutrality is that the element of entertaining itself is phenomenally the same whether it is involved in a neutral attitude toward a proposition or a neutral attitude toward an action:

(F) Entertaining that p and entertaining φ-ing involve the same phenomenal attitudinal feature.

There is a Marx Brothers film in which a waiter is asked for coffee without cream and replies "We're out of cream today, sir, can I give you coffee without milk?" The reason this is funny is that there is no difference between coffee without cream and coffee without milk. By the same token, there is no phenomenal difference between the absence of truth-commitment and the absence of value-commitment.

So far, I have offered a characterization of entertaining in terms of 1–7 and A–F. This did not take us outside the realm of neutral attitudes. In the next section, I turn to connections between entertaining and a wider circle of notions more central to doxastically committal cognition.

5. Entertaining and the Cognitive Attitudes

The discussion in this section will progress through three main themes: the connection of entertaining to thinking (§5.1), to judging (§5.2), and to believing (§5.3). The discussion will have to be relatively brief, inasmuch as one could easily dedicate a chapter or a book to each of these issues.

5.1. Entertaining and Thinking

What is the relation between episodes of entertaining and episodes of thinking? Before we can address this question, we must note the variety of reports that can be made using think talk:

- I think that Jimmy is tall
- I am thinking that Jimmy is tall
- I am thinking about Jimmy being tall
- I am thinking about/of the proposition that Jimmy is tall
- I am having a (or the) thought that Jimmy is tall
- I am having a thought about Jimmy being tall
- I am having a thought about the proposition that Jimmy is tall

These all report propositional attitudes. In addition, there is think talk that reports non-propositional attitudes (I think about/of Jimmy, I am thinking about/of tall people). A full answer to the question about the relation between entertaining and thinking will (i) map out the web of interrelations among all these thought-attitudes and then (ii) identify the relation of entertaining to each node in that web. Here I will restrict myself to preliminary remarks on entertaining's relation to central thought-attitudes.

It is plain that thinking *that* Jimmy is tall is a doxastically committal propositional attitude. In thinking that a is F, one commits to the obtaining of a state of affairs. In other words, thinking-that is a *cognitive* attitude. There may still be an interesting connection between entertaining and thinking-that, as we will see later. But it is not an immediate connection.

By contrast, thinking about (or of) the proposition that Jimmy is tall seems noncommittal. In thinking about the proposition, one does not commit to Jimmy really being tall. As Cassam (2010: 84) puts it, "someone who wonders whether P is thinking—thinking about P, as we would say—but is not mentally affirming that P." That is, the thought episode remains doxastically neutral. Arguably, then, we may say this:

(8) S is thinking about the proposition that p iff S entertains that p.

Note, however, that one is thinking about the proposition that Jimmy is tall also when one does doxastically commit to ("mentally affirms") it. So thinking about the proposition that p is not *merely*-entertaining that p; it is entertaining that p in the sense of apprehending p.

A more delicate question is how to treat "I am thinking about/of Jimmy being tall," and more generally reports that use imperfect nominals as the grammatical object of "thinking of."[19] One view is that thinking about a's being F is the same as thinking that a is F, and should be treated as a variant of thinking-that. Another view is that just as thinking about a concrete particular a does not require thinking that a exists, and thinking about a property F does not require thinking that F is instantiated, so thinking about the state of affairs of a's being F does not require thinking that it *obtains*. A third view is that reports of the form "S is thinking about a's being F" are used sometimes as suggested in the first view and sometimes as suggested in the second view. To my ear, this third view seems most accurate. I suspect that "thinking about *a* being F" is just ambiguous as between thinking that *a* is F and thinking about the proposition that *a* is F.

Most commonly, however, "thinking about/of" is used to describe non-committal *objectual* attitudes. Right now I am thinking of a flying zebra, and do so without thinking that there is one.[20] One could suggest that objectual thinking-of is simply a non-propositional counterpart of entertaining. But more interestingly, objectual thinking-of may be *implied* in entertaining: entertaining that my acquaintance immasked a starveling implies thinking of my acquaintance and thinking of a starveling. More generally:

(9) If S entertains that F*a* (or that *a*R*b*), then S thinks of *a* (or of *a* and *b*).

Thus objectual thinking-of is in some sense an *aspect* of entertaining. What makes this possible is that thinking of *a* is "existentially neutral" with respect to *a*.

To summarize the discussion thus far: thinking comes in two separate varieties, thinking-that and thinking-about/of. There are substantive ties between entertaining a proposition and thinking about the proposition or about concrete particulars associated with it. So far, no ties have been claimed between entertaining that *p* and thinking *that p*. The reason is that while entertaining that *p* is doxastically neutral, thinking that *p* is doxastically committal.

It is worth distinguishing *occurrent* thinking-that from *standing* thinking-that. Occurrent thinking-that can be correctly ascribed only when a certain mental event takes place in the subject, typically the performing of the right kind of cognitive act. Having an occurrent thought that *a* is F involves at least performing the mental act of predicating F of *a*. By contrast, standing thinking-that can be correctly ascribed even when the subject performs no mental act, indeed when she is fast asleep. She only needs to have a standing commitment to the truth of the relevant proposition. It is natural to use "S thinks that *p*" for the standing variety and "S is thinking that *p*" for the occurrent variety, as the progressive tense suggests a psychologically real *process*.

In a quasi-stipulative vein, we may use the terms "belief" and "judgment" to denote these two varieties of thinking-that. For belief is not an act, but a state, whereas judgment is an act rather than a state. We can appreciate this by considering the appropriateness of the progressive tense again (see Williamson 2000: 35). It is grammatical (if awkward) to say not only that S judges that *p*, but also that S is *judging* that *p*; by contrast, it is *ungrammatical* to say that S is *believing* that *p*—one can only say that S believes that *p*. Accordingly, one can correctly say of someone in a dreamless sleep that she believes that *p*, but not that she judges that *p*.

In the bookkeeping scheme adopted here, then, thinking divides into (i) thinking-about/of and (ii) thinking-that, which in turn divides into (ii.i) occurrent thinking-that, or judgment, and (ii.ii) standing thinking-that, or belief. This subsection only made claims about the connection between entertaining and (i). The next two make claims about the connection between entertaining and (ii.i) and (ii.ii) respectively.

5.2. *Entertaining and Judging*

It might be suggested that one could in fact *analyze* entertaining in terms of occurrent thinking-that, that is, judging. The analysis would construe entertaining as a judgment from which the element of affirmation has been somehow removed, or withheld, or bracketed, so that one ends up "withholding judgment" about *p*. In a slogan: entertaining equals judging minus affirming.

However, it is hard to see what supports this analysis of entertaining. It is particularly hard to see what is supposed to make it preferable to the opposite analysis, which could be summarized in a competing slogan: judging equals entertaining plus affirming.[21]

One consideration that supports "judging = entertaining + affirming" is that it is in general more natural to analyze a whole in terms of its parts than the parts in terms of the whole. Certainly this is so when the parts are items modally separable from each other. Thus, we are not tempted to understand a door as a house minus walls, windows, and so on. It should be equally odd to understand entertaining in terms of subtraction from judging. Furthermore, arguably "judging minus affirming" would at most capture *considering*, the engaged variety of entertaining, as it suggests a mental activity in which the plausibility of the proposition entertained is in the subject's sights. A person "withholds judgment" only when the question of whether to assent or dissent arises. Withholding judgment puts the issue of affirmation on the table, so to speak. But in contemplation (entertaining in the disengaged mode), affirmation does not enter the picture—it is neither asserted nor withdrawn, but simply absent. It would seem, then, that "judging minus affirming" is *too narrow* to capture entertaining.

This recommends rejecting an analysis of entertaining as "judging minus affirming." Two options remain open: either (*a*) we analyze judging as entertaining plus affirming, or (*b*) we treat judging and entertaining as mutually unanalyzable primitives. On (*a*), judging that *p* is a superposition of mental affirmation upon a perfectly neutral act of entertaining or apprehending *p*. This is the view of Brentano (1874), Whitehead (1929), and Soames (2010). But is there a reason to prefer it over (b)?

What is at stake in this choice is not the number of primitives. If (b) is true, then entertaining and judging are both primitives. If (a) is, judging is not a primitive, but *affirming* still is (for all we have said). Whether our primitives here are entertaining and judging or entertaining and affirming, they are two. So the number of primitives is not at stake.

Other matters are at stake, however. Most importantly, if (a) is true, we should expect a certain phenomenal commonality between judging and entertaining, since entertaining is a component or aspect of judging. In contrast, if (b) is true, we should expect no phenomenal commonality between entertaining and judging. Secondly, the two views differ on the question of whether judging is phenomenologically simple or structured: according to (b), it is likely simple; according to (a), structured. Relatedly, while both views posit an entertaining primitive and a "cognitive" primitive, according to (b) the cognitive primitive is a self-standing attitude (judging), whereas according to (a) it is an attitude-*component* or attitude-*modification* (affirming). These are three substantive differences between the two views.

Even with these substantive differences laid out, it is difficult to assess which view is more plausible. My own introspective sense is that there really is a phenomenal commonality between entertaining and judging, though a very subtle one: that of having the relevant proposition present before my mind. This is Whitehead's "propositional feeling" mentioned above. It is a phenomenologically real aspect, it seems to me, of entertaining, judging, and mere-entertaining alike. In merely-entertaining, affirmation is refused. In judging, it is accepted. In entertaining, it is neither refused nor accepted—all we have is the bare act of apprehending the proposition. If so:

(10) S judges that *p* iff S entertains-and-affirms that *p*.

I suspect, however, that others will reject the phenomenological claims just made, and sincerely profess to find no phenomenal commonality between judging, entertaining, and mere-entertaining.

A more theoretical consideration supporting 10 concerns the potential for a unified account of several propositional attitudes. The various cognitive attitudes, for example, could be understood as resulting from different affirmation-related modifications of the same underlying act of entertaining (see Soames 2014; more on this later). The emerging picture is of a group of cognitive acts with an entertaining core modulated by an affirmation-related element. In its most developed form, the picture would offer a unified account of *all* cognitive attitudes, or perhaps even all attitudes (cognitive or otherwise), in terms of a core act of entertaining/apprehending variously modified.

5.3. *Entertaining and Believing*

What about the standing, dispositional cognitive attitudes, such as belief? Given that entertaining is an occurrent act, it is hard to see how entertaining could be understood in terms of belief (or a belief-component). It may nonetheless be possible to understand belief partly in terms of entertaining, as I will now argue. The idea is to combine 10 above with the view that believing is just being disposed to judge. It would follow that believing is just being disposed to entertain-and-affirm.

Consider Searle's (1990, 1992 ch.7) "connection principle": every unconscious intentional state must be *potentially* conscious. This principle connects the unconscious to the conscious. We might formulate a parallel principle connecting the standing to the occurrent: every standing intentional state must be potentially occurrent. Or better: for S to be in a standing state with propositional content p, S must be disposed to be in a corresponding occurrent state with propositional content p. If we adopt such a principle, one substitution instance would be the following: S standingly thinks that p only if S is disposed to occurrently think that p. Recall, now, that we have determined to use "belief" for standing thinking-that and "judgment" for occurrent thinking-that. So the principle could be restated as follows: S believes that p only if S is disposed to judge that p (see Smithies 2012). Call this the *belief-judgment connection principle*.

The principle is highly plausible. The argument for it may be summarized thus: if S is not disposed to occurrently think that p, then S does not dispositionally think that p; if S does not dispositionally think that p, then S does not standingly think that p; if S does not standingly think that p, then S does not believe that p; therefore, if S is not disposed to judge that p, then S does not believe that p.

As a one-way conditional, the belief-judgment connection principle falls short of an *account* of belief. However, a case could be made for the converse conditional: if S is disposed to judge that p then S believes that p. In fact, this sufficiency claim seems if anything less controversial than the necessity claim. Plausibly, any explanatory work one might summon dispositional thinking-that to perform could be shouldered more economically by dispositions to think-that (Audi 1994). If so, there is no conceivable rationale for positing any aspect of dispositional thinking-that (believing) over and above what is involved in the disposition to think-that (the disposition to judge).

With the two conditionals in place, we can embrace the biconditional: S believes that p iff S is disposed to judge that p. The biconditional itself could serve as an account of judgment in terms of belief just as well as of belief in terms of judgment, but since it is more natural to account for the dispositional in terms of the occurrent, it is plausible to suggest that for S to believe that p

just is for S to be disposed to judge that *p*. When "S believes that *p*" is true, its truthmaker is the fact that S is disposed to judge that *p*.

The conjunction of 10 above with this biconditional leads straightforwardly to the following:

(11) S believes that *p* iff S is disposed to entertain-and-affirm that *p*.

This is meant as an account of belief partially in terms of entertaining: to believe something is to be disposed to entertain something and affirm what one entertains. When "S believes that *p*" is true, its truthmaker is that S is disposed to entertain-and-affirm that *p*.

One objection to 11 is that belief also involves dispositions to act (at least in the presence of appropriate desires), and it is unclear why we should privilege the disposition to conscious judgment more than the disposition to action. Indeed, according to some we should rather privilege the disposition to action (Schwitzgebel 2013).[22]

The basis for my response will fully emerge only in Chapter 5, where I will discuss Gendler's (2008a) distinction between belief and *alief*. The central point, though, is simply this: there are clearly two different states, which tend to coincide but frequently diverge, such that one is characterized by the disposition to consciously judge and the other is characterized by the disposition to act. It is to some extent just a terminological issue which one we should call belief, but for a variety of reasons, which will come through in Chapter 5, it is better to reserve the term to the former state.

It might be objected that 11 is too narrow: we believe that 231.857 > 143.769 but do not have the disposition to entertain this proposition. One might propose moving to the conditional disposition to affirm that *p if* the subject entertains that *p*. Here the subject is not required to be disposed to entertain that *p*, but only to be so disposed that if and when she does entertain *p*, she would affirm what she entertains. However, this newer requirement is too broad: we can imagine a subject who does not believe that *p*, but would *come to see* the plausibility of *p*, and thus to judge that *p*, *if* she entertained that *p*. So subjects have more conditional dispositions of this sort than they have beliefs.

However, in the sense in which the subject is not disposed to entertain that 231.857 > 143.769, she is also not disposed to judge so. And yet we saw there are very good reasons to think that believing that *p* entails being disposed to judge that *p*. This suggests that the problem should be overcome through a more refined specification of the relevant disposition. A full specification of the character of a disposition—the kind of specification that *individuates* dispositions—must refer to (i) triggering conditions and (ii) manifestation conditions. (The vase's disposition to break when dropped has dropping as its triggering condition and breaking as its manifestation condition.) I am now going to propose triggering and manifestation conditions for an entertaining-connected disposition plausibly coextensive with belief.

First, a subject may have the disposition to entertain and affirm that 231.857 > 143.769 in a variety of relatively specific triggering circumstances. One obvious triggering circumstance involves the subject being *asked* whether 231.857 > 143.769. But there are many other circumstances that might causally trigger the subject's entertaining of this proposition: a business transaction requiring a cost-benefit analysis in which the costs and benefits sum up just this way; a calculation of the lengths in miles or kilometers of two routes from her residence to her destination that come out this way; and so on. Let us collect all these triggering circumstances, however extraordinary, under the label "*p*-entertaining-triggers." Crucially, any subject who believed that *p* all along *would* be disposed to judge that *p* when the *p*-entertaining-triggers obtain. Thus I propose the *p*-entertaining-triggers as the triggering conditions of the disposition I claim is coextensive with believing that *p*.

As for its manifestation conditions, these cannot be just the circumstances in which the subject ends up affirming that *p*, since some subjects may come to acquire new beliefs as a result of entertaining certain propositions. However, when subjects acquire new beliefs in this way, the affirmation of the proposition entertained is not immediate but instead mediated by further reasoning and/or research. Suppose S believes that Kotarbiński studied with Twardowski in Lvov, while S* does not believe this but might come to believe it were she to entertain the proposition. The difference between them is that S* would require at least one more thought than S to affirm the proposition. Typically, this would require some preliminary research, but even if S* is lazy, and affirms the proposition because "Kotarbiński," "Twardowski," and "Lvov" are all Polish-sounding names, she would still need to have that extra thought about Polish sounds. By contrast, it is at least *possible* for S to affirm the same proposition upon entertaining it *without* having any other thought (and more generally without the mediation of any further mental states). Let us call the manifestation conditions special to S the "immediate-affirmation conditions." These are the manifestation conditions I claim characterize the disposition that coextends with belief.

The result is an understanding of the disposition to entertain-and-affirm that *p* in terms of the disposition to *immediately* affirm that *p* when *p*-entertaining-triggers obtain. We may therefore sharpen 11 as follows:

(12) S believes that *p* iff S is dis posed to immediately affirm that *p* when *p*-entertaining-triggers obtain.

Interestingly, this analysis reveals quite a bit of structure in the notion of belief, which is often taken to be an attitudinal simple in contemporary philosophy of mind. As noted above, however, this does *not* mean that the theory of attitudes has no need for a cognitive primitive in addition to the primitive of entertaining; rather, it means that the cognitive primitive is an attitude-component rather than an attitude: the component we have been calling affirmation.

Once belief is understood in terms of entertaining, a number of related cognitive attitudes plausibly follow suit. Thus, insofar as being convinced that p is just strongly believing that p, we may assert:

(13) S is convinced that p iff S is disposed to immediately and strongly affirm that p when p-entertaining-triggers obtain.

Insofar as suspecting that p is just weakly believing that p, we may say:

(14) S suspects that p iff S is disposed to immediately and weakly affirm that p when p-entertaining-triggers obtain.

Other cognitive attitudes might admit of more creative accounts in terms of entertaining.

∽෨෮∾

To conclude this section, entertaining has close connections, and seems to lie at the core of, many of the central cognitive attitudes: thinking-about, thinking-that, judging, believing, being convinced, suspecting. Most importantly, far from being primitive, belief (standing thinking-that) can be analyzed as the right disposition to entertain and affirm. Still, there must be a cognitive primitive in the theory of attitudes. This is either the attitude of judging (occurrent thinking-that) or the element of affirming, a phenomenal component of judging. I have offered some inconclusive considerations supporting the latter option.

6. Entertaining and Conative (and Mixed) Attitudes

One might be tempted to accept all of the above and still *classify* entertaining-phenomenology as just a species of cognitive phenomenology. After all, entertaining (especially considering) propositions is often part of our cognitive activity. The problem with this, however, is that entertaining can take part just as well in practical reasoning. More deeply, given the attitudinal neutrality of entertaining-phenomenology, there is no more reason to classify it as cognitive than as conative. In this section, I want to suggest that claims parallel to those made above about entertaining and cognitive states can be made about entertaining and conative states.

To the extent that we found it plausible to understand judgment as entertaining modulated by the element of affirming, perhaps something similar could be said of desire. Thus, there might be in the conative domain a phenomenal element of *approval*, corresponding to the element of affirming in the cognitive domain, such that desiring something can be understood as just entertaining it and approving of what one entertains. In a slogan: desiring = entertaining + approving.

However, "desiring" (like "thinking that" and unlike "judging") can be used to denote either an occurrent act or a standing state. Since entertaining is always occurrent, we may at most claim this:

(15) S occurrently desires that p iff S entertains-and-approves of p.

At the same time, a standing desire (such as the desire to stay alive) could be understood, again in analogy with the cognitive case, as the disposition to experience an occurrent desire. If so, the following would also suggest itself:

(16) S standingly desires that p iff S is disposed to entertain-and-approve of p.

The disposition to entertain-and-approve would have to be carefully delineated, as it was in the cognitive case. The *reasons* to accept 15 and 16 would also, presumably, closely parallel those for accepting the parallel accounts of judgment and belief.

As before, the account of occurrent desire in terms of entertaining plus approving would not dispense with a conative primitive. It would only cast the conative primitive as an attitude-*component* or attitude-*modification* rather than a self-standing attitude. There is no economy of primitives here, but there is a claim of phenomenal commonality among entertaining, judging, and occurrently desiring—all three involve a shared phenomenal component of apprehending a proposition, of having the proposition before one's mind.

In addition to cognitive and conative attitudes, there are "mixed" attitudes, which involve combinations of both. The simplest case is being glad that p, which involves both believing that p and desiring that p. Other mixed attitudes include disappointment, hope, and many other emotional attitudes. For example, to be disappointed that p plausibly involves being that p and desiring that $\sim p$.

One might hold that gladness that p does not just *involve*, but is *exhausted by*, the compresence of belief that p and desire that p. Within a framework that highlights a core act of entertaining, the account would be simply: occurrent gladness = entertaining + affirming + approving; standing gladness = disposition to undergo occurrent gladness. That is:

(17) S is occurrently glad that p iff S entertains-and-affirms-and-approves of p.
(18) S is standingly glad that p iff S is disposed to entertain-and-affirm-and-approve of p.

As before, the details would have to be ironed out. Similar though more complicated accounts might apply to other "mixed" propositional attitudes, such as disappointment, hope, and the like—provided these are *exhausted* by certain combinations of belief and desire (Gordon 1987).

The general approach suggested here would replace the functionalist belief-desire story, where all propositional attitudes are accounted for in terms of various belief-desire combinations, with an *entertaining* story, so to speak, where (*a*) all occurrent mixed propositional attitudes are accounted for in terms of a core episode of entertaining suitably modulated by affirmation-related and approval-related elements, and (*b*) all standing mixed propositional attitudes are accounted for in terms of dispositions to enter the corresponding occurrent states.

7. Summary: A Ramsey Sentence for Entertaining

The project of understanding all the propositional attitudes (partly) in terms of entertaining is extremely ambitious. But the claim that entertaining cannot be understood in terms of belief and desire, nor any other pair of cognitive and conative attitudes, is much more modest, and already represents a deep challenge to the functionalist orthodoxy on the attitudes. We can appreciate this by noting that the functionalist theorizes about mental states mostly in terms of their functional role and intentional content, and appeals to causal connections among mental states and to the environment to account for both in naturalistically kosher terms. But for both functional role and intentional content, it is *less obvious* how these causal treatments might proceed with regard to entertaining.

Consider first functional role. At the level of token acts of entertaining, there are many that seem completely divorced from behavior, including mental behavior such as reasoning. Furthermore, there are features of entertaining as a type, such as phenomenal intensity, whose functional contribution is dubious. If two subjects contemplate that p (that is, entertain p in the disengaged mode) but one's contemplative episode is more phenomenally vivid than the other's, it is not clear what difference we should expect in their functional roles. It is hard to *rule out* such a difference; still, it is *less obvious* how such story about one would go than the standard story about the functional roles of belief and desire.

Similarly for intentional content. The standard approach in the functionalist orthodoxy accounts for attitudes' intentional content in terms of broadly causal relations to the environment. The direction of the causal relation changes with the attitude's direction of fit: a belief's content is determined by the part of the world that it is *caused by* in the right way, a desire's by the part of the world that it *causes* in the right way (Dretske 1988). Since entertaining has no direction of fit, it is unclear what causal connections it is required to bear to the environment, and what causal direction they would take. Thus, when I contemplate the proposition that I can fly to Persia, my contemplation neither causes nor is caused by the state of affairs of my being able to fly to Persia. More generally, contemplating some state of affairs is dissociated from the subject's causal transactions with the world in a way belief and desire are not. Perhaps a special causal-naturalist approach could be devised from within the functionalist framework, but again it is *less obvious* what the story would be.

More generally, it seems to me that the great emphasis in the philosophy of mind of the past half-century on naturalizing mental phenomena, typically through reductive explanations in terms of structure and/or function, has often tempted philosophers to overlook mental phenomena whose essential profile *seems* independent of structure and function. In appearing cut off from the environment, on the one hand, and behavior, on the other, entertaining *appears* to resist understanding in terms of structure and function. To that extent, it represents a distinctive challenge for the program of naturalizing the propositional attitudes. It is doubtful that entertaining defies *ultima facie* demystification. But one may reasonably suspect that its scant treatment in contemporary philosophy of mind is owed in part to its uncomfortable fit with the project of causation-based naturalization. In this respect, the disregard of entertaining is patterned somewhat after the disregard of phenomenal consciousness that has characterized the philosophy of mind of much of the second half of the twentieth century. And in some palpable way, entertaining—especially contemplative entertaining—is the purest manifestation of a private, subjective state constitutively divorced from the external world.

A consequence of this neglect is that our present understanding of entertaining is surprisingly patchy (in comparison with not only belief and desire but also intention, imagination, emotion, and so on). This predicament would be disconcerting for any propositional attitude, but is acutely so when the attitude in question is the third leg of the attitudes' stool. My goal in Part II of this chapter has been to make initial observations *en route* to a nonreductive characterization of entertaining.[23] In the process, a number of theses about entertaining have been articulated that collectively generate a rather specific profile, Theses 1–18 and A–F. These can be used to produce what I called in Chapter 1 a sophisticated Ramsey sentence: one using a disjunction of conjunctions of different subsets of theses, and where the more a thesis is central to the notion elucidated, the more disjuncts it appears in.

By far the most central claims about entertaining are D and E (its doxastic and axiological neutrality) and 3 (entertaining as apprehending). They might, in fact, be nonnegotiable, in the sense in which being spatiotemporal is a nonnegotiable condition for being a mango. In that case, they would have to appear in *every* disjunct of the sophisticated Ramsey sentence. Also relatively central to the notion of entertaining that p are A–B (phenomenal intensity), F (entertaining that p and entertaining φ-ing), 1 (entertaining and mere-entertaining), 4–5 (considering and contemplating), 8–9 (entertaining and thinking-about). Less central are C and 7 (presentational phenomenology), as well as a variety of claims regarding a potential role for entertaining in grounding other central attitudes: 10–12 (judging and believing), 13–14 (being convinced and suspecting), 15–16 (desire), 17–18 (gladness), and 6 (supposition). These claims about entertaining are possibly of the greatest philosophical significance (10 being especially significant), but that does not make them central to the nature of entertaining. On the contrary, we generally have the sense that the more substantive and interesting a claim, the farther it is from being "definitional." In the present framework, this translates into presence in fewer disjuncts of the Ramsey sentence.[24]

The resulting Ramsey sentence bears improvement in a variety of ways. First, some of the theses figuring in it I floated mostly in a speculative capacity, and would need to be much more thoroughly substantiated. Secondly, some are formulated in less-than-transparent terms ("having the project of figuring out whether p," "strongly/weakly affirming," "approving of p"). Thirdly, some invoke phenomena that would require a substantive account before they can be fully appreciated (phenomenal intensity, presentational phenomenology, the right disposition to judge or desire). Still, the present Ramsey sentence, skeletal though it is, does give fuller texture to the notion of entertaining that p than it had received from most of the functionalist literature.

Conclusion

Chapters 1–3 have made the case for three primitive types of phenomenology going beyond perceptual and algedonic. They are cognitive phenomenology, conative phenomenology, and the phenomenology of entertaining. More accurately, corresponding to cognitive and conative phenomenology is the phenomenology of being in an attitudinally neutral state. The experience of entertaining is just the paradigmatic attitudinally neutral state, in the same way the experience of making a judgment is the paradigmatic attitudinally truth-committed state and the experience of deciding-and-then-trying the paradigmatic attitudinally value-committed state. The essential aspect of the attitudes themselves are the attitudinal features of presenting-as-true, presenting-as-good$_G$, and mere-presenting.

So far, then, I have endorsed *five* second-layer phenomenal primitives: perceptual, algedonic, cognitive, conative, and that associated with neutral attitudes such as entertaining. All of these are needed to adequately *describe* the phenomena of consciousness. In the next chapter, I consider another candidate primitive: emotional phenomenology.[25]

4

Emotional Phenomenology

This chapter recommends a reductivist account of emotional phenomenology. Once we appreciate the richness and complexity of perceptual, cognitive, and conative aspects of emotional experience, I will suggest, it is hard to motivate positing an additional sui generis emotional phenomenology.

I argue for this in a somewhat circuitous way. In Part I, I note that standard critiques of feeling theories of emotion have tended to construe the feel (read: phenomenal character) of emotional experiences implausibly thinly. A more accurate portrayal would construe it as involving potentially complex and sophisticated cognitive and conative elements. Combined with certain further considerations, this revives the prospects for a feeling theory of emotion. However, this fuller account of emotional "feel" makes it harder to find place for irreducible emotional phenomenology. In Part II, I consider a number of possible attempts at doing so; I argue that they are unconvincing.

1. Emotion and Emotional Phenomenology

The immense variety of emotional phenomena is well known. Arguably, the most paradigmatic are the experiences of *feeling sad* and *feeling happy*. (Their paradigmatic status stands in curious contrast to their paucity of philosophical treatment.) But there are many more experiences uncontroversially emotional, including feeling glad, ashamed, frustrated, disappointed, angry (enraged), afraid (terrified), jealous, humiliated, proud, excited, (over)joyed; feeling affection, love, admiration, respect, grief, guilt, indignation, dislike, antipathy (animosity); feeling close to someone, feeling moved by something, being in love, and more. Other experiences appear to be borderline cases of emotional experience: feeling nervous, giddy, bored, being startled, being amused, lusting, and indeed desiring.

It is very much an open question whether there is anything common and peculiar to uncontroversially emotional states. It has become common to deny that there is—to claim that emotions "do not constitute a natural kind" (see notably Griffiths 1997). Even if emotions are a natural kind after all (Charland

2002), it is a further question whether there is a *phenomenal* feature common and peculiar to their conscious occurrences. I will discuss this more fully in §6. But if there is such a phenomenal common-and-peculiar feature, we may refer to it as *emotional phenomenology per se*. We might then ask whether emotional phenomenology per se is reducible to other types of phenomenology or on the contrary is sui generis.

Even if there is no emotional phenomenology per se, emotional experiences may still instantiate some phenomenal property irreducible to other types of phenomenology they exhibit. This would be a sui generis emotional phenomenology as well. To address this issue, however, we must start by considering what are the other types of phenomenology exhibited by emotional experience. I approach this question via consideration of the so-called feeling theory of emotion.

The pre-philosophical, "naïve" view of emotions is that they are essentially feelings—often complicated and subtle feelings, eluding straightforward literal description, but feelings nonetheless. I am persuaded that this is a rather good view, notwithstanding common wisdom in philosophical circles. Standard objections taken to be fatal to the view have less merit to them than is commonly thought, it seems to me, and a proper development of the naïve view could produce an eminently plausible "feeling theory" of emotion.

The James-Lange theory (James 1884, Lange 1885) identifies emotion with feelings of *bodily occurrences*. These occurrences are claimed to be typically visceral, but sometimes also muscular or skin-related. On this view, at least some changes in one's viscera, muscles, and skin are *felt*, and one's feeling of them *constitutes* one's emoting—the emoting *just is* the feeling of such bodily events. Presumably, feeling a bodily event is a matter of proprioceptively perceiving that event. So on the James-Lange theory, emotions are just proprioceptive perceptions. To emote is to proprioceive, to experience a certain proprioceptive phenomenology.

To formulate the theory more precisely, let us adopt the thought that what a philosophical theory of emotion is supposed to do is to provide identity and existence conditions for emotional states. We can then offer a more spelled-out statement of the James-Lange theory in terms of what makes an emotional state the emotional state it is (identity conditions) and what makes it an emotional state at all (existence conditions):

(JLT) For any emotional state E, what makes E the emotional state it is (rather than another emotional state), and an emotional state at all (rather than a non-emotional state), is that E has the proprioceptive phenomenology it does (rather than another proprioceptive phenomenology), and has one at all (rather than having only non-proprioceptive phenomenology or no phenomenology).

The more "portable" version of this, if you will, is the simple equation "emotion = proprioceptive phenomenology."[1]

The apparent simplicity of the James-Lange theory hides a layer of complexity, however. For it is profitably factorized into two distinct theses. One concerns the *nature* of emotion, what *individuates* emotional states. The other concerns the *feel* of emotion, what gives emotional states their phenomenal character. The thesis about the *nature* of emotion is precisely that the nature of emotion is one and the same as the feel of emotion: emotional states individuate by their phenomenal characters. The thesis about the *feel* of emotion is that it is one and the same as the feel of proprioceptive perception: the phenomenal character of emotion is exhausted by the phenomenal character of proprioception.

It is easy to see that these two theses together *entail* the James-Lange theory. To do so, we need only frame the two theses—call them NATURE and FEEL—in terms of identity and existence conditions:

(NATURE) For any emotional state E, what makes E the emotional state it is, and an emotional state at all, is that E has the emotional phenomenology it does, and has one at all.

(FEEL) For any emotional state E, what makes E have the emotional phenomenology it does, and have one at all, is that E has the proprioceptive phenomenology it does, and has one at all.

The portable versions here would be "emotion = emotional phenomenology" and "emotional phenomenology = proprioceptive phenomenology" (respectively). It is clear that the conjunction of NATURE and FEEL entails JLT. It is also clear that a *generic* "feeling theory" of emotion is committed only to NATURE. The generic theory insists that the nature of emotions is captured by their feel, what it is like to experience them; it is altogether silent on the question of what emotional feel is in fact like, what the characteristic phenomenology of emotion is.

The James-Lange theory has attracted more attention than followership. It is often dismissed as hopeless, for reasons we will encounter shortly, with only rare exceptions (Prinz 2004). But my view is that later generations of scholars have drawn exactly the wrong lesson from the theory's demise. They have tended to accept the Jamesian view of emotional phenomenology as exhausted by proprioceptive phenomenology (FEEL), rejecting only the claim that such phenomenology captures the nature of emotion (NATURE).[2] A certain collusion between these two tendencies may be observed: it is partially the starving of emotional phenomenology—its reduction to a relatively simple, unsophisticated kind of feel—that made it singularly unfit to capture the essence of emotion.

My own inclination is to take exactly the opposite path, adopting NATURE (or rather a variant thereof) and rejecting FEEL. My contention is that a more accurate portrayal of emotional phenomenology would cast it as rich and multi-faceted, involving not only proprioceptive components but also cognitive and conative ones. Once emotional phenomenology is appreciated in its full glory, it becomes a much better candidate for capturing the essence of emotion. The result is a feeling theory of emotion, though of distinctly non-Jamesian bent. I call this the *new feeling theory* of emotion. (Its precise formulation will emerge as the discussion unfolds.) What I want to argue below is that the main reasons to reject the James-Lange theory fail to carry over to the new feeling theory.

Extant objections to the James-Lange theory are many, but two are standard and paramount. One is that the theory leaves out the cognitive dimension of emotion, offering an impoverished picture of them. The other is that emotions can occur not only consciously but also unconsciously, and when they do they are deprived of any phenomenology, proprioceptive or otherwise. The next two sections address these objections in turn, arguing that, although cogent when targeting the old (James-Lange) feeling theory of emotion, they have little or no force against the new feeling theory of emotion (when properly developed).

I. The Phenomenal Nature of Emotion

2. Emotion, Feeling, and the Cognitive

My agenda in this section is threefold. First, I want to articulate and respond to what I will call the "cognitivist objection" to the feeling theory of emotion (§2.1). Secondly, I want to use my response to undercut the apparent attraction of so-called cognitivist theories of emotion (§2.2). Finally, I want to use the considerations raised in the course of the discussion to articulate a first approximation of a *new* feeling theory of emotion; a second and closer approximation will emerge in §3.

2.1. Emotional Phenomenology and Cognitive Intentionality

The charge that the James-Lange theory leaves out the cognitive dimension of emotion has sometimes been framed in terms of *intentionality*. The claim is that emotions cannot be mere bodily feelings, because they are *about*, or are *directed at*, certain things. Bare bodily feelings, by contrast, are not directed at anything—they are mere sensations (see Dewey 1894).

In this form, the objection can be overcome simply by denying that proprioceptive phenomenology is nonintentional. According to intentionalists about phenomenal consciousness (e.g., Dretske 1995), *all* phenomenal properties are reducible to intentional properties. This applies also to the proprioceptive phenomenology characteristic of emotions. For note that James does not identify emotions with bodily occurrences themselves, but rather with *feelings of* bodily occurrences. The "of" here is the "of" of intentionality: the experiential feel is *directed at* the bodily occurrence. It is thus possible to hold that (*a*) emotional phenomenology is nothing but proprioceptive phenomenology and (*b*) proprioceptive phenomenology is intentional.[3]

We can debate the plausibility of this account, but its very *coherence* shows that the James-Lange theory is not inherently incapable of accounting for the intentionality of emotion. One may identify emotion with proprioceptive phenomenology and still hold that emotion is essentially intentional, so long as one accepts an intentionalist account of proprioceptive phenomenology. What the objector must insist on, therefore, is not just that emotion has intentionality, but that it has a *specific kind* of intentionality, one that is distinct from any intentionality implicated in proprioceptive phenomenology and is directed at the world outside the body.

The natural way to develop this objection is to argue that emotion has a specifically *cognitive* intentionality. "Cognitive intentionality" is to be understood here in terms of *what* and *how* intentional objects are presented. We need not develop a systematic account of cognitive intentionality to note that it is distinguished from proprioceptive intentionality in that it is not directed only at *bodily* events but also at *worldly* events (or objects or states of affairs), where "worldly" is used technically to contrast with "bodily." The "cognitivist objection," so understood, may be expressed as follows: 1) emotions involve a cognitive intentionality; 2) proprioceptive phenomenology does not involve cognitive intentionality; therefore, 3) emotions are not exhausted by proprioceptive phenomenology.

In this form, the objection is quite powerful. It is hard to see how one might resist Premise 2, and while Premise 1 is more controversial, on this score I am satisfied that the common wisdom on emotion is correct: emotion does involve presentation of worldly particulars, events, and states of affairs. As an adolescent, I experienced grief at my grandfather's death; somewhat trivially, the grief was intentionally directed at my grandfather and his death, not at inner bodily changes (if such there were) consequent upon the realization and emotional processing of his death. Similarly pedestrian observations apply to almost all emotions (Kenny 1963, Lazarus 1994). Thus the cognitivist objection, when properly understood, undermines the James-Lange theory rather straightforwardly.[4]

Where I think common wisdom overreaches is in claiming that the objection undermines not just the James-Lange theory, but the feeling theory of emotion as such. Recall that the James-Lange theory is just one feeling theory—the one committed to FEEL. The *generic* feeling theory, consisting merely of NATURE, is much more flexible than the James-Lange variety, and, I contend, has the resources to withstand the cognitivist objection. Adapted to target the generic feeling theory, the cognitivist objection would have to look like this: 1) emotions involve a cognitive intentionality; 2) emotional phenomenology does not involve cognitive intentionality; therefore, 3) emotions are not exhausted by emotional phenomenology. (In this version, Premise 2 is about *emotional* phenomenology, not just *proprioceptive* phenomenology.) As I argue in the rest of this subsection, this objection can be handled by rejecting Premise 2.[5]

When I consider carefully my early grief episode about my grandfather's death, I find that a central element of it was the experience of *loss*. What was lost, clearly, was not any bodily occurrence, but a person—a person of special importance. Thus the experience of loss had a cognitive intentionality, insofar as it was directed onto a worldly, non-bodily object. What I want to emphasize is that the loss was also *phenomenal*—it affected very distinctively the overall way it was like for me to undergo my episode of grief. It is not as though my grief consisted in bodily sensations accompanied by a bloodless, unfelt, unconscious, non-experienced representation of loss. It is not as though the appreciation of loss was a mental event occurring in me subpersonally, with only proprioceptive feelings actually showing up in consciousness. On the contrary, the awareness of loss itself showed up in consciousness—it was "experientially encoded." In that respect, the loss of my grandfather was not only *represented*, but *experienced*. We do not really understand what it is like to *feel* grief if we cast the element of loss-awareness as external to it. Thus although the awareness of loss was certainly an *intentional* component of my grief episode, the intentionality in question was of a distinctively experiential or phenomenal variety.

In this respect, understanding the intentionality involved in such emotional episodes invites the notion of phenomenal intentionality: the component of grief naturally called "the experience of loss" is clearly a both phenomenal and intentional, but moreover, the phenomenality and the intentionality are inextricably tied together.[6] This is effectively what Goldie (2002) calls (in this very context) "feeling-towards," an inherently *directed* kind of phenomenal feeling.

The experience of loss essential to grief is, moreover, an instance of *cognitive*-phenomenal intentionality. It is the kind of phenomenal intentionality exhibited by cognitive-phenomenal states, states possessed of cognitive phenomenology. Loss is a relatively abstract feature, not the kind of thing we could perceive. At the same time, the appreciation of loss still has a mind-to-world direction of fit. It presents-as-true that loss has occurred (or presents-as-real the loss). All this casts loss-awareness as cognitive. In fact, there may be many other cognitive-phenomenal components in grief. Many who have lost dear ones will be familiar with the experience of trying to grasp the nonexistence, the ceasing-to-be, of the grieved person, a ceasing-to-be that feels elusive and at some level ungraspable for at least a few hours. This element of attempted grasping, too, is an entirely cognitive phenomenon, but an experienced one nonetheless—another aspect of the (typical) cognitive phenomenology of grief. These elements appear to involve a kind of cognitive intentionality that is inextricably tied with a corresponding phenomenal character, a distinctively cognitive kind of phenomenal character. That is, they appear to involve cognitive-phenomenal intentionality.

Similar observations apply to other emotions. The phenomenology of frustration and the phenomenology of indignation certainly often involve bodily feelings, but they also involve much more than that, including—centrally—an experienced cognitive appreciation of a failure (for frustration) or an injustice (for indignation). It has been argued that the proprioceptive phenomenology of frustration and indignation is in fact indistinguishable, and the only element that separates them is cognitive. Solomon (1976) argues, more generally, for the proprioceptive indistinguishability of many emotion pairs. He proceeds to infer from this a *phenomenal* indistinguishability, but he does so only due to an illicit acceptance of the Jamesian conception of emotional phenomenology as exhausted by proprioceptive phenomenology. Once we reject the Jamesian conception, it is clear that even if frustration and indignation are indistinguishable with respect to their proprioceptive phenomenology, they are still distinguishable in terms of their *overall* phenomenology.

It is noteworthy, in this connection, that from a first-person point of view we can, effortlessly and noninferentially, distinguish disappointment from indignation. If such effortless noninferential knowledge of a mental feature is a symptom of its status as phenomenal, then plausibly, the effortless and noninferential knowledge of a mental *difference* is a symptom of that difference being phenomenal. The existence of such knowledge of the difference between frustration and indignation would then suggest that the difference between the two is phenomenal: their overall phenomenology must be different. If their proprioceptive phenomenology is *not* different, then there must be some non-proprioceptive phenomenology along which they do differ. A natural thought is that the difference is in cognitive phenomenology. A similar reasoning applies to many proprioceptively indistinguishable emotion pairs.

In addition to its cognitive element, emotional phenomenology often involves a *conative* component as well—one feels like "doing something about it." In addition to the experienced appreciation of a wrong, feeling indignant typically involves also an experienced nudge (of varying phenomenal intensity) to *rectify* the wrong. Depending on its phenomenal intensity, and the feasibility of rectification, the nudge may not be powerful enough to issue in action. Even then, there is a felt force in the direction of action nonetheless. It is an open question whether feeling this nudge is *constitutive* of such moral emotions as indignation or merely a contingent-but-stubborn feature of them. My own sense is that it is constitutive: one's emotional experience does not qualify as genuine indignation if one feels no nudge whatsoever to rectify the wrong. The same applies to many other (including nonmoral) emotions. Feeling rage, for example, involves a felt desire to exact revenge, inflict violence, or otherwise evince excess energy. To abstract away from this felt desire is, as far as I can see, to abstract away from rage proper.

In addition, it is clear that standard emotions exhibit an *algedonic* phenomenology. It is customary to distinguish *positive* from *negative* emotions. This seems to come down to whether experiencing the emotion *feels good* or *feels bad*. If so, some emotions—the positive ones—involve a phenomenology of pleasure and some—the negative—one of displeasure. It is an open question whether the algedonic phenomenology of emotional states affects their identity and existence conditions.[7] But algedonic phenomenology would be a component of emotional phenomenology regardless.

It is thus entirely implausible, borderline perverse, to construe emotional phenomenology as consisting in nothing but proprioceptive phenomenology. Indeed, while visceral phenomenology can be quite vivid, it is otherwise quite peripheral in the overall experience of most emotions. Cognitive and conative forms of phenomenology are much more central. Experiences of indignation and rage, for example, are completely disfigured if we overlook their cognitive and conative components and consider them only in their emaciated visceral phenomenology. From the first-person perspective, they would be literally unrecognizable. Thus it is hard to conceive of a cognitive and conative zombie who nonetheless experiences rage or indignation. This partial zombie would feel various vibrations and excitements in his viscera and skin; to say on this basis that he feels indignant, or enraged, despite lacking any conceptual appreciation of any worldly state of affairs and any motivation for action, would be extremely odd. It is hard to see what could make such a view attractive to anyone in the first place—unless it is tacitly assumed that all phenomenology is sensory.

To summarize, notwithstanding the philosophical tradition of treating all phenomenology as sensory, it is a rather obvious fact that the phenomenology of emotion is rich and multi-faceted—sufficiently so, certainly, to make room for cognitive intentionality. Recall that the cognitivist objection to the feeling theory proceeded as follows: 1) emotions involve a cognitive intentionality; 2) emotional phenomenology does not involve cognitive intentionality; therefore, 3) emotions are not exhausted by emotional phenomenology. We can now comfortably and in good conscience reject Premise 2, and with it the entire objection.

2.2. On Cognitivist Theories of Emotion

The above considerations undercut not only the cognitivist objection to the generic feeling theory, but also the main theoretical overreaction it has inspired, namely, the development of "cognitivist theories" that deny any phenomenal component in the essence of emotion. According to such theories, emotions are just judgments of a certain sort (often: "evaluative" judgments) (Solomon 1976, Nussbaum 2001), or else combinations of judgments and desires (Marks 1982, Gordon 1987). Such cognitive accounts are standardly presented as *opposing* feeling theories. The suppressed assumption is evidently that feelings cannot be cognitive or conative, that is, that there is no cognitive or conative phenomenology. This is the assumption I reject.

It is instructive that cognitive theorists have typically felt pressure to use the term "judgment" rather than "belief." For as we saw in Chapter 3, unlike belief, judgment is essentially a conscious act: it is something that one consciously does, and that there is something it is like for one to do. There is no duality of terms in the case of desire, but it is notable that often in the course of discussing this aspect of emotion, cognitive theorists employ (what are most naturally interpreted as) phenomenal descriptors. Thus, it is common to stress that the relevant desire may be *strong* or *intense* (see, e.g., Marks 1982).

With this in mind, I contend that the animating sensibilities behind cognitive theories of emotion can perfectly well be accommodated in a new feeling theory of emotion, one which allows emotional phenomenology to encompass cognitive and conative elements. What is responsible for the anti-feeling slant of cognitive theories is a "separatist" prejudice (Horgan and Tienson 2002): the notion that mental states separate into (i) those which are essentially and universally phenomenal though occasionally and accidentally intentional and (ii) those which are essentially and universally intentional though occasionally and accidentally phenomenal. Against the background of separatism, accepting the cognitive dimension of emotion does lead rather directly to rejecting the feeling theory. But separatism is forsooth quite implausible: on the one hand, perceptual and bodily experiences seem possessed of intentionality, and on the other, cognitive and conative states seem possessed of phenomenology (as argued Chapters 1 and 2).

It may be objected that I am casting as substantial, deep, and important what is in fact nothing but a verbal matter. Cognitive theorists simply use the term "feeling" to denote not just any old conscious state, but a bodily or visceral one. They need not oppose the notion that emotions are essentially feelings if that notion is *not* taken to imply that emotions are raw bodily sensations with no cognitive dimension. There is nothing in the letter or spirit of their view that precludes their embrace of the "new" feeling theory of emotion, where the term "feeling" is used quite differently from how they use it.

My response is threefold. First, insofar as cognitive theorists are happy to embrace the new feeling theory of emotion, I have no quarrel with them. I nonetheless suspect the objector is overplaying her openness to the substantive core of the new feeling theory. The substantive core is the claim that emotions are essentially phenomenal states. It may well be that some cognitive theorists are open to this, and simply use "feeling" to denote not just any phenomenal states but specifically bodily or visceral ones. I suspect, however, that many are committed to the stronger claim that the nature of emotions cannot be understood in terms of their overall phenomenology, whatever one's view of their overall phenomenology. This is, in any case, a sociological issue not much more titillating than any verbal issue. What matters to me is only the consistency of two ideas: that emotions have a cognitive dimension, and that they are essentially phenomenal.

Secondly, unlike terms such as "phenomenology" and "proprioceptive," the term "feeling" is *not* a term of art. The term enters the theory of emotion not by way of theoretical postulation, but via the mundane, pretheoretic use of such expressions as "feeling angry," "feeling scared," and "feeling frustrated." To use it in a technical sense divorced from its role in such mundane expressions is to court confusion. Now, in its mundane sense, "feeling angry" is not used to denote a specifically proprioceptive phenomenology, but whatever phenomenology turns out to be linked with anger. So insofar as cognitive theorists use "feeling" to denote specifically proprioceptive phenomenology, my claim would be simply that they ought not.

Thirdly, even if cognitivism were considered just a version of the new feeling theory, and thus not immediately problematic for the view I wish to defend, it would still be a very specific version, to which we may not want to commit. According to this specific version, the identity and existence conditions of emotional phenomenology are fully determined by cognitive phenomenology, or else by a combination of cognitive and conative phenomenology. This is not obviously implausible, but there is no reason for the new feeling theory to rule out other options: that emotional phenomenology is a combination of cognitive, conative, *and proprioceptive* phenomenology; that it consists in cognitive and *algedonic* phenomenology; and so on. If we just focus on proprioceptive, cognitive, conative, and algedonic phenomenology, we have on our hands fifteen coherent accounts of the existence and identity conditions of emotional phenomenology: one for each possible combination of at least one among them (given that n items admit of $2^n - 1$ combinations). The version appealing solely to cognitive and conative phenomenology is just one of these, and not the most antecedently plausible.

Corresponding to the fifteen combinations of proprioceptive, cognitive, conative, and algedonic phenomenology, then, are fifteen versions of the generic feeling theory of emotion. The feeling theory that appeals exclusively to proprioceptive phenomenology in accounting for emotional phenomenology is only one of them, and one of the least plausible. Arguably, the most prima facie plausible is that which appeals to all four types of phenomenology. This would amount to:

(FEEL*) For any emotional state E, what makes E have the emotional phenomenology it does, and have one at all, is that E has the combination of proprioceptive, cognitive, conative, and algedonic phenomenology it does, and has such a combination at all.

Note that FEEL* makes no commitment on the *nature* or *essence* of emotion; it is a thesis merely concerning emotional feel, silent on the question of emotional nature. At the same time, FEEL* is *consistent* with a feeling theory of emotion, and provides the resources for such a theory to resist the cognitivist critique of the old feeling theory of emotion. Conjoined with NATURE, it would generate a Relaxed Feeling Theory of emotion:

(RFT) For any emotional state E, what makes E the emotional state it is, and an emotional state at all, is that E has the combination of proprioceptive, cognitive, conative, and algedonic phenomenology it does, and has such a combination at all.

Despite retaining the commitment to the phenomenal nature of emotion, RFT survives the cognitivist critique that undermined the James-Lange theory.

3. Emotion, Feeling, and the Unconscious

The other major objection to the old feeling theory of emotion is the Freudian-inspired one that much of our emotional life is unconscious, and when it is it involves no feel whatsoever (unconscious states do not *have* a phenomenal feel). If so, neither NATURE nor RFT can be right. For some emotional states are not such in virtue of their phenomenal feel.

It may be, however, that a variation on NATURE is still tenable. Consider again Searle's (1992) "connection principle," already discussed in Chapter 3. According to it, every intentional state is potentially conscious. Given that every conscious state has phenomenal character, the connection principle entails that every intentional state potentially has phenomenal character. If one held that every emotional state is intentional, it would follow that every emotional state potentially has a phenomenal character. This would be an alternative connection principle, one connecting not intentional and conscious states but emotional and phenomenal states. As in the last chapter, the obscure potentiality talk can also be replaced by disposition talk, resulting in something like the following thesis: subject S is in an unconscious emotional state with the content that *p* only if S has a disposition to enter a phenomenally conscious emotional state with the content that *p*. For example, S is unconsciously afraid of her father only if S is disposed to be consciously afraid of her father.

How would a connection principle of this sort help the cause of a feeling theory of emotion? It may inspire a weakened version of NATURE that relaxes the connection between the identity and existence conditions of emotion, on the one hand, and emotional phenomenology, on the other. Perhaps it is false that what makes an emotional state the emotional state it is, and an emotional state at all, is the emotional phenomenology it *actually* has. It may yet be true that what makes an emotional state the emotional state it is, and an emotional state at all, is the emotional phenomenology it *potentially* has or is *disposed* to have.

There are many problems with this kind of move. First, Searle's original connection principle is open to straightforward counterexamples (Davies 1995, Kriegel 2011 ch.4); the alternative principle (connecting emotionality with phenomenality) is in all likelihood equally susceptible.[8] Secondly, Searle's own argument for his connection principle is highly problematic (Fodor and Lepore 1994, Kriegel 2003b), and moreover does not carry over to the alternative (emotionality-phenomenality) connection principle, leaving the latter unmotivated.[9] Finally, either principle is in fact far weaker than what a feeling theory of emotion would require: the former imposes a *necessary* condition on the existence of an emotional (or intentional) state, whereas the latter requires also a *sufficient* condition for the existence of such a state, one which moreover is sufficient for the *identity* of the state.

The literature on these matters offers a number of possible responses. Some authors have offered what are in effect alternative connection principles that are not potentiality-based (Loar 2003, Kriegel 2011 ch.4). Others have offered alternative arguments for their connection principle (Loar 2003, Bourget 2010, Kriegel 2011 ch.1, Smithies 2012), including some that may well carry over to the case of emotion. Rather than sift through this ever-growing literature, I will proceed by articulating the most generic kind of connection principle that would be needed and then propose a plausibility argument in its favor.

As noted above, NATURE is falsified by the existence of unconscious, nonphenomenal emotional states. Still, the *spirit* of a feeling theory could be preserved if some essential connection could be established between any emotional state and emotional phenomenology. The generic form of such a connection would require some relation R, such that every emotional state E must bear R to some phenomenal emotional state(s), so that it is in virtue of E bearing R to the phenomenal states it does that E is the emotional state it is. R may be the relation of *potentially being* or that of being *disposed to bring about*, but it may also be some other nontrivial relation (various trivializing mechanisms would have to be neutralized). A strengthened connection principle would claim that bearing

R is both necessary and sufficient for (and moreover *grounds*) E's being the emotional state it is and an emotional state at all. The result would be the following variation on NATURE:

> (NATURE*) There is a relation R, such that for any emotional state E, what makes E the emotional state it is, and an emotional state at all, is that E bears R to the emotional phenomenology it does, and bears R to an emotional phenomenology at all.

NATURE* effectively constitutes an emotional-phenomenal connection principle sufficiently strong to underwrite a feeling theory of emotion. That the spirit of the feeling theory of emotion is preserved here can be appreciated from the fact that NATURE* is not merely a thesis offering necessary and sufficient conditions for a state being emotional, but a thesis about what *makes* a mental state emotional—about the *grounds* of its status as emotional. In fact, NATURE* is a relaxation of NATURE, insofar as NATURE is just NATURE* but with R construed specifically as the *having* or *instantiating* relation.

The argument I will sketch in support of NATURE* is non-demonstrative and proceeds in two phases. The first phase concerns a central problem of the philosophy of mind that has received oddly little attention in recent decades: the question of what constitutes the "mark of the mental," that is, what makes a given state *mental*. I will argue (mostly by elimination) that the most promising view is that mental states are distinguished from nonmental phenomena in being suitably related to phenomenal states. The second phase of the argument will suggest that this leads naturally to NATURE*, through two considerations of general theoretical unity.

I start, then, by considering possible approaches to the mark of the mental.

Intentionality as the mark of the mental. The notion of the mark of the mental is due to Brentano (1874), who argued that intentionality is it. The claim is that a state is mental just in case it is intentional. Some have argued that intentionality is too *narrow* to mark the mental, claiming that some mental states (moods, for example) are nonintentional (Searle 1983).[10] The more serious challenge, however, is that intentionality appears too *broad*: linguistic expressions, traffic signs, and paintings all seem to be about something, be contentful, yet are clearly not mental.

Privileged intentionality as the mark of the mental. It may be retorted that although nonmental phenomena are sometimes intentional, they are so only parasitically and derivatively—they derive their intentionality from mental states. This may suggest *underived* (or "intrinsic") intentionality as the mark of the mental. However, it is highly questionable whether underived intentionality is perfectly coextensive with mentality. On the one hand, it has sometimes been argued that linguistic expressions are possessed of the very same underived intentionality as mental states (see Millikan 1984 ch.3, Speaks 2006). Meanwhile, other philosophers have argued that in truth only *phenomenal* mental states are nonderivatively intentional (McGinn 1988, Bourget 2010, Kriegel 2003b, 2011). What both camps have in common is an insistence on the equal status of nonphenomenal mental states and linguistic expressions. Both camps are impressed by the following question: what might endow subpersonal states in visual cortex, say, with an intentionality inherently different from that of linguistic expressions? They both track the environment, play a certain functional role within their respective systems, and so forth. Yet one is mental and the other is not.[11]

Functional role as the mark of the mental. Given the prominence of functionalist theories of mind in the past half-century, it might be thought that mental states could be distinguished from nonmental phenomena by their having a functional role. Put this way, the suggestion is clearly unworkable, as many nonmental phenomena play a functional role in relevant systems (Goldman 1993).

Privileged functional role as the mark of the mental (I). What this suggests, however, is that there may be a privileged functional role *peculiar to* mental states. A mental functional role would have to be distinguished somehow from a nonmental functional role. The distinction would advert either to the nature of the *role* or to the nature of its *occupant*. It is hard to see, however, how a role could do the job. It is unclear why, for any given functional role, there could not be some element in some entirely nonmental system (an ecological system, say) that played an isomorphic role. This consideration generates an a priori suspicion that a privileged functional role would always be too broad a mark for the mental if it adverts to the role rather than the occupant.

Privileged functional role as the mark of the mental (IIa). One suggestion that appeals to the nature of the occupant might be that mental states play an *intra-cranial* functional role. But this is doubly problematic. On the one hand, there are hormonal states of the brain that are clearly nonmental but play an intra-cranial functional role (this is a problem of breadth). On the other hand, there are extra-cranial states that some philosophers have argued are mental (Clark and Chalmers 1998), precisely on the grounds that they play the same functional role as unquestionably mental states (this is a problem of narrowness). In addition, there appears to be something arbitrary and superficial about the appeal to the cranium: even if all mental states are in it after all, that would appear to be an accidental feature of the world.

Privileged functional role as the mark of the mental (IIb). A more "scientific-sounding" variant of the preceding suggestion might appeal not to *intra-cranial* functional role but to something like *neuro*functional role. However, the above problems appear to apply with similar force: some neurofunctional states are likely nonmental; some mental states may be realized in non-neural substrate (Putnam 1967), perhaps in silicon chips following corrective surgery, or in an "extended state" partially constituted by artifacts; and the neural (as opposed to non-neural) realization of the mental in any case appears to be accidental rather than essential to the mind.[12]

"*State of a mind.*" These considerations might suggest that what makes a mental state mental is not so much the properties it has in isolation, but rather its being a state *of a mind*. Thus a mark of the mental should first demarcate mental *systems* and only then elucidate mental *states* in terms of those. The question here, of course, is how to demarcate mental systems. This question seems no easier than that of demarcating mental states, and approaches appealing to intentionality and functional role would likely be susceptible to similar difficulties.

A "phenomenal prototype" mark. Elsewhere, I have developed an account of the mark of the mental that (i) casts the concept of mind as a prototype concept and (ii) identifies the prototype with phenomenal states (Horgan and Kriegel 2008). A prototype concept is one whose instances qualify as such in virtue of resembling certain prototypes, or more generally bearing some crucial relation to prototypes (Rosch 1973). For example, the concept of furniture appears to be a prototype concept: for something to qualify as a piece of furniture, it must resemble sufficiently the prototypical pieces of furniture—tables and chairs (Rosch 1975). If the concept of mind is also a prototype concept, then states qualify as mental in virtue of bearing the right relation to prototypical mental states. Now, it is highly plausible that the prototypical mental states are all phenomenally conscious. In particular, it seems to me that the prototypical mental states are visual experiences, conscious thoughts, and experienced sadness and happiness—all phenomenally conscious states. It follows that:

(PP) There are a relevant-resemblance relation R and some phenomenal state(s) P, such that for any mental state M, M is a mental state at all because M bears R to P.

This can be understood either as an empirical hypothesis about the folk concept of mind or as a philosophical thesis about a more nuanced, more developed concept of mind (or both). In a way, PP is not so much a claim as a claim-schema, insofar as there are many different ways to construe the relevant-resemblance relation and identify the relevant phenomenal states. In any case, note that PP does not require a mental state to bear R to phenomenal states *of the same subject*. That would rule out zombie minds. PP is consistent with zombie minds: they are minds in states that bear R to phenomenal states of *other* minds.

There are other potential and actual mark theses that likely collapse into a phenomenally based mark under reasonable assumptions. Consider, for example, the claim that the mark of the mental is introspectibility: all and only mental states are introspectible (Farkas 2008, Tartaglia 2008). Regardless of how plausible this is, depending on one's account of introspection this may well collapse onto a phenomenally based mark thesis. For it is quite plausible that all and only introspectible states are phenomenal, or potentially phenomenal, or otherwise necessarily related to phenomenal states. Likewise for the notion that the mark of the mental is *privacy* (Ducasse 1961): in all probability, once the notion of privacy is adequately elucidated, it would turn out that all and only phenomenal states are private in the relevant sense. (Full argumentation for the kind of collapse I am claiming would require a foray into the nature of introspection and privacy that would take us too far afield, so I will leave the case in this germinal form.) However, PP seems to me the better phenomenally based mark of the mental, mostly for reasons of extensional adequacy.[13]

PP leads to NATURE* through two non-demonstrative considerations having to do with general theoretical unity. Observe, first, that PP concerns only the *existence* conditions of mentality, without commenting on *identity* conditions. But typically, existence and identity conditions do not really come apart: the existence condition is simply the determinable (or genus) of which the identity conditions are determinates (or species).[14] So: if what makes a state mental is that it is suitably related to phenomenal states, then it is natural to suppose that a mental state is the mental state it is in virtue of being suitably related to the phenomenal states it is.

The second consideration of theoretical unity I wish to raise is this. The thesis just formulated comments on the mark of the *mental*, not the mark of the *emotional*. Arguably, however, it recommends—in virtue of enhancing theoretical unity—a parallel thesis targeting more specifically the emotional, as a subdomain of the mental: what makes an *emotional* state the emotional state it is (and an emotional state at all) is that it is suitably related to the states with emotional phenomenology it is (and related to such states at all). This last is effectively NATURE* as formulated above.

Thus given the generic phenomenally based mark of the mental, there are general theoretical considerations that create a presumption in favor of a phenomenally based mark of the emotional—NATURE*. This is a *defeasible* presumption, of course, which may be defeated by special undermining or rebutting considerations recommending a picture of the mind *not* committed to NATURE*.[15] Still, until a case for a different and better mark thesis is presented, and/or concrete defeaters for the inference from the mark thesis to NATURE* are offered, we are well justified—*prima facie* and *defeasibly* justified, but justified nonetheless—in holding NATURE*.

I conclude that, although the existence of unconscious emotional states undermines the old feeling theory's identification of emotion with emotional feel, a subtler thesis of the same spirit is not only tenable but highly plausible. This subtler thesis maintains that while some emotional states are unconscious, and thus involve no feel, all emotional states must be somehow connected to emotional feelings, and the connection in question is in fact what *makes* them the emotional states they are and emotional states at all. Within this framework, it goes to the essence of emotion that it is suitably connected to a certain kind of feeling.

4. The New Feeling Theory of Emotion

In §2, I formulated an account of emotional feeling/phenomenology that is considerably subtler than the old feeling theory's; this was FEEL*. When we combine FEEL* with NATURE*, we obtain what I call the New Feeling Theory of emotion:

> (NFT) There is a relation R, such that for any emotional state E, what makes E the emotional state it is, and an emotional state at all, is that E bears R to the combination of proprioceptive, cognitive, conative, and algedonic phenomenology it does, and bears R to such a combination at all.

Here R is most naturally construed as the disjunctive relation of either *having* or *relevantly resembling* something that has (the right phenomenal combination), where the notion of relevant resemblance would have to be duly unpacked.

According to NFT, the identity and existence conditions of emotional states are indirectly determined by a certain type of phenomenology; not the emaciated phenomenology designated by James and Lange however, but a rich phenomenology including, among other things, cognitive phenomenology. NFT is doubly subtler and more plausible than the James-Lange theory: first insofar as NATURE* is subtler and more plausible than NATURE, secondly insofar as FEEL* is subtler and more plausible than FEEL.

It might be objected that we can perfectly well conceive of a creature with no emotional experiences who nonetheless has unconscious emotional states. Just as someone could harbor suppressed anger at her father without ever bringing it to consciousness ("getting in touch with it"), so someone could in principle harbor a variety of emotional states without ever bringing *any* to consciousness. Indeed, subjects suffering from alexithymia lack any awareness of their emotions and yet behave in ways characteristic of certain emotions (Sifneos 1973).

My response has two parts. First, while alexithymics appear incapable of identifying and classifying their emotional states introspectively, there is no evidence that they do not *experience* them, that is, that they have no phenomenal emotional states. Having emotional phenomenology is one thing, introspecting it is another. Secondly, nothing about NFT requires S's unconscious emotional states to bear R to emotional experiences *of* S. S's unconscious mental state may qualify as emotional in virtue of bearing R to a conscious emotional experience undergone by S*. Certainly this could be so if R is a relation of relevant similarity: different subjects can clearly have relevantly similar mental states.[16]

Another objection might be that some emotional states simply have no cognitive element associated with them. Robinson (1995) argues that a mental state such as startle belongs to the "emotion spectrum" but involves no cognitive dimension. According to Robinson, the popularity of cognitive theories of emotion is due in large part to philosophers' tendency to concentrate on sophisticated, "intellectual" emotions. Once this is avoided, we can appreciate startle for what it is: an emotional state with no cognitive aspect whatsoever.

However, as Robinson recognizes, there is something a little uncomfortable about taking startle to be an *emotional* state. It is not obvious that the folk would categorize startle as an emotion, nor that there is some scientifically based demarcation of the emotions which clearly rules startle in. This is presumably because, whether startle is an emotion or not, it is certainly not a *paradigmatic* emotion. There may well be no deep fact of the matter as to whether it is.[17] Or, it may be a limit case of emotion. Now, when we reflect on *why* startle is non-paradigmatic and potentially a limit case, it seems that its lack of cognitive depth has something to do with it. One view might be that unquestionably emotional states are connected in the right way to a combination of all four types of phenomenology, but certain limit cases might involve only three out of the four. (Plausibly, startle involves conative, proprioceptive, and algedonic elements.) Another view might be that startle exhibits a limit case of cognitive phenomenology, say insofar as it involves some kind of minimal appreciation of potential danger, so that the match between the property of being emotional and the property of involving cognitive phenomenology survives: startle is a limit case of both!

I conclude that the widespread rejection of feeling theories of emotion as obviously inadequate has been premature. By taking a refined view of the phenomenology characteristic of emotional experiences, and of the essential connection between emotional states and the phenomenology, we obtain a theoretically refined and dialectically resourceful feeling theory.

It is noteworthy that NFT manages to protect the feeling theory of emotion from the two most prominent objections to it without positing a sui generis emotional phenomenology. One *could* devise a view that did: the view that E is the emotional state it is (and at all) because E bears R to a primitive emotional phenomenology, or because E bears R to a combination of phenomenologies one of which is irreducibly emotional. In the remainder of this chapter, however, I argue that there is no good case for such a primitive emotional phenomenology. Once defending the feeling theory forces us to appreciate the richness and complexity of cognitive, conative, proprioceptive, and algedonic components in emotional experience, it is hard to make the case that such a further element is needed.

II. The Reducibility of Emotional Phenomenology
5. Is There a Case for Primitive Emotional Phenomenology?

The question of primitive emotional phenomenology can be framed in terms of the kind of triad discussed in the Introduction. Consider:

1) There exists emotional phenomenology.
2) Emotional phenomenology is irreducible to perceptual, algedonic, cognitive, conative, and entertaining phenomenology.
3) Perceptual, algedonic, cognitive, conative, and entertaining phenomenology ultimately exhaust all phenomenology.

In arguing for reductivism about emotional phenomenology, I will be rejecting (2). To defend a primitive emotional phenomenology, in contrast, is to deny (3). Some philosophers have defended such a primitive emotional phenomenology on introspective grounds (Stocker 1996)—emotional experiences just *seem* to them to go beyond the proprioceptive, algedonic, cognitive, and conative.[18] This does not strike me as an unreasonable claim. As I consider an episode of rage, I seem to find in it a quality uncomfortably classified as proprioceptive, algedonic, cognitive, or conative. Still, I cannot report that this impression descends on me with a great force. It is hard to judge whether out of the soup of proprioceptive, algedonic, cognitive, and conative phenomenologies there could not emerge this particular rage-ish quality which I notice. Perhaps the molecular phenomenology of rage is composed of atomic proprioceptive, algedonic, cognitive, and conative phenomenologies in a non-transparent way. It would thus be useful to have some other handle on the phenomenology, to increase confidence in one direction (primitivist) or the other (reductivist).

What are some possible argumentative strategies for a primitive emotional phenomenology? The strategies employed in Chapters 1–3 to argue for primitive cognitive, conative, and entertaining phenomenology seem to me considerably less promising in this case.

Chapter 1 developed a conceivability argument for primitive cognitive phenomenology. The argument relied crucially on a thought-experimental scenario in which a conceivable subject had an explanatory-gap-able mental life despite lacking sensory phenomenology (that is, despite being a sensory zombie). In the present context, a parallel thought-experiment would envisage a subject lacking proprioceptive, algedonic, cognitive, and conative phenomenology who nonetheless leads a gap-able mental life; a proprioceptive, algedonic, cognitive, and conative zombie who nonetheless harbored emotional states. This creature would have no bodily feelings, no pleasure and pain, no conscious thoughts, and no felt motivation of any sort, but for which the distinctive philosophical anxiety would still press. For my part, I find it strictly impossible to form a positive conception of such a creature. Perhaps I could be told the right story to make this subject come alive in my imagination. Until then, this seems to me a closed route to primitive emotional phenomenology.

Chapter 2 marshaled a sequence of contrast cases to isolate a primitive conative phenomenology. These involved pairs of conscious episodes intuitively distinguishable in their overall phenomenology but indistinguishable in their sensory and cognitive phenomenology. In the present context, a parallel argument would have to adduce a pair of conscious episodes E_1 and E_2, such that (i) intuitively, the overall phenomenology of E_1 and E_2 is different, and (ii) intuitively, the proprioceptive, algedonic, cognitive, and conative phenomenology of E_1 and E_2 is the same. Again I find myself unable to think of an appropriate pair. Part of the problem is the sheer complexity of what I am asked to imagine.

Chapter 3 offered an epistemic argument for a primitive phenomenology of entertaining. The argument proceeded centrally by (i) noting that we have distinctively first-person knowledge of our entertainings and (ii) undermining potential reducers of what is thereby known. The upshot was that positing a directly introspectible primitive phenomenology of entertaining is the best explanation of our first-person knowledge of our entertainings. In the present context, the first part of a parallel argument would be straightforward: plausibly, we also have distinctively first-person knowledge of our emotional experiences. However, we also have here a ready-made potential reducer of what is thereby known, namely, the combination of proprioceptive, algedonic, cognitive, and conative phenomenology. Moreover, the hypothesis that we acquire distinctively first-person knowledge of our emotional experiences by directly introspecting that combination is at least in one respect superior to the hypothesis that we do so by directly introspecting a primitive emotional phenomenology: it is more parsimonious. Thus all three argumentative strategies employed in previous chapters seem unpromising when applied to emotional phenomenology.

In the extant literature, the most developed argument for primitive emotional phenomenology is due to Montague (2009). Montague allows that emotional experiences have sensory (including algedonic) and cognitive phenomenology, but insists that in addition they also have a sui generis emotional phenomenology. Her argument for this proceeds as follows.

Suppose I apply for a grant for which only one applicant can be successful. My application is unsuccessful, and I am sad that they gave the grant to someone else. But—good news!—it turns out that the person who got the grant is none other than my best friend and favorite philosopher Jimmy. I am happy they gave it to him. I am happy about this even after learning that we were the only two applicants—though I am still sad that I did not get the grant. Montague's claim is that, when we examine closely the phenomenal intentionality of this episode, we realize that being happy that Jimmy succeeded is irreducible to believing that Jimmy succeeded and/or to desiring that Jimmy succeed. As far as desire is concerned, one can be happy that Jimmy succeeded without feeling any motivational pull toward that state of affairs (which already obtains anyway), hence without properly desiring that Jimmy succeed. As for belief, claims Montague, its content is too coarse-grained to capture that of emotion.

We can appreciate this by noting an asymmetry between belief and emotion. It is well known that belief contexts are opaque, so the following is invalid:

1) I believe (judge) that Jimmy succeeded;
2) Jimmy's success = my failure; therefore,
3) I believe (judge) that I failed.

However, the following appears *valid*:

1) I believe (judge) that Jimmy succeeded;
2) I am fully aware that Jimmy's success = my failure; therefore,
3) I believe (judge) that I failed.

Accordingly, I can perfectly rationally believe that Jimmy succeeded while disbelieving that I failed, but only if I am unaware that Jimmy's success just is my failure. We may signal this by saying that belief contexts are opaque but not *hyper*opaque. Emotion contexts, by contrast, are not only opaque but also hyperopaque. To be sure, the following is invalid:

1) I am happy that Jimmy succeeded;
2) Jimmy's success = my failure; therefore,
3) I am happy that I failed.

But so is the following:

1) I am happy that Jimmy succeeded;
2) I am fully aware that Jimmy's success = my failure; therefore,
3) I am happy that I failed.

That is, full awareness of the identity does not void the rationality of being happy about Jimmy's success while sad about my failure. Thus happiness is irreducible to belief or judgment: the former is hyperopaque, the latter merely opaque.

I am going to present two responses to this argument. The first has to do with a hidden conative component in happiness, different from desire; the second with a distinction regarding the proper objects of happiness. The two responses are not incompatible, each has something to it, but the second may go more to the heart of the matter.

First, it is true that being happy or sad about events that have already occurred (such as the grant application outcome) does not involve desire. We generally do not have desires about the past, at least not when we believe it is unalterable. Hence being happy about Jimmy's success does not involve desiring it. However, we may nonetheless have *wishes* regarding the unalterable, including the past. Thus my sadness about my failure to get the grant very much appears to imply that I wish I had gotten it. Arguably, my happiness about Jimmy's success at getting the grant likewise involves the wish that he had gotten it. Such fulfilled wishes (wishes for what had in fact taken place) are much harder to notice than frustrated wishes (wishes about what had not taken place), but arguably they are there all the same. If so, happiness does involve a conative phenomenal element, though not that of desire.

Secondly, note that we can be happy about two sorts of things: facts and events. I can be happy about (the fact that) I strolled in the park or I can be happy about the (event of) my stroll in the park. Thus happiness takes both facts and events as intentional objects.[19] It is natural to use the locution "happy *that*" for the former and "happy *about*" for the latter: "I am happy that I strolled in the park" reports fact-happiness, "I am happy about my stroll in the park" reports event-happiness.

This is important, because it is highly plausible that facts and events individuate very differently (Vendler 1967, Bennett 1988). For example, the fact that I strolled in the park and the fact that I strolled in the park *slowly* are two different facts: the latter is a much more specific, more determinate fact, incorporating as it does a slowness constituent. By contrast, (the event of) my stroll in the park and (the event of) my *slow* stroll in the park are one and the same: it is the same stroll, just more fully described in one case.

This matters for the evaluation of such inferences as used above to argue for emotional irreducibility. Consider again the third inference: 1) I am happy that Jimmy succeeded; 2) Jimmy's success = my failure; therefore, 3) I am happy that I failed. The first premise uses "happy that" talk, which suggests that what is at stake is fact-happiness rather than event-happiness. Consistency would require us, then, to interpret Premise 2 as concerned with facts rather than events. But given the fine-grained individuation of facts, the fact that Jimmy succeeded is *not identical* to the fact that I failed (not any more than the fact that I strolled in the park is identical to the fact that I strolled in the park slowly). If so, Premise 2 is simply false. This provides us with a diagnosis of why the conclusion is false that does not assume the inference itself is invalid. The inference itself is perfectly valid but leads to a false conclusion due to a false premise. (The same diagnosis applies to the fourth inference, whose second premise is "I am fully aware that Jimmy's success = my failure." Since "fully aware" is a success verb, this premise cannot be true when interpreted as concerned with facts.)

To make the case that these inferences are indeed invalid, then, Montague must construe the second premises as concerned with events. The event of Jimmy's success at getting the grant is indeed identical to the event of my failure to get the grant. But this forces us to interpret the rest of the reasoning as concerning events. The argument now looks a tad different:

1) I am happy about the event of Jimmy's success at getting the grant;
2) Jimmy's success at getting the grant = my failure to get the grant; therefore,
3) I am happy about the event of my failing to get the grant.

This is indeed invalid, and demonstrates the opacity of emotion contexts. What about their alleged hyperopacity? Consider:

1) I am happy about the event of Jimmy's success at getting the grant;
2) I am fully aware that Jimmy's success at getting the grant = my failure to get the grant; therefore,
3) I am happy about the event of my failing to get the grant.

Here the intuition of perfect rationality is no longer firm. It is rational for me to be *ambivalent* about the relevant event: I can be happy about one *aspect* of it and sad about another, with the relevant *event-aspects* constituting different *facts*. But to be at once happy and sad about the event itself, as a whole, could be rational only if I do not fully grasp that this is one and the same event. But then Premise 2 is no longer true: I am not fully aware that Jimmy's success *is* my failure. I must be somehow confused about that, or have a confused or indistinct awareness of that. Thus it is far from clear that emotion contexts are hyperopaque.

In summary, the inferences exploited in Montague's argument for primitive emotional phenomenology are ambiguous as between fact-happiness and event-happiness. Interpreted consistently as concerning fact-happiness, they support neither the opacity nor the hyperopacity of emotion contexts, as they involve a false premise. Interpreted consistently as concerning event-happiness, they support the opacity of emotion contexts but not their hyperopacity.

I conclude that there is at yet no case for an irreducible emotional phenomenology. On the one hand, the argumentative strategies deployed in Chapters 1–3 seem unpromising in this area. At the same time, the strongest argument in the extant literature faces serious difficulties.

6. Emotional Phenomenology and Phenomenal Attitudinal Features

In Chapters 1–3 I argued for three types of primitive nonsensory phenomenology. I also suggested what the core phenomenal feature characteristic of each is. Cognitive phenomenology is characterized by the phenomenal attitudinal feature of presenting-as-true; conative phenomenology by the phenomenal attitudinal feature of presenting-as-good$_G$; entertaining phenomenology by that of mere-presenting. If emotional experience could be shown to exhibit a fourth attitudinal phenomenal feature, on a par with the above three and irreducible to them, that would create a presumption in favor of a primitive emotional phenomenology.

One dimension or facet of reality often cited in conjunction with the true and the good is *the beautiful*. An immediate suggestion may therefore be that emotional phenomenology is a sui generis phenomenal directedness at the beautiful. Just as judging that there is still one cookie left presents-as-true that there is still one cookie left, and wanting there to be one cookie left presents-as-good there being one left, so being happy about there still being one cookie left presents-as-beautiful that there is still one cookie left. To accommodate the existence of negative emotions, the view might refer to aesthetic value in general, covering both the beautiful and the ugly. The idea is that the distinctive feel of presenting-as-beautiful something is characteristic of all positive emotional experiences, while negative emotional experiences (such as being disappointed that there is still one cookie left) are characterized by the feel of presenting-as-ugly.

The immediate problem with this suggestion is that it does not resonate phenomenologically in any way. (I am hoping this sentiment is shared by the reader.) In the standard sense of "beautiful," it simply sounds false that happiness, gladness, excitement, and so on present something as beautiful. One can be glad that one paid this month's bill without experiencing the paying of the bill as beautiful in any recognizable sense. The only way the suggestion could be workable at all is if it employed a sufficiently rarefied notion of beauty. However, it is not at all clear what this notion might be like, or what illumination is gained by attaching the term "beauty" to it.

There may yet be some value V, such that emotional experiences are characterized by presenting-as-V their intentional objects. In the remainder of this section, I consider two possible stories about what V might be. I am ambivalent about both: they seem reasonably plausible, but face certain difficulties as well. In the absence of more decisive considerations in their favor, I am tempted to provisionally adopt the more parsimonious option of reductivism about emotional phenomenology.

6.1. Emotion and Presenting-as-Important

One *kind* of suggestion posits a Fourth Great Value alongside the true, the good, and the beautiful, and claims that this fourth value is the "formal object" of emotional experience. The Christian French philosopher René Le Senne (1961) maintained that in addition to truth, goodness, and beauty, there is also *love*, which is the formal object of *faith* (specifically religious faith). A similar view could be fashioned for emotional phenomenology instead of faith phenomenology. Naturally, this approach could work only if a suitable substantive fourth value could be identified.[20] Leaving matters schematic, by not specifying what the fourth value might be, would not do: the suggestion would then amount to matching a sui generis attitudinal feature to a sui generis emotional phenomenology—not a particularly illuminating package. The resulting thesis is coherent, but virtually impossible to evaluate.

One suggestion for the fourth great value, beside the true, the good, and the beautiful, is *the important*. The idea is that while we can believe and desire many things, only some of them are important, and those are the ones we emote about. On this view, when I am angry about the Trayvon Martin affair, my experience involves the judgment that the affair took place, and the wish that it had not, but in addition also a sui generis component proprietary of anger. The judgment component presents-as-true that the affair took place, and the wish component presents-as-bad that it did, but the sui generis emotional component presents-as-important the affair's occurrence.

The view is phenomenologically, psychologically, and theoretically appealing. Phenomenologically, it resonates much more than the presents-as-beautiful suggestion. In harboring certain judgments and wishes about the Trayvon Martin affair, I am representing as true and good/bad various aspects of the affair. But in *getting angry* about it I also represent the affair as "a big deal," as something worth getting agitated over. It is natural to say, moreover, that there is a kind of intensity emotional experiences vary along, depending on how committed they are to the importance of what they present—the angrier I get, the more important the affair is experienced to be.

Psychologically, it certainly seems true that emotions often function to draw our attention to the salient aspects of a circumstance. It might therefore be claimed that they do so in virtue of involving a proprietary emotional phenomenology of directedness at the important. There is, in any case, a clear *need* for a mechanism dedicated to the representation of importance, since many things can be believed and wanted regardless of their importance, and these should be ranked somehow for the system to have cognitive and conative priorities. To be sure, one might simply *judge* that something is important. But then one might also judge that something is good. Yet the conative domain is needed for a *dedicated* representation of the good. Accordingly, when one judges that *x* is good, as opposed to wanting *x*, one's judgment only presents-as-true that *x* is good, as opposed to presenting-as-good *x*. Likewise, when one judges that *x* is important, as opposed to being happy about *x*, one's judgment only presents-as-true that *x* is important, as opposed to presenting-as-important *x*. Only the latter is a *dedicated* representation of the important. We may speculate that this is what emotion is *for*—distinguishing the importantly true from the unimportantly true and the importantly from unimportantly good.

Theoretically, the suggestion is appealing in applying uniformly to positive and negative emotions. Both present their objects as worth getting agitated over. This identifies a substantive commonality shared by positive and negative emotional experiences (which may account for why emotions seem pretheoretically to form a natural kind).[21]

It might be objected that many trifle events seem capable of rendering us disproportionately agitated. Our partner's polite smile to a good-looking neighbor can send us into intense flights of jealousy, our child's completely age-appropriate accomplishment can unleash an insensible surge of pride, and so on. To that extent, the tie between emotion and importance could be claimed to be much more tenuous than here suggested. However, while it is true that we can get disproportionately emotional about certain things, it is also true that many of our judgments are false, and many of our desires are for what is in fact bad (even bad *for us*). It remains that the *appropriateness conditions* of emotional experiences—what makes them appropriate to undergo or not undergo—make reference to the important. In the same sense in which we *ought* the have beliefs about what is true and desires about what is good, we also *ought* to have emotions about what is important. Failing to is just emotional misrepresentation. (This is why we consider it *criticizable* to undergo certain emotional experiences when we deem insignificant the matters emoted about.)

In fact, these considerations pave the way to an abductive inference for the importance view. If the appropriateness conditions of emotions refer to importance, then the following principle holds: it is appropriate to emote about *x* iff (and insofar as) *x* is important. Call this principle the Emotion-Important Connection (EIC). Why is EIC true? Something must explain this connection between emoted and important. Plausibly, what explains it is an internal connection between emoting and presenting-as-important: M is an emotional state iff M presents-as-important some *x*. Clearly, if this is true, then it would stand to reason that EIC should hold. Just as it is fitting to believe only the true *because* it is the nature of belief to present-as-true its content, and it is fitting to desire only the good *because* desire essentially presents-as-good its object, so it is fitting to emote only about the important *because* emotion essentially presents-as-important its object.

The notion that emotional experience is characterized by irreducible presenting-as-important raises worries about extensional adequacy. It is natural, for example, to take boredom as at least a borderline case of emotional experience. Yet boredom clearly does not present-as-important its object.[22]

There is a deeper problem, however, with the importance view: almost everything said above in its favor can be said, perhaps even more plausibly, with respect to *attention*. I have in mind here not only *perceptual* attention, as when we visually attend to the important part of a painting, but also purely *intellectual* attention, as when we attend to the key issue in a philosophical problem. Psychologically, it is very natural to think that attention is our dedicated mechanism for representing what is important. And phenomenologically, attention feels very much geared to what matters, what merits focusing on.

This raises the possibility that the connection between emoted and important is not basic, but derives from a deeper connection between attention and importance. The idea is that EIC is not *constitutive* but *contingent*. It can be factorized into two separate connections: (i) a constitutive connection between attention and importance, and (ii) a contingent connection between emotion and attention. On this model, the mechanical setup of the mind is such that our emotions tend to *draw* our attention to matters of potential importance. The attention itself is constitutively a representation of the important; the emotions are just a tool for guiding this kind of representation. Plausibly, they are not the only tool—thought and reasoning can be used as well. They are just a useful tool among others. This model offers us an alternative explanation of EIC: it is appropriate to emote about the important because emotions guide attention and it is appropriate to attend to the important. In this explanation, emotion's connection to the important is significant but contingent rather than essential.

The following consideration supports this alternative explanation. If we imagine taking away the presentation of importance from an act of attending (or an attentive act), the attention itself seems to disappear. There is nothing left over in attention once we have removed the element of importance-representation from it. By contrast, if we imagine taking away the presentation of importance from an emotional experience, much remains in our imagination: namely, the cognitive, conative, proprioceptive, and algedonic aspects of emotional phenomenology. Thus importance-representation goes to the essence of attention much more than emotion.

6.2. *Emotion and Presenting-as-Good$_{specific}$*

It is often remarked that emotions are inherently evaluative. Happiness about *x* casts it as good, sadness about *x* casts it as bad. More generally, positive emotions embody positive evaluations, negative ones negative evaluations. The presently defended reductivism about emotional phenomenology has a straightforward account of this: emotional phenomenology incorporates a conative element characterized by the attitudinal feature of presenting-as-good$_G$. However, a primitivist might argue that emotional experiences present-as-good in a sui generis way. We already noted that one can *judge* that x is good, but *wanting* x casts x as good in a sui generis way. There might be a third way of casting something as good, special to emotional experience. And this might undergird a primitivist account of emotional phenomenology—as long as the primitivist can identify a concrete attitudinal difference between conative evaluation and emotional evaluation.

According to Deonna and Teroni (2012 ch.7), the evaluativeness of emotions is not an aspect of their content but of the attitude they employ.[23] To that extent, Deonna and Teroni's account fits squarely within the attitudinal framework here explored. For Deonna and Teroni, what is special about emotions is that their attitudinal evaluation is inherently tied up with the bodily changes so highlighted by the James-Lange theory. Indeed, the bodily sensation itself does the evaluating.[24] We may put this by saying that emotions are somatically (or viscerally) encoded evaluations. A primitivist about emotional phenomenology could use Deonna and Teroni's account to suggest that the attitudinal phenomenal feature characteristic of emotional experiences is that of *somatically-presenting-as-good$_G$*. This is the property common and peculiar to all emotional experiences (in virtue of which they form a natural kind). Clearly, this feature is irreducible to mere-presenting, presenting-as-true, and *non*somatically-presenting-as-good$_G$.

A different categorical attitudinal difference between emotion and the will is proposed by Brentano (1907 §21). For Brentano, being happy that p and desiring that p (or being happy about x and wanting x) both frame their object as good. Only the latter, however, is subject to a certain rationality constraint. Suppose that, pleasantly full and short on cash, I *have* to choose between the chocolate cake and the cheesecake for dessert. In the circumstances, then, my having the chocolate cake for dessert and my having the cheesecake for dessert are incompatible. Only one can come to be. Here, I can rationally be *happy with* both the chocolate cake and the cheesecake. But I cannot rationally *want* both the chocolate cake and the cheesecake. More generally, having positive emotions toward incompatibles is rational, but the will has to make an unambiguous determination, presumably so it may *pursue* one of the options.[25] Thus conative states are, but emotional states are not, subject to the following rationality constraint: S rationally wants x in circumstance C only if for any y in C, if y is incompatible with x, then S prefers x to y (likewise: S rationally desires that p in C only if for any q in C, if q is incompatible with p, then S prefers that p over that q). One way to put this is say that positive emotions frame their objects as *prima facie* good (or good$_{PF}$), whereas states of the will frame theirs as *ultima facie* good (or good$_{UF}$).[26] A primitivist about emotion might use this Brentanian idea to suggest that the attitudinal phenomenal feature characteristic of emotional experiences is that of *presenting-as-good$_{PF}$* (or More generally *presenting-as-valueable$_{PP}$* to cover negative emotions as well). This is the property common and peculiar to all emotional experiences (in virtue of which they form a natural kind). Clearly, this feature is irreducible to mere-presenting, presenting-as-true, and presenting-as-good$_{UF}$.

There is something plausible about both Deonna and Teroni's view and Brentano's. Both face certain difficulties, however. Deonna and Teroni's treats bodily changes as the *vehicles* that encode emotional evaluations. Being afraid of a dog, they tell us, is a matter of being in a bodily state that is evaluatively directed at the dog. But as we saw in §2, the somatic constituent of emotional phenomenology is not the bodily states and changes themselves, but the *proprioceptive perception of* those bodily states and changes. The bodily changes are thus not vehicular properties of an emotional experience, they are aspects of its overall content. They are intentional objects internal to the subject's body, which may mislead us to think of them as mere sensations, or vehicles—but this would be an illusion. To that extent, bodily changes are not part of what does the directing of emotions, but of what emotions are directed at; not part of what encodes emotional content, but part of what is encoded. Meanwhile, Brentano's view is vulnerable to certain charges of extensional inadequacy. For it is commonly thought that we can have conflicting desires, even when we are aware of the conflict; yet desire is paradigmatically conative, not emotional. Brentano might retort that talk of rationally held conflicting desires is misguided, or perhaps more plausibly that desire is not as paradigmatically conative as is widely thought (the real paradigm being decision). All these moves, however, entrain their own difficulties and represent liabilities of the view.

In any event, the dialectical implications of the Deonna/Teroni-inspired and Brentano-inspired primitivisms for the organizing question of this book are not straightforward. This is the question of how many second-layer phenomenal primitives we ought to posit. Even if there are several kinds of presenting-as-good, presumably there are not only phenomenal differences among them but also some phenomenal commonality, insofar as all are presentings-as-good. It would then be natural to hold that experiences exhibiting presenting-as-good form a second-layer phenomenal category on a par with experiences exhibiting presenting-as-true and experiences exhibiting mere-presenting. Emotion would be a *species* of this category, hence at most a *third*-layer phenomenal primitive. This may well be Brentano's view: he considers that emotion and the will belong to a single "fundamental class" of mental phenomena (Brentano 1874 II ch.8); this class has no good name in ordinary language, he tells us (1874: 199), but may be labeled "interest."[27] Emotion, characterized by presenting-as-good$_{PP}$ and will, characterized by presenting-as-good$_{UP}$ are two subclasses of interest. On the emerging picture, in addition to perceptual and algedonic phenomenology, at the second layer of phenomenal determinables there is a cognitive phenomenology of presenting-as-true, an entertaining phenomenology of mere-presenting, and an interest-phenomenology of presenting-as-good; the last comes in two varieties, conative and emotional, which are primitive third-layer phenomenologies. The number of *second*-layer phenomenal primitives is unaffected, in this picture—only the taxonomy is.

Recall, in any case, that the reductivist about emotional phenomenology has her own readily available account of the evaluative character of emotions—it is simply inherited from the conative component of emotional experiences. From the reductivist's point of view, the difference between conative and emotional experience is simply this: conative experiences present-as-good *primitively*, or *in and of themselves*, whereas emotional experiences present-as-good *derivatively*, or *by courtesy* (of conative states, that is). Both are different from judgments about the good, which do not present-as-good anything, but merely present-as-true that something is good.

Conclusion

In this chapter, I have argued for two important claims. The first is that emotional phenomena are essentially phenomenal, in that their identity and existence conditions are ultimately given by reference to emotional phenomenology. The second is that emotional phenomenology is in all likelihood reducible to a combination of proprioceptive, algedonic, cognitive, and conative phenomenology; or more cautiously, that there is as yet no compelling case for a primitive emotional phenomenology. This leaves us, then, with five second-layer phenomenal primitives.[28]

5

Moral Phenomenology

In recent metaethics, there has been a growing interest in *moral phenomenology*, the subjective feeling of our morally relevant mental states (Horgan and Timmons 2008, Kriegel 2008). Part of the problem in this area is that it is far from clear what those mental states *are*. Accordingly, I will first offer an account of the nature of morally relevant states (Part I), then address the question of their phenomenal character (Part II). I will argue that moral phenomenology does not constitute a new second-layer phenomenal primitive, instead reducing to cognitive and emotional phenomenology.

Before starting, a terminological point. The mental states that embody our moral commitments are commonly referred to in the metaethical literature as "moral judgments." Use of this term is not intended, however, to commit to a substantive view of moral commitments as cognitive. (This is why noncognitivism is one of the views about moral judgment!) Since in this book the term "judgment" *is* used with this substantive connotation, I will simply refer to the relevant mental states as moral *commitments*. This does raise a new problem, insofar as "commitment" connotes a merely dispositional state, the kind that would not exhibit any phenomenology. Still, as we have seen in previous chapters mental dispositions are best understood in terms of their manifestations in occurrent conscious states. The question of moral phenomenology, then, can be understood as a question about the phenomenology of conscious manifestations of moral commitments.

I. The Nature of Moral Commitment
1. "The Moral Problem"

In the opening chapter of his book *The Moral Problem*, Michael Smith (1994) articulates the organizing problem of contemporary metaethics, as he sees it, in terms of a triad of highly plausible but hard to reconcile theses. Smith's own triad is not formally inconsistent, but is readily adapted into one that is:

1) Cognitivism: Moral commitments purport to be about objective matters of fact.
2) Internalism: Moral commitments are inherently motivational.

3) Humean Psychology: Mental states, including moral commitments, cannot both have objective purport and be inherently motivational.

Smith calls his triad "the moral problem," a term I will use for my own triad instead.[1]

Smith does not quite offer a positive argument for the cognitivist thesis in his triad, but only defends it against counter-arguments.[2] Presumably, this is because he takes cognitivism to be antecedently plausible. It is an interesting question, however, what *makes* it antecedently plausible. One answer is that it is simply *intuitive* that moral commitments have objective purport. Another answer, which seems to go deeper, is that the objective purport of moral commitments is *phenomenologically* manifest, in that what it is like for a subject to have (a conscious manifestation of) a moral commitment often involves a feeling as of homing in on an objective matter of fact. The advantage of appealing to phenomenology rather than intuition here is that an objectivistic phenomenology would explain *why* we have the intuition, whereas the intuition would not explain any phenomenology. So appeal to phenomenology involves added explanatory depth.

To be sure, positive arguments for cognitivism, perhaps of a more theoretical bent, may be available as well. Probably the best known rests on the Frege-Geach Problem. The Problem is that if moral commitments were *not* cognitive states, they could not play the kind of inferential role in reasoning and deliberation—which includes inferential interaction with cognitive states—that they appear to (Geach 1960).[3] Various more or less technical responses to this argument are available (see Gibbard 2003 for a particularly ingenious one), but in any case the deep source of plausibility of cognitivism does not seem to be such theoretically sophisticated considerations. Cognitivism just *seems* right, and the source of this seeming, I contend, is something like the phenomenology of moral commitment.

Smith (1994 ch.3) does offer a positive argument for the internalist thesis in his triad. The argument has been widely discussed, and I will only sketch it in the barest outlines here. Smith observes that, as a matter of contingent fact, moral commitments to φ-ing and motivations to φ are reliably compresent in the good and strong-willed person. This fact requires explanation. The most straightforward explanation is that there is an "internal," constitutive connection between moral commitment and motivation: moral commitments are "practical," in the sense that they are inherently motivating. (It should be recalled that the term "internalism," as originally introduced by Falk [1945] and Frankena [1958], was intended to intimate an "internal connection" between moral commitment and motivation.) The alternative explanation would have to be that there is a merely "external," causal connection between the two, due to the fact that the good and strong-willed person tends to have a psychologically real desire to do whatever it turns out she ought to do. This alternative explanation is implausible, according to Smith, because it is implausible to ascribe such a desire to all good and strong-willed persons (not because it is more plausible to ascribe to them the opposite desire, but because it is more plausible to ascribe to them no relevant desire). This is effectively an argument from inference to the best explanation: the explanandum is the reliable compresence of moral commitment and corresponding moral motivation in the right kind of agent, and the best explanans is that moral commitments are inherently motivating, that is, that there is a constitutive connection between moral commitment and moral motivation.

Unfortunately, the objective purport of moral commitments and their inherently motivational nature are uncomfortable bedfellows.[4] The tension between them can be brought out through what Smith calls "Humean Psychology." This is the traditional idea that the mind divides into two independent departments—reason and the will, the cognitive and the conative, or what have you—and mental states belong to either one or the other but not both. The problem is that objective purport characterizes one type of mental state, the cognitive one, whereas motivational role characterizes the other, conative type. The core of Humean Psychology is the claim that there are no unitary mental states which boast both inherent motivational force and objective purport, states both cognitive and conative. Such states are sometimes referred to as "besires"—half belief, half desire—and Smith argues that the notion of besire is incoherent.

What is the rationale for Humean Psychology and its ban on besires? Commentators have focused on Smith's argument from "direction of fit," but this focus strikes me as misguided. The direction-of-fit argument is that mental states cannot involve both the belief attitude and the desire attitude toward the same content, because it is a conceptual truth that when the state of affairs making up the state's content goes out of existence, the desire attitude tends to persist whereas the belief attitude tends to desist. The problem with this argument is that philosophers sympathetic to besires typically do not hold that moral commitments involve the belief attitude and the desire attitude *toward the same content*. Rather, they typically hold that a moral commitment to φ-ing involves a belief attitude toward the content <I ought to φ> and a desire attitude toward the content <I φ>. Thus their view is unthreatened by the argument from direction of fit. What threatens it is rather Smith's (subsidiary) argument from *modal separability*: the belief that one ought to φ and the desire to φ are modally separable in that each could exist in the other's absence, which means that they do not make up a *unitary* mental state. And it is precisely the point of Humean Psychology that beliefs and desires are distinct states rather than unitary ones. What exactly hangs on the unitariness of moral commitments is not entirely clear from Smith's discussion, but the following is a natural thought. Suppose moral commitment to φ-ing consisted in believing that one ought to φ and desiring to φ. The question would then arise of whether moral commitments motivate in virtue of their desire component or their belief component. The answer is clearly that they motivate, in the first instance, in virtue of their desire component. But if they motivate purely in virtue of their desire component, and their belief component is only contingently conjoined to their desire component, then their belief component is inessential to their motivational force. The cognitive representation of the (objective) moral facts is entirely severed from motivation: one does not φ *because* one (re)cognizes that one ought to φ.[5] This sort of worry would not arise if the belief and desire components were unitary, at least in the sense that the desire component could not exist without the belief component (such that the desire were not "modally separable" from the belief). For then the belief component would inherit the motivational efficacy of the desire component in virtue of being a necessary precondition of it: without the belief component, there would be no desire component, and without the desire component, there would be no motivation.

The ban on besires is thus *not* a ban on any propositional attitude with a cognitive component and a conative component that can be denoted with a simple term. Being disappointed that p involves believing that p and desiring that q (where $q = \sim p$), but disappointment is not a besire. For its components are modally separable, which casts it as a mere sum of two elements rather than an organic whole. Here the distinction between "mere sum" and "organic whole" can be cast in terms of Simons' (1987) mereological distinction between sums and complexes. Intuitively, the idea is that complexes involve an essential interconnection among the elements, whereas a sum is but the mere compresence of those elements. Consider the parts of an Ikea table lying about in a box, pre-assemblage, and the same parts put together so as to form a functional desk. The former is a mere sum of the parts, the latter a complex. Accordingly, it is possible to destroy the desk without destroying any of its parts, namely by destroying the interconnection among them; but the sum it is possible to destroy only by destroying one of the parts. More generally: a collection C of parts $P_1, \ldots, P_n$ is a sum iff the only way to destroy C is to destroy a P_i; C is a complex iff it is possible to destroy C *without* destroying any P_i. To say that a besire is a *complex* of belief and desire is thus to say that it involves an essential connection between its belief and desire components, so that it is possible to destroy the besire without destroying either component. By contrast, disappointment is a mere sum of belief and desire—it is impossible to destroy the disappointment state without destroying either.

A final clarification concerns the claim that belief is not "inherently motivating." To say this is not yet to say that beliefs are motivationally impotent or epiphenomenal. Rather, it is to say that there is only an "external," contingent connection between belief and motivation, as opposed to the "internal," necessary connection exhibited by decision, desire, and other conative states. That the connection of belief to motivation lies in-between the two extremes of epiphenomenalism and internal/necessary connection seems to be precisely the prima facie plausible position on the motivational character of belief.

In summary, all three theses comprising the moral problem have much to recommend them. Yet they cannot all be true. Arguably, this is indeed the organizing problem of contemporary metaethics, at least since Mackie's (1977) groundbreaking *Ethics: Inventing Right and Wrong*, which explicitly pitted these theses, or ones very like them, against each other. Contending with all the dialectical pressures in this area has led twenty-first-century moral psychology to a number of positions offering rather convoluted portraits of moral commitment. Copp's (2002) "realist expressivism," Kalderon's (2005) "hermeneutic moral fictionalism," Horgan and Timmons' (2006) "cognitivist expressivism," Ridge's (2006) "ecumenical expressivism," and Campbell's (2007) "robust hybrid view" are prominent examples; there are others. The merits and demerits of such views deserve separate discussion. In the next section, I propose that a neat, unconvoluted portrait of moral commitment is afforded by recent developments in the philosophy of action, backed by advances in cognitive-scientific models of cognitive architecture.

2. Dual-Process Architecture, the Alief/Belief Distinction, and Moral Commitment

In a series of publications, Tamar Gendler (2008a, 2008b) has argued for a distinction between belief and what she calls "alief." Gendler's argument for the distinction is a serviceability argument: the distinction is indispensable for explaining a whole slew of phenomena, typically involving "belief-behavior mismatch." After embedding Gendler's distinction in a dual-process model of cognitive architecture (§2.1), and applying it to moral mentation (§2.2), I will argue that the distinction affords an elegant way to (dis)solve the apparent tension between the inherently motivational role of moral commitments and their manifestly objectivistic phenomenology (§2.3). More specifically, I will argue that moral commitments come in two varieties, moral aliefs and moral beliefs, and it is only (conscious manifestations of) the former that are inherently motivating and only (conscious manifestations of) the latter that have an objectivistic phenomenology.

2.1. Dual-Process Architecture and the Alief/Belief Distinction

There is a long philosophical tradition of theorizing the operation of the faculty of thought in the image of logic: thought is taken to be guided by deductive and inductive logic, such that, at least in the well-functioning thinker, causal connections between mental states somehow follow logical connections (deductive or inductive) between these states' contents. There is also, however, a more recessive strand in philosophical theorizing about thought, dating back at least to Hume, that offers an alternative model: far from following logical relations, causal connections among thoughts are seen as determined by certain *laws of association* among their contents. Hume himself offered three such laws—resemblance, contiguity, and causality—but his followers among nineteenth-century British associationists, from Hartley to Lewes, refined and developed these laws more systematically. Thereafter emerged a debate between "rationalist psychology" and "associationist psychology" as to which model captures better the actual operation of thought (this served as precursor to the modern-day debate between "classical" and "connectionist" architecture).

So which is it: does thought operate along rationalist or associationist lines? Here is an interesting answer: Both! There are really two complementary faculties operative in us, one conforming to the rationalist model and one to the associationist model. A classical statement of this two-system approach is offered by Sloman (1996: 3):

> One system is associative because its computations reflect similarity structure and relations of temporal contiguity. The other is "rule based" because it operates on symbolic structures that have logical content and variables and because its computations have the properties that are normally assigned to rules. These systems serve complementary functions and can simultaneously generate different solutions to a reasoning problem.

As it turns out, this dual-process architecture is quite common in the cognitive system: dual-process models have been offered, and have gained much traction, for memory (Barrett et al. 2004), learning (Sun et al. 2005), and decision-making (Kahneman 2003, 2011).[6] If this is such a general architectural feature of the human mind, it stands to reason that it might characterize the faculty of thought as well. And indeed Sloman and others have offered wide-ranging empirical evidence suggesting that it does.

Wherever there is a duality of mental *processes*, there is likely also a duality of *products*. Thus the associationist system likely produces one mental state, the rationalist system another.[7] No such distinction has been drawn in the cognitive-scientific literature, but I contend that Gendler's alief and belief are well-suited to play the theoretical roles of "product of the associationist system" and "product of the rationalist system" (respectively).[8] Gendler's distinction can be appreciated either through examples or through a more theoretically informed elucidation of the notion of alief.

Gendler herself offers myriad examples; here is a particularly simple one: unless one is particularly reflective regarding such matters, when one sees a sign exclaiming "glasses: $9.99," one tends to form the belief that the glasses cost $10 but the alief that they cost $9. When one subsequently hurries to buy the glasses, even though one is in need of none, it is typically one's alief that guides one's actions.

Consider another example. Every day S bikes to her office. Today, however, they are predicting rain. Hearing this, S decides to take the car. After eating breakfast, brushing her teeth, replying to a couple of emails, and taking her notes, S goes out and assertively heads toward the bike shed in the yard, never for a moment stopping to think that the car is parked on the street. It is not plausible to say that S believes the car is in the shed, nor that S believes she should bike to campus. No: S believes she should take the car, and believes it is not in the shed. Her belief mismatches her behavior—which frustrates causal explanation of the latter by the former. What causally explains S's behavior is that she *alieves* she should bike to campus. This alief has been formed through years of pleasant routine associating mornings, sheds, bikes, and so on. Arguably it causally explains S's shed-bike-retrieval behavior *most* mornings (even on days S's alief and belief converge), but is appreciated to do so thanks to the occasional belief-behavior mismatch.

As for the more theoretical characterization of alief, this can be offered either through specification of alief's *explanatory role* in the theory of action or through a more substantive characterization of the likely *occupant* of said role. The *role* appears to be this: an alief is a mental state whose occurrence explains (perhaps causally) our behavior in cases where our behavior does not match our beliefs, but may be operative when our behavior matches our beliefs as well. What exactly *occupies* this explanatory role is something Gendler is somewhat tentative about and offers only a "provisional" characterization of: she proposes that an alief is a mental state whose content consists in a cluster of representational, affective, and motivational components "associatively linked" (that is, tending to co-occur). Thus, the full content of one's alief about the glasses might be something like <$9 for glasses. Exciting! Get them!>. This has three components: the first (<$9 for glasses>) is representational; the second (<Exciting!>) is affective; the third (<Get them!>) motivational.

❧❧

The centerpiece of Gendler's case for the alief/belief distinction is simply the observation that the distinction is indispensable for explaining a host of behaviors otherwise utterly perplexing. The glass-purchase and bike-retrieval behaviors are cases in point, but Gendler (2008a, 2008b) offers a wide and varied range of cases that call for a unified explanation in terms of causally operative aliefs. Call this the *serviceability argument* for alief.

In addition to the serviceability argument, Gendler also offers a principled argument that aliefs are irreducible to beliefs. The argument is that alief is hyperopaque whereas belief is not. As we saw in Chapter 4, belief is not *hyperopaque*, in that the following is perfectly valid:

1) S believes that a is F;
2) S is fully aware that $a = b$; therefore,
3) S believes that b is F.

Thus, one *can* validly reason as follows:

1) Jimmy believes that the glasses cost $10;
2) Jimmy is fully aware that the glasses are the most discounted item in the store; therefore,
3) Jimmy believes that the most discounted item in the store costs $10.

By contrast, alief *is* hyperopaque. As we will see momentarily, aliefs are the products of automatic processes insulated from top-down penetration. Because of this, a person's explicit awareness of the coreferentiality of referring expressions/concepts does not affect her aliefs' intentional content. Accordingly, one cannot validly reason thus:

1) Jimmy alieves that the glasses cost $9;
2) Jimmy is fully aware that the glasses are the most discounted item in the store; therefore,
3) Jimmy alieves that the most discounted item in the store costs $9.

More generally, the following is invalid:

1) S alieves that a is F;
2) S is explicitly aware that $a = b$; therefore,
3) S alieves that b is F.

This asymmetry in inferential licensing (if you will) precludes the reduction of alief to belief. Call this the *argument from hyperopacity*.

The case for alief rests centrally on the arguments from serviceability and hyperopacity. But another attractive feature of alief, as a posit in the theory of reasoning, concerns explanatory unity. Given the prevalence of dual-process models in cognitive science, a model positing a duality of causally operative mechanisms in the domain of reasoning—a belief-producing mechanism and an alief-producing mechanism—integrates smoothly into a satisfyingly unified account of human cognition and action. Indeed, it is natural to hypothesize that the alief-producing mechanism is one and the same as Sloman's associationist system and the belief-producing mechanism one and the same as his rationalist ("rule-based") system.

Understanding the alief/belief distinction in the context of dual-process/two-system models in cognitive science also helps us claim certain important differences between the two more confidently. As noted in Chapter 3, in such models the two processes or systems are typically divided into a Low Road and a High Road. The low-road system is typically fast, efficient, automatic, subpersonal, domain-specific, guides on-the-fly action, inflexible, and evades monitoring and control. The high-road system is the converse: slow, inefficient, personal, flexible, wide-ranged, consciously and explicitly controllable and manipulable, and linked to action only indirectly. We can expect the same differences to apply to the alief- and belief-producing mechanisms. An *alief* would be produced by processes that are typically automatized, relatively uncontrollable, architecturally connected to motor output, and inaccessible to consciousness. A *belief* would be produced by more deliberate and controllable processes that have a more indirect impact on action but are often conscious.[9]

Much more can be said about the notion of alief and the distinction between alief and belief. My hope is that the present discussion has given the notion of alief sufficient texture to proceed to the main mandate of this section: the application of the alief/belief distinction to *moral commitment*. One clarification is necessary, though. In Chapter 3, I suggested that (in its ordinary use) "belief" always denotes unconscious states consisting in the disposition to enter certain conscious occurrent states naturally denoted by "judgment." If so, Gendler's distinction between aliefs and beliefs is better thought of as a distinction between, on the one hand, (conscious and unconscious) aliefs, and on the other hand, (unconscious) beliefs and (conscious) judgments. In what follows, I will conduct the discussion mostly in Gendler's terms, thus using "belief" to denote conscious states as well. In the final section, however, I will revert to the terminology supported by Chapter 3, since that section concerns specifically the phenomenal character of conscious states of both types.

2.2. Moral Commitments, Moral Beliefs, and Moral Aliefs

The need for a distinction between belief and alief does not depend on any particular subject matter: thoughts about anything below or above the moon may have the characteristics of belief or of alief. Thus we have every reason to expect that moral commitments can also come in two varieties: moral aliefs and moral beliefs. This expectation is confirmed by all three types of consideration used to support the alief/belief distinction in general: (i) its explanatory indispensability vis-à-vis cases of belief-behavior mismatch, (ii) the difference in inferential profile (the issue of hyperopacity), and (iii) explanatory unity with "the best science of the mind we've got" (as Fodor used to say).

On the one hand, Gendler-style examples of belief-behavior mismatch are easy to come by in the moral domain. Discrepancy between a person's honest proclamations of moral principle and their ongoing moral practice is a familiar phenomenon. As "implicit bias" studies have consistently shown, many who would never consciously assent to a racist proposition, such as <black men are generally more dangerous than white men>, nonetheless show stubborn traces of racist dispositions in their behavior.[10] It is tempting to describe this precisely as a situation in which we have anti-racist beliefs but racist aliefs (Gendler 2008b). Insofar as racism is a normatively charged attitude (it represents certain races as *worse* in certain respects than others), it is natural to say that this is a case of moral alief diverging from moral belief.

This kind of "negative" belief-behavior mismatch—where a blameworthy moral attitude lies beneath the surface of a praiseworthy attitude—is routinely pointed out in the public and private spheres. Its converse, "positive" mismatch receives much less attention but is a common occurrence as well. Arpaly (2002) writes of her undergraduate student who brandishes her copy of Ayn Rand's *Atlas Shrugged* and passionately extols the virtues of selfishness, all the while helping her peers to prepare for exams, volunteering at the local soup kitchen, and so on. It is tempting and plausible to describe this student as holding egoistic beliefs but altruistic aliefs. Insofar as egoism is a morally charged attitude (representing oneself as having disproportionately greater moral weight than others), it is natural to say that this is a case of moral belief diverging from moral alief.[11]

Unsurprisingly, like all aliefs, moral aliefs are hyperopaque. This is in contradistinction with moral beliefs, which are not. Thus, the following bit of reasoning is valid:

1) Jimmy believes that black men are crime-prone;
2) Jimmy is explicitly aware that blacks are the second largest minority group in the United States; therefore,
3) Jimmy believes that men of the second largest minority group in the United States are crime-prone.

But the following is not:

1) Jimmy alieves that black men are crime-prone;
2) Jimmy is explicitly aware that blacks are the second largest minority group in the United States; therefore,

3) Jimmy alieves that men of the second largest minority group in the United States are crime-prone.

Thus moral aliefs are very different from moral beliefs.

As for explanatory continuity with cognitive-scientific research, given the prevalence of dual-process architecture in our cognitive system, it is natural to hypothesize that it subserves moral cognition as well.[12] The idea is that the execution of moral-cognition tasks is subserved by two independent neurophysiological and/or computational underlying mechanisms, an associationist low-road mechanism and a rationalist high-road mechanism. Presumably, these two mechanisms would produce mental states that would bear characteristic properties: the former would produce moral aliefs, the latter moral beliefs.

As a matter of fact, dual-process models of moral cognition have flourished in twenty-first-century cognitive science, as several cognitive and social psychologists have been more or less independently led to propose them (see Greene and Haidt 2002). These dual-process models are typically *not* billed as distinguishing a rationalist system from an associationist one, but as distinguishing a rationalist system from a *sentimentalist* one. Thus whereas the high road is taken to be rational and rule-based, the low road is cast as sentimentally grounded, driven by (often socially conditioned) affective responses evolutionarily preceding any capacity for rational processing. However, there are various ways in which the associationist and sentimentalist systems could be assimilated. After all, the low-road sentimentalist process is typically theorized in the models under consideration as habitual, fast, efficient, and so on, just as the alief-forming associationist mechanism is supposed to be. Furthermore, like aliefs the mental states the sentimentalist typically appeals to have primarily affective content but feature representational and motivational elements as well.

This could suggest that sentimentalist construals of low-road moral cognition could be subsumed under an associationist construal, with the associationist system cast as trafficking heavily in "sentimental states." Conversely, the associationist system implicated in moral cognition could be reduced to the sentimentalist system, insofar as one might hold that aliefs are in reality nothing but sentiments. After all, the affective component is central to their characterization, and although they boast cognitive and motivational components as well, so do emotions (as we saw in Chapter 4). Thus one could hold that the real occupants of the alief role are simply (some) emotions. In other words, the mental states that we must posit to causally explain belief-discordant behavior are familiar emotional states. (More on this in §3.) Whether we subsume the sentimentalist system often referred to in dual-process models of moral cognition under the associationist system responsible for producing (moral) aliefs, or conversely reduce that associationist system to the sentimentalist one, the existing dual-process models of moral cognition lend support to the applicability of the alief/belief distinction to moral commitments.

⊷⊶

We can apply the above general characterizations of alief and belief here too: moral alief is produced by uncontrollable and automatized processes architecturally connected to motor output and inaccessible to consciousness; moral belief is a mental state with a moral content produced by more deliberate and controllable processes that have a more indirect impact on action but are often conscious. It is worth pausing to dwell on the differential connection of moral alief and belief to action and to consciousness, as displayed in the normal unreflective subject.

As operative in everyday life, moral aliefs are formed by subpersonal processes that are never conscious. This may sometimes result in aliefs that are themselves unconscious, but often the alief itself is conscious. (Compare: visual processes are typically unconscious, but their products are often conscious visual experiences.) However, much more essential to aliefs is their action-guiding profile. As we have seen, aliefs govern behavior as it freely unfolds in the normal go of things, where explicit deliberation is not called for. Thus, Arpaly's supposedly Randian student may proclaim disdain for altruism, but what guides her action are by and large altruistic aliefs, which in the normal go of things trump her egoistic beliefs. This direct connection to behavior is, moreover, *constitutive* of alief: a mental state would not *be* an alief if it was not architecturally connected to motor output in a way that enables direct impact on ongoing behavior; it is part of what makes an alief an alief that it is connected to behavior in the requisite way. In this respect, alief is an inherently motivational state *par excellence*.

Moral beliefs, by contrast, are dissociated from ongoing action; their impact on action is typically much more indirect, often concerning the long term. Perhaps after years in the cradle of Randian ideology, undergoing Aristotelian reeducation of her behavioral habits, Arpaly's student could slowly become a better egoist. But this would only be because her beliefs would have finally refashioned her aliefs in their own image. It is relatively rare that a belief trumps an alief in immediately triggering behavior.[13] It may happen on occasion that, in conjunction with some desire, a moral belief may guide action over the objections, so to speak, of a contradictory moral alief (e.g., when the Randian student resists helping a peer on some particular occasion on ideological grounds). But among the innumerable actions we perform in the course of a day, many more are caused by aliefs.[14] And in any case, as the products of a high-road system, moral beliefs are not *architecturally* connected to action in the way moral aliefs are. What characterizes moral beliefs more centrally is their conscious accessibility: they "live" in personal-level cognition, where the subject typically has immediate, noninferential, first-person awareness of them and their contents.

As a result, the phenomenal profile of belief—the subjective feel of being aware of a proposition and presenting it to oneself as true or plausible—is much more essential to them. From the inside, believing that involuntary servitude is wrong, as opposed to merely entertaining it, *feels* just as objectively compelling as believing that water is H_2O (as opposed to merely entertaining it). This is precisely the objectivistic phenomenology of moral belief mentioned in §1.

2.3. Dual-Process Cognitivist Internalism

If all this is right, then the distinction between moral aliefs and beliefs may hold the potential for a dissolution of the "moral problem." The theses in the inconsistent triad from §1 concern "moral commitment," but in light of this section's discussion, that term is seen to be potentially equivocal: in one sense, it might denote moral belief; in another, moral alief. (I say "potentially equivocal" because strictly speaking the term, if used along the lines of terminological regime proposed here, would be a *univocal* term denoting the genus of which moral belief and alief are both species. In practice, however, the recommended regime need not be in force, and the term could be used equivocally to denote either one species or the other. As it happens, I think this is exactly what is going on.) Once we disambiguate "moral commitment," I want to argue, we find that there is no single sense of the term for which all three theses are compelling.

Recall that the cognitivist thesis in the triad is a thesis about the phenomenology of (conscious manifestations of) moral commitment: that it has an objective purport. As we have just seen, this is highly plausible for moral *beliefs*. But is it plausible for moral aliefs? Consider a racist moral alief of the sort we have been discussing. Its content may be thought of as <Black man. Scary! Must get away!> There is in fact a representational or cognitive component in this content (<Black man>), and this component does involve a phenomenology as of being directed at an objective matter of fact. But this component has no moral or normative dimension to it at all—it is purely descriptive. It is the affective and motivational components (<Scary! Must get away!>) that involve a normative or moral dimension. "Scary" expresses a thick normative concept, and "Must get away!" encodes imperative, action-guiding content. These, however, do not involve any objectivistic feel. What this means is that although a moral alief has a phenomenology as of being directed at an objective matter of fact, it does not have this phenomenology *qua moral*. Thus despite its representational or cognitive dimension, which makes it purport to be about *some* objective facts, there are no *moral* objective facts that this alief purports to be about.

Recall, next, that the internalist thesis in the triad requires moral commitments to be inherently motivating. Once we draw the alief/belief distinction, however, we see that this is antecedently plausible only for moral *aliefs*. Moral beliefs, once clearly divorced from moral aliefs, are freed from this theoretical burden, and seen to be more removed from action and motivation. Although on occasion they may conspire with some pro attitude to bring about an action, and have a role in the long-term shaping of aliefs, they are not *architecturally* linked to action and thus not *constitutively* motivational.

It would seem, then, that for each disambiguation of "moral commitment," we can comfortably and in good conscience adopt only two of the three theses comprising the moral problem: cognitivism and Humean Psychology about moral beliefs, internalism and Humean Psychology about moral aliefs. In other words, we can reject internalism about moral beliefs (they are not constitutively, or architecturally, connected to action) and we can reject cognitivism about moral aliefs (they do not, *qua moral*, purport to be about objective matters of fact). Thus there is no single kind of moral commitment for which all three theses in the triad are compelling.

The triad can now be dissolved into two perfectly valid (and plausibly sound) arguments about the nature of different kinds of moral commitment. The first concerns moral aliefs:

1) Moral aliefs (qua moral) are inherently motivating;
2) Mental states in general, including moral aliefs (qua moral), cannot both have objective purport and be inherently motivating; therefore,
3) Moral aliefs (qua moral) do not purport to be about objective matters of fact.

The second concerns moral beliefs:

1) Moral beliefs purport (qua moral) to be about objective matters of fact;
2) Mental states in general, including moral beliefs, cannot both have objective purport and be inherently motivating; therefore,
3) Moral beliefs are not inherently motivating.

The emerging picture combines cognitivism and externalism about moral beliefs with internalism and noncognitivism about moral aliefs—while holding on to Humean Psychology (see Clavien 2010 for a similar view). My contention is that this picture does justice to all the pretheoretic and dialectical pressures in the area, and integrates smoothly into an independently plausible (both empirically and conceptually) account of moral commitment. Its upshot is that both cognitivism and internalism are true of moral commitment, but in different senses. We may call this picture *dual-process cognitivist internalism*.

Dual-process cognitivist internalism avoids the Frege-Geach problem quite elegantly. Moral beliefs play the kind of inferential role in reasoning and deliberation that Geach demanded from moral commitments. The fact that *some* moral commitments are cognitive explains why these sorts of reasoning can and often do take place; and this, after all, is the Frege-Geach "datum." (It is true that in this picture moral aliefs do not exhibit the relevant inferential role, but it is not part of the Frege-Geach "datum" that *all* moral mentation are rational, rule-based bits of reasoning!)

Meanwhile, the picture affords a more precise take on Smith's argument for internalism about moral commitments—the argument from best explanation of the reliable compresence of moral commitment and moral motivation in the good and strong-willed person. As we can now appreciate, "commitment" is potentially ambiguous, so two different explananda may be at play here. First, there is the reliable compresence of motivation and *alief* in the good and strong-willed person. This is best explained by the fact that moral aliefs are constitutively connected to motivation, which indeed they are on the present picture. Secondly, there is the reliable compresence of motivation and *belief* in the good and strong-willed person. This is best explained by the fact that the good and strong-willed person would presumably bring her aliefs and beliefs into alignment. The implicit racist is not as good as she could be, and Arpaly's student not as strong-willed. In the good and strong-willed person, these sorts of divergence between alief and belief dissipate.

A common challenge to internalism is the argument from the conceivability of the amoralist (Brink 1989). It is conceivable that an agent should realize that she ought to φ and yet fail to come up with the motivation to actually φ— perhaps she is depressed, perhaps she just doesn't care enough. There are various more or less technical responses to this challenge—most notably, "inverted comma" responses (Hare 1952)—but the present picture neutralizes the challenge rather straightforwardly. In conceiving of the amoralist, we conceive of someone who *believes* that they ought to φ but who fails to *alieve* that they ought to φ. This is someone who has reasoned her way to the realization that φ-ing would be the right thing to do, but whose motivational setup, determined by associative habit, has not yet caught up with the realization. In conceiving of the amoralist, we conceive of someone whose moral beliefs are disconnected from motivation, in a way that suggests that moral beliefs are not *constitutively* connected to motivation; but none of this undermines the notion that moral *aliefs* are constitutively so connected. Thus dual-process cognitivist internalism accommodates this conceivability datum straightforwardly.

Perhaps the only dialectical pressure in this general area that still has any force as applied to dual-process cognitivist internalism is the anxiety surrounding "error theory." Moral beliefs, in the present picture, purport to be about objective matters of fact. If, as is not implausible, there simply are no objective matters of fact of a moral nature for beliefs to be answerable to—if there are no moral truthmakers, in short—then moral beliefs would have to be declared erroneous one and all. Some are willing to bite the bullet (self-professed error theorists), others are happy to posit moral facts and truthmakers (moral realists). But many, including me, are uncomfortable with either of these moves.

It is important to appreciate, however, that error theory is significantly less disconcerting in the present picture than in standard cognitivism. For in the present picture error theory about moral belief would not undermine the rational foundations of our entire moral practice, since the formation of moral beliefs is only one part—and not the major part—of that practice. In Mackie's (1977) error theory, *all* our moral commitments are beliefs, and therefore error theory about moral beliefs is error theory about all the mental states relevant to our moral life. Such a sweeping error theory is avoided in the present picture, since it does not touch our moral aliefs, which are also part of our moral life. Since moral aliefs do not have an objectivistic phenomenology *qua* moral, they do not *present themselves* in the relevant sense as directed at objective moral facts—as morally truth-apt, so to speak. Their rational underpinnings do not depend, therefore, on the existence of moral facts/truthmakers (hence on moral realism turning out to be true). Now, on a natural understanding of the notion of "practice," moral aliefs are arguably *more* essential to our moral practice than moral beliefs. For the term "practice" sends in the direction of the causally operative mental states in ongoing moral comportment, and in the present picture those are the aliefs, not the beliefs. If our moral aliefs form the core of our moral practice, and they do *not* claim any objective purport (*qua* moral), then the rational underpinnings of our moral practice are relatively secure.[15]

The primacy of alief in our moral practice can also be appreciated from a different angle, that of moral evaluation. We are routinely incensed by the self-proclaimed anti-racist when she shows traces of racist predilection in her actual behavior. Indeed, we seem to find her more blameworthy for her racist aliefs than praiseworthy for her anti-racist beliefs. (At least this is so when we evaluate *unreflective* subjects, where "unreflective" means just that the subject is not aware of any belief-alief misalignment. A *reflective* subject may be committed to changing her racist aliefs, perhaps even be in the process of self-rehabituation, and this may modify our intuitive moral evaluation of her. But as long as the subject is unreflective, so that her moral aliefs and beliefs are genuinely insulated from each other, we seem to find her more blameworthy for her racist aliefs than praiseworthy for her anti-racist beliefs.) Conversely, we are charmed by the (unreflective) self-proclaimed egoist whose actual behavior discloses deep-seated concern for others: we may find her annoying at the dinner party, but are compelled to note that "her heart is in the right place." That is to say, we find her more praiseworthy for her altruistic aliefs than blameworthy for her egoistic beliefs. (Again, this may change if and when we learn that she has embarked on a deliberate process of retraining her aliefs with the goal of becoming a better egoist.) Thus moral evaluation appears to track aliefs closer than beliefs, at least when the two are properly insulated from each other. This is not to say that people's moral beliefs are of *no* concern to us, of course; merely that they are of *lesser* concern.

There is a good reason for pegging evaluation to aliefs primarily. If in general the low-road system that puts a premium on speed over accuracy is the default system we operate on, then it is that system that evaluation should monitor for quality control in the first instance. For this is the system that guides our behavior in the normal go of things. A more ambitious way of putting the point is to say that the folk appear (for good reasons) to take a person's aliefs to constitute her *deeper* moral commitments. When aliefs and beliefs diverge, the *true moral character* of a person is reflected more accurately in her aliefs. I take this to be the deep insight behind the internalist outlook in moral philosophy: deep moral commitment, reflecting true moral character, is constitutively tied to the motivational states that govern behavior.

None of this renders moral beliefs completely irrelevant or unimportant to our moral practice. For moral beliefs, although not inherently or constitutively motivational, are not epiphenomenal either (as noted in §1). Crucially, as we have seen above, beliefs do have the capacity to affect aliefs, if only through an Aristotelian process of self-training or rehabilitation. At the same time, unlike aliefs, beliefs are formed through flexible personal-level processes that are consciously controllable and manipulable. In this way, our aliefs can be rationally influenced indirectly, even though they cannot be changed immediately or at will. And so a person fortunate enough to encounter Kant's second *Critique* in her early twenties might acquire the belief that she ought to treat others as ends rather than mere means, and through years of careful implementation might by her late twenties or early thirties possess robust treat-as-end aliefs. In this respect, we have no better tool for moral growth and moral progress than our moral belief-forming faculty. I take this to be the deep insight behind the cognitivist and rationalist outlook in moral philosophy.

In summary, dual-process architecture and the distinction between moral alief and belief conspire to dissolve the organizing problem of contemporary moral psychology: the tension between the objective purport of moral commitments and their inherently motivational role. They put forth the resources to articulate a conception of moral commitments—dual-process cognitivist internalism—as dividing into two subclasses, one boasting objective purport and one inherently motivating, in a way that still captures the deep insights behind both the outlook which emphasizes objectivistic moral phenomenology and that which emphasizes constitutive moral motivation.

II. The Reducibility of Moral Phenomenology
3. Is There a Sui Generis Moral Phenomenology?

In the metaethical literature it is not uncommon to describe a claim as phenomenological. But there are at least five different senses in which this can be meant. An author might state that her judgment that slavery is wrong has an objectivist phenomenology meaning only that (1) utterances to the effect that slavery is wrong tend to have the kind of superficial grammar that statements of objective fact typically do. Sometimes the claim means that (2) whatever the grammar of such utterances, when a normal person is asked whether her judgment that slavery is wrong purports to describe an objective fact, she typically states that it does. Sometimes it is that (3) whatever she *states*, the person *believes* (tacitly no doubt) that her judgment purports to represent an objective fact. And sometimes it is that (4) whatever the folk *in fact* believe, the *commonsensical* belief to have is that this judgment purports to represent an objective fact (where the commonsense belief is to the folk belief what competence is to performance). Only rarely is the thought that (5) when judging that slavery is wrong, one undergoes an *experience* with the sort of phenomenal character typically exhibited by experiences as of objective facts. My concern here is with this fifth notion exclusively. On this fifth notion, to claim that our commitment to the wrongness of slavery feels objective is to claim that (conscious manifestations) of this commitment instantiate a specific phenomenal property.

If moral commitments come in two distinct varieties, as argued above, then we should expect them to exhibit two different types of phenomenology: a phenomenology of moral belief and a phenomenology of moral alief. There may be some commonality between them that would justify talking of *moral phenomenology per se*. But even short of that, we may wonder whether moral aliefs and/or beliefs exhibit a phenomenology irreducible to the primitive types of phenomenology defended in previous chapters. We can put the issue in the terms of a triad:

1) There exists moral phenomenology.
2) Moral phenomenology is irreducible to perceptual, algedonic, cognitive, conative, and entertaining phenomenology.
3) Perceptual, algedonic, cognitive, conative, and entertaining phenomenology ultimately exhaust all phenomenology.

In §3.1, I argue for reductivism about the phenomenology of moral beliefs, or rather of the moral judgments that constitute their manifestations; I argue that it is just a specific kind of *cognitive* phenomenology (one associated with a moral content). In §3.2, I argue for reductivism about the phenomenology of (conscious) moral aliefs; I argue that theirs is just a specific kind of *emotional* phenomenology. The upshot is that there is no second-layer primitive moral phenomenology.

3.1. The Phenomenology of Moral Judgments

Let us start by distinguishing two aspects of the phenomenology of a judgment that *p*: its attitude-specific phenomenology and its content-specific phenomenology (Koksvik 2011). The attitude-specific phenomenology is the component of the judgment's overall phenomenal character that has to do with its being a judgment. The content-specific phenomenology is the component that has to do with its being directed at *p*.

When it comes to moral judgments, it is plausible to maintain that the moral part of their phenomenal character is an aspect of their content-specific phenomenology rather than their attitude-specific phenomenology. Plausibly, their attitudinal phenomenology is just that of judgment, and what makes the judgment *moral* is just that it takes moral propositions as content. If so, the attitude-specific phenomenology of moral judgments is simply the feel of affirming an entertained proposition. To make the judgment that slavery is wrong is just to be in a state that presents-as-true that slavery is wrong. The attitudinal phenomenology here is the same as that of judging that 2 + 2 = 4 or that Pope Benedict IX may have been eleven when elected. What distinguishes moral judgments, phenomenologically, from other judgments is their content-specific phenomenal character—the fact that they have *moral* propositional content. The question is how to characterize moral propositions, how to specify the kind of propositional content properly called moral. One natural approach is to isolate a specifically moral sense of the term "ought" (see, e.g., Harman 1977 ch.10), and accordingly a moral ought-concept expressed by that term. A moral propositional content is then one that either features this concept as constituent or suitably implies a propositional content that does. (Pursuing this approach would require actually isolating the relevant ought-concept and elucidating the notion of "suitable implication.")

The upshot seems to be that the distinctive phenomenology of moral judgment is the combination of two elements: the content-specific phenomenology associated with an ought-proposition (or a proposition suitably implied by one) and the attitude-specific phenomenology of *affirming* that content. It is the phenomenology of being directed in an "affirm-ish" way toward an ought-proposition.

If this is how we understand the distinctive phenomenology of moral judgment, it clearly does not constitute what I have called in the Introduction a second-layer phenomenal primitive. Since the attitude-specific "affirm-ish" component is phenomenally indistinguishable from the attitude-specific phenomenology of other judgments, it is just standard cognitive phenomenology. The fact that what distinguishes moral judgments from others is their content-specific phenomenology, meanwhile, suggests that the phenomenology of moral belief is at most a primitive *third*-layer phenomenal determinable. This kind of phenomenology would be a species of the phenomenal genus *cognitive phenomenology*. For the feeling of being directed in an "affirm-ish" sort of way toward a moral proposition is a species of the feeling of being directed in an "affirm-ish" way. (In fact, the picture might be even more complicated, with the phenomenology of moral judgment constituting a *fourth*-layer phenomenal determinable. The third layer would involve varieties of cognitive phenomenology, such as the phenomenology of judging, suspecting, being convinced, remembering, and so on. It is only at the fourth layer that distinctions reflecting content-specific rather than attitude-specific phenomenology emerge.)

Whether the phenomenology of moral belief is in fact primitive at a lower level of abstraction (higher level of determinacy) depends on whether the content-specific "ought-ish" phenomenology is reducible. There are, of course, perennial debates in metaethics about the corresponding metaphysical question: whether "ought-ish" states of affairs are reducible to "is-ish" states of affairs, whether moral facts are reducible to "natural" facts. The question before us is the phenomenological parallel: whether the *feeling* of being intentionally directed onto "ought-ish" states of affairs is reducible to the *feeling* of being directed onto "is-ish" states of affairs. The phenomenological question is no easier than the metaphysical one, I suspect, and I will not attempt to answer it here.[16]

Given this, any hope of a primitive moral phenomenology at the level in which we are interested, that of second-layer phenomenal determinables, rests on moral aliefs.

3.2. The Phenomenology of Moral Aliefs

Recall that according to Gendler, aliefs are clusters of associatively linked (i) representational, (ii) affective, and (iii) motivational elements. In this respect, they involve the compresence of several mental elements, somewhat as emotions do according to Chapter 4. In fact, the elements involved in emotion to some extent match those involved in alief, being as they are (i) cognitive, (ii) proprioceptive and algedonic, and (iii) conative. This may raise the suspicion that alief phenomenology is just emotional phenomenology, indeed that alief itself is nothing but emotion.

Consider the alief that the glasses cost $9. Its fully specified content, recall, is <$9 for glasses. Exciting! Get them!>. The first component is the representation of the glasses costing $9. The phenomenology of this component is that of presenting some state of affairs as obtaining. The difference between the phenomenology of this representation and the phenomenology of merely entertaining that the glasses cost $9 is thus the same as the phenomenal difference between judging and merely entertaining that the glasses cost $9. This suggests that the phenomenology associated with the representation of the glasses costing $9 is simply cognitive phenomenology. Meanwhile, the phenomenology of the motivational component, <Get them!>, is plausibly just conative phenomenology: the phenomenology of deciding to do something (in this case, getting the glasses), hence presenting-as-right some course of action. Finally, the phenomenological residue associated with the excitement is plausibly identified with the proprioceptive phenomenology of various forms of physiological arousal. Presumably, the excitement also *feels good*, which contributes an algedonic element to the overall experience. All this suggests an account of the alief's phenomenology as involving a cognitive component, a conative component, and a proprioceptive-cum-algedonic component. It underscores the suspicion that alief phenomenology is essentially emotional phenomenology.

Recall that the case for separating alief from belief (in §2.1) had three components: a serviceability argument, a hyperopacity argument, and a theoretical unity argument. There are reasons to suspect that none of these works for separating alief from emotion.

The serviceability argument was that the alief/belief distinction is necessary to account for cases of belief-behavior mismatch. But in many and perhaps all these cases, one can cite an emotion to explain the belief-mismatching behavior. Consider the glass-purchasing behavior we explained by citing the alief <$9 for glasses. Exciting! Get them!>. One could explain this behavior also simply by citing the emotion of excitement—the subject is excited about the glasses costing only $9. Since emotions in general have representational/cognitive and motivational/conative components, it is no surprise that one's feeling of excitement should involve representing the glasses' price and the motivation to purchase them. Likewise for the alief <Black man. Scary! Must get away!> called upon to explain racist traces in the behavior of reflectively enlightened agents: we could just as well cite the emotion of fear. Fear of black men can clearly survive rational reflection on the fact that they are no more dangerous than other men. At the same time, it is no surprise that fear of black men involves representing them as black men and motivating the fearful subject to avoid them.

As can be appreciated from these examples, what makes emotion a natural candidate reducer of alief is that, like aliefs, emotions boast associatively linked representational, affective, and motivational components. For example, fearing a dog typically involves a *representational* aspect, namely, that of representing the dog to be in some sense dangerous, or at least to be present. In addition, fearing a dog has a straightforward *motivational* component: it motivates the fearful to flee. Naturally, such an emotion also has an *affective* dimension, including proprioceptive and algedonic elements that go beyond the representational/

cognitive and motivational/conative ones already mentioned. Finally, the three aspects are associatively linked, in that they tend to cluster: when one represents a dog as dangerous, one tends to also be motivated to flee it and experience the distinctive proprioceptive phenomenology of fear; when one is motivated to flee a dog, one tends also to represent it as dangerous and to experience the relevant phenomenology; when one experiences the phenomenology, one tends to also represent something as dangerous and to be motivated to react suitably. Thus emotion has the same internal structure as alief, which makes it suitable to explain the belief-behavior mismatches that Gendler posits alief to explain.

Another way to put the point is this. Recall that Gendler offered two characterizations of alief: in terms of explanatory role and in terms of occupant of that role. The role was to explain behavior in cases of belief-behavior mismatch. The occupant was a state comprising associatively linked representational, affective, and motivational elements. As we have just seen, these elements characterize emotion as well. So nothing prevents us from saying, very simply, that *emotion is the occupant of the alief role*.

Consider next the argument from hyperopacity. Gendler uses the argument to make the case that alief is not reducible to a number of attitudes other than belief, for example imagination. For according to Gendler, one *can* validly reason as follows:

1) Jimmy imagines that Cicero is a good tennis player;
2) Jimmy is explicitly aware that Cicero = Tully; therefore,
3) Jimmy imagines that Tully is a good tennis player.

Perhaps intuition's verdict here is not quite as straightforward as in the case of belief, but let us concede to Gendler that imagination is not hyperopaque. Since alief is, it is impossible to reduce alief to imagination. If alief is irreducible to belief, imagination, and all other folk-psychological attitudes, it is a sui generis attitude. The problem with this is that, as we saw in Chapter 4, emotion seems hyperopaque as well—as indeed Montague (2009) argues. There is a kind of automaticity and cognitive impenetrability in emotional processing that insulates emotional content from the effects of explicit awareness. Arachnophobes are typically well aware that spiders are undangerous, but fear spiders nonetheless. Thus, the following seems invalid:

1) Jimmy is afraid that Buxter will bite him;
2) Jimmy is explicitly aware that Buxter is the fastest dog in the neighborhood; therefore,
3) Jimmy is afraid that the fastest dog in the neighborhood will bite him.

And the same goes for our recurring example of belief-behavior mismatch:

1) Jimmy is excited about the glasses costing $9;
2) Jimmy is explicitly aware that the glasses are the most discounted item in the store; therefore,
3) Smith is excited about the most discounted item in the store costing $9.[17]

And if in the final account things are a little more complicated with emotion, as I argued in Chapter 4, they are plausibly more complicated with aliefs—and in the very same ways (which, presumably, could also be divided into event-aliefs and fact-aliefs). The point is that the initial appearance of hyperopacity in emotion matches that in aliefs.

The final consideration supporting an alief/belief distinction pertained to theoretical unity with other areas of cognitive science: the prevalence of dual-process architectures in other mental domains rendered plausible a dual-process architecture for moral mentation that distinguished an alief-forming mechanism from a belief-forming one. As noted in §2.3, however, some have already offered a dual-process model for moral cognition with a sentimentalist low-road mechanism. Thus reducing alief to emotion would only enhance theoretical unity in the present context, by assimilating the alief/belief distinction for moral commitment into existing cognitive-scientific models of moral mentation.

At least provisionally, then, it is plausible to hold that alief is in reality nothing but emotion. If so, the phenomenology of alief is but emotional phenomenology. As I have argued in Chapter 4, the phenomenology of emotion reduces to a combination of cognitive, conative, proprioceptive, and algedonic phenomenology. On the present line of thought, then, the phenomenology of alief, including moral alief, is just that phenomenal combination.

It might be objected that if "Gendler cases" can be handled by citing emotions, this just shows that there are no aliefs, not that aliefs reduce to emotions. That is, it shows eliminativism rather than reductivism about aliefs. However, this depends on whether one builds into the very definition of alief that it is a primitive attitude. Here I followed Gendler in defining alief as the occupant of a certain distinctive explanatory role. I did *not* define it as the *irreducible* occupant of that role. This paves the way to an "Australian" reduction of alief along familiar Lewis-Jackson lines (Lewis 1972, Jackson 1998):

1) Alief = the (actual) occupant of the alief role;
2) The (actual) occupant of the alief role is emotion; so,
3) Alief = emotion.

This sort of Australian reduction of alief is very tidy indeed, but reality may be a tad messier. Consider Gendler's (2008a: 642; emphasis mine) precise characterization of alief: "A *paradigmatic* alief is a mental state with associatively linked content that is representational, affective and behavioral." This characterization appears to cast the concept of alief as a prototype concept, and to allow for *non-paradigmatic* or *non-prototypical* aliefs that do not have the designated kind of content but qualify as aliefs in virtue of relevantly resembling ones that do. It is natural to suppose that such non-prototypical aliefs exhibit two of the three elements associatively linked in a prototypical alief: they may be representational and affective but not motivational, representational and motivational but not affective, or affective and motivational but not representational. For example, Zimmerman (2007) invites us to contemplate the case of Hope, who had had a small trashcan under her sink for many years but then buys a big trashcan she places by the stove. On occasion, Hope still walks with trash to the sink, opens the door under it, and stoops in the hope of throwing away the trash—only to be reminded that it is now by the stove. The mental state that guides Hope to the sink is representational and motivational, but lacks any affective dimension. Still, it appears to resemble enough paradigmatic cases of alief to qualify as alief, albeit (presumably) a non-paradigmatic alief. Importantly for our present purposes, the mental state that guides Hope is also not an emotion—precisely because it lacks any affective dimension. What this means is that, strictly speaking, there are some aliefs which are not emotions. However, it remains true—for all that has been said so far—that all and only paradigmatic aliefs are emotions. Accordingly, it is also true that non-paradigmatic aliefs qualify as aliefs in virtue of resembling *emotions* in the right respects. Thus emotions can function as the unifying principle of the category of alief even if some aliefs are not emotions.

If the phenomenology of alief in general is just the phenomenology of emotion, then presumably the phenomenology of *moral* alief is a species of emotional phenomenology. At most, then, the phenomenology of moral alief would constitute a *third*-layer phenomenal primitive. Whether it would depends on whether moral aliefs exhibit an *irreducible species* of emotional phenomenology. The dialectical situation here is the same as with moral judgments. One might try to argue that there is a species of emotion, namely *moral* emotion, such that (i) the phenomenology of moral alief is nothing but the phenomenology of moral emotion and (ii) the phenomenology of moral emotion is irreducible to the phenomenology of any *other* kind of emotion. If so, there is a sense in which the phenomenology of moral alief is irreducible, though at the same time it does not go beyond emotional phenomenology. That is, the phenomenology of moral alief does not constitute a primitive phenomenal genus at the same level as cognitive phenomenology, conative phenomenology, and so on.

It would seem, then, that neither kind of moral commitment exhibits a primitive phenomenology at the relevant level of abstraction. The upshot is that moral phenomenology does not constitute a new second-layer phenomenal primitive. The second-layer phenomenal determinable involved in moral judgment is cognitive phenomenology; that involved in moral alief is emotional phenomenology, that is, the combination of cognitive, conative, proprioceptive (hence perceptual), and algedonic phenomenology.

Conclusion

As far as the search for the second-layer phenomenal primitives is concerned, the thesis of this chapter is that moral phenomenology is not one of them. To reach this thesis, I developed a fairly comprehensive and somewhat novel picture of moral commitment in general. This is what I called dual-process cognitivist internalism: the thesis that moral mentation is implemented in a dual-process architecture, with internalism being true of moral commitments produced by low-road processes and cognitivism true of moral commitments produced by high-road processes. Ultimately, on the picture I have painted forth, the high road of moral mental life is grounded in reason and produces moral beliefs and judgments, whereas the low road is grounded in sentiment and produces moral emotions. Both types of moral commitment—moral beliefs/judgments and moral emotions—may or may not involve an irreducible type of phenomenal character, but not one on a par with cognitive, conative, entertaining, perceptual, and algedonic phenomenology. On the contrary, the phenomenal character of both types of moral commitment is just a species of these other types of phenomenology.[18]

Conclusion

The Structure of the Phenomenal Realm

This chapter returns to our original question: how many second-layer phenomenal primitives do we need to posit to just be able to *describe* our conscious life? So far I have argued for three nonsensory phenomenal primitives—cognitive, conative, and entertaining phenomenology—in addition to the two widely accepted perceptual and algedonic primitives. In §1 of this chapter, I argue for a sixth primitive, though a sensory one: the phenomenology of imagination. In §2, I return to the question of taxonomy raised in the Introduction. In §3, I discuss the prospects for a seventh second-layer phenomenal primitive. Concluding remarks in §4.

1. Imagination: A Sixth Second-Layer Phenomenal Primitive

According to a traditional view, the phenomenology of imagination is not categorically different from that of perception: what it is like to imagine a dog is the same as what it is like to perceive that dog, perhaps in somewhat degraded form. In this section, I argue against this traditional view. My case for this draws heavily on Jean-Paul Sartre's (1936, 1940) work in the area. The case has two main parts: a battery of arguments against the reduction of imaginative phenomenology to perceptual phenomenology (§1.2) and a presentation of a credible primitivist alternative (§1.3). I start with some conceptual and methodological preliminaries (§1.1).

1.1. Preliminaries

Consider this very general question: What is the relationship between perception and imagination? When we consider this question, two facts pop out: (i) there is some commonality between the two, but (ii) there is a difference as well. Perception and imagination resemble in some respect(s), but differ in others. The question is how to characterize the similarity and how to characterize the difference. Thus we may replace our single question with a pair: (Q1) What is the similarity between perception and imagination?; (Q2) What is the dissimilarity between them?

These questions are still ambiguous, however, insofar as the terms "perception" and "imagination" are. The two nouns are most commonly used to denote putative *faculties* or *capacities*. These can be characterized in terms of the mental states they produce, or have the function of producing. Perception is the "faculty" that produces, or whose function it is to produce, perceptual states. Imagination is the faculty that produces, or has the function of producing, imaginative states.

Imaginative states come in many varieties (see Stevenson 2003). One distinction is between imagining an object and imagining awareness of the object: I can imagine a dog or imagine seeing a dog.[1] Another distinction is between propositional and "objectual" imagining: I can imagine that Lena Dunham is elected president or I can imagine a purple dog. It is sometimes claimed that the relationship between objectual and propositional imagining is analogous to that between perceiving and believing (see, e.g., Currie and Ravenscroft 2002, McGinn 2004). But this is misleading. It is true that both the following are admissible reports of imaginative states:

(1) S imagines O.
(2) S imagines that p.

But a corresponding duality applies to perception reportage:

(1*) S perceives O.
(2*) S perceives that p.

The relationship between 1 and 2 is analogous to that between 1* and 2*. In both 2 and 2*, a propositional attitude is reported, but one which conceptually involves a sensuous dimension. By this I mean: it is part of the *concepts* of perceiving-that and imagining-that that some sensory experiences take place when a subject perceives-that or imagines-that (at least typically). One might hold that occurrent beliefs or judgments also involve sensory experiences, but if so it is not *part of the concept* of belief or judgment that such experiences must take place. In that respect, believing is more analogous to conceiving, a kind of purely intellectual exercise of an imagination-like capacity. When one conceives that some water is not H_2O, one may experience sensory images of a watery substance, but it is not part of the *concept* of conceiving that such imagery must occur. In sum, my claim is that belief is to perception what conception is to imagination, not what propositional imagination is to objectual imagination. If we add

(3)   S conceives that *p*
(3*) S believes that *p*

we may say that the two series 1-2-3 and 1*-2*-3* parallel each other in a relevant sense.

The above distinctions reveal some ambiguity in Q1 and Q2, depending on what kind of perceptual and imaginative states they concern. Here I will focus on the following questions: (Q1*) What is the similarity between states of objectual perceiving and states of objectual imagining?; (Q2*) What is the dissimilarity between those states?

From a phenomenological perspective, it is useful to divide approaches to Q1* and Q2* into three. A traditional approach, more often implicit than argued for, is that perceiving and imagining are forsooth phenomenally indistinguishable. The only difference is extrinsic to their phenomenology: they are accompanied by different beliefs.[2] Another approach, associated with Hume, allows for phenomenal difference between perception and imagination, but only one of *degree*.[3] The difference may concern phenomenal intensity, or resolution, or determinacy, but perceptual and imaginative experiences have the same *kind* of phenomenology. A third approach insists on a *categorical* or *qualitative* difference between perceptual and imaginative experience. It posits a difference in *kind*, not just degree. We may call these the "no-difference" view, the "degree-difference" view, and the "kind-difference" view:

(ND) There is no phenomenal difference between perceiving O and imagining O.
(DD) There is a phenomenal difference-in-degree ("quantitative" difference) between perceiving O and imagining O.
(KD) There is a phenomenal difference-in-kind (qualitative difference) between perceiving O and imagining O.[4]

I will argue for KD, drawing heavily on Sartre's work.[5] The core of his case against ND consists in a quartet of epistemic arguments of the following form: if perceptual and imaginative experiences were phenomenally indistinguishable, our knowledge of whether we are perceiving or imagining would be very different from how it really is. He then presents an argument against retreat to DD. His arguments are discussed in the next subsection.

1.2. Against Reductivism about Imaginative Phenomenology

According to ND, there is no difference between perceptual and imaginative experience considered intrinsically. In the version Sartre finds most plausible, the only difference between the mind of the perceiver and the mind of the imaginer is in their second-order judgments *about* their experiences ("I am seeing a dog" vs. "I am visualizing a dog").[6] Still, claims Sartre, these judgments must have certain *grounds*: there is a *reason* why one judges in some cases that one is perceiving and in others that one is imagining. It is part of the view under consideration, says Sartre, that these judgments are based on interrelations among experiences (and standing beliefs), as opposed to intrinsic phenomenal features. When one's experience coheres well with surrounding experiences and standing beliefs and expectations—when it is *orderly*, if you will—it is judged to be perceptual. When it is incongruent and disorderly, it is judged to be imaginative.

Sartre's first argument against this view is this: if my knowledge that the dog presented by my current experience is perceived, rather than imaginary, were based on assessment of the experience's cohesion with other experiences, it would be a complex and somewhat impressive epistemic achievement. But this is false to the epistemology. I know that I am imagining a dog not by comparing my experience to indefinitely many other experiences, but *immediately*, at any rate without the mediation of any cognitive process of experience-comparison.[7] Call this the *argument from immediacy*: 1) we have immediate knowledge of whether we are perceiving or imagining; 2) if ND were true, we could not have such knowledge; so, 3) ND is false.[8]

The second argument is that knowledge of whether I am imagining or perceiving is characterized not only by immediacy but also by a warranted feeling of certainty. Compare the judgments that 2 +2 = 4 and that there is salad for lunch. The former features a characteristic absent from the latter: a *feeling of certainty*. Moreover, the feeling is not misplaced—one is warranted in having it. Such a warranted feeling of certainty appears also to characterize my current belief that I am seeing (and not merely imagining) a dog. But it is hard to see how it could have that characteristic if it were based on assessment of cohesion among complex, temporally extended series of experiences. The process of experience-comparison is too complicated to warrant certainty in its deliverances.[9] Call this the *argument from certainty*: 1) our knowledge of whether we are perceiving or imagining exhibits a warranted feeling of certainty; 2) if ND were true, it would not; so, 3) ND is false.

A third argument appeals to the *effortlessness* of first-person knowledge. If establishing that one is perceiving rather than imagining required sustained comparison with many other experiences and meticulous evaluation of their cohesion, it would be quite effortful. But, says Sartre (1936: 94), "Who has ever made so much effort to distinguish an image from a perception?" Call this the *argument from effort*.

A final epistemological argument may be called the *argument from incongruence*, as it rests on Sartre's (1936: 96) phenomenological analysis of surprising, incongruent perceptual experiences:

> I believe my friend Pierre to be in America. There I catch sight of him at the corner of the street. Will I tell myself "it's an image"? Not at all. My first reaction is to seek to find out how it is possible that he has already come back.

Pierre's presence on a Paris street is unexpected (read: inconsistent with standing expectations). It is incongruent (coheres poorly with other experiences and beliefs). But this creates no tendency to classify one's experience as imaginative. (In sufficiently bizarre settings, I might be unsure whether I am seeing Pierre or hallucinating him. But both perception and hallucination are perceptual experiences. Imaginative experiences are another thing still. In standard cases where I am unsure whether I am seeing or hallucinating O, I am still certain that I am not visualizing O.) This suggests that the experience has an independent phenomenal feature which "marks" it as perceptual, and which one picks up on regardless of one's other experiences, beliefs, and expectations.

One objection to Sartre's argumentation is that there is a more plausible version of ND that he ignores. All versions of ND distinguish perception from imagination on the basis of accompanying beliefs. But while the version Sartre considers appeals to second-order beliefs about what experience the subject has, another version appeals to first-order beliefs about the ontological status of the experience's object. A perceptual experience is accompanied by the belief that its object is real, an imaginative experience by the belief that its object is unreal. On this version of ND, we know which experience we are having simply by knowing which first-order belief accompanies it; this neutralizes Sartre's epistemological arguments. Ignoring this version of ND remains a major lacuna in Sartre's critique, which lacuna we would have to address later on.

Another potential objection is that Sartre's epistemological arguments are undermined by the Perky (1910) experiment. In it, subjects were asked to imagine bananas while staring at blank screens where increasingly clearer banana images slowly appeared; subjects typically failed to realize they were now perceiving rather than (merely) imagining bananas. This failure may suggest that our knowledge of whether we are perceiving or imagining is not as immediate as Sartre claims. However, even *if* the Perky experiments supported claims of introspective indiscriminability (and see Casey 2000: 149 on that), the subject's circumstances in the experimental settings are atypical and extraordinary. All Sartre needs for his argument is the premise that in typical, ordinary circumstances we are able to tell introspectively whether we are perceiving or imagining (immediately, effortlessly, and so on). This datum requires explanation, and the best explanation, it is claimed, is that there is a phenomenal difference between perceiving and imagining.

Might this phenomenal difference pertain simply to the enhanced intensity or resolution of perceptual experiences? This is DD. Sartre's (1936: 84; my translation) main argument against it is again epistemic:

> For a sensation to cross the threshold of consciousness, it must have a minimum intensity. If images are of the same nature, they will have to have at least this intensity. But then won't we confuse them with sensations of the same intensity? And why does the image of a cannon-blast noise not appear as a weak but real cracking?

Consider sensory perception of Hume's "minima sensibilia," say hearing the faintest audible sound of a piece of furniture cracking; compare it to an imaginative experience of a deafeningly loud cannon blast a yard away. We can also stipulate that the imagining is done with great energy and concentration whereas the perceiving is slumbersome. It is unclear in what sense the former is supposed to be "more intense" than the latter. In Chapter 3, I distinguished between sensory and phenomenal intensity. Certainly the perceiving is not more sensorily intense, since it makes no sense to say that it is *louder*: we could not even be *aware* of imaginary sounds, says Sartre, if they were less "loud" than minima audibilia. (This remark is consistent both with the idea that imaginary noises have a loudness greater than minimal and with the idea—as it seems to me, more plausible—that they do not have a loudness at all, but only imaginary-loudness.) On the other hand, the perceiving does not seem more phenomenally intense, since *ex hypothesi* the subject is more alert and "present" in the imagining.

The same sort of argument would apply to other putative differences of degree between perception and imagination. Consider the view that perception is just an experience that uses a higher-resolution format than imagination. This is certainly the case with typical instances. But one could manually stretch the corners of one's eyes to increasingly blur one's visual experience, without at any point the experience changing status from vision to visualization. More generally, when we consider the lowest resolution a perceptual experience can have consistently with the laws of nature, it is hard to believe that no imaginative experience can match *that* level of accuracy. As Byrne (2010: 17) points out:

> ... for any episode of visualizing or recalling [a strawberry], it should be in principle possible to create a physical picture of a strawberry such

that viewing the picture in certain conditions exactly reproduces the felt quality of visualizing or recalling. And this is what seems wrong [in DD]: any way of degrading the picture, such as blurring, desaturating, dimming, and so on, just yields another *perceptual* experience, plainly [introspectively] discernable from visualizing or recalling.

In other words, it is hard to see why the characteristic degraded-ness of an imaginative experience could not be matched by an intentional, willful degradation of a perceptual experience.

Another epistemological problem with DD is that it is unclear how it can allow for mixed episodes, as when I perceive the moon's front side, craters and all, and simultaneously imagine its backside, smooth and even-surfaced. DD seems to imply that my overall experience should be of a vivid cratered-moon image superimposed upon a faint smooth-moon image. But if that were the case, my introspection would surely suggest to me that I am having a perception of a crater-ish moon. In reality, it suggests to me that I am having simultaneous perceptual and imaginative experience.

It might be objected that first-person knowledge of perception and imagination can be based on the processes by which they are formed. Compare and contrast: when my visual cortex computes a 15° angle between two edges and produces a visual experience accordingly, I have no introspective insight into the process by which my experience was formed; but when I calculate 15 percent of the bill and form a thought about the proper tip, I am introspectively aware of at least some aspects of the calculation process involved. Accordingly, the visual experience feels in some sense passive, while the thought feels active. The objector suggests that this contrast applies to perception and imagination: the former feels passive and receptive, the latter active and spontaneous (see Kind 2001 §3). Thus, when I *imagine* a dog, I undergo an introspectively accessible personal-level process we might call the "creative exercise of imagination"; no such process takes place when I *see* a dog. On the objector's suggestion, I can tell by introspection whether my current experience is imaginative or perceptual by registering the presence or absence of this personal-level process. No difference need be assumed between the *phenomenal characters* of the perceiving and the imagining.[10]

The obvious problem with this is that it does not extend to mental images formed through subpersonal processes—what the Greeks called *phantasia*. When an unbidden image of a smiling octopus pops into my mind, the process producing it is introspectively inaccessible to me—the popping is something that happens to me, not something that I do. I feel receptive and passive rather than spontaneous and active. And yet I am perfectly capable of telling whether my experience is perceptual or phantasmagoric. So there must be a deeper dimension along which these differ. We may then reasonably assume that this dimension also distinguishes perception and voluntary, endogenous imagination.

The upshot is clear: there is a phenomenal difference between perceptual and imaginative experiences, and it is not merely a ("quantitative") difference in *degree* of intensity, resolution, or cetera. It is a qualitative difference between two *kinds* of experience. As Sartre puts it, it is "a difference of nature" (1936: 83), "an intrinsic distinction" (1936: 134), between two "sui generis" ways intentional objects appear to the subject (1940: 24). What might this categorical difference be?

1.3. A Primitivist Alternative

Sartre's positive view is a version of KD that appeals centrally to a difference in the *manner*, or *way*, or *mode* of intentional directedness at an object.[11] This talk of "manners" and "ways" of intentionally relating to an object may be understood in terms of the notion of *attitudinal feature* appealed to in earlier chapters. When I perceive my dog and when I imagine my dog, the dog presented in my experience is the same, and the intensity with which he is presented may be the same, but *how* he is presented is completely different. Sartre (1940: 17; my translation) writes:

> The word "image" thus designates but the relation (*rapport*) that consciousness has to the object; in other words, it is a certain way the object has of appearing to consciousness, or if we prefer, a certain way consciousness has of giving itself an object. In truth, the expression "mental image" invites confusion. It would be better to say . . . "imaging consciousness of Pierre."

Speaking of a mental image of Pierre is ambiguous as between describing (i) an awareness of a Pierre-image and (ii) an image-awareness of Pierre. Only the latter is accurate, according to Sartre. For in the latter, "image" modifies the intentional act, not the intentional object. It correctly casts the property of *being imagistic* as an attitudinal property of one's awareness. Call this the *attitudinal account* of the (phenomenal) difference between perception and imagination.

There is a traditional (and quite natural) view according to which seeing O and hearing O have the same content but differ in their mode or way of representing O. One uses a *visual* mode of representing O, the other uses an *auditory* mode; the difference is categorical. Within this framework, a proponent of the attitudinal account would insist that there is also a certain attitudinal *commonality* among all six perceptual modalities of representation, which commonality we may call the "perceptual mode." The present thought is that imagining O is as categorically different from perceiving O as seeing O is from hearing O, that is, that the perceptual and imaginative modes are as different as the visual and auditory modes are.

How should we characterize the attitudinal difference between perceptual and imaginative experience? Again drawing on Sartre, I would suggest that the deep difference pertains to whether the object is experienced as real or as unreal.[12] When I see a dog, I experience the dog as existent; when I visualize a dog, I experience the dog as nonexistent. Since the difference is attitudinal, this should be understood as the following contrast:

(P) Perceptual experience E presents-as-existent O.
(I) Imaginative experience E presents-as-nonexistent O.

It is not part of the *content* of a perceptual experience that its object is real or existent, nor part of the imaginative experience's that its object is unreal or nonexistent. But the characteristic *way* perceptual and imaginative experiences present their object is under the aspect of realness/existence or unreality/nonexistence.

Observe that this view, like the version of ND ignored by Sartre, appeals crucially to the difference between reality and unreality in distinguishing perception and imagination. However, while that version of ND builds the reality/unreality difference into the content of accompanying beliefs, the present view builds it into the attitude employed by perception and imagination themselves. This seems to me to have at least two major advantages. First, it vindicates the sense that there is an introspectible difference between the experiences of perception and imagination themselves, regardless of accompaniments. Secondly, it makes room for a perception/imagination distinction even in creatures completely lacking in the capacity for propositional thought—something that the appeal to *beliefs about* reality and unreality rules out.

On the view here defended, the characteristic phenomenal feature of imaginative experiences is the attitudinal feature of presenting-as-nonexistent. It might be objected that we can also imagine things we know to exist, as when I visualize Barack Obama. But even here, it is plausible that my imaginative experience itself presents-as-nonexistent Obama; it is just accompanied by an overriding belief that the imagined object in fact exists. Compare: looking at a Müller-Lyer display, I have a visual experience that presents-as-existent a pair of uneven lines; but the experience is accompanied by a belief that "disendorses" that content. If we try to abstract away from the accompanying beliefs, we recognize that imagining Obama in itself presents-as-nonexistent that which is imagined. As I close my eyes and picture him, the Obama hovering just there on the other side of my desk is something I am aware of as unreal; the real Obama is in the White House talking to more important people.[13]

A better objection is that while the present account suits experiences produced through voluntary exercise of the imagination, it is inadequate for unbidden imaginative experiences. When the image of a smiling octopus just pops into my mind, the octopus is not experienced as nonexistent the way it is when I deliberately conjure up an image of it. Calling these kinds of unbidden imaginative experiences "phantasmagoric experiences," we may put the objection as follows: it seems introspectively inaccurate to say that phantasmagoric experiences are attitudinally committed to the unreality of their objects. Instead, they seem attitudinally silent on their object's ontological status.

There are two possible reactions to this objection. The first and simpler is to deny that phantasmagoric experience is noncommittal in the way claimed. It might be suggested, for example, that the main difference between phantasmagoric and non-phantasmagoric imaginative experience is that only the latter involves a phenomenology of doing the imagining (a phenomenology of agency), and that this difference nowise entrains a difference concerning the way the object imagined is presented. The other reaction concedes that the objection is phenomenologically accurate, and proceeds to divide imaginative experiences into two types: the first (formed by active, deliberate, voluntary, endogenous, personal-level exercise of the imagination) present-as-nonexistent their object, but the other (formed by subpersonal processes uncontrolled by the subject) *merely-present* their objects (without taking a stand on their ontological status). The difference is somewhat analogous to the difference between disbelieving that p and entertaining that p: the former presents-as-false p, the latter merely-presents p. In a way, the present distinction between non-phantasmagoric and phantasmagoric imagination is simply the sensory analog.

The two reactions to the last objection lead to two slightly different views on the difference between perceptual and imaginative experiences. The first reaction leads to the view that while perceptual experiences present-as-existent, imaginative ones present-as-nonexistent. The second reaction leads to the view that while perceptual experiences present-as-existent, imaginative ones do not, instead dividing into a group that present-as-nonexistent and a group that merely-present. Both takes on the perceptual/imaginative distinction are versions of KD: there is a categorical phenomenal difference between perception and imagination. Here, I will adopt the second one, because it is more concessive to the objector but still supports a version of KD.

※

According to the view here adopted, then, the categorical phenomenal difference between imaginative and perceptual experiences is that the former do not exhibit the phenomenal attitudinal feature of presenting-as-existent. The emerging answers to Q1* and Q2* are straightforward: states of objectual perception and objectual imagination are similar in that they can in principle present the same object; they are different (most centrally) in presenting their object differently, in the sense of exhibiting different attitudinal features. In a slogan: perception and imagination are similar in content, dissimilar in attitude.

On this view, imaginative experiences are distinguished by the phenomenal attitudinal features they exhibit. It is reasonable to strengthen the claim to suggest that these attitudinal features are *essential* to the experiences' status as imaginative. That is, what makes an imaginative experience such is the fact that it exhibits either the property of *sensorily presenting-as-nonexistent* or the property of *sensorily merely-presenting* (when phantasmagoric). The result is the following account of the identity and existence conditions for imaginative experiences:

> For any imaginative experience E, E is the imaginative experience *it is* (rather than another imaginative experience) because it bears the content it does, and E is an imaginative experience *at all* (rather than a non-imaginative experience) because it employs the attitude it does.

For example, an imaginative experience as of a mustard-colored dog is the imaginative experience it is because it is *as of a mustard-colored dog*, and is an imaginative experience at all because it either (*a*) *sensorily presents-as-nonexistent* or (*b*) *sensorily merely-presents* the mustard-colored dog.

Remarkably, the assumptions needed to establish this kind of attitudinal approach to imaginative phenomenology are rather innocuous. One assumption is that imaginative and perceptual experiences *can* have the same content; not that they always or even typically do, but just that they *can*.[14] The second assumption is that even when they do, the subject can have a *distinctively first-personal* knowledge of which state she is in; not infallible or even otherwise privileged knowledge, but just *distinctive* knowledge. If these two assumptions are granted, it is hard to see how to avoid the attitudinal account of imaginative phenomenology. According to it, there is a categorical difference between imaginative and perceptual phenomenology—as per KD.

The upshot of this section is that in addition to perceptual and algedonic phenomenology, there are very good reasons to posit a third primitive type of *sensory* phenomenology, namely imaginative phenomenology. Imaginative phenomenology is irreducible to, indeed categorically different from, perceptual phenomenology. Obviously, it is not going to be reducible to algedonic phenomenology (imagining something is not a matter of experiencing pleasure or pain!). Since imaginative phenomenology is sensory, it presumably cannot be reduced to the nonsensory phenomenal primitives posited in Chapters 1–3 either. It must be recognized as a sixth second-layer phenomenal primitive.

2. The Question of Taxonomy

The picture we end up with cites six second-layer phenomenal primitives, three sensory and three nonsensory. Arguably, there is a measure of pleasing parallelism between the two groups: perceptual and cognitive phenomenology "belong together," conative and algedonic phenomenology "belong together," and so do entertaining and imaginative phenomenology.

Consider perceptual and cognitive phenomenology. The former is characterized centrally by the attitudinal feature of (sensory) presenting-as-existent, the latter by that of (nonsensory) presenting-as-true. Both encode a mind-to-world direction of fit: a cognitive experience, such as making the judgment that p, and a perceptual experience, such as seeming to see O, are both supposed to "get right" the world (the former does so when p is true, the latter when O exists). The concepts of existence/reality and truth are closely aligned in philosophy (see under: "truth supervenes on being"). The main difference is that truth is attributed to propositions whereas existence is attributed to objects. So it would stand to reason that propositional attitudes be characterized by presenting-as-true whereas objectual attitudes by presenting-as-existent.

Consider next algedonic and conative phenomenology. As argued in Chapter 2, conative phenomenology is characterized centrally by the attitudinal feature of presenting-as-good$_G$, where "good$_G$" denotes the most generic notion of goodness. More accurately, this is what characterizes the phenomenology of *positive* conative experiences, such as liking and approving of O; the phenomenology of *negative* conative experiences, such as disliking or disapproving of O, is characterized by the corresponding attitudinal feature of presenting-as-bad$_G$, where "bad$_G$" denotes the most generic notion of badness. The very same duality can be found in algedonic experiences: taking pleasure in O (or in the fact that p) presents-as-good$_G$ O (or p); being pained by O (or the fact that p) presents-as-bad$_G$ O (or p). Plausibly, now, algedonic presenting-as-valuable$_G$ is sensuous whereas conative presenting-as-valuable$_G$ is nonsensuous. Thus conative and algedonic experiences "belong together" in presenting-as-good$_G$ (or -bad$_G$) that which they are directed at.

Consider finally entertaining that p and imagining O. The defining characteristic of the former is its neutral attitude, the fact that it (nonsensorily) merely-presents p without committing either to its truth or to its goodness. This is paralleled most closely by the subset of imaginative experiences I called phantasmagoric, which (sensorily) merely-present their objects without commenting on their ontological status. The resemblance to other imaginative experiences, which commit to the nonexistence their objects, is weaker but still notable. This may suggest that, just as we took entertaining to be the paradigmatic "neutral attitude" in Chapter 3, so we should take phantasmagoric experiences to be the paradigmatic imaginative experiences here. Both are characterized by their "null direction of fit": they try neither to get the world right nor to right the world.

(The distinction between two kinds of imagining may pave the way to an even deeper symmetry in the emerging picture. Suppose we refuse to construe disbelieving that p as amounting to believing that $\sim p$, instead treating the former as a sui generis attitude that presents-as-false its propositional content. Then the cognitive domain would exhibit the same attitudinal dichotomy that the conative domain does: just as some conative experiences present-as-good$_G$, while others present-as-bad$_G$, we could say that some cognitive experiences, such as judging and remembering, present-as-true, while others, such as disbelieving and rejecting, present-as-false. There would then arise the question of what the sensory analogs of each are. We know that perception presents-as-existent, analogously to judgment, which presents-as-true. But now we could also suggest that non-phantasmagoric imagination presents-as-nonexistent analogously to disbelief, which presents-as-false. Phantasmagoric experiences would then remain the only sensory analog of entertaining, as truly attitudinally neutral sensory states. I think there is much to recommend this picture, but will bracket it here.)

Thus the sensory triplet and nonsensory triplet in our sextad of phenomenal second-layer primitives mirror each other to some degree: perceptual and cognitive phenomenology belong together, conative and algedonic phenomenology belong together, and entertaining/neutral and phantasmagoric/imaginative phenomenology belong together. It is not clear how best to characterize this "belonging together," but perhaps the notion of direction of fit could be recruited to serve this purpose. We may then note the rough structure in Table 6.1.

Table 6.1 **The Six Second-Layer Phenomenal Primitives**

	$W \to M$ *DoF*	$M \to W$ *DoF*	*Null DoF*
Sensory	Perceptual ph.	Algedonic ph.	Imaginative ph.
Nonsensory	Cognitive ph.	Conative ph.	Entertaining ph.

This structure raises a taxonomic question with implications for what we consider to be the second-layer primitives. For it is consistent with three different taxonomies. The first is this shown in Figure 6.1.

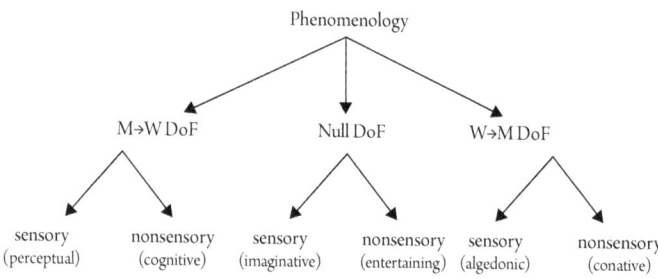

Figure 6.1. First Classification

In this first classification, there are really only three second-layer phenomenal primitives, the phenomenology of having an attitudinal feature with a mind-to-world direction of fit, the phenomenology of having an attitudinal feature with a world-to-mind direction of fit, and the phenomenology of having an attitudinal feature with a null or neutral direction of fit. The aforementioned sextad of primitives pertains only to the third layer of phenomenal determinables. Consider, however, the alternative taxonomy in Figure 6.2.

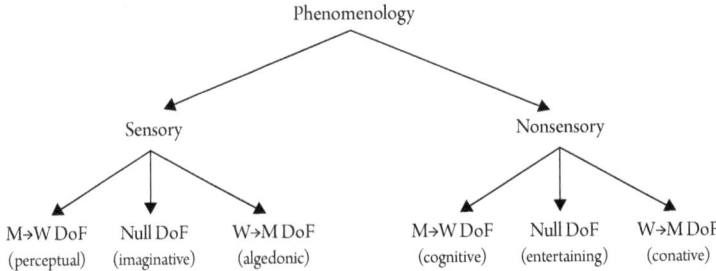

Figure 6.2. Second Classification

Here the second-layer phenomenal primitives are only two: those of sensory phenomenology and nonsensory phenomenology. And again our sextad appears only at the third layer. But consider now a third taxonomy, shown in Figure 6.3.

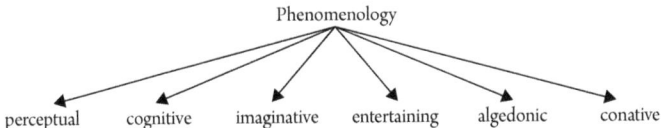

Figure 6.3. Third Classification

Here the differences between sensory and nonsensory phenomenology, on the one hand, and the different direction-of-fit phenomenologies, on the other, are ignored for taxonomic purposes; accordingly, the sextad is considered second-layer.

Plausibly, all three classifications are consistent with the picture presented in Table 6.1. This raises a number of questions and "meta-questions": How are we to decide among the three? Does it matter? Is the decision answerable to any objective matters of fact or merely pragmatic? Some of these questions were addressed *in abstracto* in §4 of the Introduction. They now appear in a concrete setting. My own inclination is to take a deflationary attitude to such questions. I am doubtful there are objective facts as to which classification is "correct." But if there are, and the first or second classification turns out to be the correct one, I would say that this only shows that my interest all along has been with the *third*-layer phenomenal primitives. Perhaps the deepest lesson from the plurality of taxonomies consistent with Table 6.1 is that figures in the style of 6.1–6.3 are not the best tools for visually representing the structure of the phenomenal realm. A collection of tables in the style of 6.1 may turn out to be more informative.

Nonetheless, it seems to me that the question of choosing among Figures 6.1–6.3 is *open* to objectivistic (or "realist") treatment—for reasons already indicated in the Introduction. If there are objective naturalness facts that make leptons "belong together" more than zebras do, there may also be naturalness facts that make, say, presenting-as-good phenomenal states "belong together" more than sensory-phenomenal states. If so, it would be more natural (in this sense) to group algedonic experiences with conative experiences than with perceptual and imaginative experiences.

On this approach, adopting the taxonomy in Figure 6.1 commits one to the substantive claim that the categories "phenomenology with mind-to-world direction of fit," "phenomenology with world-to-mind direction of fit," and "phenomenology with neutral direction of fit" are *more natural* than the categories of "sensory phenomenology" and "nonsensory phenomenology." Adopting the taxonomy in Figure 6.2 commits to the opposite claim (the former categories are *less natural* than the latter). It is plausible to interpret Figure 6.3, meanwhile, as committed to the substantive claim that the two classes of categories are *equally natural*. According to the objectivist, the facts about relative naturalness of the relevant *in re* universals are out there in the phenomena (the stream of consciousness), waiting to be discovered.

As noted in the Introduction, on this approach our evidence for naturalness claims consists in observation of objective-similarity relations. In this case, this would have to be introspective observation of similarities and dissimilarities among various token experiences. Does a perceptual experience of a mustard-colored dog objectively resemble more (i) an algedonic experience of pain in the knee or (ii) a cognitive experience of making the judgment that Spain will win the next World Cup? On the one hand, the perceptual experience shares with (i) a sensuous dimension. On the other, it shares with (ii) the feel of trying to get things right. If upon attentive introspection we end up thinking it resembles (i) more than (ii), that gives us evidence for the taxonomy in Figure 6.2. If we end up thinking it resembles (ii) more than (i), we have evidence for Figure 6.1. If we end up thinking it resembles them equally, this provides some evidence for Figure 6.3.

This is the epistemology and metaphysics of a realist approach to the choice among the three taxonomies. But one may also, of course, take a more deflationary approach to the choice. It may not really be sensible to ask what an experience objectively resembles more: there may be a category mistake in the very framing of the question. It may be sensible to ask the question but there may not be any objective facts that answer it. There may be such objective facts that are unfortunately not introspectively tractable. And so on and so forth. In many ways, a deflationary approach that dismisses the question of taxonomy as unanswerable and/or unimportant is the safer way to go. I am inclined toward this approach, but am bracketing the whole issue here.

3. A Seventh Primitive?

At the level of abstraction that interests me, then, I have argued for six phenomenal primitives. Is there any reason to think these are the *only* primitives at that level of abstraction? Not really. A scheme of three directions of fit, each admitting of a sensory version and a nonsensory version, does have an air of pleasing completeness about it. But this consideration is at most faintly suggestive. To *argue* that there is no other primitive would require considering many antecedently plausible candidates and arguing that reductivism or eliminativism is more plausible for them than primitivism.

Elsewhere, I have argued that all conscious experience exhibits a phenomenologically manifest presence to the subject, or subjective significance (Kriegel 2005a, 2009 ch.2). When I see a mustard-colored dog, there is a mustard-color-ish way it is like for me to have my visual experience. This "mustard-color-ish way it is like for me" involves two central dimensions: (i) the mustard-color-ish quality and (ii) a for-me-ness by which it is experientially given to me as subject. This for-me-ness is, on my view, a *sine qua non* of all conscious experience, and therefore an invariant aspect of the stream of consciousness. It might be suggested that this experiential for-me-ness could serve as a seventh second-layer primitive.

However, this seems like the wrong way to think of for-me-ness. For-me-ness is not a self-standing and detachable quality in its own right, but a pervasive dimension infusing all phenomenology. Thus we should not posit for-me-ness alongside such phenomenal features as presenting-as-true, presenting-as-good, and so on; instead, we should reconceive these phenomenal attitudinal features as presenting-*to-me*-as-true, presenting-*to-me*-as-good, and so on. The subjective significance or experiential givenness is a standing dimension of all of them, in virtue of which they are phenomenal features to begin with. Accordingly, we appreciate for-me-ness not by introspecting it in isolation from other phenomenal features, but by grasping what is common to all phenomenal features; this is precisely why it is a *sine qua non* of all conscious experience. From this perspective, for-me-ness does not seem like a seventh second-layer primitive so much as *the first-layer primitive*. Phenomenality as such *just is* for-me-ness. In other words, it is for-me-ness itself that divides into six species.

In Chapter 4, I considered the possibility that emotional phenomenology might be another second-layer primitive, distinguished by its attitudinal feature of presenting-as-important. Ultimately, I argued that it is more plausible to see *attention* as the mechanism constitutively dedicated to the representation of importance, with emotion bearing a nomic but merely contingent connection to attention (and thence to the representation of importance). If this is so, it might be suggested, then the *phenomenology of attention* may be a seventh second-layer primitive.

This suggestion is hampered by two considerations. First, although in ordinary language we only have predicates for two attentional properties ("attentive" and "inattentive"), plausibly the underlying reality is not binary, but involves a *continuum* from full to null attention. Secondly, although ordinary language offers us a verb for a mental act consisting essentially of attention, namely "attending to," plausibly in reality one can only have *other* mental acts which are more or less attentive. Thus, to attend to x is typically just to observe x attentively. When we take these two considerations into account, it is hard to see the phenomenology of attention as a phenomenal determinable on a par with perceptual phenomenology, cognitive phenomenology, and so on. It is more natural to think of each of these determinables as varying in the degree of attention involved in experiencing them. When S experiences perceptual phenomenology attentively to degree D_i, this experience is a specific determinate of perceptual phenomenology.

In aesthetics, there is a long tradition of discussing the nature of aesthetic experience. A traditional assumption in this debate is that aesthetic experience is something of a natural kind: although there is a variety of aesthetic experiences, there is some feature common and peculiar to them. Paintings, flowers, novels, palaces, rivers, etc. all afford very different aesthetic experiences, but these also have something in common. What they have in common may be called aesthetic phenomenology per se and suggested as a seventh primitive. Alternatively, there might be one species of aesthetic experience—one kind of encounter with one kind of beauty, or some other aesthetic property—that affords a phenomenology unlike anything else in life, a phenomenology irreproducible from any combination of other experiences we have. The experience of *encounter with the sublime* might be a good candidate. Hearing one of Bach's Brandenburg Concertos, reading one of Shakespeare's better soliloquies, witnessing one of Messi's spectacular slaloms, observing a manifestation of the aurora borealis, surveying Place de la Concorde from the entrance to Jeu de Paume: all these involve, it might be claimed, an attitudinal phenomenal feature of presenting-as-sublime the object experienced; this presenting-as-sublime is irreducible to any combination of familiar types of phenomenology.

I am open to such primitivism about the phenomenology of aesthetic experience. But I note that reductive accounts of the experience of encounter with the sublime, as a combination of several more familiar experiential elements, are also antecedently plausible. Thus we may note that encounter with the sublime involves an element of paralyzing awe; a feeling of being in the presence of ungraspable or infinite grandeur; a heightened sense of feeling alive, and of the open multitude of potentialities of life; an overwhelming but calm joy, sometimes tinged with great hope for humanity or for life itself; a dissipation of all anxiety as one fully assumes one's tiny place in the fantastic theater of the universe. It is hard to tell whether an exhaustive enumeration of the variety of perceptual, cognitive, and emotional experiences characteristic of encounter with the sublime would not exhaust all there is to the phenomenology, making appeal to a sui generis presenting-as-sublime unnecessary. More generally, I note that leading philosophical accounts of aesthetic experience tend to characterize it reductively in terms of the compresence of certain perceptual features. According to Beardsley (1958), for example, aesthetic experiences are characterized by focus, intensity, and unity. (Focus and intensity have to do with an alert attention to the object, unity with finding "coherence" and "completeness" in the object.) If this is the distinctive phenomenology of aesthetic experience, it is surely reducible. And although many now reject Beardsley's account (see Dickie 1965 for an influential critique), newer views still tend to account for aesthetic experience in terms of combinations of perceptual features (see Iseminger 2003 for review).

There are other experiences in our rich mental life that offer candidate phenomenal primitives at the right level of abstraction: existential feelings, religious experiences, and more. To argue that there are *only* six second-layer phenomenal primitives, one would need to consider all those—and others. Thus although I suspect there may be no others, my "official thesis" in this book is just this: there are at least six phenomenal primitives at the right level of abstraction—six species of for-me-ness.

4. Overall Conclusion: How We Make Sense of Ourselves

Mainstream analytic philosophy of mind of the second half of the twentieth century and early twenty-first century offers one dominant framework for understanding the human mind. It is an essentially mechanistic picture, understanding the mind in terms of its functional architecture. The fundamental architecture is this: there is input in the form of perception, output in the form of action, and input-output mediation through propositional attitudes, notably belief and desire. Perception, belief, desire, action: these are the central, recurring junctures in the continuous process we call mental life. In the literature, there are local debates aplenty on the nature of perception, the nature of action, and the nature of the attitudes. But the general framework is relatively stable. Moreover, the general approach to each of the main junctures is similar, characterizing the relevant phenomenon in terms of functional role within the system and representational connections to the environment.[15]

The framework is motivated by a cluster of methodological assumptions. The most fundamental of those is that our self-understanding should be continuous with scientific understanding as obtained through the paradigmatic natural sciences (physics, chemistry, biology). From this flow a desire for a mechanistic model of the mind; an emphasis on strictly third-personal understanding that shuns introspective insight; a conception of mental phenomena as explanatory posits, with observable behaviors as the explananda that justify positing them; and more.

I have no desire to call into question the intellectual value of the kind of self-understanding engendered by this functionalist framework. But as I argued in the Introduction, it is odd to theorize about *observable phenomena* as though they were *merely* explanatory posits, essentially bracketing our observation of them. Insofar as some mental phenomena are introspectively observable, there is a kind of insight into their nature that is *available* to us and that goes beyond that provided by the functionalist framework. This alternative self-understanding focuses on the experiential rather than mechanical aspect of mental life, freely avails itself of first-person insight, and considers that mental phenomena can be witnessed directly as opposed to merely hypothesized for explanatory benefits. It would be perverse to simply ignore this other kind of understanding and insight. Importantly, there is no immediate competition between the third-person, mechanistic, functionalist framework and the first-person, experiential, phenomenological approach—not any more than seeing and smelling a rose compete for insight into the nature of the rose.

Pursuing this kind of phenomenological understanding of the mind, I have offered a portrait of mental life at significant variance with the functionalist framework. Belief and desire have been replaced, as the paradigmatic cognitive and conative states, by the experience of making a judgment and the experience of deciding-and-then-trying (respectively). These have been characterized essentially not by their functional role and representational connections to the environment, but by two distinct phenomenal attitudinal features: (nonsensory) presenting-as-true and presenting-as-good.

In addition, I have argued for a picture of the propositional attitudes that adds a third paradigmatic type of state, on a par with the cognitive and conative paradigms: entertaining. This is characterized essentially by the phenomenal attitudinal feature of merely-presenting.

In the functionalist framework, perception and action complete the picture as entry point into and exit point out of the functional system. I have retained perception in my phenomenological alternative, but characterized it in terms of a different phenomenal attitudinal feature, presenting-as-existent. Action, however, has been replaced by algedonic experience, essentially characterized by sensuous presenting-as-valuable. Meanwhile, a sensory analog has been matched to entertaining as well, namely, (phantasmagoric) imagination.

The upshot is a framework for understanding ourselves and our mental life that replaces the functionalist picture revolving around perception, belief, desire, and action with a phenomenological picture focused on perceptual experience, making a judgment, imagination, entertaining, pleasure and pain, and deciding-cum-trying. These are all experiential phenomena. The mind also includes nonexperiential standing states, but those are characterized, qua mental, in terms of the conscious experiences they dispose one to have (for example, standing belief is essentially a disposition to make a conscious judgment).

As noted, it is not my intention to deny the intellectual value of the functionalist framework for understanding mental life; only to underline the equal value of a phenomenological counterpart. This raises the question of the relationship between the two. The answer, I think, has to do with the familiar philosophical task of reconciling the manifest and the scientific image of the world. We can envisage a future neuroscientific theory that provides a complete explanation of behavior, but in which we cannot really recognize ourselves as we appear to ourselves in our personal experience. On the opposite end of the spectrum is the immediate way we manifest to ourselves, simply in living through our stream of consciousness, but which imposes no theoretical order and rigor on the phenomena. The philosophical task is to fashion a way of making sense of ourselves that somehow lies in-between these two extremes. But this project too can be pursued from two opposing directions. One starts out from the scientific pole and asks how much of our manifest self-conception we can bring into the fold before we start losing the scientific flavor of our model. The other starts out from the manifest pole and asks how much theoretical order and rigor we can impose on the phenomena before the feeling of alienation starts setting in. The functionalist framework represents the first of these approaches to the philosophical task at hand; the alternative phenomenological framework I have pursued in this book goes for the second. Together, they allow us to narrow the chasm between the scientific and the manifest image: what needs reconciling is no longer neuroscience and lived experience, but a functionalist framework for making sense of ourselves in terms of perception, belief, desire, and action and a phenomenological framework in terms of paradigmatic conscious experiences characterized by distinctive attitudinal features.[16]

Appendix

Theses on the Phenomenology of Freedom

This appendix is a somewhat experimental piece—not in the sense in which some research is experimental but in the sense in which some music is. I am going to defend four theses about the phenomenology of freedom—another topic that has attracted attention in recent philosophy of mind—and my defense will rely on an unusual, first-personal methodology.

1. Introduction: A Framework for Studying the Phenomenology of Freedom

Over two centuries ago, Hegel (1807 §482A) wrote this:

> No idea is so generally recognized as indefinite, ambiguous, and open to the greatest misconceptions (to which therefore it actually falls victim) as the idea of freedom: none in common currency with so little appreciation of its meaning.

One way to try to overcome the murkiness and slipperiness of such a notion as freedom is through *phenomenological analysis*, whereby we seek fuller understanding of the nature of freedom, in the first instance, by investigating the modes in which it is given to us in our personal experience.[1] This Appendix is intended as a contribution to this type of phenomenological study of freedom. It divides in three: I open with conceptual and methodological preliminaries (§§2–4), then offer a first-person account of the phenomenology of freedom (§§5–10), and close with a third-person examination of a choice collection of first-person descriptions of experiencing freedom (§§11–13).

In the first part, I propose a possible framework for studying the phenomenology of freedom. I suggest that the phenomenology of freedom is a pervasive if normally unimposing type of phenomenology—which makes it particularly elusive. I suggest that the best way to study it may be to consider the first-person reports of subjects who have suffered a temporary loss of freedom, with the result that when their freedom is restored they experience it more acutely than is common. The guiding thought is that only when the phenomenology becomes thus sufficiently pronounced does it lend itself to more lucid appreciation and articulation.

In the second part of the piece, I present a first-person application of this framework: I describe and analyze the acute sense of freedom I experienced for about five hours immediately upon my release from prison, at the end of a two-month sentence, in the summer of 1992. This first-person account leads me to four main theses about the phenomenology of freedom—the one that characterized my own experience, that is. The first is simply that there *is* a (distinctive) phenomenology of freedom. The second is that this phenomenology of freedom is, in Isaiah Berlin's (1958) terminology, a phenomenology as of *negative* rather than *positive* freedom (very roughly: freedom-from rather than freedom-to). The third thesis is that the relevant phenomenology is as of compatibilist rather than libertarian freedom (roughly: as of freedom consistent with determination by prior causes). The fourth and final thesis is that the relevant phenomenology is, in the first instance, *not* a phenomenology as of *acting freely*, or even *willing freely*, but rather a phenomenology as of *being free*.

In the third part, I examine reports by other subjects temporarily deprived of freedom, in search of confirmation of the phenomenological theses presented in the second part. I focus on reports by (i) emancipated and manumitted slaves, (ii) concentration camp survivors, and (iii) recently released prisoners. This hardly exhausts the known types of captivity, let alone of unfreedom, but it will serve well as an *illustration* of a certain kind of inquiry. Although the confirmation I obtain in this part is only partial, it is substantive.

I. Conceptual and Methodological Preliminaries
2. Pervasive Phenomenology

Many first-order questions assail us when we start reflecting on the subjective experience of freedom. But the very first question that arises is second-order: why is it so difficult to answer those first-order questions with much confidence? If there is such an experience, should it not be rather transparent to us that it exists and what it is like?

Skeptics about subtle, nonsensory types of subjective experience are often motivated precisely by the epistemological difficulties that attend phenomenological inquiry. Their assumption often seems to be that if there is a phenomenology of freedom (for example), it should be obvious that there is. They assume, in effect, that knowledge of phenomenology should always be immediate and effortless. Why they think this is not always clear, but a natural diagnosis is that they are wedded to a picture of phenomenology as strongly self-intimating: whenever a person experiences a phenomenology, she *knows* that she experiences it. Ironically, then, it is a kind of epistemological inflationism that leads to ontological deflationism.

One is entitled to wonder, under these circumstances, whether a reversal of attitudes would not be appropriate: a more deflationary epistemology of consciousness might pave the way to a more inflationary ontology of it. Pain and color experiences may make themselves immediately known—they are loud, attention-grabbing experiences—but there may also be other experiences that are shyer, and as it seems to me correspondingly more charming. The experience of freedom may be one of those.

There could be many reasons why some phenomenologies are harder to notice than others. Paradoxically perhaps, one possible reason is that such experiences are pervasive in our mental life. Consider the incessant hum of the refrigerator in the background as you are engrossed in some task. Typically, you do not notice the hum—not until it ceases. It is only upon its abrupt cessation, and in view of the phenomenal contrast thus engendered in your auditory phenomenology, that you become explicitly aware both that you no longer experience the hum and that you had been experiencing it for some time.[2] Now imagine if you will a world—call it "Fridge World"—just like ours but for this minor detail: there is a background humming sound accompanying every person from birth to death. In all likelihood, in Fridge World our counterparts are entirely unaware of this component of their auditory phenomenology. We may debate whether they ever *could* become aware of it, through careful phenomenological analysis or otherwise. But two things are clear: (1) their phenomenology *has* this auditory component (by stipulation), and (2) they do not normally notice it, certainly not effortlessly or immediately. That auditory component is phenomenologically shy. (It would be a mistake to deny the possibility of Fridge World on the grounds that the auditory system would not continue to register the presence of such a stimulus. Such considerations suggest at most that Fridge World is not *nomologically* possible, but do nothing to undermine its *metaphysical* possibility [let alone its *epistemic* possibility]. For the purposes of the present thought-experiment, metaphysical possibility is certainly sufficient.)

Consider next the condition known as brunescence, characterized by a brownish-yellow hue slowly and gently permeating the subject's visual field over many years. Patients are typically unaware of this process. As their hair grows ever so slightly by the minute, so their visual phenomenology imperceptibly yellows by the hour. Exiting brunescent-cataract removal surgery, however, they are often astonished at the newfound lucidity of their visual field, and at the ignorance of its condition they had suffered so long. In this case, the induced phenomenal contrast is not between the presence and absence of a certain phenomenology (an auditory hum), but between a high and low degree of the same phenomenology (the visual yellow).

A general lesson lurks here. We can sometimes *see* a table (e.g., when it is nearby) and sometimes not (e.g., when it is far enough), but sometimes we are unsure what if anything we are seeing far off in the blurry horizon. Likewise, sometimes we clearly *introspect* an experience (e.g., of a sudden toothache) and sometimes fail to (e.g., when a mild headache has accompanied us all day), but on other occasions we are not entirely confident what if anything we are introspecting in the phenomenal jungle that is our everyday stream of consciousness. On those occasions, researchers have long attempted to magnify subjects' introspective powers, in the hope that a more discerning introspective faculty could reveal more about the realm of experience. Indeed, this was the premise behind *fin-de-siècle* introspectionist psychology. But this approach faces many pitfalls, including the possibility of reading into one's phenomenology what is not there due to prior theoretical commitments (more on this in §4). A very different and more "theoretically neutral" approach to the cognitive distance (if you will) between the introspecting and the introspected would nurture not the former but the latter: in seeking to magnify not the acuity of the introspecting, but the vivacity of the introspected, we may render it more accessible to normal, untrained introspection.[3] The Fridge and brunescence cases appear to follow this second model: they reveal a phenomenology not by introspecting experience harder but by making experience particularly vivid.[4]

We may now envision another world—call this one "Free World"—all of whose inhabitants are accompanied by an incessant, quiet, low-humming phenomenology of freedom from birth to death. Presumably, like the citizens of Fridge World, those of Free World do not normally notice this pervasive phenomenology of freedom. But for all that, the phenomenology is there.

My suspicion is that *we* live in Free World, or a world very like it. If so, there does exist a phenomenology of freedom, but in everyday life it is but a background hum of sorts. Each and every one of us experiences freedom, to some degree, more or less throughout his or her waking life. (This is perhaps why Levinas [1953: 266] remarks that "human freedom is essentially unheroic.") If this is right, then the only way to notice the phenomenology of freedom would be through cosmic perturbations in Free World: either an abrupt disappearance of freedom (analogously to the refrigerator case), or a dramatic instant drop in its level and intensity (analogously to the brunescence case). Such abrupt disappearance or dramatic drop, or for that matter the restoration of original freedom, would create a phenomenal contrast that would make the otherwise elusive—because pervasive—phenomenology of freedom more manifest to the subject. Without necessarily increasing the subject's introspective powers, it might infuse her experience with brighter phenomenal intensity that would lend it more easily to introspective appreciation.

I opened this section with the second-order question as to why it is so difficult to answer with much confidence first-order questions about the phenomenology of freedom. The answer, I suggest, is that being a pervasive and subtle phenomenology, the phenomenology of freedom is something that in the normal go of things we take for granted. It is a quiet and shy phenomenology that evades clear notice, in the way pervasive phenomenology tends to. If this is right, the best way to study the phenomenology of freedom may be to consider its manifestation in subjects who lost their sense of freedom for a certain period, such that when they regain it their experience of freedom is particularly vivid.

3. Varieties of Freedom Loss

Normally, we experience the world around us in terms of objects: we see tables *as tables*, flowers *as flowers*, and people *as people*. However, some neuropsychological conditions undermine this standard phenomenology. In prosopagnosia, for example, subjects lack the ability to recognize faces. In visual agnosia, they lack the ability to identify objects at all. Thus we can partially appreciate the aspect of identifying objects in our own phenomenology by contrasting it with the phenomenology we envisage visual agnostics as having. By the same token, if there were such a thing as *libertagnosia*, we could gain insight into the normal phenomenology of freedom by contrasting it with that of the libertagnostic. There is, in fact, no such thing as libertagnosia, at least not of a natural neurophysiological variety. There are, however, a great many familiar varieties of induced, partial, and provisional loss of freedom, often with attendant loss in the *sense* of freedom. Plausibly, the loss—both of freedom and of the sense of it—is not complete and absolute.[5] Nonetheless it is phenomenologically palpable. Certainly, I will later attest, its restoration can be phenomenologically overwhelming.

Of all forms of freedom loss, slavery is the most dramatic. As it happens, we also have something of a treasure trove for the phenomenological study of the experience of slavery, and emancipation therefrom, in the extensive literature of eighteen- and nineteenth-century slave narratives. Many of these offer acute, visceral, sometimes poetic, and often fine-grained descriptions of lived bondage and its ending. At the same time, in the present context there are certain methodological limitations in the use of the experiences of slavery and emancipation. Notably, as we will see in §11, most slaves whose accounts we can consult today were born into slavery, and thus did not enjoy a period of freedom that could afford them a clear phenomenal contrast with bondage. Relatedly, their preconceptions of freedom often come across as quasi-mythical and disconnected from the actual normal experience of freedom.

To that extent, it is more useful to consult the experiences of persons suffering temporary imprisonment. Those sent to the German concentration camps during World War II often experienced overnight a violent reversal of fortunes, affording a readily noticeable phenomenal contrast. In this respect, their experience bears some methodological advantages as compared to the experience of slaves. But both suffer from another important methodological limitation, namely, that while slavery and the concentration camp robbed a person of her freedom, they robbed her of much more: dignity and self-respect, pride, lasting happiness, and sometimes daily joy. Feelings the free person experiences comparatively infrequently suffused consciousness: resentment, distrust, fear, indignation, and often hatred. Upon rejoining the ranks of the free, the emancipated slave or concentration camp survivor was rarely struck by a pure and distilled feeling of freedom. The feeling overcoming him or her was more often an impure admixture of a great number of swirling and intermingling sentiments. In methodological terms, we would have to say that the phenomenological study of their experiences does not *control for* many variables other than freedom—it represents a "confound."

Methodologically, then, there might be some advantage in considering milder varieties of prison experience: imprisonment in which self-respect and daily joy persist, if muted, and—ideally—the only thing missing entirely is the element of freedom. To be sure, in practice it is virtually impossible to separate out the element of freedom in such a perfectly clinical manner. Still, renowned political prisoners and low-level criminal prisoners are often incarcerated in minimum-security facilities and experience a reasonably normal everyday. The experience of imprisonment in such circumstances better *approximates* the notion of a human experience differing from normal experience in the removal of only one ingredient, the feeling of freedom. Accordingly, such released prisoners' regaining of freedom is not as phenomologically intense as that following emancipation/manumission from slavery or liberation from concentration camps, but this is precisely because it compromises comparatively little. It controls better for other variables.[6]

With this in mind, §§11–13 examine a handful of spontaneous reports by manumitted and emancipated slaves, concentration camp survivors, and released prisoners. My sample will be woefully inadequate. For one thing, I will discuss only a handful of reports in each category, though I have tried to make those representative. For another, other categories of potentially useful reports will go unexamined, including by abductees and hostages, long-term bed-ridden patients, persons involuntarily institutionalized, persons suffering temporary paralysis (including, dramatically, locked-in syndrome), prisoners in penal colonies, European serfs, indentured laborers and servants, and many others. The reason for this neglect is purely technical and to do with the limitation on research resources; there is no principled reason why those further sources could not be mined for further data. Furthermore, a fuller investigation would consider also the variety of freedom experiences we commonly undergo in less dramatic circumstances: walking out of an appointment that has been the source of anxiety for some time; emerging out of a jealous and suffocating romantic relationship; the lifting of medical restrictions on certain activities; overcoming social and other inhibitions; getting out of work on a Friday afternoon (or, for an academic, coming out of the last lecture of the semester); and so forth. The examination provided here thus covers only a sliver of the domain relevant to the kind of inquiry I have in mind, and will be extremely preliminary at that.

4. Freedom Loss in Privileged Subjects

In the annals of philosophical reflection, appeal to phenomenological pronouncements as confirmation of philosophers' more theoretical constructions is not uncommon. Unsurprisingly, the phenomenology virtually always turns out to align marvelously with the theory. There are two possible explanations for this. The optimistic explanation is that philosophers are in the habit of meticulously constructing their theories around the deliverances of careful and disinterested phenomenological analysis. A more pessimistic explanation is that philosophers are tempted to heavy-handedly read into the phenomenological phenomena their preconceived theories. Here as elsewhere, the truth probably lies in the middle. But at least in the philosophy of freedom, it has often been suspected that phenomenological analysis lies downstream of theory construction—that the philosopher's assessment of what the raw feeling ought to be like is infected by his or her prior theoretical commitments. (For example, a philosopher with compatibilist leanings who was also temperamentally repelled by error theory might be tempted to read a compatibilist phenomenology into her freedom experience.) This suspicion is eminently reasonable in light of the above discussion: since the normal phenomenology of freedom is shy and elusive, its mark on the introspective faculty is often feeble and inarticulate. Because the free person's sense of freedom is typically so phenomenologically underwhelming, it is tempting to read back into it whatever one *expects* it to be like, and one's expectations in this area are likely to derive from one's theoretical commitments, especially when those are the result of thoughtful and considered reflection.

This state of affairs compromises the value of philosophers' phenomenological analyses of freedom. Recently, some researchers have concluded that it is the *layperson's* phenomenological convictions that we ought to interrogate, not the philosopher's. The reasoning is simple: the layperson typically *has no* antecedent theoretical commitments on the deep nature of freedom, and is open to being impressed upon by the sense of freedom more innocently. With this in mind, Nahmias et al. (2004) conducted seminal experimental studies intended to reveal the phenomenology of freedom in naïve subjects, that is, in subjects unversed in philosophical disputes surrounding freedom. The method is adopted from social psychology and involves undergraduate students reading vignettes concerning free choice and then filling out a questionnaire about aspects of the vignettes. From the students' answers inferences are drawn about their corresponding phenomenology.

This approach faces extraordinary methodological challenges, however. Verbal reports express *beliefs about* one's experience of freedom, not the experience itself. When a subject has the conceptual resources to correctly identify and classify her experience, this may be unproblematic. But when the experience is sufficiently subtle and elusive, rendering a subject incapable of discerning it with much clarity and articulating to herself in thought what she is experiencing, the subject is no longer in a position to form illuminating beliefs about it. I have suggested that the phenomenology of freedom is precisely of this subtle and elusive variety. If so, the conceptual resources of the folk may be unsuited for conceptualizing it with much precision and accuracy.

In other words, if the above diagnosis of the reason for philosophers' theoretical prejudices is correct—namely, that they lack independent insight into an extremely elusive and phenomenologically underwhelming experience—the approach of consulting naïve subjects in their stead does nothing to address the core problem. The average layperson's insight into the phenomenology of freedom is at least as tenuous as the philosopher's, even though in some sense it is theoretically purer. The attempt to answer the philosopher-designed questionnaire, with the philosopher still importing her presuppositions about what *might* become manifest in a phenomenology that is largely elusive to her, and the undergraduate grasping for a handle on an experience she lacks the conceptual resources to articulate in either thought or language, creates a spectacle of the blind leading the blind—or perhaps the brunescent leading the brunescent.

Partly to address this issue of conceptual sophistication, introspectionist psychologists made sure to train their subjects in the methods of careful introspection before testing and debriefing them. As noted in the Introduction, Titchener (1901–5) composed a 1600-page manual for training introspection for that express purpose. This practice was even applied to the introspectionist study of the phenomenology of freedom (Wells 1927), with the intent that subjects have the minimal conceptual sophistication needed to conceptualize and articulate all that they may encounter in their phenomenology. This method, however, does open the introspectionist to the charge that his or her subjects may be imposing *their* germinal theories onto the phenomenological data, or even that the conceptual machinery they have been handed by the investigator biases in some respects the way they approach their lived experience, creating undue expectations here and blindspots there (Nahmias et al. 2004: 171).

These charges strike me as well-founded. This is why, presented with the gulf between phenomenal vivacity and introspective acuity, it is less wise to tune up the introspective power, so it shines a more forceful spotlight on the phenomenology, than to rev up the phenomenal intensity, so it impresses upon untutored introspection with greater force. This is what happens with the kinds of subject mentioned above: the freedom experience shines brighter for a time. Other challenges are bound to attend this latter approach as well; but the approach is surely better positioned, at the outset, than those appealing to naïve subjects lacking any special intimacy with freedom or to philosophers with clear prior theoretical commitments regarding it.

Thus the subjects we should really consult, I have argued, are a select group: persons who suffered temporary loss of freedom, preferably without attendant loss of other central aspects of well-being; who have experienced acutely and vividly the restoration of their freedom; who, ideally, have no standing commitments regarding the deep nature of freedom; and who are in a position to articulate clearly that which they have experienced. This methodological approach shields us at once from the theory-laden expectations of individual philosophers and from the resourcelessness of naïve subjects.[7] As noted, later I will examine the testimonies of various authors who have suffered freedom loss at one point and have offered us quasi-phenomenological descriptions of the first moments when they regained their freedom. This sort of third-person survey of first-person reports gains special momentum, however, when conjoined with a first-person analysis of the investigator's own phenomenology. As Sartre (1947: 314) wrote:

> Freedom is one, but it manifests itself in diverse ways according to the circumstances. To all the philosophers who appoint themselves its defenders, it is permissible to pose a preliminary question: in the context of what privileged situation have you encountered the experience of your freedom?

I now turn to my own answer to Sartre's question.

II. Freedom Lost and Found: A First-Person Account
5. Background: Particulars of the Case

The privileged situation in which I encountered my formative experience of freedom was on a sunny afternoon in August 1992, and spanned approximately five hours. Earlier that day, I was released from so-called Prison Six—a military jailing facility in northern Israel—after nearly two months of imprisonment, serving a sentence for desertion.[8] At least in those days, Prison Six was comprised of three sectors: Sector A was minimum-security, Sector B was medium-security, and Sector C maximum-security. I spent the first fortnight in Sector B and the rest of my sentence in Sector A.[9] And so it came to pass that I experienced both minimum- and medium-security imprisonment before I had had the chance to form clear theoretical convictions on the philosophical nature of freedom.[10]

My tenure in Sector B was nasty, brutish, and short. When the big iron gate of the cell slams shut on the first-time prisoner, a sensational realization suddenly dawns upon him: I am in prison! The first challenge a young man faces in prison is that of projecting the right balance of toughness and respect. The prison novice must make clear that he is not to be taken advantage of, but must do so in a fashion that exudes respect for the prison magnificoes. Prison is full of strong personalities, the kind of natural leaders of men that command immediate deference, typically in inverse proportion to the frequency with which they speak. To do well in prison—which means, at bottom, to avoid being beaten up randomly as ruthlessly by an inmate whose repressed aggression has met its breaking point for some arbitrary reason—one needs to find one of those strong personalities, earn his affection and respect, and become his protégé. It is strange how one learns the rules of this new game literally within hours—the margin of error is slim and unforgiving. All this leaves precious little mental space for dwelling on one's lost freedom. Freedom is, in practice, a low-priority and profitless topic of contemplation in one's first days in prison.

How I came to the safety of protégé status, through luck more than wisdom, and on my very first night in prison no less, is an entertaining tale that unfortunately bears nowise on the phenomenology of freedom. What does bear on it is the daily routine of the prisoner. We were woken up every day at 5:30 for a head count in the Sector's central yard. Two hours later, we were to report to the eating hall for breakfast, after which we went to work: for my part, I spent my medium-security career refining my talent for cleaning and folding blankets. There was lunch, then more work, then the long-awaited hour in which we were allowed to move freely in the yard—always the high point of the day. ("Know, ye unimprisoned," wrote Jack London in *The Road*, "that traffic is as restricted inside a large prison as commerce was in the Middle Ages.") After dinner, we had a fixed time interval in which we were permitted to shower and required to shave. On the Sabbath, we did not work and had two extra sessions of yard freedom, where under watchful eyes we were allowed to congregate and laugh loudly—within reason—and, most importantly, did not have to follow any orders. Whenever we were neither working nor eating nor showering nor in the yard, we were locked in our cells.

Although the human element in Sector B was positively more terrifying, its cells were considerably emptier and more comfortable than in Sector A, which was oppressively overpopulated as I was soon to learn. In Sector A, ten bunk beds were lined up on each side of every cell, with less than a foot between them, thus accommodating forty irritable and ill-tempered young men in close confines. Once in Sector A, I was soon removed from blanket duty and given the extremely exclusive and singularly coveted assignment of kitchen work. This involved being woken up an hour earlier, at 4:30, providing sufficient time to prepare breakfast for the hundreds of Sector A inmates, as well as working until midnight, when all prisoners' dinner plates were clean and ready for use the morrow. The great virtue of this assignment, accounting for its universal desirability, is how fast it made time pass. For the prisoner has only one overarching priority, which is to be a non-prisoner, and nothing brought this vista closer with greater efficiency than the ghostly state of semi-consciousness brought forth by long days of incessant work and short nights of harsh sleep. (Left to our own devices for ten minutes, we would all put our heads on the kitchen's cold and filthy floor and fall asleep instantaneously, only to be woken up with a gentle kick moments later to resume work.)

All in all, my time in prison was not a pleasant one. There is brutality and exhaustion, and an inevitable sadness that permeates the unfree man; for years afterward I would have recurrent nightmares of being sent back. But it was also an unrepeatable experience, and an extremely instructive one at that. There was a lot of laughter, a lot of learning and hurried maturation, frequent admiration of men the likes of whom I had never met before—men unfamiliar with fear of authority and lacking any shred of respect for common standards of behavior, but with a fundamental and unshakable decency that manifested itself in irregular and unpredictable manners.

The morning I was released, my mother and sister waited for me outside the prison gates and drove me to my parents' home. After eating lunch with them, I left for a walk about the neighborhood (and the adjacent one), a walk that ended up taking five or six hours. Perhaps for the only time in all the years I spent at my parents' home, I went out for a walk without taking my dog Julie with me. I wanted to be alone.[11]

6. Phenomenological Description

I was walking extremely slowly, as if partially hypnotized. There was no rush, no purpose—nothing needed to get done. The paramount feeling I was experiencing was that of being *uncompelled*. It was very vivid before my mind that nobody could tell me what to do, that there was nothing I needed to do or could be required to do (regardless of what I might happen to want to do). Nothing was even *expected* of me. No external force was in a position to impose itself on me, take over my will, or determine what I was to do over the objections of my will.

Following in the shadow of the feeling of being uncompelled was a related but importantly different feeling of being *unconstrained*. The feeling of being uncompelled and the feeling of being unconstrained are related thus: to feel uncompelled is to feel that no external force can make one do something; to feel unconstrained is to feel that no external force can *prevent* one from doing something. The latter expresses a freedom of agency, the former a freedom of patiency (if you will). There may or may not be a *real difference* between a constraint and a compellence.[12] It remains that the *feelings* associated with being uncompelled to do something one does not want to do, on the one hand, and being unconstrained to do something one does want to do, on the other, is real. The phenomenological difference is there, and both phenomenologies I felt quite distinctly on that afternoon, though that of being uncompelled considerably more vividly.

An interesting feature of both feelings was that they were felt as *boundless*, virtually *all-encompassing*: I had the feeling that I could do (or avoid doing) *anything*—if I only wanted to. I should stress that it is indeterminate in my mind whether this feeling was *strictly* universal or just *almost*. It was also not a feeling directed at particular actions—I did not feel, for example, that I could fly. The feeling was rather that actions in general were open to me. To be sure, in reality there were indefinitely many outlandish and non-outlandish things I could *not* do or avoid doing: I could not bake a cheesecake on my own and I could not avoid wearing clothes while strolling down the street (for more than a few minutes, without interference, etc.). Not only was it false that I could not do (or avoid doing) such things, I (tacitly) *knew* it to be false. But I did not *feel* it to be false. On the contrary, I felt as though I could do, or avoid doing, more or less anything I pleased. We may call this feature of the feelings of being uncompelled and unconstrained their *boundless character*.

An even more basic feature of these feelings was what we may call their *hypothetical character*. Neither the feeling of being uncompelled nor the feeling of being unconstrained involved any pronounced phenomenology of *desire*. There was nothing I actually wanted to do or avoid doing, no action or course thereof that recommended itself to me for pursuit or avoidance. The feelings of being uncompelled and unconstrained did not involve any element of intending, desiring, or even wishing anything. Rather, they had something of a hypothetical form to them: what I felt was that *if* I wanted to do (or not do) this or that, I could. All those courses of action were *open* to me, in that I could pursue or avoid pursuing them as I pleased. But there was nothing I specifically pleased—no course of action had any special attraction on me.

Importantly, the absence of wanting brought in its train an absence of want. Having no desire for anything meant having no *unfulfilled* desire, and thus no lack. The overall experience thus felt "filled," self-contained, stable. It felt *right* to be where I was, doing what I was doing, being who I was. This is related to what is sometimes referred to as the *feeling of rightness* (Mangan 2001), and it was in vivid evidence during large tracts of those five hours.

The next powerful phenomenological element in my overall experience was an overwhelming positive affect—an unusual kind of elation or euphoria, distinguished by the lack of that energetic, enthusiastic, adrenalined strand in more common moments of euphoria. I would describe it as a sort of *passive bliss*. I was very alert, very aware, and things were felt with great clarity and acuity—as they can under the influence of certain stimulants—but I was not overtaken by any energy that needed to find its outlet, and as mentioned there was nothing in particular I felt like doing. It just felt *good*.

So far I have discussed four phenomenal elements in the experience of freedom: the feeling of being uncompelled, the feeling of being unconstrained, the feeling of rightness, and the feeling of passive bliss. (In addition, I described two *characters* of some of these elements: the boundless character and the hypothetical character.) A fifth distinctive component in my overall experience was a conspicuous *lack of anxiety*. There was nothing to worry about, or more accurately, everything to be unworried about. By this I mean that, phenomenologically speaking, this was not an absence of feeling, but a feeling of absence. It was not just that there was no feeling of anxiety. There was a positive feeling of no-anxiety, of *lightness*—of all things being liberatingly inconsequential. As before, it was not the case that everything was inconsequential, nor did I believe it to be the case. But it was what the *feeling* was like. This may be thought of as a *phenomenology of extraordinary calm*. It functioned as a shield of some sort. Negative thoughts, vengeful thoughts, worrisome thoughts, indignant thoughts, failed to make their mark on my state of consciousness. They evaporated at the entry points of my awareness like soap bubbles against a concrete wall. Thoughts of the form "I should pay that bill" and "I should clip my toenails" would not make it through. My consciousness' grounds were inhospitable to "I should" thoughts—they had space only for "I could" thoughts. The regime was of a protected peace of mind, a permeating sense of mental safety.

There seems to be some intimate connection between this feeling of lightness and the feeling of rightness. The positive feeling of *no-anxiety* just mentioned is phenomenologically similar to, and may well overlap with, the positive feeling of *no-desire* mentioned above. Still, they are distinct feelings.

My overall phenomenology during the entire episode involved also, of course, ongoing visual and other perceptual experiences, as well as any number of errant thoughts. The specific contents of perceptual experience were in one sense unremarkable: houses, trees, cars, roads, people. Yet there were distinctive phenomenal features even at that level. Three stand out; henceforth I will refer to them as "the three perceptual features." First, things were perceived very vividly, though not more brightly. If anything, there was something distinctly muted about the hues around me, something visually understated. The experiences were more vivid only in that they were more *present to the mind*. Secondly, the natural attraction point of visual space, the location in one's surrounding that magnetized my visual attention, was much farther from me than it normally is. Whereas on a regular day the space five to twenty-five yards straight ahead of me commands my visual attention, on that day the point of attraction lay about forty to sixty yards ahead and slightly to one side or the other. My gaze was somehow lifted, removed from the immediate surroundings. (Perhaps this had to do with a general sense of being removed from the world.) Thirdly, my otherwise aimless gaze seemed disproportionately attracted to trees and bushes. For whatever reason, my visual attention seemed to find botanic—or perhaps just "natural"—objects a comfortable resting point much more frequently than in ordinary life. I am not sure what to make of this, but am reminded of a line from Shakespeare's fourth Sonnet: "Nature's bequest gives nothing but doth lend / And being frank she lends to those are free."[13]

Another attentional effect could be seen in the contents of my *cognitive* phenomenology, the sort of thoughts that occurred to me. I already mentioned that negative and worrisome thoughts fell flat. But there was another systematic feature of my thought process during the episode: the relative proportion of ongoing self-awareness and world-awareness in my overall awareness was persistently balanced. In everyday life, by far most of our awareness is consumed with the world around us, self-awareness intruding only peripherally. Sometimes we enter introspective moods in which our consciousness is filled with more focal self-awareness, but these are comparatively short-lived and do not typically endure past the half-hour. On that day, however, I was acutely aware of myself and my state of mind, in quite unspecific manner, for a period of hours. This self-awareness did not crowd out world-awareness, but cohabited with it in a stable balance. I will refer to this, doubtless suboptimally, as "the cognitive feature."

There was also a temporal dimension to the episode. It had a rhythm not unlike other powerful prolonged experiences. What I describe above is based on the episode's peaks of phenomenal intensity, which recurred in intervals of twenty to thirty minutes (though my memory here feels uncertain). There were also ebbs in which the described phenomenology was less clear and distinct—though at no time did I feel quite as one does in the ordinary go of things. The phenomenological extraordinariness was stubborn. Perhaps the most powerful peak in the entire episode marked itself in my memory with great overall precision, of the sort that characterizes traumas or turning points in one's life (see under: "Where were you on 9/11?").

On a number of occasions, I became focally and reflectively aware of the very extraordinariness of the overall experience I was undergoing. Like a headache slowly becoming so painful as to command one's focal attention, the phenomenal intensity of what I was experiencing occasionally became so overwhelming that it involuntarily attracted my attention. Unfortunately, it was impossible to dwell on it overmuch: the phenomenology appeared to blur under introspective microspection. It could only flourish, apparently, in the state of the right balance between world-awareness and self-awareness. Eventually, the phenomenology started slowly dissipating, in something that was experienced as painful loss, not unlike the way one feels when the state of bewitchment following a powerful film—the feeling that says "From now on *that* is how I am going to live my life!"—starts to dissipate, leaving behind it only the oppressive banality of the present.

7. Preliminary Phenomenological Analysis

The actual flow of experience is continuous rather than discrete and is not instantly experienced as decomposing into distinct elements. So the above "mere description" is forsooth and perforce at least somewhat theoretical and analytic. I have, in fact, identified *nine* components in it: (1) the feeling of being uncompelled (with its hypothetical and boundless character), (2) the feeling of being unconstrained (ditto), (3) the feeling of passive bliss (the "nonadrenalined euphoria"), (4) the feeling of lightness (aka the phenomenology of extraordinary calm), (5) the feeling of rightness, (6)–(8) the three perceptual features, and (9) the cognitive feature (the balance of world-awareness and self-awareness). Later, I will add a tenth element.

These are components of the phenomenology of freedom, or at least *one* phenomenology exhibited by *one* personal experience of freedom. Interestingly, most are clearly not components of any *distinctive* phenomenology of freedom. Thus, the feelings of passive bliss, lightness, and rightness (items 3–5) are types of mood phenomenology one is liable to experience outside the freedom context. Likewise, the perceptual and cognitive features may characterize the experience of freedom, but they are present in other experiences as well (one may find oneself wanting to stare at trees in any number of circumstances!).

The feelings of being uncompelled and unconstrained, however, do seem to constitute a distinctive type of phenomenology of freedom. The idea of a distinctive phenomenology of freedom is one of a phenomenal feature no other experiences exhibit but freedom experiences. This means that other experiences can be distinguished from freedom experiences purely phenomenologically, and without appeal to any nonphenomenal elements. Since *only* experiences of freedom exhibit the feelings of being uncompelled and unconstrained, these are *peculiar* to the phenomenology of freedom.

For my first thesis about the phenomenology of freedom, then, I put forward simply that there is one—a distinctive one. This is a sort of zero-point thesis for any discussion of the distinctive phenomenology of freedom. We may put it simply as follows:

(T_0) There exists a distinctive phenomenology of freedom.

As noted, what constitutes this distinctive phenomenology is the compresence of feeling uncompelled and feeling unconstrained.

It is fairly clear, at the same time, that such a phenomenology of freedom is not a phenomenal determinable at the same level as cognitive, conative, and entertaining phenomenology. The feeling of being uncompelled, for example, is not as general as the "credal feeling" of judging that something is the case. There is an open question in my mind whether the feeling of being uncompelled represents a *sui generis* phenomenology at a lower level of abstraction, or on the contrary can be reduced to a combination of cognitive, conative, and mood phenomenology. I am bracketing this question in this Appendix.

What more can be said by way of characterizing this distinctive phenomenology of freedom? In other areas of phenomenological analysis, it is often useful to refer to philosophical disputes about the *nature* of certain entities to characterize parallel disputes about *experiences* as of those entities. Consider the perennial metaphysical dispute about the nature of *causation*: Humeans maintain that there is nothing more to A causing B than a constant conjunction between A and B; anti-Humeans hold that there *is* something more, an invisible "secret connexion" between A and B. Without settling this dispute about the *nature* of causation, one may use it to characterize the *experience* of causation: one view would be that perceiving A to cause B is nothing but perceiving a constant conjunction between A and B, another that it also involves a feeling as of a "secret connexion" between the two. Likewise, consider the metaphysical dispute about the nature of (ordinary, medium-sized, physical) *objects*: one view is that they are nothing but bundles of properties, another that they involve bare particulars. A parallel phenomenological dispute would afford two possible characterizations of the *experience* of objects—in terms of experiencing bundles of properties or experiencing bare particulars.

In like manner, one might hope that philosophical disputes about the *nature* of freedom could be used to formulate theses on the subjective experience of freedom. The nature of freedom is debated most centrally in two areas of philosophy: political philosophy and metaphysics. In both areas the notion of freedom is implicated in a battery of intermingled debates and is thus hard to distill clearly. Still, there are central, paramount debates that may serve us well: in political philosophy, the debate between negative and positive conceptions of political liberty; in metaphysics, the debate between compatibilist and libertarian conceptions of free will. The next two sections introduce these debates and take a stand on their phenomenological parallels (on the basis of the phenomenological description from §6). The parallel disputes concern whether freedom is *experienced* as negative or positive, and whether it is *experienced* as compatibilist or libertarian.

Appendix

8. Phenomenology of Negative Freedom

Let us start with a science-fiction vignette. Aristide is born in Haiti in 2028 and grows up in extreme poverty in Port-au-Prince's outer slums. From a young age he develops a fascination with the aurora borealis (the "northern lights"). As he turns eighteen, he resolves to travel to Scandinavia and see the aurora borealis before he dies. Initially, however, there are three problems. First, in 2032 (when Aristide was just four), after a long descent into ever greater political instability, a totalitarian regime emerged in Haiti that forbade any travel abroad. Secondly, early in the 2040s, and following the rise to power of fierce anti-immigration parties across Scandinavia, Scandinavian countries one by one closed their borders to any third-world visitors (even tourists). Thirdly, as a baker assistant Aristide makes less than a dollar a day and could simply never afford a trip to Scandinavia. Fortunately, however, three events take place over the next dozen years, and by 2058 Aristide realizes his lifelong dream and rests his weary eyes on those enchanting lights. The first thing that happens is that, in 2049, the totalitarian regime dissolves and Haitians regain the right to travel abroad. The second is that, in 2055, the anti-immigration party is thrown out of power in much heralded Swedish elections, with the new government reopening the country to third-world travelers. Finally, in 2058, Aristide wins the national lottery and pockets a handsome million dollars. His first action is to take his young family to Sweden to see the aurora borealis.

Before these three events take place, Aristide is unfree to take his coveted trip. After they occur, he is free to do so. But it is interesting to chart the different impact each event has on Aristide's freedom to take the trip. The 2049 collapse of the totalitarian regime is welcome, but even after it Aristide remains unfree to take the trip, given the Scandinavian restrictions on travel and his own lack of financial resources. Anyone claiming that this event alone makes Aristide free to go would be simply wrong. In contrast, the 2058 lottery win certainly makes Aristide free to take the trip, given the previous developments in Sweden. Anyone claiming that Aristide is still unfree to do so would again be wrong. The effect of the 2055 Swedish elections is more ambiguous. After it, neither Haiti nor Sweden prevents Aristide from taking the trip, but he still cannot afford it under any circumstances. Here arguing about whether Aristide is free or unfree to take the trip feels more like a verbal dispute. In one sense he is free to, in that no one prevents him from doing so; but in another sense he is unfree, as he still lacks the power to go. Both those claiming that he is free to go and those claiming he is not have a point—they are both right in *one* sense. It thus seems that there are two notions of freedom—"freedom$_1$" and "freedom$_2$"—such that between 2055 and 2058 Aristide is free$_1$ to go but not free$_2$.

The sense that the term freedom is ambiguous is a recurring theme in political thought. In the *New Essays on Human Understanding* (Book II, ch.21 §8), Leibniz (1765: 130) distinguishes between "freedom of right" and "freedom of fact":

> The term *freedom* is highly ambiguous. There is freedom of right and of fact. By that of right a slave is not free and a subject is so completely, but a poor man is as free as a rich one. The freedom of fact consists either in the power to want as one should, or in the power to do as one wants.

In a similar vein, Benjamin Constant (1819) distinguishes between "freedom of the moderns" and "freedom of the ancients," which correspond roughly to freedom$_1$ and freedom$_2$ respectively. Isaiah Berlin (1958) similarly distinguishes between "negative" and "positive" freedom. Debates over how exactly to characterize these distinctions, and over their very tenability, are rife in political philosophy. If nothing else, however, we may use the Aristide vignette to define two notions of freedom *ostensively*: using Berlin's terminology, we may define negative freedom as the kind of freedom Aristide gains already in 2055 and positive freedom as the kind he gains only in 2058. When subject S is free relative to action φ, we may say that (i) S is negatively free to φ iff S's situation is similar in relevant respects to Aristide's situation in 2055, and that (ii) S is positively free to φ iff S's situation is similar in relevant respects to Aristide's situation in 2058.

Berlin himself attempted to draw his distinction in terms of *freedom-from* and *freedom-to*: a person is negatively free to the extent that she is free *from* constraints, obstacles, restrictions, and so on; she is positively free to the extent that she is free *to* do or become what she wants. Thus, in 2055 Aristide is free *from* external constraints on traveling to Sweden, but he is not yet free *to* travel to Sweden. Although the suggestion is intuitive, the difficulties it faces are legion. This is not the place to rehearse them; let us only point out that the same state can arguably be equivalently described as being free *to* travel to Sweden and being free *from* the relevant financial constraints, or as being free *from* government ban on travel and being free *to* travel as one pleases. More deeply, a full specification of any state of freedom appears to involve reference to both constraints one is free *from* and courses of action one is free *to* pursue; it is only reliance on context that allows us to drop explicit reference to one of these in casual conversation (MacCallum 1967). Better to stick with the ostensive definition, then. For although the literature's trail of sorrow is awash with other failed attempts to articulate the distinction, the story of Aristide shows that there is *something there*—however hard it is to characterize generally. The story *points* at the phenomena of interest, even if it does nothing to define them. (Compare: a speaker may try to offer a definition of "the moon," but the interlocutor is more likely to grasp what is spoken of by being pointed in the right direction.[14])

There may well be a number of closely related but different distinctions in the area, so that Aristide's case is too underdescribed to discriminate among them. Still, at least one of those distinctions captures a deep and important divide in conceptions of freedom, and all those hovering about it surely inherit some of its gravity. That some distinction in the area is deep and important is clear from the fact that much of political philosophy can be organized around the question of which kind of freedom a political system ought to maximize. Russell (1919: 64) may be right that "freedom is the greatest of political goods"—but which freedom? One thesis, recognizably liberal, is that negative freedom is the highest political good. A very different thesis, more socialist-leaning, is that positive freedom is.[15] The deep divide between left and right in the political arena is arguably diagnosed by this simple question: What is freedom that a political system should maximize it? Is it the kind of freedom Aristide enjoys already in 2055, or the one he gains only in 2058?

Parallel to this political question is a *phenomenological* question: What is the freedom that shows up in the phenomenology of freedom experiences? Do freedom experiences *feel* like experiences as of negative freedom or as of positive freedom? I cannot, of course, address the question for *every* freedom experience, and will focus instead only on the particular freedom experience I described in §6: was it an experience as of negative or positive freedom? Since the distinctive phenomenal aspects of that experience are the feelings of being uncompelled and being unconstrained, the question is whether those feelings reflect a negative or positive type of freedom.

In considering this question, my sense is that the feelings of being uncompelled and unconstrained pertain to negative rather than positive freedom. We have characterized negative and positive freedom ostensively, by pointing at the kind of freedom Aristide gains already in 2055 (negative freedom) and the one he gains only in 2058 (positive freedom). Recall, now, that the feelings of being uncompelled and being unconstrained were characterized above as follows: to feel uncompelled is to feel that no external force can make me do something; to feel unconstrained is to feel that no external force can prevent me from doing something. The key phrase in these characterizations is "external force." As soon as the travel bans are lifted, and before Aristide acquires the means to act on his desire to go to Sweden, what prevents him from going to see the aurora borealis is lack of financial resources. Such lack is not an external force (certainly not *experienced* as an external force) in the sense legal restrictions, for example, are. No outside *agency* constrains his travel, and certainly none compels him not to travel.[16]

The point is *not* that Aristide himself feels uncompelled and/or unconstrained already in 2055. (Perhaps he does, perhaps he does not—the story did not comment on this.) Rather, the point is that the experience *I* had in 1992 was an experience *as of* the kind of freedom already enjoyed by Aristide in 2055. This point may be put more precisely in terms of *veridicality conditions*:[17] what was required for my 1992 experience of freedom to be accurate is only that I possess the freedom Aristide in fact possesses, in the story, already in 2055; whether in addition I possessed the freedom he comes to have in 2058 is irrelevant to the accuracy of my experience. In other words: the only type of freedom that showed up in the experience's veridicality conditions is negative freedom. One need not refer to positive freedom to specify the experience's veridicality conditions.

The zero-point thesis for our discussion of the distinctive phenomenology of freedom was that such a phenomenology *exists*. This left the task of *characterizing* that phenomenology. I now wish to add a first thesis by way of characterization:

(T_1) There is a type of experience of freedom whose distinctive phenomenology is as of negative freedom.

This thesis is obtained by application of the general method of using conceptual tools that evolved in the context of philosophical disputes about the *nature* of certain phenomena to elucidate the character of *experiences* of those phenomena. We continue with the same method in the next section.

9. Phenomenology of Compatibilist Freedom

The most prominent philosophical debate implicating the notion of freedom is surely that over determinism and free will. There are many ways to formulate the debate. Start by considering the following inconsistent triad:

(1) All our actions are causally predetermined.
(2) Some of our actions are free.
(3) Causally predetermined actions are not free.

This triad can be resolved by rejecting the third proposition: a causally predetermined action can still be free, it is natural to think, provided that what causally determines it is the agent's will. After all, intuitively an action is free when one performs it of one's own free will—because one freely chose to perform it. Unfortunately, a similar triad resurfaces for choices and decisions:

(1) All our decisions are causally predetermined.
(2) Some of our decisions are free.
(3) Causally predetermined decisions are not free.

The problem of free will is that each of these is individually plausible but they cannot all be true. Libertarianism about free will rejects the first, claiming that some of our decisions (and hence actions) are not causally predetermined. Hard determinism rejects the second, claiming that none of our decisions (and actions) are free—free will is an illusion. Compatibilism rejects the third proposition, claiming that a decision (or action) being predetermined does not preclude its being free—causal determination and freedom are perfectly compatible.

One way to think of the dispute between the compatibilist and the libertarian is as a dispute about the nature of freedom. It is antecedently plausible that one acted freely just in case one could have acted otherwise—and that one chose freely just in case one could have chosen otherwise.[18] Still, compatibilists and libertarians disagree on the nature of this "ability to do/choose otherwise" condition. In particular, they disagree about whether freedom requires the ability to do/choose otherwise given (*a*) the *actual* prior conditions or (*b*) *some* nonactual prior conditions. Compatibilists must adopt the latter interpretation: even though all our actions and choices are causally predetermined by prior conditions, still it is sometimes true that we could have acted or decided otherwise, namely, *if the (right) prior conditions had been different*.[19] Libertarians insist that this kind of ability to do or decide otherwise does not suffice to make us free. What is required is the ability to do/decide otherwise *given the actual prior conditions*. In order to be actually free, we must be able to act and choose to act otherwise given the actual history of the universe.

With this in mind, we may distinguish two notions of freedom, based on two different senses of "could have done" and "could have decided." I am not a US citizen, so am legally barred from voting in presidential elections. Because of this, I did not vote for Barack Obama in 2012. *Could* I have voted for him? In one sense, of course I could—namely, if I had been a US citizen. But in another sense, of course I could not—since I am *not* a US citizen! The first is a *hypothetical sense* of "could have done," the second a *categorical sense*. The hypothetical sense allows *nonactual* prior conditions in the assessment of what someone could do; the categorical sense allows only *actual* prior conditions. The same applies to "could have chosen" and "could have decided." Consider this bit from *Seinfeld*:

GEORGE: You should confront him!
ELAINE: Really? You would do that?
GEORGE: If I was a different person.

George would not choose to confront Elaine's foe. But *could* he choose to confront him? There is a sense in which he could not—he is too cowardly, as he well knows. But there is another sense in which he could, namely, if he was *less* cowardly. That is, given his *actual* personality, formed through the actual history of the universe (in particular his upbringing and genetics), George could not choose otherwise. But if things had been different, and George had formed a different personality (say, if his parents were less oppressive), he certainly could choose otherwise. These are the two senses of "could choose": the *categorical sense* and the *hypothetical sense*.

This ambiguity in "could have done" and "could have decided/chosen" propagates to "freely." Suppose for the sake of argument that "X acted freely" is defined as "X could have done otherwise" (Ayer 1954), or just that the latter is a necessary condition for the former. Then we obtain that there are two senses of "acted freely": X acted freely *in the hypothetical sense* just if X could have done otherwise in the hypothetical sense of "could have done"; X acted freely *in the categorical sense* just if X could have done otherwise in the categorical sense of "could have done." Similarly for "chose freely" and "could have chosen": X chose freely *in the hypothetical sense* just if X could have chosen otherwise in the hypothetical sense of "could have chosen"; X chose freely *in the categorical sense* just if X could have chosen otherwise in the categorical sense of "could have chosen."

With this distinction in place, we can frame the disagreement between the libertarian and the compatibilist rather straightforwardly, namely, as a disagreement on which notion of freedom—the hypothetical or the categorical—captures the "real" nature of freedom. The libertarian thinks it is the categorical notion, the compatibilist that it is the hypothetical notion.

⋘⋙

A parallel question pertains to the *experience* rather than *nature* of freedom: did the (distinctive) phenomenology of freedom I experienced that day in 1992 involve feeling like I could have done (and decided) otherwise *in my circumstances* or feeling like I could have done (and decided) otherwise *if the circumstances had been different*?

In addressing this question, we should start by pulling apart freedom of (overt) action and freedom of decision/choice.[20] The first question is this: regardless of whether freedom of overt action is in fact libertarian or compatibilist, is it *experienced* as libertarian or as compatibilist?

To see the answer to this, recall that in discussing the feelings of being uncompelled and being unconstrained I pointed out their *hypothetical character*: during the five-hour episode described above, there was nothing I specifically *wanted* to do or avoid doing; the feeling was rather that *if* I wanted to do or avoid doing certain things, I could. This suggests that it was no part of the feeling that I could do certain things *given* my actual desires, preferences, and choices. The feeling was silent on whether that was the case or not. What showed up in the phenomenology took only a hypothetical form: I could do this or that *if* I so desired, preferred, chose. As it pertains to overt action, then, my experience was as of compatibilist freedom.

A separate question concerns freedom of choice and decision: did I experience it as libertarian or as compatibilist (regardless of whether it *is* libertarian or compatibilist)? Here the correct answer seems to me this: Neither! On the one hand, the experience certainly did not include a feeling that I could have decided otherwise given my actual history. But neither did it include a feeling that I could have decided otherwise if I had had a different history. The experience was simply silent on both scores. The reason is simply that it did not involve much by way of deciding and choosing at all. As noted, during the entire episode I did not experience any desires to speak of (except insofar as I wanted to go on strolling, which did not involve performing any act of making a decision or choosing between alternative courses of action). Inasmuch as no decisions or choices to speak of were made, the issue of being able to choose otherwise did not arise. So it is no surprise that the experience was silent on whether I could have decided/chosen otherwise *in any sense* (categorical or hypothetical).[21]

Thus I have no thesis to offer with respect to the phenomenology of free choice. My second thesis characterizing the phenomenology of freedom is limited, then, to the phenomenology of free (overt) action:

(T_2) There is a type of experience of freedom to act whose distinctive phenomenology is as of compatibilist freedom.

Having used the two main philosophical disputes about the *nature* of freedom to characterize the *experience* of freedom, I now wish to suggest a completely different thesis about the experience of freedom, one that departs from the basic assumptions of much philosophical discourse on freedom.

10. Phenomenology of Basically Intransitive Freedom

Consider these two different everyday attributions of freedom:

(IF) I am free.

(TF) I am free to φ.

Paying homage to these attributions' surface grammar, we may call the properties they ostensibly designate "intransitive freedom" and "transitive freedom" respectively. The attributions are clearly distinct, but the properties thereby attributed may or may not be. Indeed, it is often assumed that intransitive freedom can be analyzed in terms of transitive freedom: *grosso modo*, a person is free just in case, and to the extent that, she is free to act in certain ways. The more courses of action are open to her, the freer she is. The details of how exactly to quantify transitive freedom are certainly elusive. But however that turns out, one's quantity of intransitive freedom is thought to be a function of one's quantity of transitive freedom. In "How Free: Computing Personal Liberty," Hillel Steiner (1983) proposes the following equation: a person's freedom equals the number of actions she is free to perform divided by the sum of (i) the number of actions she is free to perform and (ii) the number of actions she is not free to perform. Thus: $F(P) = A_{Pf} / (A_{Pf} + A_{Pu})$. Other authors have offered refinements and improvements on this equation (e.g., Carter 1992), but all refer to free action (hence transitive freedom) on the equation's right-hand side, by way of accounting for free personhood (intransitive freedom) on the left-hand side. This merely gives expression to the standard assumption that transitive freedom is more basic than intransitive freedom, such that the latter is to be analyzed in terms of the former.

This is an eminently reasonable assumption. After all, there are only two alternatives to it. One: transitive freedom is to be analyzed in terms of intransitive freedom. The other: transitive and intransitive freedom are mutually independent notions, such that neither is analyzable in terms of the other. Yet on the one hand it is difficult to envisage how an analysis of transitive freedom in terms of intransitive freedom could proceed, and on the other hand it is counterintuitive that the two notions are conceptually independent. It is thus highly plausible that transitive freedom is the more basic notion, with intransitive freedom analyzable in terms of it.

It is a separate question, however, how things are with the *phenomenology* of freedom. Regardless of whether transitive freedom *is* in fact more basic, we may ask whether it is *experienced* more basically. A person's freedom may be grounded in her actions' freedom without her experience of her freedom being grounded in her experience of her actions' freedom. To address this issue, let us introduce a relation of *phenomenological priority*, or *phenomenological grounding*, to parallel the more familiar relation of *ontological* priority or grounding.[22] For there are cases where A is ontologically prior to B but the experience-of-B is phenomenologically prior to the experience-of-A. Mass is ontologically more basic than weight: the weight of an apple is grounded (partly) in its mass. But the experience of weight is phenomenologically more basic than the experience of mass: insofar as we experience (cognitively?) the apple's mass, it is on the basis of first experiencing (tactilely) its weight. There are also cases where A is ontologically prior to B but neither the experience-of-A nor the experience-of-B is phenomenologically prior to the other: they are mutually independent at the phenomenological level. Good chicken broth is ontologically grounded in bony chicken pieces, celery, carrot, onion, leek, turnip, parsley, thyme, and water. But if it is *really* good, when we taste the broth we cannot recognize any of these individual flavors, as they have all fused into one simple, homogenous, unfactorizable gustatory experience. In this case, the ingredients of chicken broth are ontologically prior to the broth, but neither the broth-experience nor the ingredient-experiences are phenomenologically prior. They are all *experienced* as equally simple and partless.

A similar situation seems to me to apply to transitive and intransitive freedom. Even if transitive freedom is *ontologically* more basic than, and grounds, intransitive freedom, *phenomenologically* their experiences are mutually independent. And indeed, although in describing my episode of vivid experience of freedom I described individual aspects of it, isolating nine such, upon reflection it seems to me that there was also a phenomenological residue of *just feeling free*. This extra element—the tenth I am listing—went beyond any combination of the previous ones, experientially speaking. There was a simple, homogenous, and experientially nondecomposable feeling of being free that accompanied me, at varying degrees of vivacity, throughout that afternoon. Call this a phenomenology of *basically intransitive freedom*.

It is clear that such a basic, nondecomposable feeling of simply being free is *distinctive* of the phenomenology of freedom, just as the feelings of being of uncompelled and being unconstrained are. No type of experience can exhibit it but a freedom experience. Therefore, I am tempted to add the following third thesis to the characterization of the distinctive phenomenology of freedom:

(T_3) There is a type of experience of freedom whose distinctive phenomenology is as of basically intransitive freedom.

By this I mean that part of what is involved in the experience of freedom—at least of the type described in §6—is an experience as of intransitive freedom being basic: simple, nondecomposable, ungrounded, unanalyzable.

Collectively, Theses T_0–T_3 provide a portrait of *a* distinctive phenomenology of freedom. One immediate limitation of the portrait is that it can make no claim to *exhaustiveness*. The fact that there exist experiences with a distinctive phenomenology as of negative, compatibilist, and basically intransitive freedom in no way rules out the existence of *other* freedom experiences with *different* distinctive characters. In particular, other types of freedom loss may bring to the phenomenological fore other kinds of freedom experience: as of positive and/or libertarian freedom, for instance.[23]

It might be objected that the above portrait is not only inexhaustive but also methodologically problematic. After all, it comes from just one vivid experience by one particular person at one specific time and recalled, conceptualized, and articulated by that particular person (with a particular set of conceptual tools) at another (much later!) specific time. For all we know, it may be the portrait of a reconstructed memory of an entirely idiosyncratic experience—nothing to hang an intellectually responsible theory on. How much weight can we really give to this sort of material?

One way to put the point is in terms of the replicability or reproducibility of scientifically legitimate evidence. Recall the anti-introspectionist passage from Watson (1913: 163) that I quoted in the Introduction:

> Psychology, as it is generally thought of [i.e., by introspectionists], has something esoteric in its methods. If you fail to reproduce my findings, it is not due to some fault in your apparatus or in the control of your stimulus, but it is due to the fact that your introspection is untrained . . . In [the natural] sciences a better technique will give reproducible results. Psychology is otherwise. If you can't observe 3–9 states of clearness in attention, your introspection is poor. If, on the other hand, a feeling seems reasonably clear to you, your introspection is again faulty. You are seeing too much. Feelings are never clear.

Watson's thought is that the cornerstone of scientific inquiry is the possibility of experimental *replication* ("reproducible results"). So *phenomenological* inquiry would needs recurrent patterns in our phenomenological data set—but finding such patterns requires the element of replication.

To address these concerns, we must mine an extensive and representative data set of first-person reports of freedom experiences by a range of subjects who lost and regained their freedom in a wide variety of circumstance. In practice, this presents a problem, as no such data set exists. Still, in the final part of this Appendix, I *illustrate* how this type of inquiry *would* proceed, by actually pursuing it in (very) limited fashion. As advertised, I will examine unprompted descriptions of first moments of regaining freedom by emancipated and manumitted slaves, concentration camp survivors, and recently released criminal prisoners. From a statistical standpoint, the obvious problem with the exercise is that the sample used is comically unrepresentative. At present, it is not even clear what standards of representativeness should be operative. At the same time, the great *advantage* of the exercise is that the data are *ecologically valid*: the experiences are not artificially induced in laboratory conditions, and their reporting is entirely unprompted and often philosophically disinterested.[24] They go to the phenomenology of freedom in the wild. It is perhaps with this in mind that Brentano (1874: 39) remarks on "the value which the study of autobiographies has for the psychologist, provided that he takes due account of the fact that in this case the observer and reporter is more or less biased."

III. Varieties of Freedom Loss

11. Slavery

Perhaps the most remarkable recurrent feature in freedom reports by emancipated slaves—at least those born into slavery—is how dumbfounded the ex-slave is by the acquisition of freedom. The great writer, orator, and intellectual Frederick Douglass, who was born into slavery in 1818 and became a free man in 1838, captures this well toward the end of his autobiography (1845: 107):

> I have been frequently asked how I felt when I found myself in a free State. I have never been able to answer the question with any satisfaction to myself. It was a moment of the highest excitement I ever experienced. I suppose I felt as one may imagine the unarmed mariner to feel when he is rescued by a friendly man-of-war from the pursuit of a pirate. In writing to a dear friend, immediately after my arrival at New York, I said I felt like one who had escaped a den of hungry lions. This state of mind, however, very soon subsided; and I was again seized with a feeling of great insecurity and loneliness. I was yet liable to be taken back, and subjected to all the tortures of slavery.

Several elements stand out in this passage. The first thing Douglass mentions is the element of ineffability: he finds it hard to articulate what the sense of freedom is like. Second is an element of elation, or euphoria—"the greatest excitement ever experienced." Interestingly, the bulk of the passage is dedicated to a third element, which seems to correspond to a certain relief from anxiety, a hard-won and long-missed inner tranquility, as would be restored after escaping pirates or lions. The fourth and final comment Douglass makes about his experience of freedom in this passage is that it was short-lived, soon giving way to realistic concerns. The fact that Douglass' experience was short-lived attests to the phenomenological extraordinariness of the experience. The relief from anxiety appears to conform to the positive feeling of no-anxiety I described in what I called the "feeling of lightness." As for the element of euphoria, it is reminiscent of course of what I called the "feeling of passive bliss," though the calm and passive aspect of what *I* described is absent in Douglass' report. Most importantly, Douglass' report does not seem to make any reference to what I designated as the distinctive dimensions of the phenomenology of freedom, the feeling of being uncompelled and the feeling of being unconstrained.[25]

Douglass' narrative is particularly well known, but is quite representative. (I am saying this on the basis of consulting a data set much larger than what I will present here.) The element of not knowing how to conceptualize one's freedom is a recurring theme in slave narratives, especially by authors born into slavery. Often the main phenomenological component discerned is the feeling of lightness, the relief from anxiety. In a heartbreaking and beautifully written autobiography, Harriet Jacobs says next to nothing about finally becoming free—but does write this (1861: 180):

> I had objected to having my freedom bought, yet I must confess that when it was done I felt as if a heavy load had been lifted from my weary shoulders. When I rode home in the cars I was no longer afraid to unveil my face and look at people as they passed.

Beside the feeling of resentment over the fact that white friends bought her from her monster-master Daniel Dodge—Jacobs insisted that she should not pay Dodge for her freedom, since it was never his property to begin with—what she experiences is clearly the feeling of lightness ("a heavy load lifted") and decrease in anxiety ("no longer afraid").

Similar sentiments are shared by Moses Grandy, who was manipulated by white owners time after time and had to buy his freedom thrice over. He describes the moment of final, real, legally binding manumission thus (1844: 49):

> When, at length, I had repaid Captain Minner, and had got my free papers, so that my freedom was quite secure, my feelings were greatly excited. I felt to myself so light, that I could almost think I could fly; in my sleep I was always dreaming of flying over woods and rivers. My gait was so altered by my gladness, that people often stopped me, saying "Grandy, what is the matter?"

The same double-minded focus on euphoria ("greatly excited," gait altered) and lightness ("so light I could fly") recurs in narrative after narrative. However, the feelings of being uncompelled and unconstrained are virtually never mentioned.

For the study of the phenomenology of freedom, there would be special value in narratives by slaves born free, since they would have a sharper sense of what they lost. The problem is that, as far as the New World slavery of the sixteenth to nineteenth centuries is concerned, there is very little by way of first-hand testimony by freeborn slaves. The situation is complicated by the fact that narrating slaves' claims to have been born free are often disputed, as many wrote with the abolitionist cause in mind and were concerned to portray pre-slavery life in Africa in idyllic strokes. A good example is Olaudah Equiano (sometimes known by his slave name, Gustavus Vassa), whose autobiography describes in rare detail his birth in 1745 and first ten years of life among current-day Nigeria's Igbo. However, in a controversial essay and a follow-up book-length treatment, the cultural historian Vincent Carretta (1999, 2005) has argued that this part of Equiano's autobiography is fabricated: he was born a slave in South Carolina, and never in fact set foot in Africa. The centerpiece of Carretta's case is a pair of documents, including one from Equiano's baptism, stating he was born in South Carolina in 1747.

Equiano describes the moment his master grants his request for manumission thus (1789: 78):

> My master then said, he would not be worse than his promise; and, taking the money, told me to go to the Secretary at the Register Office, and get my manumission drawn up. These words of my master were like a voice from heaven to me; in an instant all my trepidation was turned into unutterable bliss; and I most reverently bowed myself with gratitude, unable to express my feelings, but by the overflowing of my eyes, and a heart replete with thanks to God ... My imagination was all rapture as I flew to the Register Office: and, in this respect, like the apostle Peter, (whose deliverance from prison was so sudden and extraordinary, that he thought he was in a vision), I could scarcely believe I was awake. Heavens! who could do justice to my feelings at this moment? Not conquering heroes themselves, in the midst of a triumph—Not the tender mother who has just regained her long-lost infant, and presses it to the heart—Not the weary hungry mariner, at the sight of the desired friendly port—Not the lover, when he once more embraces his beloved mistress, after she had been ravished from his arms!—all within my breast was tumult, wildness, and delirium!

What Equiano describes here is all in all rather one-dimensional: unutterable, phenomenologically overwhelming joy—an ecstatic, barely contained euphoria. The comparisons he draws to his experience—of battlefield victory, mother's love, a seaman's reprieve, and romantic and carnal love—are all instances of some of the most intense positive-affect human experiences. But they are not associated in any special way with the sense of freedom; merely with that of joy, or happiness. (One might, somewhat speculatively, take this to suggest that he in fact had no real prior sense of freedom, consistently with Carretta's claim that he was not born free.)

In any case, Equiano's report does not provide any replication of the multifaceted experience of freedom I reported above. In general, the reports of emancipation or manumission provided by North-American slaves do not appear to converge much with my report. There are only two elements for which there is systematic convergence: euphoria and lack of anxiety. These elements resonate already from everyday appreciation of freedom, however: being free feels good, and often takes the form of feeling relief—as burden dissolves, the sense of freedom rises. Unfortunately, the central elements I claimed to be *distinctive* of the phenomenology of freedom—the feelings of being uncompelled and unconstrained (as well as the feeling of just being free)—are absent in these reports, as far as I can tell. Going through sufficiently many slave narratives, one might find isolated instances that do cite such elements. But it is clearly not a general characteristic of the genre.

There are two possible explanations for this. The pessimistic explanation is that my own report is somehow idiosyncratic and unrepresentative. A more optimistic explanation is that certain factors in slavery are such that the experience of emancipation/manumission is not primarily an experience of freedom. Two such potential factors come to mind immediately. First, as noted most slave narratives we have come from people born into slavery, who consequently may have no genuine prior sense of freedom. We can imagine that in their mouths the word "freedom" stood for a whole host of intangible feelings pertaining predominantly to self-respect and (quite literally) self-possession. Secondly, slavery robs one of much more than one's freedom; in particular, it seems to me that coming out of slavery one is liable to feel most acutely the regaining of *dignity*, not *freedom*. The phenomenology of dignity may thus overwhelm that of freedom, leaving the latter comparatively subdued and not vivid enough for clear introspecting.

This brief and preliminary discussion leaves unpursued much pertinent research. First, it would be of particular interest to identify and analyze slave narratives by freeborn slaves. Secondly, my discussion has focused on slave narratives based in the transatlantic trade of the sixteenth through nineteenth centuries, but slavery has occurred at many times and places through human history, and indeed persists in modern times (most extensively in large tracts of northern Africa). Of particular interest may be the military slavery common in the Ottoman Empire. In this practice (starting in the fourteenth century), soldiers of defeated armies were taken into a special slave army, where they could become high officers and rise to leadership positions, effectively managing the empire and enjoying great wealth and respect—all the while remaining the property of the sultan. I lack the tools and competence to do the relevant research myself, but it is extremely intriguing just what the experience of these military slaves was like—both in bondage and when emancipated. In the next section, I offer another brief and preliminary discussion of freedom-experience reports, with the hope of finding greater convergence with my own report.

12. Concentration Camps

Probably the best-known Holocaust memoir is Elie Wiesel's *Night*. Wiesel's style is almost anti-phenomenological. While often poetic, the book reports event after event somewhat as they would be by a behaviorist: there is no dwelling on the fine shades of emotion anywhere, perhaps because the events themselves speak louder to the transcendent suffering that is Wiesel's subject matter. The characters in *Night* are nowhere developed in any personal, meaningful manner.

They have no individualizing characteristics of any order. They are but a mass of men and women—some named, most nameless—tumbling through an overpowering mechanical process imposed on them by equally impersonal perpetrators. All involved have lost their individual humanity and human individuality. This process of self-estrangement and self-loss climaxes in the final scene of the book, the aftermath of liberation (Wiesel 1960: 116):

> At about six o'clock in the evening, the first American tank stood at the gates of Buchenwald.
> Our first act as free men was to throw ourselves onto the provisions. We thought only of that. Not of revenge, not of our families. Nothing but bread...
> Three days after the liberation of Buchenwald I became ill with food poisoning. I was transferred to the hospital and spent two weeks between life and death.
> One day I was able to get up, after gathering all my strength. I wanted to see myself in the mirror hanging on the opposite wall. I had not seen myself since the ghetto.
> From the depths of the mirror, a corpse gazed back at me.
> The look in his eyes, as they stared into mine, has never left me.

Thus the final sentence of the book presents the author with himself as not-himself: the narrating subject can no longer feel identical to the person the war had produced ("his" eyes and "mine" are experienced as the doors of two numerically distinct souls). Looking in the mirror produces in him not just the felt quality of intriguing unfamiliarity, but the unmistakable quality of encounter with the radical other, the sort of terrifying gulf of otherness often belabored by Levinas. In normal circumstances, a person vanishes and is gone when she dies. The great horror of the Holocaust, for Wiesel, is its invention of this new and monstrous possibility: personal disappearance among the living.

It will be noted that Wiesel says nothing about the *experience* of being freed, and free. Perhaps it was not felt, the only thing felt being the desire for bread. In other writings by Holocaust survivors, however, the feeling of freedom is dwelled upon quite often. A particularly thoughtful description is offered by Ruth Klüger, a University of California–Irvine Germanist who escaped from a forced march at the age of thirteen with her mother, a friend, and three Czech women. In her memoirs, she describes the moment of escape as follows (2001: 130):

> [O]n that evening I experienced the unforgettable, prickly feeling of what it means to reconstitute yourself, not to be determined by others, to say yes or no as you like, to stand at a crossroad where there had been a one-way street, to leave constraint behind with nothing in front, and

> call that nothing good. Certainly there were reasons and causes why we found the energy to act—as there were reasons and causes why we could have continued on that desperate, doomed march. We made a choice: inebriated with hope and despair, a heady cocktail, I chose the freedom of birds that can be shot down by any hunter.

Interestingly, the second half of this passage explicitly describes a feeling as of compatibilist freedom: there were reasons and causes, Klüger insists, but they were consistent with free choice. The resulting action was not felt to be unfree even though it was felt to be causally predetermined. More interesting yet is the first part of the passage, which strikes me as describing a feeling of negative freedom that replicates the central elements of the distinctive phenomenology of freedom I described in my own case. The first phenomenal element Klüger mentions is that of regaining self-ownership ("reconstituting yourself"), but immediately afterwards she describes in effect what I called the feeling of being uncompelled ("not determined by others," "say yes or no as you like") and being unconstrained ("leave constraint behind," "nothing in front"). Indeed, the very hypothetical character of these phenomenal elements seems in evidence: Klüger does not feel the desire either to say yes or to say no, what she experiences is that she could say yes *if* she so desired and could say no *if* she thus desired. There is a crossroad—a plurality of options—where there was once a single track.

Similar elements, and other familiar ones, are related when she reports her experiences the following morning (2001: 136):

> Simply to walk down a country road of one's own volition was like conquering the world. Freedom meant getting away, rather than getting somewhere. Getting away from the lethal march, from the bedraggled crowd, from slavery's constant invasion of ego and identity. The air smelled different, more springlike, now that we had it to ourselves. Who knows what the next day is going to bring, what any next day is going to be like, so why worry?

The phenomenology of negative freedom is palpable in the second sentence: "Freedom meant getting away, rather than getting somewhere." This is freedom-from rather than freedom-to. Other elements reported are euphoria ("like conquering the world"), dignity or self-respect ("away from . . . invasion of ego and identity"), some connection to nature ("air smelled different," "springlike") reminiscent of the third perceptual feature I described, and again the feeling of lightness and no-anxiety ("why worry?").[26]

A less intellectual but otherwise very similar report is provided by Tobias Schiff, a Belgian Jew arrested by the German occupiers in 1942, at the age of seventeen. Schiff was a cook at the concentration camp Bergen-Belsen when he was liberated three years later. In a prolonged interview turned into a book on his life, he describes the moment of fully realizing he was free thus (Schiff 1995: 133–4):

> I remember that the following night, the weather was very beautiful
> I went to a field near the camp and I gave myself orders
> "now, make ten steps forward"
> I made them but on the fourth I looked
> "nobody shoots"
> and I changed the order
> "and now make ten steps to the left"
> I made them and again after two or three steps I looked
> "nobody shoots"
> so again I changed the order
> it was very exulting
> each time I verified
> "nobody shoots"
> I thought
> "I can go here, and here, I move, nobody tells me
>   anything and nobody shoots"
> I lay down in the grass, I looked at the moon
> I thought of what had happened and what was going to happen
>
> it was freedom
> at every step I thought
> "nobody shoots"
> I had to persuade myself that it was really the end
> that the nightmare had finished
> unfortunately this feeling of freedom goes away too fast

This description is much more visceral and concrete than Klüger's, but manifests similar themes. The main theme appears to be the feeling of being uncompelled ("nobody shoots," "nobody tells me anything"). The hypothetical character of the feeling is likewise evident: "I can go here, and here, I move, nobody tells me anything and nobody shoots." Schiff has no particular desire to go here or there, presumably; he simply revels in the fact that *if* he wanted to, he could. The particular actions he performs—taking four steps forward, three to the left—are completely insignificant; they do not express any desire to achieve anything through them. They express only the hypothetical character of being uncompelled: *if* there was something to be achieved by performing these actions, it could be. This is clearly the central theme of the passage. Another element in it seems to be a feeling of anticipation ("I thought . . . of what was going to happen"). A final point is that the experience of specially vivid phenomenology of freedom is short-lived: "unfortunately this feeling of freedom goes away too fast."

The themes brought up by Klüger and Schiff run through many testimonies of liberation from the concentration camps. I close with just one more passage, by Henry Oertelt, who was liberated from a Death March on 23 April 1945 by General Patton's Third Army and has lived and worked in Minnesota since 1949 (2000: 132):

> Suddenly, I began to realize that I was now, at last, a free man! The crackers and the piece of chocolate must have started my flow of adrenaline. Does this mean that I can now walk as slowly as I want to? That I can sit down any time and any moment I desire to do so? How about that! Our contemptible guards had finally disappeared.
>
> With this in Mind, Will and I realized that for the first time in years we would not have anyone shouting *"Schnell! Schnell!"* at us. So, with our precious food boxes tucked securely under our arms, we took our first careful steps of freedom in the direction of Stamsried.

Oertelt has no particular desire to walk slowly or to sit down, but if he had such a desire he could act on it. Nobody compelled him otherwise.

In general, unlike the reports by ex-slaves, those by concentration camp survivors appear to systematically converge with the first-person report I offered above. (As before, I am saying this on the basis of a larger "data set" than presented here.) This is remarkable in light of what comes through most clearly in Wiesel's report. In the camps, a person's very identity was taken away—and yet freedom was often a predominant feeling upon liberation. (This may suggest an internal connection between identity and freedom, one that would have to remain unexplored here.) In any event, imprisonment in the camps certainly compromised not only the prisoner's freedom, but also her dignity, happiness, and much more. In this respect, it is no different from the predicament of slavery. What distinguishes concentration camp survivors from typical emancipated and manumitted slaves is that the former experienced a long existence of freedom prior to captivity. This is also the case with released prisoners, to whom we turn next.

13. Criminal Prisoners

As a default penal system, the prison is a fairly modern invention. Many of the testimonies we have from ex-prisoners have in the background the cause of penal reform, and thus focus on the travails of life *inside* prison. Nonetheless, descriptions of the first moments after release are not uncommon. They represent another part of the "data set" for the sort of inquiry into the phenomenology of freedom outlined above. This particular part of the set is enormous; below are just a handful of items, admittedly picked in part for their convergence with the themes that came up in my own report.

James Newsome is a prison reform activist who spent fifteen years in prison on a wrongful conviction of murder and armed robbery, reversed in 1994 thanks to advances in fingerprint technology. In these circumstances, anger and indignation would have to be the dominant emotion. Still, Newsome's report of his feelings upon release is revealing (Vollen and Eggers 2005: 135, 137):

> The sheriff took me out. I wasn't excited at all. I was angry. It came, but it came too late. It came at a time when they had taken a lot of my life. Almost all of my twenties, every year of my thirties—how do you give that back to me? . . .
>
> You know, it's kind of strange when you're incarcerated and you come out. What made me most happy? The ability to choose whatever I wanted to do, whenever I wanted to do it. Eat whatever I wanted to. Walk wherever I wanted to. Drive. Just having the choice to enjoy some of the basic freedoms.

What is particularly interesting about this passage is the way Newsome does not cite, as a source of happiness, any concrete desire he had the opportunity to satisfy upon leaving prison. What made him happy was the mere fact that *if* he had some desire he could act on it. Here again is the hypothetical character of the feeling of being unconstrained.

Similar feelings can be found in reports of released criminals who take themselves to have been justly incarcerated. Dannie Martin, a lifelong criminal turned freelance journalist halfway through his sentence, spent eleven years in prison for bank robbery. In his coauthored memoir, he says this (Martin and Sussman 1993: 306):

> On the streets, heading to this or that appointment, I often find myself stopping and looking around, marveling that I'm alone and free, acting on my own—and with no guard watching me. In prison, there is no place to escape observation; there is someone watching our every move.
>
> And the people I'd been living with day in and day out have had two things in common: They're all grown-ups and they're all male. Having women and children around—friends and even passersby on the street—is an unbelievable wonder. It's one of the many impressions that crowd around me and even stop me on the street in mid-thought.

The first two elements coming through in Martin's report are the phenomenal vivacity of the experience of freedom and a somewhat muted euphoric feeling ("stopping and looking around, marveling"); the vivacity seems to come through again in the final sentence of the passage. Next is the feeling of "acting on my own," which is associated with not being observed by those who can *compel* him to act as *they* would like rather than on his own. The oppressive feeling of being observed is indeed vivid in my own memory, and although I do not remember that its lifting was central to my experience upon being released, I do remember that what made the feeling oppressive is precisely that being observed meant that there were limits on what I could do. The will of another was always *in a position* to take over and override my own will. All this seems to speak precisely to the feeling of being uncompelled as a central aspect of the experience of freedom upon release.

In a similar vein, Phillip Swanson, a bank robber who spent a dozen years in prison in the sixties, reports this in an interview during his parole (Erickson et al. 1973: 20-1):

> The first few days were strange. It's the turnover from the discipline. All of a sudden you've stepped out of it. You don't have somebody tellin' you when to go to bed, when to get up, when you can do this, when you can't do that. It's just a relaxed feeling now . . .
>
> Nobody's leaning on me, which is a good thing for a person in my position. I don't need anybody leanin' on me. I lean on myself now. I think that's one of the major factors behind me making this good parole is the fact they're not hassling me, you know. "You can't do this; you can't do that; keep your head this side; shine up, man." That's what they do.

Here too the feeling of being uncompelled is central—the "turnover from discipline," where nobody says "you can do this" and "you can't do that." In a way, this is the theme of the entire two paragraphs: not being told what to do. Presumably, this would *allow* one to do as one wishes (in accordance with the feeling of being unconstrained), but what it highlights immediately is the ability *not* to do what one does *not* wish to do (in accordance with the feeling of being uncompelled).

In general, the reports from released prisoners that I had occasion to consult are quite varied. They vary with several factors: how long one has been incarcerated, how roughly and how wrongly one was treated when in prison, and most importantly, how challenging free life has been to one. Many prisoners who go out into the world with a measly sum of money and no help finding employment or shelter report experiencing nothing but anxiety and self-doubt. A cloud is hanging over their head that makes any sense of freedom somewhat foreign. The reports I have quoted from give voice to only a portion of the spectrum of experiential reactions in released prisoners. Still, the recurrence of themes within that portion suggests to me a measure of replication of the report I provided in §6.

IV. Conclusions

14. Concluding Remarks and Directions for Future Research

The very preliminary third-person examination of first-person reports in Part III offers at least partial confirmation of—by way of convergence with—my own first-person report in Part II. I take the results of this preliminary examination to tentatively suggest that a fuller one might produce substantial replication of the themes in my report, casting it as representative of at least one type of phenomenology of freedom. Although the social sciences are in their historical infancy, I can (just barely!) envisage an "end of psychological and sociological inquiry" where highly specific circumstances are identified in which the feeling of being uncompelled/unconstrained is an invariant dimension of one's phenomenology of freedom.

If my conjecture is right that this is a pervasive phenomenology, so that the episodes focused on in Parts II and III are only specially vivid manifestations of an ever-present, low-humming background feeling, then the characterization I offered of the phenomenology in those privileged episodes applies in truth to a constant element in our "baseline phenomenology." We virtually always feel *to some degree* uncompelled and unconstrained—though the degrees change with the circumstances.

Even if accepted, the fact that this phenomenology is *pervasive* would not mean that it is *exclusive*. There may be other types of freedom experience, characterized by an importantly different phenomenology of freedom. I suspect that the phenomenology of freedom I have targeted here is nonetheless a particularly fundamental one, though the elucidation and defense of such a claim would require a separate investigation. In any case, much of the philosophical significance of the type of phenomenology of freedom I have targeted does not depend on its being the *only* type of such phenomenology. This philosophical significance is captured in the four theses I have defended regarding it, which may be encapsulated thus:

> There exists a *distinctive* phenomenology as of negative, compatibilist, and basically-intransitive freedom.

This is bound to have important implications for debates on political freedom, determinism and free will, and the nature of freedom. It is also of interest to the study of the phenomenal realm that is this book's concern, though as noted the distinctive phenomenology of freedom discussed here is not a plausible candidate for a second-layer phenomenal determinable.

The phenomenology of freedom served here as a platform for carrying out a general *kind* of first-person inquiry into a subtle, pervasive, non-overwhelming type of phenomenology. This sort of inquiry attempts to avoid the well-documented pitfalls of introspective research by examining the unprompted reports of privileged subjects, ones who experienced the relevant type of phenomenology with uncommon vivacity for one reason or another. It strikes me, moreover, as an advantage for the relevant type of inquiry that the investigator himself or herself falls in the group of subjects designated "privileged," liable to afford him or her first-hand insight in which to anchor interpretation of others' first-person reports. It is for this reason that I have focused here on the phenomenology of freedom. But the field of phenomena that might lend themselves to illumination through this type of inquiry, by investigators similarly well positioned to understand them, is enormous, and may include non-pervasive and/or more familiar phenomenologies. These include the phenomenology of curiosity, the phenomenology of loneliness, the phenomenology of empathy, the phenomenology of concentration, the phenomenology of self-respect, the phenomenology of affection, the phenomenology of anxiety, the phenomenology of courage, the phenomenology of boredom, the phenomenology of aesthetic delight, the phenomenology of need, the phenomenology of anger, the phenomenology of fantasizing and of daydreaming, the phenomenology of existential angst, the phenomenology of effort, the phenomenology of deep gratitude, the phenomenology of melancholia, the phenomenology of physical and mental attraction or infatuation, the phenomenology of fear of death, the phenomenology of eureka, the phenomenology of emotional exhaustion, the phenomenology of surprise, the phenomenology of grief, the phenomenology of complete understanding, the phenomenology of care, the phenomenology of intellectual engrossment, the phenomenology of caffeinated alertness, the phenomenology of jealousy, the phenomenology of play, the phenomenology of treating someone as an end, the phenomenology of disgrace, the phenomenology of self-hatred, the phenomenology of waking up, the phenomenology of athletic exertion and exhaustion, the phenomenology of doubt and uncertainty, the phenomenology of nostalgia, the phenomenology of dignity, the phenomenology of deliberation, the phenomenology of obsession, the phenomenology of personal crisis, the phenomenology of desperation, the phenomenology of feeling ticklish, the phenomenology of the *déjà vu* experience, the phenomenology of trust, the phenomenology of felt duty, the phenomenology of being intrigued, the phenomenology of shame, the phenomenology of insecurity, the phenomenology of insight and intuition, the phenomenology of togetherness and of fraternity, the phenomenology of hunger, the phenomenology of pregnancy, the phenomenology of religious faith, the phenomenology of emotional tenderness, the phenomenology of the sense of justice, the phenomenology of vitality and vigor, the phenomenology of lucid dreaming, the phenomenology of vicarious embarrassment, the phenomenology of rightness or of things feeling not quite right, the phenomenology of deep fulfillment, the phenomenology of missing someone, the phenomenology of temptation, the phenomenology of encounter with the radical other, the phenomenology of restlessness, the phenomenology of unendorsed greed, the phenomenology of humiliation, the phenomenology of vulnerability, the phenomenology of emotional burden, the phenomenology of illness, the phenomenology of valuing something dearly, the phenomenology of feeling safe, the phenomenology of impatience, the phenomenology of yearning for the extraordinary, the phenomenology of self-possession, the phenomenology of pride, the phenomenology of political indignation, the phenomenology of creative engagement, the phenomenology of romantic, parental, and filial love, the phenomenology of wonder at the world, the phenomenology of philosophical contemplation, and more.[27]

NOTES

Introduction

1. The triad could be put in more overtly metaphysical terms thus: 1) Some cognitive-phenomenal properties are instantiated. 2) Some instantiated cognitive-phenomenal properties are irreducible to combinations of perceptual- and/or algedonic-phenomenal properties. 3) Perceptual- and algedonic-phenomenal properties ultimately exhaust all phenomenal properties. This formulation is more precise, in a way, but also more cluttered, so in the text I stick with the simpler formulation.
2. The corresponding triad would be: 1) there exists emotional phenomenology; 2) emotional phenomenology is irreducible to perceptual and/or cognitive phenomenology; 3) perceptual and cognitive phenomenology ultimately exhaust all phenomenology. Here the eliminativist about emotional phenomenology still denies its very existence, the reductivist attempts to reduce it to a combination of perceptual and *cognitive* (rather than perceptual and *algedonic*) phenomenology, and the primitivist posits a sui generis emotional phenomenology.
3. Even within the perceptual domain, one may be particularly stingy and admit only bare sensory phenomenal properties, as in Dizzy Gillespie's confession: "I don't care much for music; what I like is sounds."
4. The former are real but reducible, the latter unreal. It might be objected that the distinction is of no substantive significance, but that depends on what one takes to be significant. Compare: we tend to be reductivists about chairs and eliminativists about ghosts, and we consider that this is a meaningful and important difference.
5. Presenting the procedure this way has the unfortunate feature that we are quantifying over nonexistents. Arguably, however, any kind of ontological theorizing has to start with *putative* existents, and would thereby be forced to speak of what may potentially turn out to be nonexistents.
6. It may be objected that this procedure presupposes that there are grounding or reducibility relations among phenomenal properties, but that it is not obvious that there are. For now, however, it is worth realizing that the procedure itself does not commit itself to this. If there are no grounding and reducibility relations among phenomenal properties, then there are no phenomenal derivatives. In other words, for no putative type of phenomenology is reductivism true. For some eliminativism is and for others primitivism is, so that there are no grounding/reducibility relations among any pair of phenomenal properties (or sets thereof). This is a stable and coherent view nowise ruled out by the framework itself.

    The same procedure can be applied, I would like to underscore, in other areas of philosophy. In metaethical discussions, there is often a debate about the conceptual interrelations between various normative notions: goodness, rightness, virtue, fittingness, justice, and so on. One could run structurally the same procedure for this question as for the one addressed in this book. (Thanks to Gwen Bradford for pointing this out to me.)

7. On the one hand, it is natural to think that some reduction relations are not in-virtue-of relations, since some reductions are a matter of identity of reduced and reducer, whereas in-virtue-of relations are asymmetric and therefore can never be a matter of identity. Conversely, it is also natural to think that some in-virtue-of relations are not reduction relations. It is sometimes thought, for example, that relations of nomic supervenience can make true "in virtue of" statements, but not "is nothing but" (i.e., reduction) statements. Thus, someone may hold that moral facts nomically supervene on certain social facts, and therefore that there is some social fact in virtue of which Jimmy's murder of Johnny is wrong. But such a person need not assent to the claim that the murder's wrongness is nothing but the relevant social fact. If all this is right, then reduction and grounding are doubly dissociable.
8. Needless to say, how to elucidate the notion of grounding is a nontrivial matter, but as noted, intuitively grounding is the relation canonically picked out by the "in virtue of" locution. For more—much more—see Fine 2001, Schaffer 2009, and Sider 2011.
9. Moreover, this is so regardless of whether there are pragmatic factors influencing the decomposition of overall experiences into parts; more on this in §5.
10. Another worry might be that it is plausible to hold that at least some types of phenomenology are *ineffable*, and that this renders impossible, perhaps unintelligible, inquiry into their ontological status. However, even types of phenomenology that are indescribable, and hence ineffable, are *namable*, and one could always use such names in the relevant inquiry. This does raise the question of how the community of inquirers can ensure that the name picks out the same phenomenology when different persons use the name. But this is just an aspect of the more general problem that the referents of phenomenal terms, whether names or descriptions, are always subjective and in some significant sense "private." This raises of course tremendous methodological challenges, which have preoccupied consciousness researchers at least since the second half of the nineteenth century. I will address some aspects of the relevant conundrums in Part II of this Introduction. My present point is that the alleged ineffability of (some) phenomenology does not generate a distinctive metaphysical difficulty with the project of identifying phenomenal primitives.
11. These features apply also outside the phenomenal realm. For example, there is a continuum connecting being six foot tall and being five foot tall, but there is no continuum between being a Mazda driver and being a Peugeot driver. Meanwhile, if you are six foot tall, you cannot also be some other height, but if you are a Mazda driver you may also be a Peugeot driver. Thanks to Tom Avery for pointing this second difference between the two relations to me.
12. Thanks to George Sher for suggesting the term to me.
13. I am assuming here that there is such a highest phenomenal determinable. This is essentially to assume that there is something in common among all phenomenal properties—this would be phenomenality as such. The assumption is not obviously necessarily true—Geoff Lee once floated before me the idea that there may be no such thing. One way to work out the claim is to say that phenomenality as such is not a "natural" property in the Lewisian sense (Lee 2013, forthcoming). For more on naturalness, see §4.
14. Gestalt psychologists have often rejected the existence of phenomenal elements, but what they meant by that was not exactly that experience lacks any parts that do not themselves have parts. Rather, what they meant is that the character of such parts is what it is in virtue of these parts' relations to the other parts (see, e.g., Koffka 1922: 543).
15. Wilson develops a version of the argument that does not require saying that determinable-color instances could have been another shade, instead allowing us to say only that they belong to types whose instances could have been another shade of. For my part, I am quite convinced of the stronger claim anyway.
16. Wilson's argument is structurally similar to the argument some two-thingists provide in the metaphysics of material constitution for numerically distinguishing the statue and the clay from which it is made (Baker 1997). Arguably, since the modal argument in this debate over material constitution is considered cogent by many, so should Wilson's parallel argument.

17. The notion of metaphysical relation would have to be properly elucidated, but whatever it turns out to be, the overall structure of the phenomenal realm can be equated with the web of all metaphysical interrelations among phenomenal properties.
18. What makes these universal is that, unlike concrete particulars, they are wholly present at different places at the same time. This is different from two kinds of concrete particular. My dog Julius is present only in one place at a time. Hawaii, meanwhile, is present at different places at the same time (both in Oahu and in Kawai, for example), but it is not *wholly* present in those places: part of Hawaii is present in Oahu, another part in Kawai). Note that in this picture, what makes something a universal is *not* that it exists outside spacetime altogether. For Armstrong, this is an essential component of a naturalistic worldview.
19. There are in fact four positions to choose among here: (i) Luciana is right and Ada is wrong; (ii) Ada is right and Luciana is wrong; (iii) both are wrong; (iv) both are right. It seems the realist can accommodate the first three positions, arguing that there are naturalness facts which are correctly tracked by Luciana's introspection, or by Ada's, or by neither. But the fourth position seems compatible only with an anti-realist view according to which there are not observer-independent facts of the matter about phenomenal similarity.
20. It is also possible to be a "resemblance nominalist" (see Rodriguez-Pereyra 2002) about phenomenal properties, claiming that there are no phenomenal universals and resemblance among phenomenal states is primitive and inexplicable.
21. They may also offer other explanations. But the realist's explanation would cite only objective features of phenomenal reality, whereas the anti-realist might cite some feature(s) of us its investigators.
22. A realist could also attempt to explain away the intuition of indistinctness among W_1, W_2, and W_3 by claiming that grounding is in fact necessary, not contingent. However, this may only force us to recast W_1, W_2, and W_3 as *epistemically* possible worlds. The intuition of indistinctness appears to survive, though perhaps substantially blunted (this may vary from person to person, and conceivably could lie downstream of philosophers' theoretical commitments).
23. In many domains, anti-realism is motivated by relativism. Thus, it has proved tempting to infer from the variance in moral systems across cultures to a degree of culture-dependence in morality. This inference can certainly be made in a dogmatic and naïve fashion, and to overly anti-realist conclusions ("anything goes"); but it could also be made in subtler and more thoughtful manners. Importantly, it is at present an open empirical question whether the facts about phenomenal structure vary across cultures and societies, across individuals in the same society, or even across life-stages in the same individuals. The more such variance in phenomenal structure turns out to exist, the more tempting an inference to anti-realism will prove to be.
24. Thanks to Will Leonard for bringing to my attention this passage.
25. According to many, there are principled reasons for this limited success. For example, Chalmers (1995) has argued that while standard cognitive science is suited to explain structure and function, the phenomenon of phenomenal consciousness is not exhausted by structure and function. Other diagnoses are possible.
26. The difference between Shepard's work and Ramachandran's is that the former relies on the scientist's own introspection to form the relevant scientific hypothesis, whereas the latter relies on others' introspective reports.
27. In fact, often an introspectively *obvious* claim is established in such a third-person way, so that no real increase in humanity's knowledge is effected in the process: the entire purpose of the exercise seems to be to showcase the scientist's ingenuity in devising a task that allows for the relevant third-person measure of what was already introspectively manifest. I am tempted to say that the operative goal of cognitive-scientific research is thus not always to increase our understanding of the mind; often it is rather to devise increasingly ingenious introspection-purged ways of ratifying ("legitimating") knowledge we already have.
28. Needless to say, in this formulation (and all sequels) "introspect" is used as a nonfactive verb (the claim is not meant to be trivial). If one cannot hear "to introspect P" as nonfactive,

we would have to introduce the notion of "seeming-introspection" and the claim would have to be reworded thus: If S seemingly-introspects having P, then S has P.

29. Consider the following view, which we may call *introspective skepticism*, and which can be factorized into these two theses: (*a*) a subject S introspecting phenomenology P is no indicator of S having P; (*b*) a subject S having P does not tend to make S introspect P. The conjunction of (*a*) and (*b*) casts introspection as entirely untrustworthy. But of course, nothing in the implausibility of introspective dogmatism supports the plausibility of introspective skepticism. More plausibly, the right view is somewhere in the middle, casting introspection as usefully but not awesomely trustworthy.

30. Thanks to Jay Garfield for pressing me on this.

31. According to Annas (2008), this phenomenology of flow is in fact the experiential signature of virtue: what it is like to be a virtuous agent is to enjoy this un-conflicted, un-bifurcated phenomenology of flow. If so, the phenomenology of virtue itself may be non-introspectible.

32. There may also be a class of extraordinarily esoteric phenomenologies (say, the phenomenology of skydiving, if such there be) that for one reason or another evade clear introspection. If so, ACR and/or NNP might need to be restricted to more ordinary phenomenologies, the kinds of phenomenology most of us experience routinely.

33. This may well be Dennett's (1991 ch.5) view, at least in the context of his discussion of Stalinesque versus Orwellian interpretations of certain experiments about consciousness.

34. It is most natural to develop the view against the background of a Russellian treatment of "P is F" as implicitly existential. Just as "The present king of France is bold" is false, because there is no x, such that x is the unique present king of France and x is bold (Russell 1905), so "P is not F" is strictly false, because there is no x, such that x is the unique phenomenology picked out by "P" and x is F. If one adopts instead a Strawsonian treatment that adverts to "neutral" truth values (Strawson 1950), one would have to say that while "P is F" is false, "P is not F" is neutral. Either way, both claims are untrue.

35. In coming to appreciate the possibility of expressivism about phenomenal report, I have benefited from conversations with Rachel Schneebaum.

36. By "incorrigibility," I mean that a subject's introspective reports cannot be justifiably corrected by another. That is, a subject S's belief about her own phenomenology, at least when introspectively based, is always more justified than any other subject's belief about S's phenomenology. (Incorrigibility in this sense is to be distinguished from infallibility: the latter means that the phenomenological belief is always *true*; the former makes no claim about truth, only about justification.)

37. In any case, the no-fact reaction does not pose a threat to the use of introspection if it is only appealed to *sometimes*—and indeed it seems that only in relatively specific circumstances would it be the most appropriate reaction.

38. Something like this view is defended in the area of moral phenomenology by Gill (2008) and Sinnott-Armstrong (2008). Gill, for example, argues that while moral judgments (e.g., that slavery is wrong) involve a phenomenology of objective import in some subjects, they do not in others.

39. Even more dramatically, suppose that despite behaving otherwise indistinguishably, S reports never experiencing emotions and S* reports sometimes experiencing them. The phenomenal variability approach would have us conclude that, quite unusually, S lacks emotional phenomenology altogether. This, again, seems far from natural an inference to make. The emotional life of people admits of great variability, but surely not as much regarding the very *existence* of an emotional life.

40. This is probably not exactly how Siewert put it to me.

41. Unnecessary anecdote: David Braddon-Mitchell once told me that when he looks at the stars he experiences *the past*. When I denied that he does, a bystander indignantly jumped to Braddon-Mitchell's defense and exclaimed: "How can you tell him what his phenomenology is?" I apologized to both.

42. Accordingly, although the expressivist approach to introspective judgments, such as "What I am feeling right now is frustration," is rather implausible (as noted in the above discussion of the no-fact view), it is much more plausible for introspective *confidence* judgments, such

as "I am highly confident that what I am feeling right now is frustration." Many occurrences of such judgments do not appear to be truth-apt descriptive statements that attempt to correctly represent an observer-independent fact of the matter (despite their surface grammar). In many, the primary function seems to be to assert one's authority over one's own internal life, that is, to *demand* dignity and respect.

43. In a debunking explanation, a cognitive reaction to *p* is shown to be formed not responsively to *p*, but to something else altogether. Thus, the Freudian debunking explanation of theistic beliefs shows that they are not formed responsively to God, but responsively to certain social pressures and emotional needs. By the same token, resistance to the introspective competence view is here shown to be formed not responsively to certain blemishes on the plausibility of the view, but responsively to certain moral commitments and expectations. In all such cases, the fact that a cognitive reaction to *p* is formed responsively to something other than *p* shows that it does not exhibit the reliabilist virtue of sensitivity (Nozick 1981) and therefore is not epistemically justified by reliabilist lights.

44. Wundt's student Titchener composed a 1600-page manual for introspection, going through which he presumably treated as competence-boosting. But this is an even worse measure of introspective competence, as its starting point is not theoretically neutral.

45. Another option here is to simply forsake appeal to introspection wherever disagreement has arisen, restricting one's introspective appeal phenomenological questions free of controversy. This appears to be the view of Bayne and Spener (2010).

46. This deductive reconstruction does not rule out the possibility of some nondeductive reconstructions of the Moore-Strawson argument and other "phenomenal contrast" arguments (Siegel 2007). For example, one might offer the following abductive reconstruction: P1) S and S* have a different overall phenomenology; P2) the best explanation of the difference in the overall phenomenology of S and S* is that there is a purely nonsensory phenomenology that S and S* differ in; therefore, C1) there is a purely nonsensory phenomenology that S and S* differ in; therefore, C2) there is such a thing as purely nonsensory phenomenology. I focus on a deductive reconstruction because of its relevance to the potential for deductive arguments for phenomenological theses.

47. P1 and P2 are clearly introspective premises, though only in the broad sense that they require some exercise of introspective abilities. In assessing them from the first-person perspective, we probably conjure up episodic memories of listening to speech we understand and speech we do not understand and introspectively examine the phenomenology of our respective experiences *as remembered*. Alternatively, we may be imagining having such experiences and introspectively examining the phenomenology of these experiences *as imagined*.

48. We may also seek *several* phenomenological propositions that are introspectively unobjectionable, even together, and yet conjointly entail, or at least support, the introspectively controversial phenomenological proposition.

49. Moreover, in the standard case the phenomenological premise(s) would cite a more general phenomenal feature than the conclusion (since the latter is supposed to be somehow deduced from the former). This means that the phenomenological premise, if it is susceptible to introspective disagreement, will be a better candidate for introspective-competence treatment than phenomenal-variability treatment.

50. Naturally, one ought to seek arguments with premises ever more introspectively uncontroversial. But this is simply to seek ever better arguments. The situation here is no different than in other areas of philosophy (Siewert 2007): we seek the best argument we can come up with, where the goodness of an argument is a function of the degree to which its premises command wider or stronger intuitive support than their conclusion.

51. Consider the analogy with Moore's "naturalistic fallacy." The neo-Moorean can accept normative facts that reduce to natural facts, as *per* Cornell realism in meta-ethics (Boyd 1988), but would have to hold that the reduction is not *a priori*, and therefore normative propositions are not *deducible* from nonnormative ("natural") propositions.

52. Elsewhere, I have indicated my hesitant preference for *a posteriori* (type-B) physicalism about phenomenal consciousness (Kriegel 2011a). I have also argued there against the plausibility of *a priori* (type-A) physicalism.

53. I say "ultimately" because, in a first instance, each phenomenological premise could be supported by a further sub-argument. However, either no premise in the sub-argument is phenomenological, in which case the argument cannot be deductive (consistently with PF), or some premise is phenomenological, in which case the same dilemma recurs. The only way to stop an infinite regress of deductive sub-argument is to support some phenomenological premise in some sub-argument directly by introspective appeal.
54. If *a priori* physicalism is true after all, then there is also a sixth possible reaction to introspective disagreements, namely, using deductive arguments with physical or neural premises exclusively and a phenomenological conclusion. Since my credence in *a priori* physicalism is relatively low (though by no means negligible), I set this sixth option aside here. In addition, there might be some seventh possible reaction that has not occurred to me. Needless to say, one should always make allowances for methodological innovations evolving through the actual practice of a type of inquiry.
55. Dorsch (2009), for example, develops an epistemic argument to the effect that our conscious judgments exhibit a phenomenology of reason-responsiveness (they present themselves as occurring in response to epistemic reasons). Such a specific phenomenal feature is hard to defend with the introspective competence view, as it raises fairly immediately the prospect of phenomenal variability.
56. Thus, elsewhere I have developed an epistemic argument to the effect that every conscious experience is such that the subject is consciously aware of its occurrence, a feature I call the "for-me-ness" of experience and consider constitutive of all consciousness (Kriegel 2009 ch.4).
57. Given that emotional phenomenology is in turn reducible to a combination of cognitive, conative, perceptual, and algedonic phenomenologies, the ultimate reduction base of moral phenomenology involves all these elements as well.
58. It is of course possible to hold that although perceptual phenomenology has this epistemic power, other types of phenomenology do not. But then some reason would have to be provided for the asymmetry. In any case, there is clear interaction here between epistemology and the search for phenomenal primitives.
59. Upon reading Tennessee Williams' *The Glass Menagerie*, one is liable to be permeated by deep sadness about the infinite fragility of sentiment. This kind of sadness has a distinctly negative affective valence. One could hold that once separated from the other components of such deep emotional sadness, the hurtful phenomenology of this negative affect is in itself the same as that of a toothache. That is, one could hold that the phenomenology of negative emotional affect reduces to the phenomenology of pain. But another view is that it is a sui generis kind of negative phenomenology. This too is a debate over phenomenal primitives.
60. For comments on an earlier draft, I am grateful to Farid Masrour, Eric Schwitzgebel, Mark Timmons, and an anonymous referee for Oxford University Press. I have also benefited from presenting parts of this chapter at the Jean Nicod Institute, Rice University, Ruhr University in Bochum, and conferences at the Royal Institute of Philosophy in Prague and the University of Copenhagen. I am indebted to the audiences there, in particular Takeshi Akiba, Adrian Alsmith, Tom Avery, Alexandre Billon, Gwen Bradford, Pietro Cattorini, John Collins, Cameron Buckner, Elvira Di Bonna, Jérôme Dokic, Coralie Dorsaz, Rasmus Thybo Jensen, Huiwon Kim, Ladislav Kvasz, Albert Newen, Søren Overgaard, Alejandro Perez Carballo, François Recanati, Louise Roeska-Hardy, Tobias Schlicht, George Sherr, Charles Siewert, Nicola Spinelli, David Suarez, Genki Uemura, and Pierre Uzan. The contents of this chapter are probably also informed by many conversations and exchanges over the years; relatively recent ones that stand out have been with Geoff Lee, Will Leonard, David Pitt, Eric Schwitzgebel, Charles Siewert, Alberto Voltolini, and Anna Welpinghus.

Chapter 1

1. For making me see the importance of focusing on the act of *making* a judgment, as opposed to the more general notion of judging, I would like to thank Martine Nida-Rümelin and Graham Peebles. If it is possible for judgments to just occur to us (as when it suddenly occurs to me that I have yet to pay this month's phone bill), *making* a judgment should be distinguished from that. In the latter, the subject acts as an epistemic *agent*.

2. Some arguments in the literature do not fit comfortably into either. These include arguments by Lurz (2006), Klausen (2008), Tennant (2009), Nes (2012), and Chudnoff (2015 ch.4) that I will not discuss here, as well as some due to Goldman (1993) and Horgan (2011) that I will.
3. A related form of argument presents a single cognitive experience that is supposed to be phenomenally overwhelming enough to appreciate its cognitive phenomenology. Under this heading we may include Goldman's (1993) and Mangan's (2001) discussion of tip-of-the-tongue phenomenology, Siewert's (1998, 2011) and Horgan and Potrč's (2010) discussion of delayed understanding, and Siewert's (2011) and Chudnoff's (2013b) discussion of intellectual gestalt shifts. Personally, I find that these arguments are better used to fix ideas about what sort of phenomenon the proponent of cognitive phenomenology has in mind. Opponents will typically find ways to offer a reductive account of the relevant phenomenology.
4. Other arguments for cognitive phenomenology that use the contrastive strategy are developed by Peacocke (1998), Siewert (1998), Horgan and Tienson (2002), Kriegel (2003a), Pitt (2004), and Chudnoff (2013b).
5. For some responses to these arguments for cognitive phenomenology, see Robinson 2006, Carruthers and Veillet 2011, Prinz 2011. When it comes to the Moore-Strawson argument, critics typically reject the claim that the best explanation of the phenomenal contrast is the presence of cognitive phenomenology: a superior explanation is that understanding French alters the purely sensory profile of the episodes, by affecting the parsing and foreground/background structure of one's auditory stream of consciousness. When it comes to the Goldman-Pitt argument, critics typically deny that without cognitive phenomenology we would be unable to have the kind of first-person knowledge of our cognitive states, instead offering alternative accounts of how we might.
6. Thanks to Angela Mendelovici for putting the observation to me in these terms.
7. Zangwill himself suggests that the best way to construe direction of fit is as a *normative* property. But it is not clear how it can remain a *psychological* property at that point. For background on the notion of direction of fit, see Anscombe (1957) and Searle (1983).
8. In saying this, I am rejecting (admittedly, without argument) dispositional essentialism: the view that properties are dispositional "all the way down" (Shoemaker 1979).
9. I thank Davor Bodrozic for pointing this out to me.
10. Something like this seems to be the view of Franz Brentano (1874 II ch.7). For more on this, see Kriegel 2015.
11. Objectual perceiving (as when I see the rain), while not naturally described as presenting-as-true, is very naturally described as presenting-as-*real*. That is, in perceiving an object, we are mentally committed to the reality of the object perceived. The properties of presenting-as-true and presenting-as-real seem to be close cousins.
12. It may be claimed that there is still a sense in which it is I who is doing the thinking, in that all thinking involves a subtle phenomenology of agency or authorship of one's thought. However, if we take at face value the reports of thought-insertion patients, this subtle sense of authorship may well be characteristic of *normal* cognitive states, but it is not a *universal*, let alone *necessary*, characteristic of it (see Graham and Stephens 2000). Certainly the phenomenology of doing-the-thinking is missing in these cases, though some might argue that doing-the-thinking itself still occurs.
13. This is typically motivated by the thought that this move is required in order to account for illusion and hallucination: the difference between veridical and nonveridical representations of the brown table is that only in the former are the relevant universals instantiated (Johnston 2004).
14. For a thesis coming close to claiming that we *can* perceive numbers, see Maddy (1980). Naturally, a nominalistic assay of numbers is required for this to be at all viable. Although the matter is delicate, due to a level of unclarity surrounding the notion of abstractness, such an assay tends to undermine the status of numbers as abstracta.
15. Naturally, some philosophers have argued that moral perception *is* possible (Harman 1977 ch.1, Audi 2013).
16. As Malika Auvray pointed out to me, it is common in the neuroscientific literature to take activity in visual cotext to be sufficient for a phenomenon being visual—but the view is explicit in some philosophers as well (e.g., Grice 1962).

17. Thus many properties represented in visual phenomenal states can also be represented in nonphenomenal states—even colors can be represented by tacit beliefs and blindsight states. As for functional role, it is notoriously controversial what the functional significance of phenomenology is. Thus there are both philosophical (Chalmers 1996 ch.5) and scientific (Libet 1985) reasons to doubt whether phenomenal character contributes to a state's functional role at all (or more plausibly, very much). Some philosophers insist that phenomenology has a special functional role in that it is poised to affects beliefs and desires in some way (Tye 2000), but it is fairly clear that in the absence of phenomenology something could fill the same functional role. Conversely, even if phenomenology plays a certain role in the actual world, it is not obviously an epistemically necessary (i.e., *a priori*) feature of it that it does—it may also play a different role in some other epistemically possible world.
18. I will say more about the nature of the explanatory gap below.
19. For approaches along these lines, see Block 1995: 382, Kriegel 2009 ch.1, Carruthers and Veillet 2011.
20. Note that this characterization appeals to a gap between F and *physical* properties, not *neural* properties. It thus skirts Bayne's (2009) concern that various types of philosophers, such as phenomenal externalists (e.g., Dretske 1996), can be concerned with the possibility of cognitive phenomenology but deny that there is an interesting explanatory gap between neural and phenomenal properties. Even phenomenal externalists should be concerned about a gap between phenomenal and *physical* properties, including non-neural physical properties.
21. Tyndall was apparently a mathematician of some renown. This passage is quoted from Tennant (2007: 753). Everything I know about Tyndall I learned from that paper.
22. For Tyndall, these further facts concern physical-phenomenal relations. A modern variant might give the ideal epistemic agent perfect knowledge of the physical facts and perfect reasoning capacities, and maintain that the agent would nevertheless be unable to deduce the phenomenal facts.
23. Leibniz (1714 §17) writes: "Suppose that there be a machine, the structure of which produces thinking, feeling, and perceiving; imagine this machine enlarged but preserving the same proportions, so that you could enter it as if it were a mill. This being supposed, you might visit its inside; but what would you observe there? Nothing but parts which push and move each other, and never anything that could explain perception." Chalmers (1995: 64) writes: "The critical common trait among [the easy problems of consciousness] is that they all concern how a cognitive or behavioral function is performed . . . The hard problem of consciousness, in contrast, goes beyond problems about how functions are performed. Even if every behavioral and cognitive function related to consciousness were explained, there would still remain a further mystery: Why is the performance of these functions accompanied by conscious experience? It is this additional conundrum that makes the hard problem hard."
24. Naturally, there are other possible diagnoses of the explanatory gap: it has sometimes been claimed that the statement "Pain is nothing but c-fiber firing" is *unintelligible* to us at our present state of knowledge (Nagel 1974); sometimes that the subjective and perspectival can find no place in an objective conception of the world (Nagel 1986); sometimes that there is at least an appearance of some sort of *category mistake* in reducing the phenomenal to the physical (Kriegel 2009); sometimes that the explanatory gap arises due to the existence of two different kinds of concepts that can pick up phenomenal properties, physical and phenomenal, such that there are no a priori connections between the two (Vettier and Carruthers 2011). Fiala (2012) discusses a number of possible diagnoses of the explanatory gap, and defends what he calls the "intuition-only" diagnosis, according to which the gap is nothing but a particularly forceful intuition of distinctness. In any case, what unifies all these diagnoses seems to be the notion that an ideal epistemic agent—a perfectly informed and perfectly reasoned agent—would be unable to produce a *reductive explanation* of phenomenal facts and properties in terms of physical facts and properties. She could not produce a full reductive explanation of phenomenal properties by appealing exclusively to physical properties. If we adopt this general construal of the explanatory gap, the gap-based

characterization of phenomenality would entail that a property F is phenomenal just in case an ideal epistemic agent could not reductively explain F in terms of physical properties.
25. The modified characterization of the phenomenal would be this: For any property F, F is a phenomenal property iff there is a rationally warranted appearance that an ideal epistemic agent could not reductively explain F in terms of physical properties.
26. The appeal to a mere appearance of an explanatory gap could also handle what Chalmers calls type-F monism (sometimes called "Russellian monism" or "panprotoexperientialism," and associated with Spinozistic neutral monism). On this view, phenomenal properties arise from proto-phenomenal properties, rather than from physical properties construed as the properties studied in physics. The appeal of the view is that although phenomenal properties arise (in some sense) from protophenomenal ones, there is no explanatory gap between the two. However, since this is the appeal of the view, it is clear that the view is motivated by consideration of the problem of the explanatory gap, which suggests that proponents of the view (type-F monists) are impressed by the rationally warranted *appearance* of an explanatory gap. At the same time, those proponents would not take the explanatory gap to be a gap between phenomenal and *physical* properties, but between phenomenal and *proto-phenomenal* properties. Taking this into account would therefore force us to revise the original biconditional as follows: For any property F, F is a phenomenal property iff there is an explanatory gap between F, on the one hand, and physical and protophenomenal properties, on the other hand.
27. At the same time, in other places Block often seems to think of the explanatory gap as unique to phenomenal consciousness. This is particularly clear when he offers his own characterization of the phenomenal in terms of the explanatory gap: "I mentioned the explanatory gap partly by way of pointing to P-consciousness [phenomenal consciousness]: *that's* the entity to which the mentioned explanatory gap applies" (Block 1995: 382; italics original, and page reference is to the reprint).
28. This category may also include alleged explanatory gaps between color and other manifest properties (on the one hand) and microscopic/scientific properties (on the other), between intentionality and neuro-functional properties, and between dispositional properties and their categorical bases. Thus, it is often thought that any explanatory gap pertaining to color derives from a corresponding explanatory gap pertaining to color phenomenology—though this is certainly not a universal view (see Shoemaker 1994, Byrne 2006). Similarly, it is often thought that there is an explanatory gap for intentionality that has to do with the fact that some intentionality is phenomenally constituted (Horgan and Tienson 2002). Likewise, it is sometimes thought that the problem of consciousness is what brings out an explanatory gap between dispositional and categorical properties, because it is only in the case of consciousness that we have independent access to the categorical property. Obviously, all this would have to be defended much more fully ultimately, but here I am merely sketching a strategy to securing fixing the reference of "phenomenal" so it uniquely picks out the property we are pretheoretically interested in.
29. Of course, it may also be that the normativity gap does derive from the phenomenality gap, especially if we adopt a broadly subjectivist account of normativity: response-dependent realism, fitting attitude analysis, buck-passing account, ideal observer theory, and sensibility theory are only some of the options here. In addition, eliminativism about normativity is much more compelling than about consciousness—most antirealists, expressivists, noncognitivists, nondescriptivists, and so on reject the existence of normative properties. Furthermore, even within the framework of objectivist realism about normative properties, while there is clearly an issue regarding the *reduction* of normativity, it is less common to expect any reductive *explanation* of normative properties in terms of nonnormative ones. Thus the problem of reduction does not present itself as a problem about *explainability* here.
30. Within the Chalmers-Kim model, (apparent) failure of reductive explanation must be due to either (apparent) failure of functionalization or (apparent) failure of identifying what plays the relevant functional role. Presumably, however, in the case of phenomenal consciousness the problem is *not* that nothing in the physical realm (apparently) turns out to play the

specified functional role. So it must be the apparent failure functionalization that explains the apparent resistance to reductive explanation. For more on all this, see Kriegel 2009 ch.8.
31. For the debate on property-exemplification versus bare-particular accounts of states, see Davidson 1969, Kim 1976.
32. To repeat, this characterization is not intended as capturing the deep essence of phenomenal consciousness—*that* we grasp through introspective ostension or acquaintance, I maintain—but rather to provide an informative characterization that does not prejudice the debate over cognitive phenomenology.
33. For a more critical discussion of these kinds of argument, see Bayne 2009 and Dumitru Ms.
34. Once we take this cluster-of-symptoms approach, we may also bring into the cluster other features that are plausibly symptomatic of phenomenality. In particular, there may exist *epistemic* symptoms of phenomenality. Thus, Siewert (2011) argues that a special and distinctive kind of knowledge is appropriate to seek for phenomenal states, so phenomenality motivates a unique type of curiosity. And as already noted, Goldman (1993) and Pitt (2004) have presented epistemic arguments for cognitive phenomenology that rely on the claim that phenomenal states can be known in a special and distinctive manner. Such epistemic features, while controversial as criterial of phenomenality, may be quite plausible as symptomatic, and thus indicative, of it. (One might still hold that the explanatory gap is in some sense the most direct symptom, precisely because it is least theoretically laden.) The advantage in this cluster-of-symptoms approach is that it is more agile than any suggestion for a *criterion* of phenomenality. The disadvantage is that any argument for a controversial type of phenomenology using it would be onerous to both mount and evaluate. It would consist in a cluster of sub-arguments appealing to single symptoms. Perhaps, however, this is all we can hope for in this area.
35. This is not to deny that CPP is, once grasped, also simply intuitive. For my part, I find that relatively untutored introspective examination of my own stream of consciousness suggests that it has both sensuous and intellectual components, both of which appropriate objects of the aforementioned philosophical anxiety. And I note that Tyndall suggests the same in the passage quoted above: in articulating his "explanatory chasm," he mentions *thoughts* alongside *feelings*. Arguably, however, the presence or absence of an explanatory gap is not something directly accessible to introspection, and requires a more sustained *argument*.
36. Long-term survival prospects for congenital analgesia patients are known to be dim, and our algedonic zombie is even worse off, but in our thought-experiment we can stipulate that the world is fortuitously cooperative, so that the algedonic zombie survives and lives a long and respectable life.
37. I will say more about this element of vivacity below. For instructive discussion of intellectual gestalt shifts, see Chudnoff (2013b).
38. It may well be that the ability to imagine Zoe's mental life as my own is derivative from an ability to use empathy in imagination to imaginatively simulate another's inner life. That is, it may be that in the first instance I imagine the relevant inner life from the outside, so to speak, and only in a second instance import the imagined mental life into my "subjectivity." It is for this reason that I stipulated that Zoe is your daughter, rather than *you*.
39. Chudnoff (2011b) proposes to account for it in terms of the presence, in addition to any seeming fact-awareness (or propositional awareness) involved in the episode, of a seeming item-awareness, where the item is relevantly connected to the relevant fact/proposition. I will discuss Chudnoff's account of presentational phenomenology more fully in Chapter 3.
40. The objector may press that we cannot rule out some further putative type of phenomenology which would both be a plausible prima facie reducer and potentially present in the Zoe scenario. However, for any potential type of noncognitive phenomenology, it is unclear why an augmented thought-experiment that would stipulate it out of Zoe's mental life could not be devised (with no noticeable effect on the explanatory-gap intuition). Furthermore, as with conative phenomenology, in considering further potential noncognitive phenomenologies, we should keep in mind that many might turn out to be of the sort that cognitive

phenomenology skeptics are opposed to anyway. In any case, I take it to be the skeptic's burden to adduce a specific candidate.

41. Compare: if we want a theory of cells, we account for them in terms of the molecules making them up; if we then want a theory of molecules, we account for them in terms of the atoms composing them; ditto for atoms and their constituent subatomic particles. But when we reach the elemental particles of matter, the only way to characterize them is by specifying as exhaustively as possible their lawful interrelations. The same applies in the domain of phenomenology: we can account for complex experiences in terms of their elemental phenomenal constituents, but we can account for the latter only in terms of their interrelations. The envisaged Ramsey sentence for making a judgment attempts to do something like that. Interestingly, this is more or less how Bolzano (1837 §34) proceeds in his discussion of judgment.

42. Many of the platitudes to be discussed below emerged during a 2.5-hour seminar discussion at the University of Fribourg in April 2013, which allowed me to see many central aspects of the phenomenology of making a judgment that I would never have been able to appreciate by myself. I am greatly indebted to the audience in that session, in particular Davor Bodrozic, Coralie Dorsaz, Hannes Mathiessen, Jacob Naïto, Martine Nida-Rümelin, Michael O'Leary, Graham Peebles, Gianfranco Soldati, and Samet Sulejmanoski.

43. The element of finality in the act of judgment-making should be distinguished from the element of absoluteness. The former has a delicate character: although making a judgment seems to involve the feeling of deciding to "close the investigation," it does *not* seem to involve the feeling that one could never decide to "reopen the investigation." This is what recommends speaking of "provisional finality." We should keep in mind that the paradoxical ring of the expression does not reflect any incoherence in the characteristic described.

44. Dominated by a strong desire to judge that p, I may decide to expose myself only to evidence for p and avoid all sources of information likely to reveal counterevidence. But there is a sense in which that would make judgment depend on the will only *indirectly*. To accommodate this, I propose that we construe "involuntary" to mean "not directly dependent upon the will." (How to draw the direct/indirect distinction is a difficult question. But in any case judgment's merely indirect dependence on the will can show up in the phenomenology without the grounds or nature of indirect dependence showing up.)

45. For comments on an earlier draft, I am grateful to Eli Chudnoff, Farid Masrour, Angela Mendelovici, Boyd Millar, Michelle Montague, Indrek Reiland, Eric Schwitzgebel, and an anonymous referee for Oxford University Press. For useful exchanges, I thank Malika Auvray, Chris Kahn, Benji Kozuch, and Geoff Lee. I am also grateful to audiences at the University of Fribourg, the University of Georgia, and the University of Guelph, in particular Yuri Balashov, Davor Bodrozic, Chuck Cross, Tony Dardis, Coralie Dorsaz, Peter Lopson, Mark McCullagh, Hannes Mathiessen, Jacob Naïto, Martine Nida-Rümelin, Michael O'Leary, Graham Peebles, Beth Preston, Brad Richards, Patricia Sheridan, Gianfranco Soldati, Christian Stephens, Samet Sulejmanoski, and Sarah Wright.

Chapter 2

1. For an argument that the two states cannot be identified from a functionalist point of view, see Lewis 1988. But arguably the difference is also phenomenologically manifest.
2. One often encounters in the literature reductive accounts of some conative states in terms of others: for example, of intention in terms of desire or the right combination of desire and belief (Anscombe 1963, Audi 1973). Through a series of intra-conative reductions of this sort, it is possible to end up with the view that ultimately there is only *one* conative primitive—desire, say—and that all other conative phenomena can be accounted for in terms of it plus some other element or specification. But this still commits to a conative primitive. The idea that *all* conative states are reducible to nonconative phenomena is much stronger, and is standardly taken to be implausible. However, this is not exceptionless. Stampe (1986) accounts for desire in terms of perception of the good; Price (1989) defends the thesis that desiring p is just believing that p is desirable against certain objections.

3. For example, Lewis' (1988) argument that desire cannot be reduced to belief is based on the notion that the *theoretical role* of desire in decision theory is one that it could not perform if it was just a kind of belief. But Lewis could also hold that the *phenomenal* properties of desire are inessential to the relevant theoretical role.
4. In a similar vein, Horgan et al. (2003) distinguish between a first-person and third-person phenomenology of agency, and identify the phenomenology of doing with the first-person variety exclusively.
5. It is also possible to maintain that in fact Jean-Paul has performed a single action that falls under four action types (or that admits of four descriptions); in fact, there is much to recommend this view (see Hornsby 1980 ch.1). However, we could readily redefine the more-basic-than relation I am interested in over action-types or (or over action-descriptions) rather than actions.
6. This is a first approximation only, but it will do for our purposes. For discussion of complications that must be taken account of in a satisfactory account of basic action, see Hornsby 1980 ch.6 and Enc 2003 ch.2. It is quite plausible that all *overt* basic actions are muscle-contractings, and I will conduct the discussion as though this is indeed so, but nothing I will say is supposed to be hostage to this assumption. I conduct the discussion as though this is assumed because it simplifies the presentation and is moreover independently plausible. My view on these matters is in general in line with Hornsby's (1980): muscle-contractings are the basic overt actions, but there are (non-overt) actions even more basic than them: tryings. I will discuss tryings in due course.
7. Note well: the objection is not that we *experience* a temporal gap between the experience of muscle contraction and the muscle contraction itself, but that there *is* such a gap. The objection concerns the temporal order itself, not any experience of temporal order.
8. James (1890: 493–4) writes: "all our ideas of movement, including those of effort which it requires, as well as those of its direction, its extent, its strength, and its velocity, are images of peripheral sensations, either 'remote,' or resident in the moving parts, or in other parts which sympathetically act with them . . ." And later (1890: 501): "An anticipatory image, then, of the sensorial consequences of a movement . . . is the only psychic state which introspection lets us discern as the forerunner of our voluntary acts."
9. Indeed, this was the primary motivating factor in James' adoption of his forward-looking proprioceptive view. James (1890: 499) writes: "*There is no introspective evidence of the feeling of innervation.* Wherever we look for it and think we have grasped it, we find that we have really got a peripheral feeling or image instead—an image of the way in which we feel when the innervation is over." Therefore (1890: 493; my italics): "Bain, Wundt, Helmholtz, and Mach defend [the feeling of innervation] most explicitly. But in spite of the authority which such writers deservedly wield, I cannot help thinking that they are in this instance wrong—that the discharge into the motor nerves is *insentient.*"
10. I am bracketing here issues to do with Libet's (1985) experiments and whether they indicate that such signals start traveling 200 milliseconds before the conscious experience of decision occurs. Obviously, if this is so it would be greatly vexing to the proponent of the innervation theory. But Libet's experiments (and their correct interpretation) are much more controversial than the introspective inaccessibility of brain-to-muscle energy currents ought to be.
11. Ginet makes many specific claims about this proprietary volitional/conative phenomenology that we need not commit to here. One of his central theses (Ginet 1990 ch.1) is that it is the presence of this volitional phenomenology that accounts for the difference between (i) actions and (ii) events the subject causes that are not action. Although I am sympathetic to Ginet's theory of action, which is developed around this primitive phenomenal quality, nothing in this chapter commits to any position on these wider issues.
12. That short step would be to rule out any *other* reducers of the relevant phenomenology. But since the tactile, visual, proprioceptive, and cognitive phenomenologies are the most threatening candidates for reducers, their failure to reduce this type of conative phenomenology makes it very likely that the thesis of the primitive *conatus* is true.

13. The distinction thus foreshadows Chalmers' (1996 ch.1) thesis of the "double life of mental terms": mental terms can be used to express two systematically different concepts, grounded in two different conceptions of mentality. One conception characterizes mental phenomena third-personally in terms of their causal and functional relations to the environment and to each other; the other characterizes them first-personally in terms of their subjective feel, their phenomenal character. The main point appears to be that the third-person approach focuses on the *mechanical* dimension of mental life whereas the first-person one focuses on its *experiential* dimension.
14. This can be seen already in William James' (1890: 487; italics original) seminal work on the will: "*voluntary movements must be secondary, not primary functions of our organism.* This is the first point to understand in the psychology of Volition. Reflex, instinctive, and emotional movements are all primary performances." Ricœur (1950: 20–1) describes this attitude expressively: "[The] rule that gives the natural sciences their force leads to constructing man like a house, that is to say first laying the foundations for a psychology of the involuntary and then topping these lower functional floors with an additional floor called the will."
15. All translations from the French are mine, though I have been assisted by Erazim Kohak's excellent 1966 translation into English. Page references are to the reprint.
16. From Ricœur's discussion, it is not entirely clear (to me at least) whether he means this in-my-power-ness to be constitutive of the notion of a project, or to characterize some projects and not others. Accordingly, it is not clear whether it is *the project* as such that can be designated the formal object of decision, or just a subset of projects, namely those that are in my power.
17. The term "internalism" comes from Falk (1945), who uses it to indicate that there is an "internal connection" between moral commitments and motivation. The issue will be discussed more fully in Chapter 5.
18. It has sometimes been argued that one of these notions can be analyzed in terms of the other. (Perhaps an action is right in virtue of leading to a good state of affairs. Perhaps a state of affairs is good in virtue of an ideal subject finding it right to bring it about.) This debate is orthogonal to our present concerns.
19. The "primarily" is significant. Both actions and states of affairs can be used to describe the intentionality of both desiring and deciding. You want the beggar to *have* the extra dollar, but you also want to *give* him the dollar; you decide to give him the dollar, but you also decide that he shall have that dollar. Still, the natural order of explanation in each case is opposite. You want to give the beggar the dollar *because* you want him to have it—you want the right in virtue of wanting the good. But you decide that he shall have it *by* deciding to give it to him—you decide the good in virtue of deciding the right. We may say that at the fundamental, nonderivative level, you want the good state of affairs to obtain and decide to perform the right act.
20. It might be objected that sometimes we decide to do the wrong thing, where this means not just that we decide to do what, unbeknownst to us, happens to be wrong, but that we decide to do something wrong *qua* wrong. A similar objection is sometimes leveled against internalist accounts of moral commitment, and while Hare's (1952) "inverted commas" response has faced resistance, it is clearly the way to go with decision: the decided is "wrong" only by standards *other than* the subject's (or more accurately other than the decision's).
21. In this respect deciding is more like intending than desiring. Unlike desire, intention aims primarily at the right, not the good. Insofar as we can intend that some state of affairs obtain, it is only in virtue of intending to perform some action that would lead to it. Meanwhile, the complete "opposite" of deciding is wishing, which aims primarily at the good (I wish for world peace, construed as a grand state of affairs) and is not connected to action even hypothetically (I wish the Armenian genocide had never happened, but feel no pull to action as a result).
22. For Ricœur (1950: 259), this relationship of "filling" or "realization" between decision and action finds expression in their respective temporal phenomenologies. We have already

noted that deciding is phenomenally oriented toward the future. In the very same sense, acting is phenomenally oriented toward *the present*.

23. I suppose some kind of disjunctivist could deny that phenomenology is an entirely mental phenomenon. Here (and elsewhere) I will ignore this kind of disjunctivism. Note that it is much stronger than just externalism about phenomenology, since the latter can be, and indeed usually is, combined with externalism about the mental that allows the phenomenal to be internal to the mental even if it is external to something else.

24. It is true that the result of one's action is a change in the painting's location, but that change is not what is tried (in the first stance)—it is what is desired. What is tried is the moving of the painting—an act. (These claims should more properly be made about what is tried and what is desired *basically* and *primarily*. As we saw in §4, there are derivative ways of talking about what is tried and desired that mix things up.)

25. It is of course true that some decisions and consequent actions are effortless, in the sense that there is no special difficulty involved in them. But this is *relative* effortlessness. There is also an *absolute* sense of effort in which we can say that trying always mobilizes *some* effort, although sometimes the effort is so comparatively minimal that we consider the trying (relatively) effortless. One might reasonably hope that understanding the feeling of effort in this absolute sense could shed light on the phenomenology of trying.

26. Following de Biran, it has been something of a recurring theme that the feeling of effort constitutes an introspective proof of the existence of libertarian free will (see, e.g., Laporte 1947 and Campbell 1957). Even James (1890 ch.26) saw it necessary to concede that in *some* cases of willing a phenomenal element is present in the form of the feeling of effort, and Dewey (1897) followed in his steps.

27. It would seem, then, that Ricœur is right, contrary to James, that conative phenomenology involves an element referring to realization in action, an element of moving from disposition to manifestation, from chargedness to discharge; but he is wrong that conative phenomenology must therefore involve an action-phenomenology. Rather, it is trying-phenomenology that is built into conative phenomenology. It remains that the phenomenology of decision is unlike how James thought of it and very like how Ricœur did.

28. It may be objected that sometimes we try to do something without first explicitly deciding to do it. But this objection depends on too demanding a conception of decision. It is true that the most phenomenologically vivid (and thus most paradigmatic) decisions are deliberate, thoughtful, and "explicit." But throughout the day we make a great many more small decisions, "thoughtless," "implicit" decisions that impose on our ongoing conscious experience only very lightly. These decisions have the same phenomenal character as the more paradigmatic ones, but theirs is much more subdued and peripheral. It simply suffers from lower phenomenal intensity, but is otherwise the same as paradigmatic decisions'. My contention is that trying always implicates a decision, though typically of this phenomenologically unimposing variety.

29. Many such elements may be such that appreciating them is necessary for understanding Aristide's decision. Arguably, one does not fully grasp the decision if one does not grasp that Aristide is perceiving the cake as nearby and smelling nice. Regardless, the perceptual experience is not literally part of Aristide's *conative* phenomenology—and neither is his consent.

30. As such, it would already represent a major contribution toward the characterization of conative phenomenology. But it might also go beyond that. Suppose, for the sake of argument, that the folk concept of the will (or even a more refined, scientific or philosophical concept) behaves as a prototype concept: a mental state qualifies as conative just if it resembles (sufficiently and relevantly) certain prototypical exercises of the will. It would then be natural to take *deciding and then trying* as at least one such prototype, perhaps even *the* prototype. Then mental states might qualify as conative solely in virtue of resembling it. In that case, any descriptive account of the phenomenology of deciding-cum-trying would in effect deliver an account of conative phenomenology simpliciter: to have a conative phenomenology would just *be* to have a phenomenology that resembles (sufficiently, relevantly) the phenomenology of deciding-cum-trying.

31. For comments on a previous draft of this chapter, I would like to thank Thor Grünbaum, Eric Schwitzgebel, Mark Timmons, and an anonymous referee. I have also benefited from presenting materials from this chapter at the Pratt Institute and at the University of Copenhagen's Center for Subjectivity Research. I would like to thank the audiences there, in particular Adrian Alsmith, Rasmus Thybo Jensen, John McGuire, Søren Overgaard, Katherine Poe, and Dan Zahavi.

Chapter 3

1. Brentano often puts the claim in terms of classes of *mental* phenomena. But since he holds that there are no unconscious mental states, this effectively divides *conscious* phenomena into three fundamental classes. Whether Brentano's notion of consciousness is the phenomenal notion is a trickier question, which depends partly on one's conception of the phenomenal. In chapter 1, I argued that the best way to fix the reference of "phenomenal" is in terms of what produces the appearance of an explanatory gap. In this sense, it is clear that Brentano's concern is with the phenomenal notion of consciousness, since it is the notion he is ultimately dualist about (see Brentano 1874: 51).
2. Note that although this consideration mentions introspection, it is not introspectively based, in a sense that it is not for introspective reasons that we are compelled to believe it: we do not *introspect* the introspective discriminability of propositional attitudes.
3. Overall, Goldman sketches four arguments for the "phenomenological parity" of the attitudes. Here I am concerned with the third of these. Goldman (1993: 24) writes: "My third argument is from the introspective discriminability of attitude strengths. Subjects' classificational abilities are not confined to broad categories such as belief, desire, and intention; they also include intensities thereof. People report how firm is their intention or conviction, how much they desire an object, and how satisfied or dissatisfied they are with a state of affairs. Whatever the behavioral predictive power of these self-reports, their very occurrence needs explaining . . . The most natural hypothesis is that there are dimensions of awareness over which scales of attitude intensity are represented."
4. Pitt (2004: 7) writes: "Normally—that is, barring confusion, inattention, impaired functioning, and the like—one is able, consciously, introspectively and noninferentially (henceforth, "Immediately") to do three distinct (but closely related) things: (a) to distinguish one's occurrent conscious thoughts from one's other occurrent conscious mental states; (b) to distinguish one's occurrent conscious thoughts each from the others; and (c) to identify each of one's occurrent conscious thoughts as the thought it is (i.e., as having the *content* it does). But (the argument continues), one would not be able to do these things unless each (type of) occurrent conscious thought had a phenomenology . . . different from that of any other type of conscious mental state (proprietary)." In Pitt's hands, this argument appeals to a special case of inference to the best explanation, which we may call "inference to the *only* possible explanation." But this is not an essential feature of the reasoning, and the argument can certainly be set out as a standard inference to the best explanation.
5. Thanks to Victor Kumar and David Pitt for independently raising this possibility with me.
6. Early introspectionists such as Oswald Külpe and Narziss Ach attempted to adduce *actual* cases of imageless thought, as does Siewert (1998). To my mind, however, the best cases may be merely possible ones. The Zoe thought-experiment was supposed to produce one such. This thought-experiment, I contend, demonstrates the possibility of entertaining a (mathematical) proposition without any capacity for sensory imagery.
7. Brentano (1874: 205) writes: "But even if in certain cases the act of taking something to be true coincides with the greater intensity of a presentation, the presentation is not, on that account, itself a judgment. That is why the error in question may disappear, while the vividness of the presentation persists. And in other cases we are firmly convinced of the truth of something, even thought the content of the judgment is anything but vivid."
8. It might be objected that it is impossible for us to entertain such necessarily false propositions, on the grounds that there are no such propositions for us to entertain. The suggestion might be that we truly entertain in such cases are only the *sentences* used to express

the alleged proposition. But it is unclear what motivates this restriction. In the sensory domain, we seem capable of visualizing an Escher triangle, even when we *know* it to be logically impossible (I argue for this in Kriegel 2011 ch.3). It is unclear what would motivate a disanalogy in the case of propositional attitudes.
9. Thanks to Eli Chudnoff for this point.
10. Relatedly, Brentano (1874 Bk II ch.7) distinguishes two dimensions of intensity along which judgments (cognitive phenomenology) can vary, one to do with the degree of conviction in the proposition judged and one to do merely with the degree of vividness with which the proposition is present before the mind; according to Brentano, presentation (entertaining-phenomenology) exhibits only the second dimension. He writes: "Furthermore, in presentations the only intensity involved is the greater or less sharpness and vividness of the phenomenon. When love and hate enter in, however, a new kind of intensity is introduced—a greater or lesser degree of energy, vehemence or moderation in the strength of these feelings. In an altogether analogous manner, we also find an entirely new kind of intensity when judgment is added to presentation. For it is obvious that the greater or lesser degree of certainty in conviction or opinion is more closely related to the differences in the intensity of love than to differences in the strength of presentations." (1874: 223)
11. Thanks to Lizzie Kriegel and Joseph Tolliver for helpful discussion of this issue.
12. Gilbert (1991: 107) writes: "Is there a difference between believing and merely understanding an idea? . . . [I argue] that (a) the acceptance of an idea is part of the automatic comprehension of that idea and (b) the rejection of an idea occurs subsequent to, and more effortfully than, its acceptance."
13. Mandelbaum (2010: 13) writes: "If I tell you that I'm about to read a list of sentences all of which are false and then I read the sentences, it seems plausible that you would not automatically believe these sentences in the way that you may, for example, automatically get excited when hearing of a rare and tantalizing opportunity. However, in what follows I will argue that this plausible assumption is false: . . . just as emotions are insensitive to our background beliefs, so too is belief formation initially insensitive to our background beliefs. More specifically, I will argue for the claim that, whenever we entertain a proposition, we automatically believe that proposition. The plausible idea that we can entertain a proposition while withholding assent from it is a myth . . ."
14. Incidentally, this framework requires a story about what distinguishes the proposition that *p* from the proposition that *q*, and accordingly what distinguishes the acts of entertaining that constitute the former from those that constitute the latter. Obviously, the difference cannot be that the former are suitably related to *p* whereas the latter to *q*, on pain of circularity. One (but not the only) noncircular answer would appeal to the phenomenology: it is possible to claim that entertaining that *p* has a different phenomenal character from entertaining that *q*. On this version of the "propositions as types" view, *p* is nothing but a type of entertainings, namely, the *p*-ish entertainings (where *p*-ish-ness is explicated in terms of brute phenomenal character). This would give phenomenology a central role in the metaphysics of propositions. Needless to say, nothing in Soames' writing suggests a penchant for this way of going. But the result is a coherent and internally stable position nonetheless.
15. This outlook requires a robust distinction between content and attitude (or in the case of language, content and force). Perhaps not accidentally, Hanks (2007) rejects this distinction. His case for this is too elaborate to take on here, as it involves three different plausibility considerations. But it should be noted that at least one central line of argument cannot be used in the present context, as it *presupposes* that there is no such thing as entertaining. Hanks argues that acts of assertion underlie "assertive propositions," acts of interrogation underlie "interrogative propositions," and imperative acts underlie "imperative propositions," but there is no type of act that underlies propositions *simpliciter*. Because of that, there is no content that remains the same across different attitudes. However, if there is such an act as mere entertaining (in thought if not in language), then propositions *simpliciter* could be identified with entertaining types. Thus the present line of argument *presupposes* that there is no entertaining, and could not be used in the present dialectical

context. The other parts of Hanks' case are the claims that there is no conclusive argument *for* the attitude-content distinction and that the distinction renders the so-called unity of the proposition mysterious. I think there are plausible responses to both of these charges, but cannot pursue the matter here.

16. It is important not to confuse the phenomenology of neutrality and the phenomenology of disengagement. Entertaining is doxastically neutral on the truth of *p* whether engaged or disengaged. The element of engagement does not undermine neutrality: it introduces a doxastic *concern* but not a doxastic *position*. (Thanks to Indrek Reiland for a very useful exchange on these issues.)
17. If my claim about the fringe versus center of ordinary usage turns out to be false, we could move to treating "consideration" and "contemplation" as used here as *entirely* technical rather than *quasi*-technical.
18. In Kriegel 2009, I distinguish between two aspects of an experience's phenomenal character. In the reddish way it is like for me to have an experience of a red tomato, we can distinguish a *reddish* component and a *for-me* component. The former I call "qualitative character," the latter "subjective character." Plausibly, the two types of intensity distinguished in the text are attributes of these two different components of phenomenal character. Sensory intensity is an attribute of qualitative character; phenomenal intensity is an attribute of subjective character. On this construal, the more acutely for me the experience is, the more present the experience is to my mind, and the more vivid it is to me. (It might be better, within this framework, to call them "qualitative intensity" and "subjective intensity" respectively.)
19. These nominals are called imperfect because they contain traces of the verb. They are to be contrasted with perfect nominals, such as "*a*'s F-ness," in which the verb disappears altogether (for more on this, see Vendler 1967, as well as Kriegel 2005b).
20. There is also a usage that ties "thinking about/of" to memory: when I say "I am thinking of Jimmy," I express an episode of reminiscing about Jimmy. In this case I do commit to Jimmy's existence (in an eternalist sense). But this is not the only usage of the locution, not even a central one. When I say "I am thinking of a flying zebra," I am clearly not expressing a reminiscing but an imagining.
21. If the Gilbert model were correct, that *might* support the first analysis. But as I argued in §3, the Gilbert model is at most adequate for low-road reasoning; it is inadequate for high-road reasoning. And in any case, it is unclear how to translate a psychological claim about the formation of mental states into a philosophical claim about their internal structure.
22. This objection was presented to me separately by Bruno Leclercq and Eric Schwitzgebel.
23. To repeat myself, the characterization is nonreductive in that it does not attempt to account for entertaining in terms of other *attitudes*. It is not meant to be nonreductive in the sense of positing a nonphysical feature of the world. For all that has been said here, entertaining is nothing but E-fiber firing.
24. Some of the claims made in the above discussion, such as 2, pertain not to entertaining that *p* but entertaining φ-ing, so we might want to leave them out of the Ramsey sentence for entertaining *that p*—Thesis F notwithstanding.
25. For comments on previous drafts of all or parts of this chapter, I am grateful to Margherita Arcangeli, David Chalmers, Eli Chudnoff, George Graham, David Pitt, Indrek Reiland, and Eric Schwitzgebel. I also benefited from presenting parts of this chapter at Kings' College London, Northwestern University, University of Fribourg, University of South Denmark, an NEH summer institute on "investigating consciousness" at the College of Charleston, and conferences at Rice University and Willamette University. I am grateful to the audiences there, in particular Davor Bodrozic, Alex Byrne, Cristian Coseru, Tim Crane, Sandy Goldberg, Benj Hellie, Avram Hiller, Robert Howell, Ivan Ivanov, Søren Harnow Klausen, Pete Mandik, Michelle Montague, Martine Nida-Rümelin, Nikolaj Nottelmanm, Casey O'Callaghan, David Papineau, François Recanati, and Galen Strawson. Finally, I also benefited from conversations with Margherita Arcangeli, Lizzie Kriegel, Victor Kumar, and Joseph Tolliver as well.

Chapter 4

1. It is not entirely clear whether James (or Lange, for that matter) thought that every feeling of bodily occurrence constituted an emotion or only the converse, that every emotion was constituted by a feeling of bodily occurrences. If the latter is the case, then we would have to refine the portable version of the thesis to "emotion = subset of proprioceptive phenomenology." A corresponding change to the spelled out articulation of JLT would require specifying a *kind* of proprioceptive phenomenology. (Similar adjustments would be called for in the case of the other indented theses to be discussed later in this section, but I am not going to remark on this again.) It is noteworthy that James' contemporaries appear to have taken him to mean the former. Thus, Cannon (1915) argues against James that the same visceral changes that sometimes occur in emotional states can also occur in non-emotional states. This would be a criticism of James only if he was committed to the thesis that every feeling of bodily occurrence constituted an emotion.
2. The rejection of the feeling theory of emotion is well documented and is in fact the starting point for many philosophical discussions of emotion of the past century. The implicit acceptance of the Jamesian account of emotional *phenomenology* has been less highlighted, but see Armstrong 1968 ch.8 and Tye 1995 ch.4. Here is a representative passage from Armstrong (1968: 180; italics original): "I suspect that this close connection between emotion and bodily sensation explains why we speak of 'feeling' emotions. The etymologically original sense of the word 'feel' seems to be that connected with tactual and bodily perceptions (see *O.E.D.*). Bodily perceptions (that is, sensations) are phenomenologically conspicuous in first-person experience of emotions, and so we speak of *feeling* angry. (And where the sensations are absent, it is natural to speak of *being* angry, but not *feeling* it.)"
3. This used to be Tye's (1995: 126; italics mine) explicit view: "Suppose you suddenly feel extremely angry. Your body will change in all sorts of ways: for example, your blood pressure will rise, your nostrils will flare, your face will flush . ... These physical changes are registered in the sensory receptors distributed throughout your body. In response to the activity in your receptors, you will mechanically build up a complex sensory representation of how your body has changed, of the new body state you are in. In this way, you will feel the bodily changes. The feeling you undergo *consists in* the complex sensory representation of these changes." More recently, Tye (2008) has incorporated other intentional elements into his account.
4. An objection might be that the grief proper is exhausted by the proprioceptive awareness of bodily changes, but is regularly *accompanied* by a thought that constitutes an appreciation of an external cause of those bodily changes. However, if this were the case, then in principle the grief could occur *without* the accompanying thought (in sufficiently extraordinary circumstances). But for my part, I find it impossible to imagine a grief with no awareness of a grievesome event, exhausted entirely by bodily sensations. That kind of experience is not recognizable to me as grief.
5. This is not to say that I reject the argument's conclusion as well. In the next section, I will argue that the conclusion is strictly speaking true, though a modification thereof can be produced that retains the spirit of the feeling theory of emotion.
6. For more on the notion of phenomenal intentionality, see Kriegel 2013. A crucial aspect of the phenomenal intentionality of emotions is that there cannot be intentional difference between two emotional states without a corresponding phenomenal difference. (This does not yet entail that the phenomenal is somehow more *basic* than the intentional.)
7. This would be the case if (i) there are two different emotional states that differ only in their relation to algedonic phenomenology and/or if (ii) there is an emotional state and a non-emotional state that differ only in that the former but not the latter is suitably related to algedonic phenomenology. The first pair would substantiate the relevance of algedonic phenomenology to the identity conditions of emotional states, the second its relevance to their existence conditions.

8. Davies' (1995) counter-example is of subpersonal computational states in the visual system—Marr's (1982) "2.5D sketches." Different examples also involving subpersonal mental states—whether computational or neural—are provided in Horgan and Kriegel 2008 and Kriegel 2011 ch.4. It is plausible that, just as the visual system has computational and neural states that are not even potentially conscious, so the emotional system has such states. Thus, surely some emotional processing in the amygdala results in cerebral states that qualify as emotional but that are not even potentially conscious.

9. Searle's argument is that the intentionality of mental states exhibits an aspectual shape (e.g., they can represent Venus as Phosphorus without representing it as Hesperus), and this is a feature that only consciousness can bring into the picture—brute neural states cannot discriminate between Phosphorus and Hesperus. (For fuller discussion, see Kriegel 2011 ch.4.) This argument is problematic in a number of ways, discussed by the commentators cited in the main text. In addition, it is a substantive claim that emotional states' intentionality also features aspectual shape, though arguably quite a plausible one (see Montague 2009).

10. In recent years, and contrary to a long tradition, more and more philosophers have come to think that moods are intentional but have a somewhat peculiar intentional profile (Crane 1998, Seager 1999, Mendelovici 2013). The earliest explicit statement of this view that I know of is in Solomon (1976: 173): "Euphoria, melancholy, and depression are not about anything in particular (though some particular incident might well set them off); they are about the whole of our world, or indiscriminately about anything that comes our way, casting happy glows or somber shadows on every object and incident of our experience."

11. The general strategy of ruling out nonmental phenomena by homing in on a particular, privileged kind of intentionality may yet be viable: appeal to underived intentionality is only one version of that general strategy. But some concrete suggestion would have to be presented that would at least get the extension right.

12. There might be some other way to specify a privileged kind of functional role allegedly common and peculiar to mental states, but again a concrete proposal would have to be made before this could be evaluated.

13. The existence of non-introspectible subpersonal representations in the visual system suggests that the introspection-based mark is too narrow. Meanwhile, Ducasse's suggestion is also clearly too narrow, as many unconscious states are not private in all but the most esoteric senses of the term. For both Farkas/Tartaglia and Ducasse, then, it makes sense to route their mark theses through the whole system: a mental state is a state of a system capable of entering introspectible/private mental states. The probable co-extension of the introspectible/private with the phenomenal would then make the suggestion collapse onto a phenomenally based mark. In the same vein, one might hold that a state is mental just in case it is a state of a system capable of entering states possessed of phenomenal intentionality (something like this appears to be in the background of Horgan and Graham 2009). This is clearly a phenomenally based mark thesis.

14. Consider the view that properties are just funds of causal powers (Shoemaker 1979). It would be extremely odd, and very much in need of justification, to maintain causal existence conditions for properties but reject causal identity conditions (or conversely). Similarly, those who hold that events are just triples comprising an object, a property, and a time (Kim 1976) typically also hold that events *individuate* in terms of such triples; those who hold that concrete particulars are "spacetime worms" (Sider 2001) tend to hold that different particulars are just different worms; and so on.

15. For that matter, the very case for the phenomenally based mark of the mental I have adopted was non-demonstrative, insofar as it relied on a merely partial argument by elimination. That, too, then, was merely a prima facie case for that mark thesis.

16. It is often noted that different subjects' mental states can be strictly type-identical. If we think of similarity as *partial* type-identity, it is obvious that S's unconscious emotional state may be similar in relevant respects to S*'s conscious emotional state.

17. One reason there might not be a fact of the matter is that some states might resemble the paradigm in a real but far from overwhelming way, so that we are tempted to see them as falling in a gray area between clearly emotional and clearly non-emotional states.
18. Presumably, adding algedonic, entertaining, and non-proprioceptive perceptual phenomenology is not what will make a difference, as these are not prima facie plausible candidates for the reduction base of emotional phenomenology.
19. This distinction pertains to what we may call "transitive happiness," the kind of happiness reported by a transitive verb. There is also what we might call "intransitive happiness," reported by the corresponding intransitive verb. It is an open question what the relationship between the two might be. One view is that "S is happy" just means "S is happy about S's life/existence." This would analyze intransitive happiness in terms of transitive happiness. Another view, however, would reject any such analysis.
20. Certainly "love" would not make a plausible candidate. For one thing, it appears to confuse a mental act with how it presents its object. We may call the formal object of love "the lovely," but it is no more plausible that emotion's formal object is the lovely than that it is the beautiful. The same issues of extensional adequacy arise.
21. Every language seems to have a simple noun for emotions as a group. Why would that be if emotion did not seem, at a pretheoretic, folkloresque level, to constitute a natural kind? This would be nicely accommodated by the idea that all emotions present-as-important what they do.
22. Thanks to Anita Konzelmann Ziv for raising the issue of boredom to me.
23. Deonna and Teroni (2012: 77) write: "the fact that emotions have evaluative properties amongst their correctness conditions traces back to the fact that they are specific attitudes—namely evaluative attitudes—and not to the fact that they have a specific content."
24. Deonna and Teroni (2012: 79): "the emotionally relevant bodily changes are experienced as distinct stances we adopt towards specific objects. That is to say, we should conceive of emotions as distinctive types of bodily awareness, where the subject experiences her body holistically as taking an attitude towards a certain object . . ."
25. Brentano (1907: 150; italics original) writes (or rather *says*—this essay was dictated when Brentano was already blind): "If someone *desires*, or *wills*, or *wants* that an object be one of [incompatible] things, then he cannot at the same time reasonably desire, will, or want that it be the other. But one can *look favorably upon* the object being one of these things and at the same time also look favorably upon its being the other."
26. Brentano (1907: 151): "Suppose there are three mutually incompatible goods, A, B, and C; I might prefer B to A, but also prefer C to B, with the result that B, though preferred to A, is no more wanted, willed, or desired than A is. We must say, therefore, that in order to become an object of will, want, or desire, the thing that is loved must be preferred, not only to some one thing that is incompatible with it, but also to every possible object that is thought to be incompatible with it. But the simpler type of love, which does not thus involve wanting, willing, or desiring, is directed upon things considered in abstraction from the actual circumstances in which they occur."
27. This is not an implausible view. Recall that at the beginning of Chapter 2, I offered a long list of conative phenomena. In retrospect, some of them, such as liking and hoping, are naturally classified as emotional phenomena as well. This may inspire a picture in which there is a single spectrum leading from the paradigmatically emotional to the paradigmatically conative, with many intermediate states that involve a mixture of the emotional and the conative. At the same time, for many items on that list it is hard to see what emotional element there might be to them. This includes deciding, valuing, preferring, choosing, planning, trying, and striving.
28. For comments on a previous draft of this chapter, I would like to thank Kim Hyoung Sung, Angela Mendelovici, and Eric Schwitzgebel. I have also benefited from presenting the chapter at the University of Geneva's Swiss Center for Affective Sciences. I would like to thank the audience there, in particular Julien Deonna, Akiko Frischhut, Clare Mac Cumhaill, Olivier Massin, Michele Davide Ombrato, Graham Peebles, and Anita Konzelmann Ziv. Finally, I also benefited from a lone conversation with Victor Kumar.

Chapter 5

1. Smith's own triad is this: 1) moral judgments express beliefs about objective matters of fact (the "objective pretensions" of moral judgment); 2) if a person makes a moral judgment, then *ceteris paribus* s/he is motivated to act accordingly (the "practicality" of moral judgment); 3) action can be caused only by a combination of a means-end belief and a desire for the relevant end ("Humean psychology").
2. In particular, he focuses on a destructive dilemma adapted from Ayer (Smith 1994 ch.2). The dilemma concerns whether the putative objective facts allegedly targeted by moral judgments would be natural or nonnatural facts. If nonnatural, then the *a priori* supervenience of moral facts on natural facts would be utterly inexplicable. If natural, a second dilemma arises, concerning whether moral facts' being natural is an a priori or a posteriori truth. On the one hand, this cannot be *a priori*, because there are no complete analyses of moral terms in natural terms; but it cannot be *a posteriori* either, because that would make it impossible to recover certain platitudes about morality. Smith chooses the natural horn of the dilemma, claiming that, a priori, the facts allegedly targeted by moral judgments are natural facts; this aprioricity does not require complete analyses of moral facts in natural terms, he insists, but only what he calls "summary definitions."
3. For example, one can reason as follows: if my sister did not visit my father in hospital yesterday, then I ought to do so today; she did not; therefore, I ought to. This type of inferential interaction appears to require a cognitive/descriptive content. If we construe moral commitments as having only a conative/imperative content, they would not integrate as well into this form of reasoning. For the following seems ill-formed: if my sister did not visit my father in hospital yesterday, then visit him today!; she did not; therefore, visit him today!
4. Philosophers who have upheld both cognitivism and internalism include notably McDowell (1979) and McNaughton (1988).
5. Someone could, of course, adopt the view that moral mentation involves a desire element that controls moral action and a belief element that tends to co-occur with it but without providing any independent input into moral action. It is not clear, however, that the belief element deserves then to be called a *moral* belief in the relevant sense. It is a moral belief in the limited sense that its subject matter is moral, but not in the more robust sense that it guides the agent's moral action (and perhaps more generally her moral life). In other words, it is a purely descriptive mental state (akin to mathematical belief and other beliefs about abstract subject matters) with no normative dimension.
6. In the discussion to follow, I use the terms "cognitive" and "cognition" in the way it is used in cognitive science—to cover virtually any mental process, faculty, etc. To that extent, I do not use it as I did in earlier chapters, to denote cognitive states as opposed to other kinds of states. I do so because the dual-process architecture I am discussing is drawn from the cognitive-scientific literature, and because consistency of usage across chapters could be readily established by replacing "cognitive" with "mental" and "cognition" with "mentation" throughout the discussion that follows.
7. It is probably the wrong question to ask whether these two products are of the same "general kind." Kind generality comes in degrees: a dog and a hamster belong to the same general kind at one level (they are both mammals) but not at another (they are not both rodents). Likewise, the products of the associationist and rationalist systems are probably of the same kind at one level of generality but not at another. The more appropriate question is therefore this: just *how* similar and dissimilar are the products of the two systems?
8. To my knowledge, Gendler herself does not embed the two states in a dual-process account of thought and reasoning in print, but she is certainly sympathetic to doing so (Gendler, personal communication). In any case, I contend that the two are natural allies and can be combined to articulate a picture of thought and reasoning that is compelling both empirically and conceptually.
9. The listed characteristics of low-road and high-road systems may also inspire a certain speculation about design rationale for a dual-process architecture: that it has to do with

the inescapable speed-for-accuracy trade-off in cognition. In many cases, the cognitive system is well served by employing two distinct mechanisms that hit different trade-off optima. In the normal go of things, and as long as things go fine, the system defaults to the fast-but-inaccurate ("quick and dirty") mechanism; it is only in circumstances of error, conflict, or delay, or when the stakes are particularly high, that the system is liable to shift to the accurate-but-slow mechanism. Note that if this is the teleological rationale for dual-process architecture, it again stands to reason that thought would involve such an architecture, using by default an associationist mechanism good enough for the purposes of everyday life and reverting to the rationalist, rule-based mechanism when greater accuracy is called for.

10. This tendency is even registered in differential activation of the amygdala (associated with threat detection) in the presence of startling white and black faces (Amodio et al. 2003). Thus the phenomenon is supported by both behavioral and neural evidence—the two kinds of evidence typically appealed to in cognitive science. Needless to say, it is also familiar from everyday life.

11. We can envisage many other cases of this form. Suppose someone converts to a particularly conservative religion late in life, and accordingly adopts a strong anti-homosexual stance, but for a while at least treats homosexuals with as much respect, openness, and affection as anybody else; feels no disgust, resentment, or other ill will towards them; and so on. It is natural to say that during that period this person has anti-homosexual beliefs but no such aliefs.

12. Let me remind the reader that here I use the terms "cognitive" and "cognition" to cover any mental process, faculty, etc., not just those that are properly cognitive as opposed to conative, emotive, etc.

13. By this I mean that it is much more common for the alief to trump the belief than for the belief to trump the alief. (I do *not* mean that the trumping of alief by belief is rare by some independent standard.) That this is so falls out of the dual-process picture presented here, but is also independently plausible: as we consider ongoing behavior in unreflective mode throughout the day, we observe that aliefs normally "run the show," beliefs supplanting them only when some conflict arises in the system.

14. In saying this, I do not mean to intimate that the matter of individuating and counting actions is trivial. But however issues about action counting are resolved, it will turn out that many more are caused by aliefs than by beliefs.

15. An independent challenge could ultimately arise that would undermine in a principled manner the rational foundations of our moral alief formation. Although vindication of our commonsensical moral aliefs would not require them to be *true* (in the sense of representing appropriate facts), it *would* require them to be justified in some other way. It is of course epistemically possible that our commonsensical moral aliefs lack the relevant justification. But until such a principled challenge is actually mounted, the rational underpinnings of our moral practice, being founded on traffic in moral aliefs primarily and beliefs only secondarily, remains provisionally secure. To repeat, this is meant as an essentially conceptual claim about the notion of a practice.

16. It should be noted that in the metaphysical domain there is also the live option of going eliminativist with respect to the "ought-ish" states of affairs, whereas in the phenomenological domain the eliminative option, while coherent, is considerably less plausible. For denying the very existence of the feeling of being intentionally directed onto "ought-ish" states of affairs is hard to take seriously.

17. If the same applies to all other emotions, we can state more generally that the following sort of inference is invalid: 1) S emotes that a is F (or about a's being F); 2) S is explicitly aware that $a = b$; therefore, 3) S emotes that b is F (or about b's being F).

18. For comments on a pair of previous drafts, I am greatly indebted to Miri Albahari, Tamar Gendler, Michael Gill, Victor Kumar, Eric Schwitzgebel, and Mark Timmons. For important conversations and exchanges, I would like to thank Matt Bedke, Mike Bruno, Tamar Gendler, Terry Horgan, Cole Mitchell, and Mark Timmons.

Conclusion

1. When I imagine seeing a dog, there is a further distinction between imagining myself as part of the scene, with the imaginative state representing explicitly both the dog and me, and imagining the scene as seen from my viewpoint, construed as a sort of zero point of perceptual space.
2. This view is discussed somewhat sympathetically by Russell (1921 ch.8), who nonetheless does not end up endorsing it, despite adopting an analogous view regarding the difference between perception and episodic memory (1921 ch.9).
3. Hume writes: "An idea assented to FEELS different from a fictitious idea, that the fancy alone presents to us: And this different feeling I endeavour to explain by calling it a superior force, or vivacity, or solidity, or FIRMNESS, or steadiness" (*Treatise*, I.iii.vii; emphasis original).
4. DD is intended to exclude KD, something that the present formulations leave to implicature. We can fix this by adding "mere" to DD, or else defining the second account of the relationship between perceptual and imaginative phenomenology in terms of DD&~KD. In all three theses, we probably have to add a qualifier such as "typically."
5. Sartre offers us not one but two book-length phenomenological treatments of "the image." According to Simone de Beauvoir (1960: 168–71), the two were originally written as a single book, to be titled *The Image*, but the publisher (F. Alcan) accepted for publication only the first half, which was to become *The Imagination* (Sartre 1936). The second half was published four years later by Gallimard as *The Imaginary* (1940). Both books are organized around the question of the relationship between images and perceptions. The first presents a critical survey of failed accounts of imagination along the lines of ND and DD, with a diagnosis of their underlying error. The second develops a positive account of imagination in a KD vein.
6. Sartre (1936: 91; my translation, italics original) describes the view he targets as follows: "We begin again with the assertion that sensation and image are identical in nature. We assert once more that an *isolated* image does not distinguish itself from an *isolated* perception. But this time the discrimination will be the product of a judgment-act (*acte judicatif*) of the mind." (In quoting Sartre, I will often stick to the excellent English translations of his two books now available. Occasionally, however, I will offer my own translation, rarely very different from the published ones.)
7. Sartre (1936: 93) writes: "Rather than the nature of the image as such [i.e., as being an image] being revealed to us by immediate intuition, we must finally make use of a system of infinite references in order to affirm of a content that it is an image or a perception . . . Nobody will accept that recourse to a system of infinite references is needed to establish the discrimination between an image and a perception. Let everybody consult their internal experience."
8. If we wanted to formulate the argument with greater precision, we might offer: for some subject S and any experience E, such that S is a healthy human adult in normal circumstances and E is either a perceptual experience or an imaginative experience, 1) S knows whether E is perceptual or imaginative immediately; 2) if ND, then S does not know whether E is perceptual or imaginative immediately; therefore, 3) ~ND.
9. Sartre (1936: 93) writes: "the discriminative judgment will only ever be *probable* . . . We thus arrive at a paradoxical conclusion: far from the deep nature of the image being revealed to us by an immediate and certain knowledge, we will *never* be *sure* that such and such psychic contents on such and such a day and such and such an hour were really truly an image. Introspection is entirely deprived of its rights . . ."
10. This objection would be particularly embarrassing to Sartre, since he is explicitly committed to spontaneity as a distinguishing mark of imagination (Sartre 1940 ch.1 §4).
11. Here is a representative passage (Sartre 1936: 132–3; italics mine): "The image of my friend Pierre is not a vague phosphorescence, a wake left in my consciousness by the perception of Pierre. It is a form of organized consciousness that relates, *in its manner*, to my friend Pierre. It is one of the possible *ways of aiming* at the thing, Pierre . . . [Accordingly,] image is only a name for a certain *way that consciousness aims at its object*."

12. Sartre's view here strikes me as needlessly complicated, and involving some inaccuracies, however. Nonetheless, the fundamental idea is sound, and goes in the direction suggested in the text. Thus, Sartre (1940: 24–5; my translation) writes: "Every awareness posits its object, but each in its own manner. Perception, for example, posits its object as existent... The intentional object of imaging awareness has this peculiarity that it is not there and it is posited as such, or that it does not exist and is posited as nonexistent, or that it is not posited at all." The verb "to posit" is unfamiliar in analytic philosophy of mind, but in the Husserlian tradition it is commonly used to describe precisely the kind of attitudinal feature of an intentional act whereby it presents its object in a specific way. In this passage, Sartre distinguishes different manners of positing the object, but the distinctions he makes change at different points of Sartre 1940 and are somewhat confused.
13. Some might also hold that we cannot imagine Obama *himself*, as opposed to just an Obama-like object. Imaginative reference might be claimed to be "descriptive" rather than singular. If so, the imaginative experience proper presents-as-nonexistent an Obama-like object.
14. Thus we may concede that typically the content of perception presents a higher-resolution scene than that of imagination—as long as sometimes the resolution can be the same. Likewise, we may note that perceptual experience always presents its object as spatially located relative to the subject, whereas it is possible to imagine the same object in an entirely aspatial manner—as long as it is also possible to imagine the object as spatially located just the way a perceived object is spatially located.
15. Thus, a belief is the belief it is because of the part of the world that suitably causes it, and is a belief at all because of its distinctive functional role in mediating perception and action. A desire is the desire it is because of the part of the world that it suitably causes, and is a desire at all because of its own functional role in the same mediation. Perception is recognized to also have a phenomenal character, though the hope is that the latter can be unpacked in terms of functional role and representational content: often, the idea is that a perceptual experience has the phenomenal character it does in virtue of representing what it does, and has one at all in virtue of having the right functional role, namely, being poised to directly affect beliefs and desires (Tye 1995). Action, meanwhile, is construed as a motor output essentially characterized in terms of the belief-desire pair bringing it about: a motor output constitutes action at all because suitably caused by such a pair, and constitutes the specific action it does in virtue of being caused by the specific pair it is (Dretske 1988).
16. For comments on drafts of relevant material, I am grateful to Margherita Arcangeli, David Chalmers, Matthew Eshleman, Eric Schwitzgebel, Jonathan Webber, and Kenneth Williford. For useful exchanges, I would like to thank Margherita Arcangeli, Steven DeLay, Anya Farennikova, Joëlle Proust, Charles Siewert, and Kenneth Williford.

Appendix

1. This approach is natural because, remarkably, freedom is nowadays commonly conceived of, sought, and valued primarily for its appearance in inner experience. The Alabama slave awaking on the morning of January 1, 1863, fortunate to be among the twenty thousand slaves freed at once as that day's Emancipation Proclamation went into immediate effect in all of all Alabama, this slave, if kept in ignorance and unaware that he is now a free man, feels as oppressed as he did the previous morning. Conversely, a woman awaking in a hospital unaware that she has just started her life as a disabled person is not free to move as she once was, but until she realizes her new predicament she is as merry as any master of limbs. Thus Hannah Arendt (1978: 5; italics original) writes this: "It would be rather easy to trace the idea of Freedom historically: how it changed from being a word indicating a political status—that of a free citizen and not a slave—and a physical fact—that of a healthy man, whose body was not paralyzed but able to obey his mind—into a word indicating an *inner* disposition by virtue of which man could *feel* free when he actually was a slave or unable to move his limbs."

2. It is possible to maintain that the refrigerator hum was not actually experienced before its cessation, and instead a memory of it was instantaneously formed immediately thereafter. But this is not how things seem from the first-person perspective. The phenomenology is as of having heard it before it stopped.
3. Of course, one could also combine both approaches—apply magnified introspective powers to magnified introspected items—to launch an expedition to the limits of the humanly introspectible.
4. Koksvik (2011) distinguishes two uses of phenomenal contrast thought-experiments. One is dialectical, where the contrast, or an intuition thereof, functions as a premise in a(n abductive) argument for the existence of some distinctive phenomenology. The other is ostensive, where the contrast is used simply to make a certain experience more phenomenologically overwhelming to a skeptical subject. In these terms, my suggestion is to interpret the present use of phenomenal contrast as ostensive rather than dialectical: as a device of introspectionist inquiry intended to make a phenomenology more amenable to introspective discerning rather than a device of philosophical argumentation.
5. The hard compatibilist would reject this claim, of course, claiming that we never really have any freedom to lose. However, most hard determinists would agree that we have a *sense* of freedom that we can lose. In the exposition of the case in the main text, I am assuming that hard determinism is false and there is a freedom we can lose. But a more cumbersome exposition could be devised that would not assume that, assuming instead only that there is a sense of freedom we can lose.
6. A curious upshot is that the phenomenologist finds herself in need of the prisoner's services to pursue her investigation here. For the just-released prisoner experiences acutely the return of her phenomenal freedom as the just-operated-upon brunescence patient experiences acutely the return of her visual field's lucidity. In his 1938 essay enigmatically titled "Fluctuations on Freedom," the French poet Paul Valéry (1945: 56) wondered: "But wherefrom then can come this idea that man is free; or else the other, that he is not? I know not whether it is philosophy that started it or else the police." Perhaps it is philosophy that posed the question and the police that makes the answer possible.
7. To that extent, it has some commonality with Michael Gill's (2008) historical method of surveying medium-sized samples of introspectively resourceful writers from across the ages.
8. Prison Six is located fifty-odd miles north of Tel Aviv, and houses both military prisoners and criminal prisoners who have committed their crimes during military service. A year earlier, I had been drafted into mandatory three-year service in the Israeli Defense Forces (IDF). After a few months of service, I decided I wanted out. The most practical option in those days was to desert, turn oneself in after a time (not too short), and hope for a dishonorable discharge after a reasonably short prison sentence. This was my gambit, and fortunately it was successful: I was officially dishonorably discharged in October of 1992.
9. A prisoner awaiting trial would always be placed in Sector B for the first fortnight. A military judge would typically see him then for a quick, essentially *pro forma* trial, whereupon prisoners the likes of me—read: distinctly undangerous—would be transferred to Sector A.
10. By that point, I had read works on political freedom by Marx, Herzen, Fromm, and even Berlin—in all of whom I found great insight—and was superficially acquainted with the problem of determinism and free will, but did not have any deep convictions on the nature of freedom.
11. This desire for lonesome strolling is reported by released prisoners quite often. Jacques Angelvin, a French actor and television personality who was busted for heroine traffic in 1962 in New York (as part of the battle against the "French Connection"), writes of his return to France five and a half years later: "In the days that followed, I felt like walking, walking, wandering the streets, alone, taking the measure of my freedom" (1968: 257).
12. The noun "compellence" comes from the 2005 economics Nobel laureate Thomas Schelling, who contrasts it with "deterrence" as two types of coercion (1984: 321; italics original): "By 'deterrence' I mean inducing an adversary or a victim *not* to do something, to continue not doing something. The word takes the presupposition 'from' . . . It is the more passive kind of

coercion. By 'compellence' I mean inducing a person *to do* something through fear, anxiety, doubt, etc. 'Compel' takes the presupposition 'to.' My dictionary contains no word specialized toward this more active kind of coercion, so I coined the word."
13. Wilbert Rideau, who spent forty-four years at Louisiana's notorious Angola prison, explains in his memoir his fascination with trees after his release in terms of the absence of any trees inside the prison (Rideau 2010). But Prison Six had a view on beautiful woods on hills and mountains surrounding the prison.
14. Furthermore, no history of botched definitions of "the moon" would convince us there is no such thing. Although pointing at Aristide's predicament in 2055 does not have quite the same force as pointing at the moon, it is intended to function similarly as an "ostensive definition."
15. The central competition in contemporary Western civilization between the American model and the European model can be seen through these lenses. At the level of ethos, at least, the American model aspires to maximize negative freedom, the European one positive freedom. Personally, I suspect this is one of those instances where the ethos exists to mask lived practice. Consider that work is, at its core, a trading of negative freedom for positive freedom. In practice, Europeans are on the whole much less attracted by this trade-off than Americans. In this respect, then, it is Europeans who value their negative freedom primarily and Americans their positive freedom. The European spirit follows more closely the one attributed by Montesquieu (1758) to the ancient Greeks in Book IV, ch.8 of *The Spirit of Laws*: "One should realize that in the Greek *polis* . . . all work and all professions that might lead to earning money, were considered unworthy of free men."
16. It may be objected that there is an external force preventing him from doing so, namely, his lack of funds. But I use the expression "external force" advisedly, in a way meant to distinguish it from "external factors" and other expressions that do not imply any *agency* in the preventing. This is both central to Berlin's discussion of negative liberty and crucial for ensuring that the negative/positive distinction is substantive.
17. Many experiences have accuracy conditions, conditions under which the world is the way the experience presents it to be. If one undergoes a visual experience as of a three-headed kangaroo sitting in one's armchair, the experience is accurate just if there is such a kangaroo in one's armchair and inaccurate otherwise. Certainly freedom experiences have accuracy conditions: they are accurate if one is free and inaccurate if one is unfree. Leonard (Ms) illustrates this succinctly: "Consider Locke's man who chooses to remain in a room the door of which has been secretly locked: he may have a phenomenology of freedom with respect to leaving the room even though he is not free to do so . . . Consider [next] the case of the prisoner whose cell door has been secretly unlocked: he experiences no phenomenology of freedom with respect to leaving the cell even though he is free to do so."
18. Not every compatibilist accepts this. Many compatibilists today hold that we are sometimes free to act or choose a certain way even though we could not act or choose otherwise (Frankfurt 1969).
19. Here it is important to distinguish between two claims—one plausible and one not. The implausible claim allows *every* prior condition to be changed when assessing whether an agent could have done/chosen otherwise. The plausible claim allows only *some* prior conditions to be changed in this way. For example, prior conditions that have to do with the personality and deep character traits of the agent cannot be changed. The implausible claim is certainly refuted by counterexamples due to Frankfurt (1969). But the plausible claim can be tailored to avoid counterexamples of that sort. Indeed, it can take examples as guides for determining which of the conditions one can change in the assessment of "could have done/chosen otherwise" in order to obtain the otherwise plausible result that an agent acts/chooses freely only if she could do/choose otherwise.
20. The divide is specifically between freedom of *overt* action and freedom of decision/choice, because deciding and choosing are themselves types of action, though not *overt* ones (in the relevant sense): typically at least, deciding or choosing is something that we do, not something that happens to us.

21. To be sure, during those five hours some trivial choices did have to be made, for example when the road forked and I could no longer stroll straight ahead. But these aspects of the overall episode were *not* phenomenologically intensified in the way that made it vivid enough to introspectively discern structure in. Our adopted phenomenology yielded data only on the phenomenology of (overt) action.
22. Although more familiar, the ontological relation is stalked by bitter debate as well—but see Fine 2001 for illuminating discussion.
23. Certainly there is a long tradition of philosophers who maintained that the existence of a libertarian freedom is phenomenological and introspectively manifest—see, e.g., Sartre (1943), Laporte (1947), Campbell (1957), Lehrer (1960), Strawson (2004).
24. In addition, the reports are not the result of forced-choice answers to experimenters' questions, which may involve preconceptions and expectations on the experimenters' part. This feature shares with Stillman et al.'s (2011) method of eliciting autobiographical reports of free and unfree actions from subjects. However, the latter method does not get (i) at unprompted reports, nor (ii) at the reports of subjects who have felt the phenomenology of freedom particularly vividly.
25. It is possible of course that those dimensions hide under the ineffable part of Douglass' experience—what he could not formulate *to himself* with any satisfaction. But it remains that the report does not provide positive evidence for their presence.
26. Thus the only phenomenal features I reported that are *not* replicated in this report are the feeling of rightness, the other two perceptual features, the cognitive feature, and the feeling as of basically intransitive freedom.
27. This piece is dedicated to all my brothers and sisters locked down, and to my great-grandfather Maurice Fragman, who died in Majdanek. Research for it was supported by a grant from the American Philosophical Society. For comments on a previous draft, I would like to thank Oisin Deery, Shaun Nichols, David Rudrauf, Eric Schwitzgebel, and Itay Shani. For useful conversations and exchanges, I am grateful to Lizzie Kriegel, Margaret Modlinger, Shaun Nichols, and Charles Siewert.

BIBLIOGRAPHY

Amodio, D., E. Harmon-Jones, and P. Devine 2003. "Individual Differences in the Activation and Control of Affective Race Bias as Assessed by Startle Eyeblink Response and Self-Report." *Journal of Personality and Social Psychology* 84: 738–753.
Angelvin, J. 1968. *Mes prisons américaines*. Paris: Plon.
Annas, J. 2008. "The Phenomenology of Virtue." *Phenomenology and the Cognitive Sciences* 7: 21–34.
Anscombe, G. E. M. 1957. *Intention*. Oxford: Basil Blackwell.
Arcangeli, M. 2014. "Against Cognitivism about Supposition." *Philosophia* 42: 607-624.
Arendt, H. 1978. *The Life of the Mind, vol. II: Willing*. New York: Harcourt Brace and Company.
Aristotle. 1911. *Nicomachean Ethics*. Trans. D. P. Chase. London: J. M. Dent.
Armstrong, D.M. 1968. *A Materialist Theory of the Mind*. London: Routledge.
Armstrong, D. M. 1978. *Universals and Scientific Realism, vol. I: Nominalism and Realism*. Cambridge: Cambridge University Press.
Arpaly, N. 2002. "Moral Worth." *Journal of Philosophy* 99: 223–245.
Audi, R. 1973. "Intending." *Journal of Philosophy* 70: 387–403.
Audi, R. 1994. "Dispositional Beliefs and Dispositions to Believe." *Noûs* 28: 419–434.
Audi, R. 2013. *Moral Perception*. Princeton: Princeton University Press.
Ayer, A. J. 1954. "Freedom and Necessity." In his *Philosophical Essays*. New York: St. Martin's Press.
Baker, L. R. 1997. "Why Constitution Is Not Identity." *Journal of Philosophy* 94: 599–621.
Balzac, H. de 1835. *Le Père Goriot*. Paris: Garnier-Flammarion, 1966.
Barrett, L. F., M. M. Tugade, and R. W. Engle 2004. "Individual Differences in Working Memory Capacity and Dual-Process Theories of the Mind." *Psychological Bulletin* 130: 553–573.
Bayne, T. 2008. "The Phenomenology of Agency." *Philosophy Compass* 3: 1–21.
Bayne, T. 2009. "Perception and the Reach of Phenomenal Content." *Philosophical Quarterly* 59: 385–404.
Bayne, T. 2011. "The Sense of Agency." In F. Macpherson (ed.), *The Senses*. Oxford: Oxford University Press.
Bayne, T. and D. J. Chalmers 2003. "What Is the Unity of Consciousness?" In A. Cleeremans (ed.), *The Unity of Consciousness: Binding, Integration, Dissociation*. Oxford: Oxford University Press.
Bayne, T. and M. Montague 2011. *Cognitive Phenomenology*. Oxford: Oxford University Press.
Bayne, T. and M. Spener 2010. "Introspetive Humility." *Philosophical Issues* 20: 1–22.
Beardsley M. C. 1958. *Aesthetics*. Indianapolis: Hackett.
Bengson, J. Forthcoming. "The Intellectual Given." *Mind*.
Bennett, J. 1988. *Events and Their Names*. Oxford: Oxford University Press.

Berlin, I. 1958. *Two Concepts of Liberty.* Oxford: Clarendon. Reprinted in his Four Essays on Liberty. Oxford: Oxford University Press, 1969.
Block, N. J. 1978. "Troubles with Functionalism." In C. Savage (ed.), *Perception and Cognition: Issues in the Foundations of Psychology.* Minneapolis: University of Minnesota Press.
Block, N. J. 1986. "Advertisement for a Semantics for Psychology." *Midwest Studies in Philosophy* 10: 615–77.
Block, N. J. 1995. "On a Confusion about the Function of Consciousness." *Behavioral and Brain Sciences* 18: 227–247. Reprinted in N. J. Block, O. Flanagan, and G. Guzeldere (eds.), The Nature of Consciousness. Cambridge MA: MIT Press.
Block, N. J. and R. Stalnaker 1999. "Conceptual Analysis, Dualism, and the Explanatory Gap." *Philosophical Review* 108: 1–46.
Bolzano, B. 1837. *Theory of Science.* Trans. R. George. Berkeley: University of California Press, 1972.
Bourget, D. 2010. "Consciousness Is Underived Intentionality." *Noûs* 44: 32–58.
Boyd, R. 1988. "How to Be a Moral Realist." In G. Sayre-McCord Geoffrey (ed.), *Essays on Moral Realism.* Ithaca NY: Cornell University Press.
Bratman, M. 1987. *Intention, Plans, and Practical Reason.* Cambridge MA: Harvard University Press.
Brentano, F. C. 1874. *Psychology from an Empirical Standpoint.* Trans. A. C. Rancurello, D. B. Terrell, and L. L. McAlister. London: Routledge and Kegan Paul, 1973.
Brentano, F. C. 1889. *The Origin of Our Knowledge of Right and Wrong.* Trans. R. M. Chisholm and E. H. Schneewind. London: Routledge and Kegan Paul, 1969.
Brentano, F. C. 1907. "Loving and Hating." In Brentano 1889.
Brentano, F. C. 1911. "Appendix to the Classification of Mental Phenomena." In Brentano 1874.
Brink, D. 1989. *Moral Realism and the Foundations of Ethics.* Cambridge: Cambridge University Press.
Browne, A. and R. Sun 2001. "Connectionist Inference Models." *Neural Networks* 14: 1331–1355.
Buber, M. 1923. *I and Thou.* Trans. R. G. Smith. London: Continuum Books, 2001.
Byrne, A. 2006. "Color and the Mind-Body Problem." *Dialectica* 60: 223–244.
Byrne, A. 2010. "Recollection, Perception, Imagination." *Philosophical Studies* 148: 15–26.
Cameron, R. P. 2007. "The Contingency of Composition." *Philosophical Studies* 136: 99–121.
Campbell, C. A. 1957. "Has the Self 'Free Will'?" In his Selfhood and Godhood. London: Routledge.
Campbell, R. 2007. "What Is Moral Judgment?" *Journal of Philosophy* 104: 321–349.
Cannon, W. B. 1915. *Bodily Changes in Pain, Hunger, Fear, and Rage.* New York: Appleton.
Carretta, V. 1999. "Olaudah Equiano or Gustavus Vassa? New Light on an Eighteenth-Century Question of Identity." *Slavery and Abolition* 20: 96–105.
Carretta, V. 2005. *Equiano, the African: A Biography of a Self-Made Man.* Athens: University of Georgia Press.
Carruthers, P. 2006. "Conscious Experience vs. Conscious Thought." In U. Kriegel and K. W. Williford (eds.), *Self-Representational Approaches to Consciousness.* Cambridge MA: MIT Press.
Carruthers, P. and B. Veillet 2011. "The Case against Cognitive Phenomenology." In Bayne and Montague 2011.
Carter, I. 1992. "The Measurement of Pure Negative Freedom." *Political Studies* 40: 38–50.
Casey, E. 2000. *Imagining: A Phenomenological Study*, 2nd ed. Bloomington: Indiana University Press.
Cassam, Q. 2010. "Judging, Believing and Thinking." *Philosophical Issues* 20: 80–95.
Chalmers, D. J. 1995. "The Puzzle of Conscious Experience." *Scientific American,* December 1995: 62–68.
Chalmers, D. J. 1996. *The Conscious Mind.* New York: Oxford University Press.
Chalmers, D. J. 2002. "Consciousness and Its Place in Nature." In D. J. Chalmers (ed.), *Philosophy of Mind: Classical and Contemporary Readings.* New York: Oxford University Press.
Chalmers, D. J. 2012. *Constructing the World.* New York: Oxford University Press.
Chalmers, D. J. and F. Jackson 2001. "Conceptual Analysis and Reductive Explanation." *Philosophical Review* 110: 315–361.

Charland, L. C. 2002. "The Natural Kind Status of Emotion." *British Journal for the Philosophy of Science* 53: 511–537.
Chisholm, R. 1957. *Perceiving: A Philosophical Study*. Ithaca NY: Cornell University Press.
Chudnoff, E. 2011a. "The Nature of Intuitive Justification." *Philosophical Studies* 153: 313–333.
Chudnoff, E. 2011b. "What Intuitions Are Like." *Philosophy and Phenomenological Research* 82: 625–654.
Chudnoff, E. 2013a. "Gurwitsch's Phenomenal Holism." *Phenomenology and the Cognitive Sciences* 12: 559–578.
Chudnoff, E. 2013b. "Intellectual Gestalts." In U. Kriegel (ed.), *Phenomenal Intentionality: New Essays*. New York: Oxford University Press.
Chudnoff, E. 2015. *Cognitive Phenomenology*. New York: Routledge.
Clark, A. and D. J. Chalmers 1998. "The Extended Mind." *Analysis* 58: 7–19.
Clavien, C. 2010. "An Affective Approach to Moral Motivation." *Journal of Cognitive Science* 129–160.
Cohen, L. J. 1992. *An Essay on Belief and Acceptance*. Oxford: Clarendon.
Cohen, S. 2008. "Fundamental Equality and the Phenomenology of Respect." *Iyyun* 57: 25–53.
Constant, B. 1819. "The Liberty of the Ancients Compared with That of the Moderns." In B. Fontana (ed.), *Constant: Political Writings*. Cambridge: Cambridge University Press, 1988.
Copp, D. 2002. "Realist-Expressivism: A Neglected Option for Moral Realism." *Social Philosophy and Policy* 18: 1–43.
Crane, T. 1998. "Intentionality as the Mark of the Mental." In A. O'Hear (ed.), *Contemporary Issues in Philosophy of Mind*. Cambridge: Cambridge University Press.
Currie, G. and I. Ravenscroft 2002. *Recreative Minds: Imagination in Philosophy and Psychology*. Oxford: Oxford University Press.
Dancy, J. 1993. *Moral Reasons*. Oxford: Blackwell.
Danto, A. 1965, "Basic Actions." *American Philosophical Quarterly* 2: 141–148.
Davidson, D. 1969. "The Individuation of Events." In N. Rescher (ed.), *Essays in Honor of Carl G. Hempel*. Dordrecht: Reidel.
Davies, M. 1995. "Consciousness and the Varieties of Aboutness." In C. Macdonald and G. Macdonald (eds.), *Connectionism: Debates on Psychological Explanation*, vol. II Oxford: Blackwell.
de Beauvoir, S. 1960. *The Prime of Life*. Trans. P. Green. New York: Paragon, 1992.
de Biran, M. 1812. *Essai sur les fondements de la psychologie*. Paris: Vrin, 1812.
Dennett, D. C. 1991. *Consciousness Explained*. Boston: Little, Brown.
Deonna, J. and F. Teroni 2012. *The Emotions*. New York: Routledge.
Dewey, J. 1894. "The Theory of Emotion." *Psychological Review* 1: 553–569.
Dewey, J. 1897. "The Psychology of Effort." *Philosophical Review* 6: 43–56.
Dickie, G. 1965. "Beardsley's Phantom Aesthetic Experience." *Journal of Philosophy* 62: 129–136.
Dorsch, F. 2009. "Judging and the Scope of Mental Agency." In L. O'Brien and M. Soteriou (eds.), *Mental Actions*. Oxford: Oxford University Press.
Douglass, F. 1845. *Narrative of the Life of Frederick Douglass, an American Slave*. Forgotten Books.
Dretske, F. I. 1981. *Knowledge and the Flow of Information*. Oxford: Clarendon.
Dretske, F. I. 1988. *Explaining Behavior*. Cambridge MA: MIT Press.
Dretske, F. I. 1993. "Conscious Experience." *Mind* 102: 263–283.
Dretske, F. I. 1995. *Naturalizing the Mind*. Cambridge MA: MIT Press.
Dretske, F. I. 1996. "Phenomenal Externalism." *Philosophical Issues* 7: 143–59.
Ducasse, C. 1961. "In Defense of Dualism." In S. Hook (ed.), *Dimensions of Mind*. New York: Collier.
Dumitru, M. Ms. "The Phenomenology of Thought."
Ehrenfels, C. von 1897–1898. *System der Werttheorie*. Leipzig: Reisland.
Enç, B. 2003. *How We Act*. Oxford: Clarendon Press.
Equiano, O. 1789. *The Interesting Narrative of the Life of Olaudah Equiano*. Wilder Publications.
Erickson, R. J., W. J. Crow, L. A. Zurcher, and A. V. Connett 1973. *Paroled but Not Free*. New York: Behavioral Publications.
Falk, W. D. 1945. "Obligation and Rightness." *Philosophy* 20: 129–147.
Farkas, K. 2008. *The Subjective Point of View*. Oxford: Oxford University Press.

Fiala, B. 2012. "Explaining the Explanatory Gap." PhD Dissertation, University of Arizona.
Fine, K. 2001. "The Question of Realism." *Philosophers' Imprint* 1.
Fodor, J. A., and E. Lepore 1994. "What Is the Connection Principle?" *Philosophy and Phenomenological Research* 54: 837–845.
Frankena, W. K. 1958. "Obligation and Motivation in Recent Moral Philosophy." In A. Melden (ed.), *Essays in Moral Philosophy*. Seattle: University of Washington Press.
Frankfurt, H. 1969. "Alternate Possibilities and Moral Responsibility." *Journal of Philosophy* 66: 829–839.
Frith, C. D., S.-J. Blakemore, and D. M. Wolpert 2000. "Explaining the Symptoms of Schizophrenia: Abnormalities in the Awareness of Action." *Brain Research Reviews* 31: 357–363.
Gallie, W. B. 1956. "Essentially Contested Concepts." *Proceedings of the Aristotelian Society* 56: 167–198.
Galton, F. 1880. "Visualised Numerals." *Nature* 22: 494–495.
Gärdenfors, P. 2004. *Conceptual Spaces: The Geometry of Thought*. Cambridge MA: MIT Press.
Geach, P. T. 1960. "Ascriptivism." *Philosophical Review* 69: 221–225.
Gendler, T. S. 2008a. "Alief and Belief." *Journal of Philosophy* 105: 634–663.
Gendler, T. S. 2008b. "Alief in Action (and Reaction)." *Mind and Langage* 23: 552–585.
Georgalis, N. 2006. *The Primacy of the Subjective*. Cambridge MA: MIT Press.
Gibbard, A. 2003. *Thinking How to Live*. Cambridge MA: Harvard University Press.
Gilbert, D. T. 1991. "How Mental Systems Believe." *American Psychologist* 46: 107–119.
Gilbert, D. T., R. W. Tafarodi, and P. S. Malone 1993. "You Can't Not Believe Everything You Read." *Journal of Personality and Social Psychology* 65: 221–233.
Gill, M. B. 2008. "Variability and Moral Phenomenology." *Phenomenology and the Cognitive Sciences* 7: 99–113.
Gillet, C. and B. Rives 2005. "The Nonexistence of Determinables: Or, a World of Absolute Determinates as a Default Hypothesis." *Noûs* 39: 483–504.
Ginet, C. 1986. "Voluntary Exertion of the Body: A Volitional Account." *Theory and Decision* 20: 223–245.
Ginet, C. 1990. *On Action*. Cambridge: Cambridge University Press.
Goldie, P. 2002. "Emotions, Feelings, and Intentionality." *Phenomenology and the Cognitive Sciences* 1: 235–254.
Goldman, A. I. 1993. "The Psychology of Folk Psychology." *Behavioral and Brain Sciences* 16: 15–28.
Goodman, N. 1954. *Fact, Fiction, and Forecast*. London: Athlone Press.
Gordon, R. 1987. *The Structure of Emotion*. Cambridge: Cambridge University Press.
Graham, G. and L. Stephens 2000. *When Self-Consciousness Breaks: Alien Voices and Inserted Thoughts*. Cambridge MA: MIT Press.
Grandin, T. 1996. *Thinking in Pictures*. New York: Vintage.
Grandy, M. 1844. *Narrative of the Life of Moses Grandy, Late Slave in the United States of America*. Boston: Oliver Johnson.
Greene, J. and J. Haidt 2002. "How (and Where) Does Moral Judgment Work?" *Trends in Cognitive Sciences* 6: 517–523.
Grice, H. P. 1962. "Some Remarks about the Senses." In R. J. Butler (ed.), *Analytical Philosophy*. Oxford: Basil Blackwell.
Griffiths, P. 1997. *What Emotions Really Are*. Chicago: University of Chicago Press.
Hájek, A. and P. Pettit 2004. "Desire Beyond Belief." *Australasian Journal of Philosophy* 82: 77–92.
Hanks, P. 2007. "The Content-Force Distinction." *Philosophical Studies* 56: 141–164.
Hanks, P. 2011. "Structured Propositions as Types." *Mind* 120: 11–52.
Hanks, P. 2013. "First-Person Propositions." *Philosophy and Phenomenological Research* 86: 155–182.
Hare, R. 1952. *The Language of Morals*. Oxford: Clarendon Press.
Harman, G. 1977. *The Nature of Morality*. Oxford: Oxford University Press.
Harman, G. 1990. "The Intrinsic Quality of Experience." *Philosophical Perspectives* 4: 31–52.
Hawley, K. and F. Macpherson 2011 (eds.). *The Admissible Contents of Experience*. Oxford: Blackwell.
Hegel, G. W. F. 1807. *The Phenomenology of Spirit*, trans. A. V. Miller. Oxford: Clarendon Press, 1977.

Horgan, T. M. 2011. "From Agentive Phenomenology to Cognitive Phenomenology: A Guide for the Perplexed." In Bayne and Montague 2011.
Horgan, T. and U. Kriegel 2008. "Phenomenal Intentionality Meets the Extended Mind." *Monist* 91: 347–373.
Horgan, T. M., and M. Potrč 2008. *Austere Realism: Contextual Semantics Meets Minimal Ontology*. Cambridge MA: MIT Press.
Horgan, T. M. and M. Potrč. 2010. "The Epistemic Role of Morphological Content." *Acta Analytica* 25: 155–173.
Horgan, T. M. and J. Tienson 2002. "The Intentionality of Phenomenology and the Phenomenology of Intentionality." In D. J. Chalmers (ed.), *Philosophy of Mind: Classical and Contemporary Readings*. New York: Oxford University Press.
Horgan, T., J. Tienson, and G. Graham 2003. "The Phenomenology of First-Person Agency." In S. Walter and H. D. Heckmann (eds.), *Physicalism and Mental Causation: The Metaphysics of Mind and Action*. Exeter: Imprint Academic.
Horgan, T. and M. C. Timmons 2006. "Cognitivist Expressivism." In T. Horgan and M. Timmons (eds.), *Metaethics after Moore*. Oxford: Oxford University Press.
Horgan, T. and M. C. Timmons 2007. "Moorean Moral Phenomenology." In S. Nuccetelli and G. Seay (eds.), *Themes from G. E. Moore*. Oxford: Oxford University Press.
Horgan, T. and M. C. Timmons 2008. "Prolegomena to a Future Phenomenology of Morals." *Phenomenology and the Cognitive Sciences* 7: 115–131.
Hornsby, J. 1980. *Actions*. London: Routledge & Kegan Paul.
Huemer, M. 2001. *Skepticism and the Veil of Perception*. Lahman MD: Rowman & Littlefield.
Hume, D. 1739. *A Treatise of Human Nature*. http://ebooks.adelaide.edu.au/h/hume/david/h92t/index.html.
Husserl, E. 1901. *Logical Investigations*, vol. II. Trans. J. N. Findlay. London: Routledge, 2001.
Iseminger G., 2003. "Aesthetic Experience." In J. Levinson (ed.), *The Oxford Handbook of Aesthetics*. Oxford: Oxford University Press.
Jacob, P. 1998. "What Is the Phenomenology of Thought?" *Philosophy and Phenomenological Research* 58: 443–448.
Jacobs, H. 1861. *Incidents in the Life of a Slave Girl*. Rockville MD: Arc Manor.
Jackson, F. C. 1982. "Epiphenomenal Qualia." *Philosophical Quarterly* 32: 127–136.
Jackson, F. C. 1998. *From Metaphysics to Ethics: A Defence of Conceptual Analysis*. Cambridge: Cambridge University Press.
James, W. 1884. "What Is an Emotion?" *Mind* 9: 188–205.
James, W. 1890. *The Principles of Psychology*, vol. II. New York: Cosimo, 2007.
Johnston, M. 2004. "The Obscure Object of Hallucination." *Philosophical Studies* 120: 113–183.
Kahneman D. 2003. "A Perspective on Judgement and Choice." *American Psychologist* 58: 697–720.
Kahneman, D. 2011. *Thinking, Fast and Slow*. New York: Farrar, Straus and Giroux.
Kalderon, M. E. 2005. *Moral Fictionalism*. Oxford: Oxford University Press.
Kant, I. 1789. *Critique of Practical Reason*. Trans. T. K. Abbott. http://www.gutenberg.org/ebooks/5683.
Kekulé, F. A. 1865. "Sur la constitution des substances aromatiques." *Bulletin de la Société chimique de Paris* 3: 98–110.
Kenny, A. 1963. *Action, Emotion and Will*. London: Routledge and Kegan Paul.
Kim, J. 1976. "Events as Property Exemplifications." In M. Brand and D. Walton (eds.), *Action Theory*. Dordrecht: Reidel.
Kim, J. 1998. *Mind in a Physical World*. Cambridge MA: MIT Press.
Kind, A. 2001. "Putting the Image Back in Imagination." *Philosophy and Phenomenological Research* 62: 85–109.
Klausen, S. H. 2008. "The Phenomenology of Propositional Attitudes." *Phenomenology and the Cognitive Sciences* 7: 445–462.
Klein, M. 1981. "Context and Memory." In L. T. Benjamin Jr. and K. D. Lowman (eds.), *Activities Handbook for the Teaching of Psychology*. Washington DC: American Psychological Association.
Klüger, R. 2001. *Still Alive: A Holocaust Girlhood Remembered*. New York: Feminist Press.

Kobes, B. W. 1995. "Telic Higher-Order Thoughts and Moore's Paradox." *Philosophical Perspectives* 9: 291–312.
Koffka, K. 1922. "Perception: An Introduction to the *Gestalt-theorie*." *Psychological Bulletin* 19: 531–585.
Koksvik, O. A. K. 2011. "Intuition." PhD Dissertation, Australian National University.
Kotarbiński, T. 1929. *Gnosiology: The Scientific Approach to the Theory of Knowledge*. Trans. O. Wojtasiewicz. Oxford: Pergamon Press, 1966.
Kriegel, U. 2002. "PANIC Theory and the Prospects for a Representational Theory of Phenomenal Consciousness." *Philosophical Psychology* 15: 55–64.
Kriegel, U. 2003a. "Consciousness as Sensory Quality and as Implicit Self-Awareness." *Phenomenology and the Cognitive Sciences* 2 (2003): 1–26.
Kriegel, U. 2003b. "Is Intentionality Dependent upon Consciousness?" *Philosophical Studies* 116: 271–307.
Kriegel, U. 2004. "Consciousness and Self-Consciousness" *The Monist* 87: 185–209.
Kriegel, U. 2005a. "Naturalizing Subjective Character." *Philosophy and Phenomenological Research* 71: 23–56.
Kriegel, U. 2005b. "Tropes and Facts." *Metaphysica* 6: 83–90.
Kriegel, U. 2007. "The Phenomenologically Manifest." *Phenomenology and the Cognitive Sciences* 6: 115–136.
Kriegel, U. 2008. "Moral Phenomenology: Foundational Issues." *Phenomenology and the Cognitive Sciences* 7: 1–19.
Kriegel, U. 2009. *Subjective Consciousness: A Self-Representational Theory*. Oxford: Oxford University Press.
Kriegel, U. 2011a. "Self-Representationalism and the Explanatory Gap." In J. Liu and J. Perry (eds.), *Consciousness and the Self*. New York: Cambridge University Press.
Kriegel, U. 2011b. *The Sources of Intentionality*. New York: Oxford University Press.
Kriegel, U. 2013. "The Phenomenal Intentionality Research Program." In U. Kriegel (ed.), *Phenomenal Intentionality*. New York: Oxford University Press.
Kriegel, U. 2015. "How to Speak of Existence." *Grazer Philosophische Studien*.
Kriegel, U. Ms. "Ontology: Existence or Fundamentality?"
Lange, C. G. 1885. *Om sindsbevægelser*. Kjøbenhaven: Jacob Lunds Forlag.
Laporte, J. 1947. *La conscience de la liberté*. Paris: Flammarion.
Lazarus, R. 1994. "Appraisal: The Minimal Cognitive Prerequisites of Emotion." In P. Eckman and R. J. Davidson (eds.), *The Nature of Emotions*. New York: Oxford University Press.
Lee, G. 2013. "Materialism and the Epistemic Significance of Consciousness." In U. Kriegel (ed.), *Current Controversies in Philosophy of Mind*. New York: Routledge.
Lee, G. Forthcoming. "Alien Subjectivity and the Importance of Consciousness." In A. Pautz and D. Stoljar (eds.), *Themes from Block*. Cambridge MA: MIT Press.
Leibniz, G. W. 1714. *La monadologie*. Ed. E. Boutroux. Paris: LGF, 1991.
Leibniz, G. W. 1765. *Nouveau essais sur l'entendement humain*. Paris: Hachette, 2000.
Lehrer, K. 1960. "Can We Know That We Have Free Will by Introspection?" *Journal of Philosophy* 57: 145–157.
Leonard, W. N. Ms. "Satisfying the Phenomenology of Freedom."
Le Senne, R. 1961. *Traité de morale générale*. Paris: Presses Universitaires de France.
Levinas, E. 1948. *Le temps et l'autre*. Paris: PUF, 2001.
Levinas, E. 1953. "Liberté et commendement." *Revue de metaphysique et de morale* 3: 264–272.
Levinas, E. 1961. *Totalité et infini: Essai sur l'extériorité*. The Hague: Martinus Nijhoff.
Levine, J. 1983. "Materialism and Qualia: The Explanatory Gap." *Pacific Philosophical Quarterly* 64: 354–361.
Levine, J. 2001. *Purple Haze: The Puzzle of Consciousness*. New York: Oxford University Press.
Lewis, D. K. 1966. "An Argument for the Identity Theory." *Journal of Philosophy* 63: 17–25.
Lewis, D. K. 1972. "Psychophysical and Theoretical Identifications." *Australasian Journal of Philosophy* 50: 249–258.
Lewis, D. K. 1983. "New Work for a Theory of Universals." *Australasian Journal of Philosophy* 61: 343–377.

Lewis, D. K. 1988. "Desire as Belief." *Mind* 97: 323–332.
Libet, B. 1985. "Unconscious Cerebral Initiative and the Role of Conscious Will in Voluntary Action." *Behavioral and Brain Sciences* 8: 529–566.
Loar, B. 2003. "Phenomenal Intentionality as the Basis for Mental Content." In M. Hahn and B. Ramberg (eds.), *Reflections and Replies: Essays on the Philosophy of Tyler Burge*. Cambridge, Mass.: MIT Press.
London, J. 1907. *The Road*. New York: Macmillan.
Lormand, E. 1996. "Nonphenomenal Consciousness." *Noûs* 30: 242–61.
Łukasiewicz, J. 1970. *Selected Works*. Ed. L. Borkowski. Amsterdam: North-Holland.
Lurz, R. W. 2006. "Conscious Beliefs and Desires: A Same-Order Approach." In U. Kriegel and K. W. Williford (eds.), *Self-Representational Approaches to Consciousness*. Cambridge MA: MIT Press.
MacCallum, G. C., Jr. 1967. "Negative and Positive Freedom." *Philosophical Review* 76: 312–334.
Machery, E. 2009. *Doing without Concepts*. New York: Oxford University Press.
Mackie, J. L. 1977. *Ethics: Inventing Right and Wrong*. New York: Penguin.
Maddy, P. 1980. "Perception and Mathematical Intuition." *Philosophical Review* 89: 163–196.
Mandelbaum, E. 2010. "The Architecture of Belief." PhD Dissertation, University of North Carolina at Chapel Hill.
Manfredi, M., G. Bini, N. Accornero, A. Berardelli, and L. Medolago 1981. "Congenital Absence of Pain." *Archives of Neurology* 38: 507–511.
Mangan, B. 2001. "Sensation's Ghost: The Non-sensory Fringe of Consciousness.' *Psyche* 7.
Marks, J. 1982. "A Theory of Emotion." *Philosophical Studies* 42: 227–242.
Marr, D. 1982. *Vision*. San Francisco: W.H. Freeman.
Martin, D. M. and P. Y. Sussman 1993. *Committing Journalism*. New York: Norton.
McDowell, J. 1979. "Virtue and Reason." *The Monist* 62: 331–350.
McGeer, V. 2004. "The Art of Good Hope." *Annals of the American Academy of Political and Social Sciences* 592: 100–127.
McGinn, C. 1988. "Consciousness and Content." *Proceedings of the British Academy* 76: 219–239. Reprinted in N. J. Block, O. Flanagan, and G. Güzeldere (eds.), *The Nature of Consciousness: Philosophical Debates*. Cambridge MA: MIT Press, 1997.
McGinn, C. 2004. *Mindsight: Image, Dream, Meaning*. Cambridge MA: Harvard University Press.
McNaughton, D. 1988. *Moral Vision*. Oxford: Blackwell
Mele, A. R. 2009. *Effective Intentions: The Power of Conscious Will*. New York: Oxford University Press.
Mendelovici, A. 2010. "Mental Representation and Closely Conflated Topics." PhD Dissertation, Princeton University.
Mendelovici, A. 2013. "Pure Intentionalism about Moods and Emotions." In U. Kriegel (ed.), *Current Controversies in Philosophy of Mind*. New York: Routledge.
Merleau-Ponty, M. 1944. *Phenomenology of Perception*. Trans. C. Smith. London: Routledge and Kegan Paul, 1962.
Millikan, R. G. 1984. *Language, Thought, and Other Biological Categories*. Cambridge, Mass.: MIT Press.
Montague, M. 2009. "The Logic, Intentionality, and Phenomenology of Emotion." *Philosophical Studies* 145: 171–192.
Montesquieu, C. de 1758. *L'esprit des lois*. Paris: Gallimard, 1995.
Moore, G.E. 1903. *Principia Ethica*. Cambridge: Cambridge University Press.
Moore, G. E. 1953. "Propositions." In his *Some Main Problems of Philosophy*. London: Routledge.
Nagel, T. 1974. "What Is It Like to Be a Bat?" *Philosophical Review* 83: 435–450.
Nagel, T. 1986. *The View from Nowhere*. Oxford: Oxford University Press.
Nahmias, E., S. Morris, T. Nadelhofer, and J. Turner 2004. "The Phenomenology of Free Will." *Journal of Consciousness Studies* 11: 162–179.
Nelkin, N. 1989. "Propositional Attitudes and Consciousness." *Philosophy and Phenomenological Research* 49: 413–430.
Nes, A. 2012. "Thematic Unity in the Phenomenology of Thinking." *Philosophical Quarterly* 62: 84–105.

Nisbett, R. and T. Wilson 1977. "Telling More Than We Can Know: Verbal Reports on Mental Processes." *Psychological Review* 84: 231–259.
Nozick, R. 1981. *Philosophical Explanations*. Cambridge MA: Harvard University Press.
Nussbaum, M. 2001. *Upheavals of Thought: The Intelligence of Emotions*. Cambridge: Cambridge University Press.
Oertelt, H. 2000. *An Unbroken Chain: My Journey through the Nazi Holocaust*. Minneapolis: Lerner.
O'Shaughnessy, B. 1973. "Trying (as the Mental 'Pineal Gland')." *Journal of Philosophy* 70: 365–386.
Paul, S. K. 2012. "How We Know What We Intend." *Philosophical Studies* 161: 327–346.
Peacocke, C. 1998. "Conscious Attitudes, Attention, and Self-Knowledge." In C. Wright, B. C. Smith, and C. Macdonald (eds.), *Knowing Our Own Minds*. Oxford: Oxford University Press.
Perky, C. W. "An Experimental Study of Imagination." *American Journal of Psychology* 21: 422–452.
Pitt, D. 2004. "The Phenomenology of Cognition; or What Is It Like to Think that P?" *Philosophy and Phenomenological Research* 69: 1–36.
Price, H. 1989. "Defending Desire-as-Belief." *Mind* 98: 119–127.
Prinz, J. 2004. *Gut Reactions: A Perceptual Theory of Emotion*. Oxford: Oxford University Press.
Prinz, J. 2011. "Conscious Thought." In Bayne and Montague 2011.
Pryor, J. 2005. "There Is Immediate Justification." In M. Steup and E. Sosa (eds.), *Contemporary Debates in Epistemology*. Oxford: Blackwell.
Putnam, H. 1967. "The Nature of Mental States." Originally published as "Psychological Predicates," in W. H. Capitan and D. D. Merrill (eds.), *Art, Mind, and Religion*. Reprinted in D. M. Rosenthal (ed.), *The Nature of Mind*. Oxford: Oxford University Press.
Ramachandran, V. S. and E. M. Hubbard 2001. "Psychophysical Investigations into the Neural Basis of Synaesthesia." *Proceedings of the Royal Society* 268: 979–983.
Ramsey, F. P. 1931. "Theories." In his *The Foundations of Mathematics and Other Logical Essays*, ed. R. B. Braithwaite. London: Routledge & Kegan Paul.
Revonsuo, A. 2010. *Consciousness: The Science of Subjectivity*. New York: Psychology Press.
Rey, G. 1988. "A Question about Consciousness." In H. Otto and J. Tueidio (eds.), *Perspectives on Mind*. Norwell: Kluwer Academic Publishers.
Ricœur, P. 1950. *Le volontaire et l'involontaire*. Paris: Aubier. Reprinted as *Philosophie de la volonté: Le volontaire et l'involontaire*. Paris: Editions Points, 2009.
Rideau, W. 2010. *In the Place of Justice*. New York: Alfred A. Knopf.
Ridge, M. 2006. "Ecumenical Expressivism: The Best of Both Worlds?" *Oxford Studies in Metaethics* 2: 302–336.
Robinson, J. 1995. "Startle." *Journal of Philosophy* 92: 53–74.
Robinson, S. W. 2006. "Thoughts without Distinctive Non-imagistic Phenomenology." *Philosophy and Phenomenological Research* 70: 534–561.
Rodriguez-Pereyra, G. 2002. *Resemblance Nominalism*. Oxford: Oxford University Press.
Rosch, E. H. 1973. "Natural Categories." *Cognitive Psychology* 4: 328–350.
Rosch, E. H. 1975. "Cognitive Representations of Semantic Categories." *Journal of Experimental Psychology* 104: 192–233.
Rosen, G. 2006. "The Limits of Contingency." In F. MacBride (ed.), *Identity and Modality*. Oxford: Oxford University Press.
Rosenthal, D. M. 1990. "A Theory of Consciousness." ZiF Technical Report 40, Bielfield, Germany. Reprinted in N. J. Block, O. Flanagan, and G. Güzeldere (eds.), *The Nature of Consciousness: Philosophical Debates*. Cambridge MA: MIT Press, 1997.
Russell, B. 1905. "On Denoting." *Mind* 14: 479–493.
Russell, B. 1910. "Knowledge by Acquaintance and Knowledge by Description." *Proceedings of the Aristotelian Society* 11: 108–128.
Russell, B. 1919. *Proposed Roads to Freedom: Socialism, Anarchism, and Syndicalism*. New York: Henry Holt.
Russell, B. 1921. *The Analysis of Mind*. London: Routledge, 1995.
Sartre, J.-P. 1936. *L'imagination*. Paris: F. Alcan. Trans. K. W. Williford and D. Rudrauf. New York: Routledge, 2012.
Sartre, J.-P. 1940. *L'imaginaire*. Paris: Gallimard.

Sartre, J.-P. 1943. *L'Etre et le néant*. Paris: Gallimard.
Sartre, J.-P. 1947. *Situations I*. Paris: Gallimard.
Schaffer, J. 2007. "From Nihilism to Monism." *Australasian Journal of Philosophy* 85: 175–191.
Schaffer, J. 2009. "On What Grounds What." In D. Manley, D. J. Chalmers, and R. Wasserman (eds.), *Metametaphysics: New Essays on the Foundations of Ontology*. New York: Oxford University Press.
Schaffer, J. 2010. "Monism: The Priority of the Whole." *Philosophical Review* 119: 31–76.
Schelling, T. C. 1984. *Choice and Consequence*. Cambridge MA: Harvard University Press.
Schiff, T. 1995. *Revenir: Drancy—Auschwitz—Bergen-Belsen*. Paris: Talus d'approache.
Schwitzgebel, E. 2011. *Perplexities of Consciousness*. Cambridge MA: MIT Press.
Schwitzgebel, E. 2013. "A Dispositional Approach to the Attitudes." In N. Nottelmann (ed.), *New Essays on Belief*. Basingstoke: Palgrave-Macmillan.
Seager, W. 1999. *Theories of Consciousness*. London: Routledge.
Searle, J. R. 1983. *Intentionality*. Cambridge: Cambridge University Press.
Searle, J. R. 1990. "Consciousness, Explanatory Inversion and Cognitive Science." *Behavioral and Brain Sciences* 13: 585–642.
Searle, J. R. 1992. *The Rediscovery of Mind*. Cambridge MA: MIT Press.
Shepard, R. and J. Metzler 1971. "Mental Rotation of Three-Dimensional Objects." *Science* 171: 701–703.
Shoemaker, S. 1979. "Identity, Properties, and Causality." *Midwest Studies in Philosophy* 4: 321–342.
Shoemaker, S. 1994. "Phenomenal Character." *Noûs* 28: 21–38.
Sidelle, A. 2002. "Is There a True Metaphysics of Material Objects?" *Philosophical Issues* 12: 118–145.
Sider, T. 2001. *Four-Dimensionalism*. Oxford: Oxford University Press.
Sider, T. 2011. *Writing the Book of the World*. New York: Oxford University Press.
Siegel, S. 2005. "The Phenomenology of Efficacy." *Philosophical Topics* 33: 265–284.
Siegel, S. 2007. "How Can We Discover the Contents of Experience?" *Southern Journal of Philosophy* (supplement) 45: 127–142.
Siewert, C. 1998. *The Significance of Consciousness*. Princeton NJ: Princeton University Press.
Siewert, C. 2007. "In Favor of (Plain) Phenomenology." *Phenomenology and the Cognitive Sciences* 6: 201–220.
Siewert, C. 2011. "Phenomenal Thought." In Bayne and Montague 2011.
Sifneos, P. E. 1973. "The Prevalence of 'Alexithymic' Characteristics in Psychosomatic Patients." *Psychotherapy and Psychosomatics* 22: 255–262.
Simons, P. 1987. *Parts: A Study in Ontology*. Oxford: Clarendon Press
Sinnott-Armstrong, W. 2008. "Is Moral Phenomenology Unified?" *Phenomenology and the Cognitive Sciences* 7: 85–97.
Sloman, S. A. 1996. "The Empirical Case for Two Systems of Reasoning." *Psychological Bulletin* 119: 3–22.
Smith, M. 1994. *The Moral Problem*. Oxford: Blackwell.
Smithies, D. 2012. "The Mental Lives of Zombies." *Philosophical Perspectives* 26: 343–372.
Soames, S. 2010. *What Is Meaning?* Princeton: Princeton University Press.
Soames, S. 2014. "A Cognitive Theory of Propositions." In J. C. King, S. Soames, and J. Speaks (eds.), *New Thinking about Propositions*. New York: Oxford University Press.
Solomon, R. 1976. *The Passions*. New York: Doubleday.
Speaks, J. 2006. "Is Mental Content Prior to Linguistic Meaning?" *Noûs* 40: 428–67.
Stampe, D. 1986. "Defining Desire." In J. Marks (ed.), *The Ways of Desire*. Chicago: Precedent.
Steiner, H. 1983. "How Free: Computing Personal Liberty." In A. Phillips-Griffiths (ed.), *Of Liberty*. London: Cambridge University Press.
Stevenson, L. F. 2003. "Twelve Conceptions of Imagination." *British Journal of Aesthetics* 43: 238–259.
Stillman, T. F., R. F. Baumeister, and A. R. Mele 2011. "Free Will in Everyday Life: Autobiographical Accounts of Free and Unfree Actions." *Philosophical Psychology* 24: 381–394.
Stocker, M. 1996. *Valuing Emotions*. Cambridge: Cambridge University Press.
Strawson, G. 1994. *Mental Reality*. Cambridge MA: MIT Press.

Strawson, G. 2004. "Free Agents." *Philosophical Topics* 32: 371–402.
Strawson, P. F. 1950. "On Referring." *Mind* 59: 320–344.
Sun, R., P. Slusarz, and C. Terry 2005. "The Interaction of the Explicit and the Implicit in Skill Learning: A Dual-Process Approach." *Psychological Review* 112: 159–192.
Tartaglia, J. 2008. "Intentionality, Consciousness, and the Mark of the Mental: Rorty's Challenge." *Monist* 91: 324–346.
Tennant, N. 2007. "Mind, Mathematics, and the *Ignorabimusstreit*." *British Journal for the History of Philosophy* 15: 745–773.
Titchener, E. B. 1901–5. *Experimental Psychology: A Manual of Laboratory Practice*. London: Macmillan.
Titchener, E. B. 1912. "The Schema of Introspection." *American Journal of Psychology* 23: 485–508.
Travis, C. 2004. "The Silence of the Senses." *Mind* 113: 57–94.
Tye, M. 1995. *Ten Problems of Consciousness*. Cambridge MA: MIT Press.
Tye, M. 2000. *Consciousness, Color, and Content*. Cambridge MA: MIT Press.
Tye, M. 2008. "The Experience of Emotions: An Intentionalist Theory." *Revue Internationale de Philosophie* 62: 25–50.
Valéry, P. 1945. *Regards sur le monde actuel, et autres essais*. Paris: Gallimard.
Vendler, Z. 1967. "Facts and Events." In his *Linguistics in Philosophy*. Ithaca NY: Cornell University Press.
Vollen, L. and D. Eggers (eds.) 2005. *Surviving Justice: America's Wrongfully Convicted and Exonerated*. San Francisco: McSweeney's.
Watson, J. B. 1913. "Psychology as the Behaviorist Views It." *Psychological Review* 20: 158–177.
Weiskrantz, L. 1986. *Blindsight*. Oxford: Oxford University Press.
Wells, H. M. 1927. *The Phenomenology of Acts of Choice*. Monograph Supplement, *British Journal of Psychology*. London: Cambridge University Press.
Whitehead, A. N. 1929. *Process and Reality* (corrected ed.). New York: Simon and Schuster, 1979.
Wiesel, E. 1960. *Night*. Trans. S. Rodway. New York: Hill & Wang.
Williams, B. 1979. "Internal and External Reasons." In R. Harrison (ed.), *Rational Action*. Cambridge: Cambridge University Press.
Williamson, T. 2000. *Knowledge and Its Limits*. Oxford: Oxford University Press.
Wilson, J. 2012. "Fundamental Determinables." *Philosophers' Imprint* 12(4).
Wittgenstein, L. 1953. *Philosophical Investigations*. Trans. G. E. M. Anscombe. Oxford: Blackwell, 2001.
Wundt, W. M. 1874. *Principles of Physiological Psychology*. Trans. E. B. Titchener. New York: Sonnenschein, 1904.
Yirmiya, N., C. Kasari, and P. Mundy 1989. "Facial Expressions of Affect in Autistic, Mentally Retarded and Normal Children." *Journal of Child Psychology and Psychiatry* 30: 725–735.
Zahavi, D. 2004. "Back to Brentano?" *Journal of Consciousness Studies* 11: 66–87.
Zangwill, N. 1998. "Direction of Fit and Normative Functionalism." *Philosophical Studies* 91: 173–203.
Zimmerman, A. 2007. "The Nature of Belief." *Journal of Consciousness Studies* 14: 61–82.

INDEX

action 36, 58, 74, 76–82, 85–91, 95–6, 107, 116, 122, 135–6, 163, 165, 167, 170–2, 179, 202–3, 216, 221–8, 236–7, 255–7, 264–5, 267, 270
action, phenomenology of *see* phenomenology of doing
alief 122, 163–83, 265
agency, phenomenology of 1, 3–5, 37, 77–8, 82, 193, 250, 255
 see also conative phenomenology
algedonic phenomenology 3–6, 9, 34, 36, 39–40, 48, 53–61, 71, 73, 75, 96, 99–100, 104, 128, 136, 138–9, 145–8, 155, 157–8, 176, 178–9, 181, 183–4, 194–8, 202, 244, 249, 253, 261–3
apprehending 96, 111, 117–20, 127
 see also entertaining
Aristotle 13, 170, 175
Armstrong, D. 5, 13–4, 246, 261
attitudinal features 43–4, 53, 65–6, 70, 74–5, 86–8, 95–6, 98, 100, 103–6, 116, 124, 128, 152–3, 156, 191–203, 267
Audi, R. 121, 251, 254

Bayne, T. 5, 41, 75, 82, 258, 251, 253
behavior 83–5, 97, 107, 111, 126–7, 163–70, 174–5, 179–81, 202–3, 215, 234, 251, 258, 265,
belief 36, 42–4, 74, 91–4, 97, 100–111, 116, 118–27, 137, 149, 154, 161–83, 185–8, 192, 201–3, 212, 247–8, 251, 254–5, 258–9, 264–5, 267
Block, N. 47, 51, 251–2
Brentano, F. 10, 20, 66, 74, 83, 99–100, 104–5, 120, 141, 156–7, 230, 250, 258–9, 263,
Byrne, A. 189, 252, 260

Carruthers, P. 4, 31, 150–2
Chalmers, D. 7, 32, 49–53, 61, 142, 246, 251–3, 256, 260, 267

Chudnoff, E. 8, 36, 59, 62, 115, 250, 253–4, 259–60
Cohen, L.J. 43, 65
cognitive phenomenology 1–5, 9, 12, 14, 23–4, 26, 30–47, 53–71, 73–8, 82–3, 96–101, 104–7, 124, 128–9, 132–9, 145–8, 152, 155, 157–60, 171, 176–84, 195–201, 218–20, 228, 244, 249–51, 253–4, 256, 259, 270
cognitivism, ethical 35, 159–60, 163, 171–5, 183, 252, 264
compatibilism (about free will) 35, 206, 211, 220, 224–7, 229, 236, 241, 268–9
conative phenomenology 3, 12, 33–6, 40–4, 53, 61–2, 71–100, 104, 110, 114, 124–6, 128–9, 132, 135–9, 145–58, 161–3, 176–84, 195–8, 202, 220
consciousness, stream of 1–3, 6
consciousness, phenomenal 3, 5
contemplation 93, 112–5, 119, 126–7, 243
 see also entertaining
content 3, 41, 43, 45–6, 48, 62–3, 65–7, 74, 83, 86, 101, 105, 108–110, 114–5, 121, 126, 140–1, 149, 154, 156–7, 161, 164–6, 169–172, 176–8, 180–2, 191, 194, 196, 217–8, 259–60, 263–4, 266–7
 see also intentionality

decision 34, 72–3, 76, 83–96, 100, 111, 128, 157, 163–4, 179, 202–3, 224–7, 255–8, 263, 270
Deonna, J. 156–7, 263–4
desire 2, 34, 42–4, 72–4, 84–7, 91–7, 100–3, 109–10, 112, 116, 122–9, 136–7, 149–50, 153–7, 161–3, 170, 201–3, 215–7, 226–7, 235–9, 251, 254–8, 263–4, 267–8,
determinables 9–18, 28–9, 34–5, 49, 52, 96, 144, 157, 178, 182, 200, 220, 242, 245
Dewey, J. 79, 132, 257
doing, phenomenology of 76–82, 135, 193, 216–7, 221, 223, 226, 250, 255
 see also conative phenomenology

283

Index

Dretske, F. 63, 126, 133, 251, 267
dual-process models 35, 116, 163–75, 181, 183, 264–5

eliminativism 3–8, 26, 50–1, 75–6, 141, 181, 199, 244, 252, 265
emotion, cognitivist theories of 132–9, 146
emotion, conscious *see* emotional phenomenology
emotion, feeling theories of 5, 27, 34–5, 129–41, 144–6, 156, 261
emotion, unconscious 132, 139–40, 144–6, 263
emotional phenomenology 1–2, 5, 9, 26–7, 33–6, 40, 53–61, 70–1, 128–41, 144–59, 176–83, 199–201, 242–4, 247–9, 261–3
entertaining 33–4, 52, 57, 63, 65, 70, 96–128, 147–8, 152, 158, 171, 176–9, 183–4, 193–7, 202–3, 220, 258–60, 263
error theory 26, 173–4, 211
explanation, reductive 48–52, 127, 252–3

functional role 42–4, 48, 52, 58–9, 102–3, 126, 142–3, 201–2, 251, 253, 262, 267

Gendler, T. 122, 163–8, 178–81, 264, 266
genus 9–10, 17, 144, 171, 178, 182
Gilbert, D. 116–8, 259–60
Ginet, C. 74, 81–2, 90, 255–6
goodness 43–4, 74–5, 82, 87, 94–6, 98–100, 105, 109, 116, 128, 136, 152–8, 160–1, 173, 179, 195–9, 202, 223, 244, 255–7, 263
Gordon, R. 126, 137

Hanks, P. 106, 109, 260
happiness 129, 143, 148–56, 210, 233, 238–9, 263
Horgan, T. 8, 63–4, 67–9, 137, 143, 159, 163, 250, 252, 255, 262, 266
Hume, D. 160–1, 164, 171, 186, 189, 220, 264, 266
Husserl, E. 83, 267

imagination 15, 20–1, 34–5, 80, 83, 113, 127, 180, 184–98, 202–3, 248, 260, 266–7
intensity, phenomenal 58–9, 104, 114, 126–8, 137, 153–4, 186, 189–91, 208–10, 213, 218, 233, 257–8, 270
intention 72–3, 84, 88, 111, 127, 216, 254, 256, 258–60
intentionality 46, 48, 60, 82, 87, 89, 92–5, 114, 121, 126, 132–43, 149–52, 157, 166, 178, 191, 252, 256, 261–2, 265, 267
internalism (ethical) 35, 85, 159–60, 171–5, 183, 256, 264
introspection 3, 13–33, 40, 47, 62–3, 80, 100–3, 108–10, 120, 143–8, 188–93, 198–9, 202, 208–213, 230, 234, 242, 246–9, 253, 255, 257–8, 262, 266, 268, 270
introspectionism 25–6, 208, 212, 230, 258, 268

Jackson, F. 7, 53, 181
James, W. 5, 27, 79–80, 85, 88, 130–5, 139, 145, 156, 255–7, 261
judgment 38–46, 56, 62–79, 82–3, 86, 99–100, 104–9, 116–25, 128, 137, 149, 152–4, 156, 158–9, 167, 176–9, 182–3, 185, 187, 195–8, 202–3, 220, 247–50, 255, 258–9, 264, 266

Kim, J. 52, 253, 262
Koksvik, O. 62–3, 177, 268

Lange, C. 27, 130–3, 139, 145, 156, 261
Leibniz, W. 49, 222, 251
Levine, J. 58–9
Lewis, D. 14, 64, 181, 245, 254–5

Mackie, J. 163, 174
Mandelbaum, E. 106–9, 259
materialism 50–2
see also physicalism
McGinn, C. 142, 185
Montague, M. 5, 148–51, 180, 254, 261–2
Moore, G.E. 30–2, 40, 248, 250
moral phenomenology 33–6, 136, 159–63, 171–2, 175–83, 247–9, 251
motivation 8, 56, 61–2, 85, 129, 136, 147, 159–63, 165, 169–75, 178–82, 256, 264

Nagel, T. 51, 251
Nes, A. 69, 250

pain 36, 49–50, 54–5, 74, 147, 203, 207, 218–9, 249, 251
see also algedonic phenomenology
perception *see* perceptual phenomenology
perceptual experience *see* perceptual phenomenology
perceptual phenomenology 3–6, 9–10, 34–7, 39–40, 45, 53–8, 61–2, 70, 73, 75–6, 78, 81, 90–1, 96, 99, 104, 115, 128–9, 147, 157, 176, 183–203, 217, 219, 236, 244, 249, 257, 263, 266–7, 270
physicalism 4, 32, 69, 249
see also materialism
Pitt, D. 4, 32–4, 40, 100–1, 163, 249–50, 253, 258, 260
pleasure 36, 74, 147, 203
see also algedonic phenomenology
primitivism 4–8, 34, 38–9, 53, 61–3, 72–5, 81–3, 99, 147, 156–7, 184, 191, 199–200, 244
Prinz, J. 4, 31, 131, 250
psychology 22, 25–6, 83–4, 97, 106–8, 160–4, 172, 175, 180, 208, 212, 230, 241, 245, 256, 260, 264
psychology, introspectionist *see* introspectionism

Ramachandran, V. 22, 246
Ramsey sentence 38, 64–70, 83, 95–6, 110, 126–8, 254, 260

Reductivism 4–8, 35–6, 72, 75–82, 129, 147, 152, 155, 158, 176, 181, 187, 199–200, 244, 250, 254
Ricœur, P. 83–96, 256–7
rightness 74, 83, 87–9, 94–6, 163, 179, 244, 256
rightness, feeling of 24, 216–9, 243, 270
Rosch, E. 48, 143
Russell, B. 105, 223, 247, 252, 266

sadness 55, 129, 143, 148–51, 155, 215, 249
Sartre, J.-P. 83, 184–92, 213, 266–7, 270
Schaffer, J. 7–8, 18, 245
Schwitzgebel, E. 29, 122, 249, 254, 258, 260, 263, 266–7, 270
Searle, J. 121, 139, 140–1, 250, 262
sensory phenomenology 1–4, 30–1, 34–5, 41, 45–6, 54–61, 71, 74, 97, 136, 147–8, 184, 193–9, 244, 250, 259–60
Shepard, R. 22, 246
Siegel, S. 78, 248
Siewert, C. 4, 28, 41, 47, 247–50, 253, 258, 267, 270

Sloman, S. 107, 164, 167
Soames, S. 109, 120, 259
species 5, 9–10, 17, 87, 124, 144, 157, 171, 178, 182–3, 199–201
Stocker, M. 5, 147
Strawson, G. 30–1, 40, 247–8, 250, 261, 270
supposition 105, 110, 113–4, 128

Teroni, F. 156–7, 263–4
thinking of 98, 109, 116–9, 124, 260
thinking that 47, 98, 116–21, 124–5
Timmons, M. 67–9, 159, 163, 249, 258, 266
Titchener, E. 20, 25, 212, 248
trying 34, 42, 72–3, 81–4, 88–96, 100, 128, 203, 255, 257–8, 263

Watson, J. 35, 230
Whitehead, A. 99, 120
Wilson, J. 11, 245
Wundt, W. 10, 29, 80, 90, 248, 255

zombies 28, 53–5, 60–1, 69, 136, 143, 147, 253

www.ingramcontent.com/pod-product-compliance
Ingram Content Group UK Ltd.
Pitfield, Milton Keynes, MK11 3LW, UK
UKHW042006230426
12048UKWH00009B/578